THE COMANCHE BARRIER TO SOUTH PLAINS SETTLEMENT

By
RUPERT NORVAL RICHARDSON

Edited by
KENNETH R. JACOBS

With a new introduction by
A. C. GREENE

EAKIN PRESS ◆ Fort Worth, Texas
www.EakinPress.com

Copyright © 1996
By Eakin Press
Published By Eakin Press
An Imprint of Wild Horse Media Group
P.O. Box 331779
Fort Worth, Texas 76163
1-817-344-7036
www.EakinPress.com
ALL RIGHTS RESERVED
1 2 3 4 5 6 7 8 9
Paperback ISBN 978-1-68179-178-4
Hardback ISBN 78-1-68179-306-1
eBook ISBN 978-1-68179-308-5

ALL RIGHTS RESERVED. No part of this book may be reproduced in any form without written permission from the publisher, except for brief passages included in a review appearing in a newspaper or magazine.

Table of Contents

List of Illustrations	iv
Editor's Note on the Centennial Edition	v
Introduction by A. C. Greene	vii
The Tribe and the Country	1
First Relations with the White Men	21
New White People in Texas	39
Sam Houston and Peace	54
The Period of the Mexican War	66
Increasing Confusion	78
Establishing Contact on the Arkansas	89
War Trails Beyond the Rio Grande	97
The Texas Reservation	106
Enemies on Every Border	118
When the White Men Fought Each Other	135
The Last Treaties	147
The Quakers in Charge	164
The Quaker Policy Is Modified	174
The Last Wars	184
Notes	193
Bibliography	249
Index	255

List of Illustrations

	facing page
A Note on the Photographs	32
Tabaloso Comanche	33
Comanche brave	48
Comanche squaw	49
"Dog Eater," Comanche chief	112
Comanche, one of twelve raiders into Texas, the only one who returned	113
Comanche braves	128
Kwahadi Comanche camp	129
Quinine, Kwahadi Comanche	176
Comanche captive (Mexican boy)	177
Medicine Bluffs Pathway, near Fort Sill, Indian Territory	192
Medicine Bluffs Pathway, near Fort Sill, Indian Territory	193

Editor's Note on the Centennial Edition

This edition of the *Comanche Barrier* is published in honor of Rupert N. Richardson's long service to Hardin-Simmons University and for his many contributions to southwestern history. The first edition was printed in 1933 during the Depression and to minimize publication costs approximately thirteen thousand words were deleted from the original manuscript. Therefore, the purpose of this edition is to restore the *Comanche Barrier* to its original form using Dr. Richardson's own words and style as much as possible.

Unfortunately the editor of the first edition used some type of permanent ink in the editing process. Consequently, I was only able to completely retrieve eleven thousand of the deleted words from the original manuscript. Much of the edited material was located in the explanatory footnotes and as far as possible I have left that material in the footnotes. This avoids having to provide additional transitional words and phrases of my own to transfer that material into the text. I have used my own words only when they were necessary for transition purposes. All of the new material is identified by a vertical bar before and after each addition.

I would like to thank my dean, Dr. Lawrence Clayton, who encouraged this undertaking and also provided funds in the initial stages of the book. Special thanks are extended to Tom Taylor for his interest and publication expertise and to Randy Armstrong and Bill Curtis. The original idea of the centennial edition was theirs and they are most responsible for its publication. My deepest gratitude I reserve for Miss Jill Post, my graduate-student assistant, whose aid in deciphering the edited manuscript was incalculable.

Kenneth R. Jacobs
Hardin-Simmons University

Introduction

I hold as close a set of professional memories of *The Comanche Barrier to South Plains Settlement* as if it were one of my own works. I am a native of West Texas, and I was more than partially raised by a great-grandmother born on the forward edge of the frontier in San Saba County, in 1862. Thus, from her stories and remembrances, when I was a youngster the phrase "The Comanches" became more terrifying to me than "The Devil"—which is a significant demonstration of terror, seeing that I also spent years amidst a fundamentalist religious aura wherein The Devil lurked with all the danger and ominous opportunism of the frontier Indians.

Like so many who grew up surrounded by remnants and relics of the frontier, I only recognized "the Indians" in an unidentified way. Oh, I was not completely ignorant of tribal identities. I knew the Apaches, the Comanches, the Wichitas, the Kiowas, Caddoes, Tonkawas were Texas Indians, somewhat different from those Native Americans who helped the Pilgrims institute Thanksgiving, and that the Cherokees had developed an alphabet. (Although, I'll admit, thanks to Hollywood, it would have been difficult to name any Indian chiefs other than Cochise and Geronimo.) And I was not alone. It was to be many years before the writers of Texas history textbooks could lift their eyes beyond Stephen F. Austin, the Heroes of the Alamo, Sam Houston, and the Battle of San Jacinto to include more than one or two paragraphs about the remainder of Texas and the problems of settlement.

Therefore, in the summer of 1959, when I began working on a series of newspaper stories about the forts of West Texas, I discovered I was in trouble. I was not troubled by the need to separate popular myth from historic reality. I knew that Robert E. Lee did not command, much less establish, Fort Phantom Hill and I knew that "Indian Emily" hadn't really saved Fort Davis, in the Big Bend, from her marauding kinsmen because of her love for a U.S. cavalryman.

My historical trouble was with the Comanches. One cannot write a history of anything in 19th century West Texas without writing about the Comanches. It was the Comanches against whom the federal forts were built, it was the Comanches who seemed to inspire the fiercest and cruelest responses of the Southwestern pioneers, and it was the Comanches whose gradual surrender (if we want to call it that) ended the most frightful indigenous threat to settlement of the region. But all I had in my head about them was a vague, undated bag of jumbled particles.

So, that July afternoon in 1959 I made an appointment to see the man I supposed knew, or could point me toward someone who knew, about the Comanches. It was Dr. Rupert Norval Richardson, at that time the Emeritus President of Hardin-Simmons University and outstanding professor in the history department. Rupert Richardson was highly recommended to me and my efforts by my wife, Betty, who had worked in his office when she was a student at HSU. I knew who he was, and had attended high school with his son, Rupert Jr. but not having taken any history courses at HSU I was not privileged to have known the depths of his expertise concerning Southwestern history and the lore of West Texas in particular. It took us less than thirty minutes (I flatter myself) to establish a recognition that stemmed from our love of regional history and our experiences from having been born in and remaining in West Texas. As I related some of my great-grandmother's trials and tribulations on the West Texas frontier, Dr. Richardson quickly related some parallel or accompanying incident that would not only enlighten my understanding of the regional history but sometimes expand the very tale I had been told.

From that afternoon I carried away dozens of ideas, memories, and a load of admiration for the man which time has not diminished. Dr. Richardson and I were to see more and more of one another through the years and as I took my own writing further and further, he was both kind and appreciative. When I was made a member of the Texas Institute of Letters (he had long been so honored), his was the first congratulation from "on high" that I received, and I never asked for a favor or a fact that he didn't graciously respond.

Which returns me to that 1959 afternoon. When I suggested he must have done germinal research on the Comanches, Dr. Richardson (he once said to call him "Rupe," or "Dr. Rupe," that "Dr. Richardson" created a gulf between fellow historians) smiled modestly and suggested I read his first book, *The Comanche Barrier to South Plains Settlement*. To cover my embarrassment at not having checked on his work beforehand, I went into a semi-elaborate rationalization of how difficult it was for me to use library reference books, how likely I was to damage them when using them "in the field," and other quasi-explanatory ceremonies screening my guilt.

At which he arose and went into an adjoining room, bringing back an unopened copy of the book, published in 1933 by the distinguished California

Introduction

history publisher The Arthur H. Clark Company, and long out of print. I turned it over in my hands, and as a former rare book dealer, noted the book's wonderful overall quality, from paper to binding, the strength of the design, the appositive affinity of type to text . . . and Dr. Richardson said, "There are only a few of these left . . . you can put it to good use, I am sure, and better it be used than hidden away in some locked case." I was not just flattered, I was flattened by this gesture. But having been a book merchant and recognizing the real value, not just of the contents but of the volume itself, I insisted I must give him the catalogue price, praying to myself that the catalogue price could be extracted from a newspaperman's biweekly paycheck. He shook his head negatively, I persisted. I offered $25, which I thought might be half the volume's catalogue price, he smilingly resisted. Finally, desperate that I not insult him and embarrass myself, I said I would only accept the book if he would let me reimburse him for what it had cost him. He reluctantly agreed, pencilling the cost on a corner of the fly-leaf. $7.00. I have the book before me as I write, the figure in his hand. (And never, in the years after, until his death at age ninety-six, would I have dreamed of calling Dr. Rupert Norval Richardson . . . Rupe.)

There have been several books on the Comanche Indians published since the 1933 appearance of *The Comanche Barrier*. At least two of them first rate. But none succeeds so well in picturing the Comanches of the final years, the resolute but doomed tribesmen who only came in off the high plains and open prairies and ended their terror when the world they understood had disappeared. There is displayed an evident admiration for this people as a fiercely independent, obsolete society, the least adaptable to white ways of any of the tribes, yet the most adaptable to the life of the nomadic horseman-hunter-warrior, flaunting his freedom with an earned arrogance.

Rupert Richardson has put together a table of tribal organization, as little organization as the Comanches had: four major divisions that, in effect, were four individual tribes; but, as he puts it, ". . . the Comanche tribe (if there was such a thing) was never united in historic times." The author attempts to explain the Comanches; not defending, but offering sound and thoroughly researched explanations. He doesn't accuse, he doesn't blame, but he doesn't soft-pedal atrocities of which the Comanches were capable. He shows, under the precepts of their tribal culture, why certain activities took place, why most overtures of the whites failed, and why so many "westernized" ideas could not be applied to the Comanches. And the Comanches had few affiliations. As the Biblical verse says, ". . . his hand against every man and every man's hand against him." I cannot believe that even a surface understanding of any of the Plains Indians can be had without studying *The Comanche Barrier*. It is one of the few Native American histories that does not need revision, either for its facts or its approach to cultural and moral appraisals. And when we observe that Richardson the historian was also Richardson son of the frontier (born in 1891), we know how high was the mountain of inherited prejudice to be topped before he could offer balanced and unbiased research and commentary.

As to particulars, Rupert Richardson gives details from both sides of the tragic Council House "fight" of 1840 which offers a basis for understanding the Comanches' reluctance ever again to accept Texan overtures to peace. Representatives of the Republic of Texas with alleged peaceful intent, lured a large group of Comanche leaders into a house in San Antonio and, on getting vague answers to demands for which the chiefs possibly had no way of supplying information, locked the doors and slaughtered as many of them as they could, only some women and old men who had not been in the building managing to escape.

The tragic story of the Comanche reservations along the Brazos River in the 1850s (and the subsequent assassination of Robert Neighbors, the Indian Agent who had tried to save his tribal charges) saddens us through the short-sightedness and rascality of some Texas frontier "spokesmen." But the history of white and Comanche relations is not one-sided. At other agencies, in Kansas and Oklahoma, the hard-headedness of some of the Comanche bands blasted the hopes of even their fellow tribesmen and rendered helpless some of those conscientious officials whose attempts were sincerely motivated toward helping.

One of the most valuable portions of *The Comanche Barrier* is the chapter on the famous Adobe Walls battle, a chapter which comes from the Indian side and relates the fascinating background, especially the role of Isatai, the young Comanche medicine man and prophet who, convincing the leaders of his magic and his visions, created that one final, failing cooperative effort on the part of several tribes to reclaim their buffalo hunting grounds.

In 1982 when I was preparing a list of titles for my book *The Fifty Best Books on Texas*, among my instant choices was *The Comanche Barrier to South Plains Settlement*. I said of it then:

> This is straightforward history, done well and done professionally by a writer I consider the equal to any historian the Southwest has produced. Richardson's scholarship works exactly the way a reader wants it to: it fills in the gaps, it informs you when the scene is clouded, and it supports its contentions and conclusions . . . a model of historical viewing and information. Dr. Richardson does not slide off into ancestral praise and aboriginal condemnation; his eye is constantly upon his topic, and that other "I," the first person

Introduction

pronoun, is not once used by the author. Only in the final paragraph does he let a few words of the romantic (which, in reality, any good historian should be) come through: "They were finally defeated in the unequal conflict, but what a magnificent fight they made! . . . But even yet, if we look by the light of an August moon across a Texas prairie dotted here and there by gnarled mesquite and mottes of scrubby oak, surely we shall see phantom warriors as of old—Comanches."

A. C. Greene

CHAPTER ONE

The Tribe and the Country

About the beginning of the eighteenth century, the Comanche Indians left their country between the Yellowstone and Platte rivers and moved into the South Plains. Here they fought with the Apaches, drove them away to the south and west, and took possession of the land. For one hundred fifty years they made forays against both the red and white people along the border of their territory, and resisted the approach of all intruders. Thus they represent the most significant human element in retarding the occupation and settlement of the plains region south of the Arkansas river. Their peaceful relations with the white people were comparatively slight, and for this reason they were able to resist both the civilization and the vices of their more advanced neighbors. They fought desperately, and in scores of encounters all the way from the Platte to the plains of Durango they avenged real or imaginary wrongs and made the Spaniard and the Anglo-American pay with blood for the country taken from them. And even to this day when old frontiersmen recount tales of border struggles, the Comanche and his raids will surely be described. They wrote their names indelibly in the saga of the land and are entitled to some consideration in its formal histories.

THE TRIBE

The word Comanche or Cumanche is probably of Spanish origin, but its meaning is not known. It first occurs shortly after 1700 and when adopted by Anglo-Americans a century later, it came to be spelled in various ways, Camanche, Cammanche, and Commanche being among the most common forms. The Comanches called themselves Nĕrm or Nĭm'-ma (the people).[1] The French called them Pàdoucas, after the name given them by the Kansa, Osage and other tribes between the Arkansas and Platte rivers. Also, the name Iatan, or Ietan was applied to them by certain Indian tribes.[2] The tribe belonged to the Shoshonean family, being related to the Shoshoni, Ute, Bannock, and several other Rocky mountain tribes as well as to the great Nahuatl stock in Mexico.[3] It is stated that the Comanches were the only great division of the Shoshonean family who lived entirely on the plains.

The tribe was divided into a number of bands or permanent tribal parts.[4] These bands were not family groups and were not the basis for the regulation of marriage. The gentile system did not prevail among the Comanches, and there were no restrictions on marriage except that near relatives were not expected to marry. On the other hand, these bands were more than natural social groups under the leadership of a competent individual. Chiefs might come and go, but the bands remained, and selected new chiefs to carry on the leadership of the organization. Each of these bands would divide from time to time under chiefs who would lead their people away, to be separated for months or even a year or more. Then the different divisions would unite for a few days, and matters of general interest would be considered in council.[5] But this dividing and uniting was within the band; the Comanche tribe (if there was such a thing) was never united in historic times. The different bands or main divisions remained on friendly terms the one with the other. Occasionally two or more of them cooperated in certain undertakings; there was evidently considerable intermarriage; there was no distinct boundary between their several ranges; and in many respects they were more closely related than distinct and separate tribes would be. On the other hand, it must be said that they were more like independent tribes than bands in the sense in which that term is ordinarily used, and they will be designated hereafter as bands for the reason only that there is no better term.

In comparing one band with the others, it is difficult to find any differentiating institutions. It is said that certain dances were practiced exclusively by some divisions, while other dances might be used by the whole tribe.[6] Also there were slight differences in speech. For instance, the Penatekas (southern Comanches) pronounced their words more slowly than did the Kwahadi Comanches of the Staked Plains.[7] Notwithstanding these and other slight differences that may have existed, there was evidently not much variation in the habits, customs, and institutions of the different divisions.

It is impossible to identify all of the bands, or to describe with any detail and precision more than about half of them. The Penatekas or Honey-eaters[8] inhabited Texas during the later Spanish and the Anglo-American periods, and much of the Comanche history pertains to them. They were the southernmost of the various divisions and had, according to their tradition, wandered off a great distance from the other bands so that communication between them was discontinued for a long time. Finally the northern warriors, on their way to the Mexican frontier, re-discovered these Comanches of the south. The history of this division is very much that of an independent tribe. They were not intimately associated with their northern kinsmen, and were sometimes even hostile toward them.

The extreme northern part of the Comanche country was occupied by the Yamparikas,[9] or Root-eaters. According to their own accounts they came from the Rocky mountain country, north of the headwaters of the Arkansas river, to the valley of that stream in what is now eastern Colorado and western Kansas, about 1700. Previous to this date they had inhabited a country with the Shoshoni tribe.[10] In 1786 Governor Don Juan Bautista de Anza of New Mexico stated that their country was approximately what is now Colorado north of the Arkansas [Napestle] river.[11] The accounts indicate, however, that the Yamparikas felt at home in much of the country south of that stream also.

Another numerous band was that of the Kotsotekas or Buffalo-eaters.[12] Of course buffalo meat was the favorite food of all Comanches, but this particular division, whose favorite haunt during the nineteenth century was the Canadian valley, may well have been especially associated with that animal. Like the Yamparikas, they established relations with the Spaniards in New Mexico early in the eighteenth century; and after peace was established in 1786, *Comanchéros*, traders from the New Mexico settlements, visited them frequently. The eastern and southern members of this division likewise came to be well known to the Spaniards in Texas; in fact, they are commonly referred to in the documents of the Bexar Archives as Texas or eastern Comanches.

Another Comanche division which the Anglo-Americans came to know well, if not favorably, was the Nokoni or Detsanayuka. The word *nokoni* means wanderer, and by this name the band was known to the white people of the frontier. It is said that they changed their name to Detsanayuka (bad campers —people who never take the trouble to fix up good camps since they never stay long in the same place) after the death of a chief who bore the same name as his band, Nokoni. This seems to have been in keeping with an old Comanche custom which required that any name or word made sacrosanct by association with some lamented chief or leader be set aside and never used again.[13] During the nineteenth century the Nokonies generally ranged immediately north of the Penatekas. They were never brought into treaty relationship with the Texas or United States governments before the Civil War, and they harried the frontier of Texas as much, perhaps, as any other Comanche band. These Nokoni Comanches and their neighbors, the Tenawas and Tanimas,[14] frequently associated with the Penatekas or southern Comanches and are sometimes referred to as middle Comanches. The great Penateka chief, Päh'-häh-yō'-kō, had a strong influence with these middle Comanches, and they often camped with his people.

One other band must be given notice, although it cannot be identified until towards the close of the pre-reservation period. This is the Kwahari or Kwahadi division, which was located just south of the Yamparikas before the Comanches came into the South Plains region. The two bands probably drifted south about the same time. The Kwahadies made the *Llano Estacado* or plains proper their home, and challenged all intruders. The word *kwä'-hä-dĭ* is Comanche for antelope, a term which, within itself, bears evidence of their life on the open plains where antelope were plentiful.[15] They successfully resisted all efforts of the United States government to make a treaty with them, and defied the authority of "Washington" in many an encounter. For years they scoffed at their beef-eating kinsmen on the reservation, and took great pride in their wild and independent way of living. They were the last Comanches to go to the reservation, and did not do so until they had been repeatedly drubbed by superior military forces.

There are many estimates of the population of the Comanches, but those made before the reservation period represent little more than guesses. Governor Anza of New Mexico reported that up to July 14, 1786, there had visited Santa Fé and the pueblo of Pecos that year Comanches representing a total of 593 lodges. These were the Kotsoteka, Yamparika, and Yupe[16] divisions, and, according to his way of estimating, would represent a total of six thousand souls or more. Among these Indians, twenty-three chiefs are listed. The governor stated that at least a third of the followers of these chiefs did not come in with them.[17] Furthermore, it is evident that some of the general tribal divisions were not represented at all. In this same year Anza's emissary, Francisco Xavier Ortiz, reported that in the country north and east of Pecos he visited eight *rancherías* of Kotsoteka Comanches, aggregating altogether some seven hundred lodges, each representing, he thought, ten or twelve persons.[18] If the other great bands or general tribal divisions were as populous as this, the tribe may have numbered at that time as many as twenty or thirty thousand persons. If this be approximately correct, the tribe evidently was reduced in numbers rapidly during the next half century; for during the middle decades of the nineteenth century these Indians could not have numbered more than eight or ten thousand.

The Comanche dialect seems to have been intelligible to all the tribes of the

Shoshonean family. Communication quite satisfactory, however, was held between all the prairie tribes in the sign language.[19] Comanche was the court language of the South Plains, and if the sign language proved inadequate at Indian gatherings, the proceedings would likely take place through this medium. It is said that for this reason the Comanches were the poorest "sign talkers" of the plains.[20]

The absence of any general tribal organization on the one hand, and the loose relationship that prevailed between the members of the same band on the other, made the process of organizing new tribal divisions very easy and natural. Evidently there were more bands in existence during the nineteenth century than there had been in the century preceding. By 1786 the Spaniards knew more about the Comanches than the Anglo-Americans succeeded in learning before 1850, but it may well be doubted that the Spaniards ever discerned the exact number and nature of the bands in existence during their era. The fact that there were several independent tribal divisions with no general tribal government is a matter of great historical significance, and often caused the Comanches to be charged unjustly with failure to keep their treaty obligations. A treaty would be made on the Arkansas, or in Texas, with a number of Comanche braves led by a certain great chief who described himself as the "head-chief of all the Comanches." Now every band was apt to have one or two leading men claiming such distinction. The other bands would not feel obligated to obey the treaty, and probably would not hear about it for years. Still, the government and the white people concerned might continue to labor under the impression that they had made a treaty with the "entire Comanche nation."

CHARACTERISTICS

It does not appear that a careful study of the Comanches has ever been made by a trained ethnologist. This is unfortunate, since the old Indians are fast disappearing and the habits, institutions, and traditions of the tribe are being lost beyond recovery. The Comanches were comparatively newcomers on the plains. This is indicated by the fact that most of their Shoshonean kinsmen are mountain people, by the comparatively low stature of the Comanches,[21] and by the direction of their movements in historic times. However, during the few generations that they had lived on the plains, they had come to be a typical plains tribe, possessing in the highest degree the principal plains characteristics. These characteristics, along with a few other traits that may be peculiar to the Comanches, call for as much consideration as the limited data available on the subject will permit.[22]

The Comanches were a migratory people and did not remain long in the same place. In their movements they transported their tepees and other possessions by means of the horse and travois. It is likely that they were a migratory people before the coming of the horse, using the dog as their beast of burden. There are no written accounts of this pre-horse era, and Comanche tradition on the subject is negligible. However, some conjecture about their condition at that time can be based on what has been learned about other plains tribes under the same conditions. Food was difficult to secure in a country where there was little timber to hide the hunter as he tried to stalk his game. The wild life of the plains consisted very largely of the fleet deer and antelope and the huge buffalo. That the buffalo was a stupid animal may be true, but that he was courageous, and a dangerous adversary when wounded, must also be taken into consideration. Perhaps the most effective method of hunting the buffalo (more properly bison) before the Indians had horses was that of partly decoying, partly driving, a herd of these animals over a bluff where they would be killed or crippled in falling, or would be confined in a strong inclosure at its base.[23] Journeys were shorter in this era before the horse; lodge poles were lighter, if they were transported at all, and the tepees smaller and flimsier. Life was hard for these Indians, and there was little to change its monotony. Perhaps this accounts for the small store of tradition which the modern Comanches possessed; their great day had not arrived; the tribe had not been emancipated from the drudgery and dull life that had been its lot for many generations. It took the horse to make the Comanche great as savages measure greatness. The achievements of the tribe are modern, and were accomplished on horseback.

It is difficult even to approximate the date at which the Comanches acquired horses. It may be that a few stallions and mares escaped from the early Spanish explorers; or they may have been stolen from the Mexican settlements and passed on from one Indian tribe to another until they reached the South Plains and the eastern Rocky mountains. At any rate, the first white men whose accounts indicate positively that they saw the Comanches, found them well mounted. One of these is the French explorer Bourgmont who visited a Comanche village in Kansas in 1724. He learned that the Comanches had horses and knew how to use them. They explained to him that they secured their mounts from the Spanish.[24] The Indians were excellent horsemen when Bourgmont met them, and they must have had horses in their possession for a long time. In fact, his description of their village and ways of living would apply to them quite accurately a century later. Evidently it had taken many years to make pedestrians the most superb horsemen in the world.

Regardless of the date that marked the Comanche's transition to a "horse Indian," the change, when it occurred, must have been great.[25] The modifications in our own way of living incident to the invention of the steam railway and the automobile were not more far-reaching than those that occurred when the squaws took the packs off the dogs and placed them on the ponies. Henceforth longer lodge poles and more pelts for covering could be taken along, more food could be carried, and even small quantities of water could be transported; longer journeys at a faster gait could be made. Now the tribe or band might follow the migrations of the buffalo, or at least seek new ranges when drought or snow had driven the game away. Most significant of all, the horse (which may have been used first as a pack animal only) was mounted. Now the hunter could chase and overtake the buffalo; and as he urged his pony up to a position a little behind and at the side of the fleeing quarry, guiding his mount altogether with the pressure of his knees, he was in a position to drive an arrow or a spear into the vital organs of the great beast. At the twang of the bow string, the trained hunting pony instinctively turned aside to be out of reach of the sharp horns in case the enraged, wounded animal should turn on his pursuer.[26] The bow was now made short—not more than four feet in length—the short lance came into use, and henceforth these were the favorite hunting implements even for those few Comanches who might happen to come into possession of firearms. Likewise, the shield to be used in battle must be small. This is described as consisting of two skins of the toughest buffalo hide, padded between with an inch of hair. This was laid over a light frame, about two feet in diameter, in such a way as to present a slightly convex surface.[27]

The horse was both a form of capital and a medium of exchange for the Comanche. In fact, during the nineteenth century, the horse, next to the buffalo, was the principal food for some of the bands. Horse herds could easily be transported, the Indians could find a market for horses of good quality, and they were always eager to add to their herds. Good horses were most easily obtained in the settlements of the frontier white people, and most Comanche raids were primarily for the purpose of securing these animals. If, on these forays, the braves were able to take a few scalps, the expedition was regarded as all the more successful; but the taking of human life was ordinarily a secondary matter. Each Comanche's wealth was measured by the size of his horse herd, and next to prowess on the battlefield, skill at taking horses was regarded as the greatest virtue. Chief Is-sa-keep told Captain Marcy[28] that his four sons were a great comfort to him in his old age, since they could steal more horses than any other young men in the tribe.

Superior animals were well cared for. The war horse was never ridden except in battle or on important hunts, but was led along while some less fortunate animal of poorer quality did the drudgery. "I love him very much," said Chief Sanaco to Captain Marcy when that army officer tried to purchase the Indian's favorite hunting horse. The chief fondly patted the animal on the neck and refused to consider any offer Marcy might make.[29]

The Comanches were generally regarded as being most excellent horsemen. The artist Catlin, who had seen the Sioux and other northern tribes carry on mounted drill and acrobatics, declared that the Comanches were not equalled by any other Indians on the continent.[30] The ease with which they could cling to their mounts, even while leaning over and shooting arrows under the horse's neck, especially excited his admiration. Perhaps no other tribe, with the possible exception of the Kiowas, so nearly *lived* on horseback. Unlike most other "horse" Indians, the Comanches even went mounted when on horse-stealing expeditions.

The Comanches have bright, copper-colored complexions, thin lips, black eyes and hair, and but little beard. The pronounced aquiline nose is common among them. The men are of low or medium stature and well proportioned. In former times the hard, nomadic life told severely on the women; they were ugly and aged prematurely. The dress of these Indians varied, but the men commonly wore moccasins of buckskin, and leggings which extended from the upper portion of the thigh to the foot. The seam of these leggings ran close in so that the garment was close-fitting. The border of the material beyond the seam was left loose, presenting a wide margin of flapping buckskin. A breech clout of cloth or skin was worn, and if the weather was cold, a buffalo robe or blanket was thrown over the shoulders.[31] Catlin describes the dress of the women as consisting generally of a "gown or slip, that reaches from the chin quite down to the ankles, made of deer or elk skins; often garnished very prettily, and ornamented with long fringes of elks' teeth, which are fastened on them in rows, and are more highly valued than any other ornament they can put upon them."[32]

Like that of other plains Indians, the parade dress of the Comanches consisted of many fantastic designs. The warriors often wore a coiffure of buffalo horns, or a hood made of the scalp of the buffalo with the horns attached in proper position. Feathers were worn as plumes, in pensile formation, or woven into a hood or war bonnet. Vermillion was much sought after; but if it was not to be had, colored clay would serve for paint and each warrior endeavored to bedaub himself after his own peculiar design. Bears' claws, horse hair, mules' tails, and other similar materials might be appended to the hair or slung about the body. Nose-pieces of shell, bone, or silver were popular, and ear-pendants of beads or other ornaments were common. Multiple wristbands of copper wire were ornamental and served to protect the wrist of the left hand from the slap of the bow string. On entering a battle, the warriors disrobed save for breech cloth and moccasins. Their saddles were light and they never encumbered their mounts with useless trappings. |The different written accounts together with Catlin's sketches indicate that there was considerable variation in dress, particularly that of the men. It seems that there were few if any characteristics of dress peculiar to the Comanches as distinguished from that of other plains tribes.[33]|

The food of the Comanches was principally meat. The buffalo supplied those in the northern part of the range, but the southern Comanches (Penatekas) were obliged to depend largely on smaller game and horseflesh. Meat was dried and preserved for long periods of time. An ex-captive describes this process in the following manner:

> They would make a kind of box out of rawhide, two or three feet long and about twenty inches wide, so it will fit a packsaddle. They cut the meat thin and hang it up to dry and when packing they fold the dry sheets of meat and put it in these rawhide boxes and place a box on each side of the packsaddle, and carry it with them. Many is the time I have slyly loosened the string on a box and swiped some of the dried meat. It was real good, and very palatable the way the Indians prepared it.[34]

Naturally the Indians ate fruit and vegetables whenever they could secure them, and in this matter they were not hard to please. They made a kind of bread of mesquite beans, prickly pear "apples" were consumed in season, and many roots and herbs were eaten and relished, one being commonly referred to as a species of wild potato. Pecans, grapes, plums, haws, and even the stony hackberry were regarded as delicacies. The Comanches would not eat either birds or fish, and pork seemed to them especially unclean.[35] They were all fond of tobacco, which they prepared for smoking by mixing it with dried sumach leaves and bark. They inhaled the smoke into their lungs and blew it out through their nostrils.[36] Much has been written about the gluttony of the Indians and their improvidence, but their self-restraint could be quite as pronounced as their gormandizing. Clinton Smith, the boy captive, tells how on a certain trip across the plains, when water was not found at a certain spring or lake where it was expected, the most rigid discipline was enforced in the interest of the weaker members of the band. Grim warriors, with blood-shot eyes and swollen tongues, staggered on, threatening with death anyone who might attempt to drink the few cupfuls of water carried in buffalo paunches and doled out to the little children.[37]

Polygamy was common, each brave having as many wives as he could support. It seems, nevertheless, that the great majority of warriors had only one wife each. The average man could not supply more than one family with game.

Furthermore, there was not enough difference in the number of male and female inhabitants of the different bands to have permitted a great deal of polygamy. The wife was generally purchased, but parents sometimes awarded the special bravery of a youth by giving him their daughter.[38] Horses were the coin ordinarily used in these transactions. Evidently there was little ceremony associated with courtship and marriage. A dependable informant states that the suitor simply took the horses and other goods he thought necessary or was willing to give, went to the head of the girl's family, seated himself nearby and awaited results. The girl's father then came out of his tepee and, if he was satisfied with the prospective son-in-law and the proffered goods, led out his daughter, and the transaction was closed.[39] Both maidens and married women were often stolen. Comanche standards of sexual relationship seem to have been higher in the earlier than in the later part of the historic period. Once a fugitive sought asylum at Governor Anza's house in Santa Fé, stating that all the captains were conspiring to kill him for having been discovered in adultery with one of their women.[40] It seems that sexual immorality increased during later years. The extreme disparity of age that often existed between husband and wife was probably the cause of many unconventional relations. In such cases custom permitted the injured husband to satisfy himself by taking horses from his rival. Ordinarily such matters were settled without violence, but sometimes an unfaithful woman was punished by having her nose cut off or being otherwise mutilated. The guilty man likewise might suffer injury at the hands of the enraged husband, but this was evidently not common. In fact, the idea of compounding or paying the injured party or his relatives was firmly fixed in all Comanche relations.[41] Wives frequently ran away from their husbands, and the task of keeping up with his harem sometimes represented a serious problem for the Comanche brave. It seems that the unfortunate husband received little aid from his fellows in this matter, and it was expected that each man should recover his own absconding spouse and determine the punishment to be meted out to her and the satisfaction demanded of her consort.[42]

The wives ordinarily lived apart, each woman having her own tent; but harmony prevailed, and each woman felt obligated to look after her husband's children by another wife as diligently as she cared for her own. Family life was generally pleasant; children were treated kindly. Noah Smithwick, who lived with the Penatekas some three months, stated that he never saw a woman or a child abused. |Probably contemporary writers who have left accounts of the Comanches have given undue emphasis to the practice of polygamy. No doubt the great majority of warriors had only one wife each.[43]|

Information concerning Comanche government is scant. Evidently their political institutions were few and poorly defined. In each of the main tribal divisions there were a number of chiefs. It seems that in some cases chiefs were elected, while in most cases they attained their rank by common consent because of special ability or prowess. In 1849, when the southern Comanches had lost their two most influential chiefs, the leading men of the tribe, according to their report, met in a protracted council and selected a head-chief. However, there are two distinct and conflicting accounts as to which chief was so selected, and a little later a United States army officer well acquainted with the band thought that their most influential leader was still a third chief who had never claimed election by the council.[44]

In the matter of attaining to the chieftaincy, hereditary influence was certainly slight, if indeed it existed at all. There are in historic times very few instances of the sons of prominent chiefs attaining a position in the tribe equal to that of their fathers.[45] Evidently the chiefs and leading braves in council often selected some man as their leader.[46] But the authority of such a chief lasted only so long as he was able to maintain it. Among the Comanches the man made the office and not the office the man. There was a principal or head civil chief, and a head war chief. The civil chiefs often referred to their war chiefs, and the war chiefs to their civil chiefs in such a way as to indicate that in all matters, even war, the civil chief was superior. But such superiority was probably more theoretical than real.

Important policies were determined in council, the decision of which was binding on all. In this connection, Robert S. Neighbors, long associated with the Comanches, states:

> The subjects under discussion in council are at all times open to popular opinion, and the chiefs are the main exponents of it. The democratic principle is strongly implanted in them. They consult, principally, the warrior class, and the weaker minds are wholly influenced by popular opinion. Each man endeavors to obtain as high a position as their merits allow. War chiefs commit hostilities without consulting the other tribes [chiefs?]. Any proposition or treaties proposed by the whites are discussed privately, and the answer given by the chief as the unanimous voice of the tribe. In deliberations in council, they consult each other, and one addresses the meeting. The council is opened by passing the council pipe from one to the other, and invoking the Deity to preside. It is conducted with great propriety and closed in the same manner. There is one appointed as crier or messenger, whose duty it is to fill the pipe . . .[47]

It must not be understood, however, that decisions of councils were regarded by the warriors generally as sacrosanct. Punishment for violating these decisions was certainly not common. While the great chiefs were present, the warriors would obey; but this was done more out of fear of the chief than because of any respect for law or authority in the abstract. The nomadic character of the Comanches made it impossible for the chiefs to keep in touch with their warriors at all times, and when a warrior committed an offense, his punishment generally went no further than rebuke and admonition. If that government is best which governs least, the Comanches had certainly reached a state of perfection.

As in the case of most American Indians in historic times, war was the principal occupation of the Comanches. A chief who wished to lead a party to war mounted and rode about camp, carrying perhaps a red banner tipped with eagles' feathers attached to a pole. Fighting was voluntary, but the young man who never joined such parties would likely become an object of scorn. If the proposed expedition proved to be popular, recruits were gathered rapidly, runners would be sent to inform other groups, processions would be formed, and great excitement would prevail. There was much drumming and singing in connection with these processions, and occasionally the march was stopped while the crowd was harangued by the leaders. These martial festivals, *nā'-wap-in ā'r*, might last for several weeks,[48] or the party might leave sooner for the country of the enemy. There is some evidence to indicate the existence of military societies among the Comanches, but there is not much information on this subject.[49]

A war party might consist of a few dozen or a few hundred men, depending largely upon the prominence of the leader and the conditions that called forth the expedition. The purpose of the foray might be to avenge a wrong by taking human life, or to collect horses and plunder, or both. War parties and stealing parties are difficult to distinguish, and the Indians themselves engaged in both in very much the same state of mind and carried them on after the same fashion. In their most destructive raids against the frontier, the Indians traveled (always riding) in comparatively large parties to some point near the settlements which were to be raided. Here the large party broke up into a number of small bands, and the destructive work was begun. By means of signal smokes, the different divisions kept in touch the one with the other and would unite again when they had completed their foray or when considerations of safety demanded it. In case they should be hard pressed by an enemy force too large to resist, they would again divide and sub-divide their forces so that each fleeing warrior left a separate trace and their pursuers found it impossible to punish them effectively. The following passage, taken from the narrative of the ex-captive Herman Lehmann, suggests the methods by which information was transmitted from one group to another. In this case, Lehmann's party had been on a raid against the settlements along the Llano and San Saba rivers in Texas, and were on their return journey to the Comanche country proper. He states:

> Riding in a run, night and day, never stopping to eat or sleep until we were away up in the open country, we went back to camp, only to find it deserted. Signs left on the ground there told us that a battle had taken place in which some Tonkaways with whites had been in a measure successful; that the tribe had gone to the sand hills, followed by the Tonkaways and the soldiers, and warned us to be cautious for our enemies would probably be between us and the tribe.[50]

| The Indians often used ingenious devices to throw their pursuers off the trail, one such ruse at least occasionally used being to scatter skunk musk in order to deaden the trailing sense of bloodhounds in pursuit. | The return of a war or raiding party was the signal for shouting, dancing, feasting, and riotous celebration of every description. The newly-taken scalps were hung on a pole and carried about the camp while men, women, and children took part in the rejoicing.[51] But there might be mourning as well as rejoicing, for some braves would likely not return. If the party had suffered the loss of many warriors, the whole camp broke forth in a pandemonium of wailing; captive women and children (the Comanches rarely ever took men prisoners) would be abused, tortured, or slain; and violence and frenzy reigned supreme. The female relations of slain Indians were expected to evidence their grief by shrill lamentations and self-torture, and these demonstrations they would keep up for weeks, months, and even years. Every evening or night mourners would withdraw some distance from the camp and wail until they were exhausted, meanwhile slashing their arms, faces, and breasts, and sometimes becoming bloody objects of frenzy and madness.[52]

Some notice must be taken of the Comanches' religion, although few subjects of Indian ethnology present to the investigator greater difficulties. Their religious beliefs and practices were not well defined. The "Great Spirit" was associated with the sun, and Comanches are sometimes quoted as referring to the sun as "father," while the earth was "mother." When smoking in ceremonial fashion, the first puff was blown towards the sun, and the second towards the earth.[53] However, at least some Comanches explained that the sun itself was not worshiped so much as the great creator or father of the Comanche race, who resided in or beyond the sun. This deity or person who was of gigantic stature, was the original parent of the Comanche race, and would never die. Bollaert[54] states that this being was supposed to live in the sun; but other accounts have it that he lived beyond the sun, the Indians explaining that they could not worship this great being since he was so far away. The sun was nearer and between them and the "Great Spirit," hence they worshipped the sun. Robert S. Neighbors, who was more intimately associated with the Comanches during the pre-reservation period than any other white man, distinguishes between the sun and the "Great Spirit" or the "Supreme" of these Indians.

> They use many charms, and are very superstitious. All charms are supposed to be derived from the Great Spirit, which they buy from their "medicine men." They offer Him many sacrifices. The first puff of smoke is offered to the Supreme, the second to the Sun, the third to the Earth, and after these, to whatever they venerate. The first morsel of what they intend to eat is presented to the Great Spirit, and then buried in the ground. All their implements of war are made by, or undergo charms from, their priests or magicians, who practice charms for the purpose. Their shields are made in imitation of the sun, and before going to war they are stuck upon their lances, facing the rising sun; and no person is permitted to handle or touch them except their owners. They believe that they were made by a secondary spirit, who was sent down to the earth by the Supreme. When he first made them, they were imperfect. The spirit returned to the Supreme, and told what he had made. He was then directed to return and complete his work by giving the beings he had created sense, and instruct them how to live. He taught them how to make bows and arrows, and gave them horses, etc., etc.[55]

If the Comanches had anything like general or tribal religious celebrations, these escaped the notice of observers. All accounts indicate that religion with them was largely an individual matter.[56]

The Comanches associated mystic influence with a number of different objects. The skins of certain animals, particularly the buffalo, bear, otter, and the plumes of certain birds, were believed to possess charms and were for this reason often carried in battle.[57] The oil of a beaver rubbed on the body was regarded as absolute protection from the rifle ball of the enemy.[58]

In common with most savages, they had many taboos. They would not drink from a cup when standing, a mirror was regarded as "bad medicine," sticks of wood must not be lain across the fire but instead the end must be inserted and the stick moved up to the fire as the end burned away. The wolf was regarded as a brother who often warned the Comanches of impending trouble; and if, when the Indians were on a journey, a wolf jumped up before them, looked at them, barked or howled, they would change their course and travel no farther in that direction that day. Disease and misery were attributed to the blasting breath of some secret enemy. On their journeys to Natchitoches, made frequently during the period from 1810 to 1820, the Comanches occasionally contracted diseases (probably malaria). This illness was attributed to the blasting breath of the Kichais, a Caddoan tribe through whose country they passed on the way.[59]

In the matter of medical knowledge, the Comanches are credited with being "expert in curing gun-shot wounds, and in the treatment of fractured limbs, which they bandage with neatness and good effect."[60] Likewise it is claimed that they had one or more effective remedies for rattlesnake bite. A poultice made of prickly pear leaves was sometimes applied to check inflammation.[61] The steam or vapor bath was used extensively. The patient was placed in a specially constructed oven made of boughs and covered with skins. Hot stones were placed in the center, water was sprinkled on these, and the dense hot vapor that resulted produced a profuse sweat on the patient who had been confined within the small enclosure. Meanwhile, the medicine men kept up their incantations in order that their occult powers might be added to the physical forces at work in the treatment. Generally, if the patient was able, he followed this sweat with a cold plunge. In the treatment of smallpox this remedy was nearly always fatal.[62]

When the condition of a patient became hopeless, he was generally abandoned by all except his most faithful relations and friends; and sometimes even these left him. This was not because of lack of loyalty and sympathy so much as the fear of the spirits which possessed the unfortunate one. When the sick Comanche felt death drawing near, he sometimes gave away all his property and retired to a quiet corner of the village to die. At least one Comanche chief is known to have taken the life of his wife by cutting her throat because she was hopelessly ill and was suffering.[63] The death of a member of a band generally caused the entire village to be moved, particularly if the deceased was a prominent man. No doubt this practice often served to stop the ravages of epidemics.

The Comanches generally buried their dead in sitting posture, making a grave or hole just deep enough to hold the corpse. The body was well clad; arms, ornaments, and trinkets were included in the burial. At the funerals of prominent warriors or persons of well-to-do families, horses were slain in order that the dead Comanche might enter the spirit world well mounted. A more thrifty practice, which was often made to suffice, was simply to shave off the manes and tails of the horses and mules which had belonged to the deceased.[64] The place of burial was apt to be a high hill near the place where death occurred. The grave was covered with stones, piled on, apparently, without any special system or arrangement. Some of the Comanches later adopted the scaffold method of burial in common use by some other plains tribes. In such cases, the body was wrapped in blankets on an elevated platform erected especially for that purpose.[65]

The Comanches were fun-loving and fond of games. A favorite contest was a guessing game in which two opposing sides participated. The leader of one side took a small bone in his hand and passed it or pretended to pass it on to one or two others. Each of these, in turn, pretended to have the bone and went through the motion of passing it on, everyone being careful to keep his hands closed so that it was impossible or difficult to determine which one of the several players had it. Then one of the opposing players, who thought he had detected who really had the bone, made his designation. If he was correct, his side won a point; if he was in error, his side lost a point. The other side took the bone in turn and went through the same performance. The Indians bet heavily on this game, and there was much excitement. The favorite game of the squaws and children was the "plum-stone game" in which polished plum-stones served somewhat as dice.[66]

Like most good horsemen, the Comanches were fond of horse racing and, according to the tradition of the plains, were exceedingly proficient at promoting races to their own advantage. They were good judges of horses, were good jockeys, and often exercised great ingenuity in matching profitable races. Colonel Dodge tells how Mu-la-que-top, a Comanche chief, took "a miserable sheep of a pony, with legs like churns" and beat "a magnificent Kentucky mare, of the true Lexington blood," winning some heavy bets made with the army officers and soldiers at Fort Chadbourne, Texas. The savage rider of this sheep-like pony added insult to financial injury by riding the last fifty yards of the course sitting face to his horse's tail "making hideous grimaces and beckoning to the rider of the mare to come on." It turned out that this shabby-looking pony was renowned among all the tribes of the South Plains, and that Mu-la-que-top had recently used him to win some six hundred ponies from the Kickapoos.[67]

The Comanches had no system of writing, unless the crude pictures they sometimes drew may be classed as writing. In these pictures war and the chase were favorite themes. On carefully dressed skins they often drew designs, a common one being the sun in the center with different colored rays of light radiating out in finely drawn lines. Their shields were often adorned with pictures. Their paints were made from colored chalks or clay, and their brushes of tufts of hair. For drawings of a more temporary character, charcoal often served as the pencil, and any smooth surface like a bone, a board, or the bark of a tree served for canvas. They had a system of enumeration, but apparently little knowledge of the rudiments of arithmetic. They measured long periods of time in terms of "winters" (*tōm*, meaning winter or year), and to designate short periods the phases of the moon served them. They reckoned from full moon to full moon. Their astronomical knowledge seems to have gone but little further than an acquaintance with the north "not moving" star. They were fond of singing and, although their repertoire was limited even for Indians, their music is characterized by its martial ring or soothing softness.[68]

The Comanches were generally regarded as rating higher morally than other nomadic tribes about them. They were hospitable, and would share their last morsel with a guest. In war they gave no quarter and asked none, but it was not their custom to torture unfortunate enemies.[69]

The courage of the Comanches was superb. Sometimes, when the fight became desperate, they dismounted and took off their moccasins in token of their resolve never to leave the place alive.[70] L. C. Scott, a veteran ranger, once related to the writer how his party surrounded a small band of Comanches and killed them all except one lithe youth, who took refuge in a thicket. Because of their admiration for his courage, the white men tried to persuade him to surrender, but he either did not understand their proposal, or else was determined to die under his shield. He sent a shower of arrows against his adversaries even after he had been mortally wounded; and, finally, after he had been overcome and was no longer rational, he continued to pull at the bow string—a warrior to the last.

THE COMANCHE COUNTRY AND RANGE

It has already been stated that the Comanches came from the Wyoming country, and that when white men first learned of them early in the eighteenth century, they were living in what is now Colorado and western Kansas. They continued their southward migration until about 1840, at which time their country might have been described as a blunt irregular wedge, point downward, the broad end extending from the vicinity of the great bend of the Arkansas river to the mouth of the Purgatory, the point extending almost to Austin.[71]

The topography of the country included within these boundaries varies from the hilly, undulating, and partly timbered area between the ninety-seventh and one hundredth meridians, to the level plains or *Llano Estacado* on the west. Within what was once the *Comanchería* are to be found occasional hills, canyons, and gorges which break the monotony of the prairies and plains. Along the larger streams, practically all of which run southeast, there were timber areas which extended far into the plains country. Thus the Comanches were never more than a few days' ride from some stream or canyon where wood for fires and poles for their lodges might be had, and where protecting bluffs or ridges would break the force of cold and hot winds.

The Kiowa and Kiowa Apache Indians shared with the Comanches the vast area they claimed as their home. Like the Comanches, the Kiowas were migrating southward when they first appear in history. They are known to have lived at one time as far north as the Yellowstone country, and may have been driven out by the Cheyennes and Dakotas. At any rate, they drifted southward, clashed with the Comanches, and for many years carried on a war with them. Finally, according to Kiowa tradition, the two tribes made a treaty at a date which Mooney fixes at about 1790.[72] This peace agreement has never been broken. The Kiowas soon moved into the Comanche country south of the Arkansas river, and became staunch allies of the northern Comanche bands.

The Kiowa language apparently has no connection with that of any other tribe. Their customs and characteristics were quite different from those of the Comanches. The two tribes have, nevertheless, lived in harmony and have generally been in accord in all important matters of tribal policy. Hence, in recounting the history of the Comanches, it will be necessary to make frequent reference to that of the Kiowas. The Kiowas were not, however, allied with the Penatekas, or southern Comanches, and, except when making raids against the Texas and Mexican frontiers, they were not often found south of Red river. They were not a large tribe, although they probably outnumbered any one of the several Comanche bands or tribal divisions.

The Kiowa Apaches were incorporated with the Kiowa tribe and formed a component part of its tribal circle. They were Athapascan stock, but their history is in no way connected with the Apache bands of New Mexico and Arizona. They came into the South Plains region with the Kiowas, and there is no tradition of a time when the two peoples were not associated.[73]

The range of the Comanches is an entirely different matter from their homeland proper. As late as 1802 bands of these people occasionally roamed as far north as the upper stretches of the Missouri, and during the first half of the nineteenth century, they harried Mexican settlements almost or quite as far south as Durango.[74]

Along the periphery of the extensive *Comanchería* were several powerful and warlike tribes. On the extreme northwest were their kinsmen, the Utes. On the northwest border along the upper Arkansas river were the Cheyennes and Arapahoes, who appeared in great numbers at about 1830. War frequently prevailed between the Comanches and these tribes until 1840, when a lasting peace was made with them.[75]

North of the Comanches and east of the Cheyennes and Arapahoes were the

Pawnees, a numerous and powerful confederacy of Caddoan stock, numbering as late as 1838 about 10,000 persons.[76] The confederacy was composed of four bands. Their great village was located on the Platte about 150 miles from its junction with the Missouri.

To the east and northeast of the Comanche country were the Osages, a tribe of the Sioux family. A band of these Indians drifted as far south as the Arkansas river about 1802. They were less numerous than the Pawnees, but more formidable because their association with the whites and immigrant civilized tribes enabled them to possess firearms.[77] However, the Osages had already begun the process of ceding their territory to the United States. In 1808 they had ceded rights to a portion of their lands comprising a large part of what is now the state of Missouri and the north part of Arkansas, and in a few years the Cherokees from east of the Mississippi settled in a part of that territory.[78] Other cessions were made, that of 1825 being especially significant; so that after that date the Osages were confined to a comparatively small area along the Neosho river.[79] Thus, after 1825, on a considerable portion of the eastern boundary of the Comanche country more advanced Indians from the east took the place of the Osages. This is a matter of great consequence in the history of the Comanches and all Indians of the South Plains region, and it will be given more attention later.

The Comanches had been at war for several generations with the Pawnees and Osages on the northeast and east, and these wars continued during most of the nineteenth century up to the time that the plains tribes were brought under control. However, there were periods of peace, at least between the Osages and Comanches, when disputes were settled and forgotten, and trading and friendly relations prevailed.[80]

From the Washita and Red river valleys southward almost to the location of Austin, occupying a strip of territory about 200 miles wide, were the Wichitas or Pawnee Picts, the Wacoes, and a few Tawakonies and Kichaies. Estimates made in 1824 gave this whole group a population of 2600. They were of Caddoan stock, but were generally friends and allies of the Comanches, and their attitude towards the white people was governed largely by their powerful friends from the plains. In fact, it may be said that by 1840 the Comanches occupied this country jointly with these weaker tribes.[81] To the east of this Wichita group were remnants of other tribes belonging to the Caddo family also. From time to time these bands yielded to the pressure from white settlers and drifted over to the middle Brazos region; and Caddoes, Anadarkoes, and Ionies (Hainaies) were living along the Comanche border from the middle thirties on.

Among other lesser Texas bands, various remnants of which were to be found as late as the period covered by this study, only two need be mentioned, the Tonkawa and Lipan. During the Spanish period the Tonkawas, who form a separate linguistic family, lived in central Texas. The coming of the American settlers drove them westward and northward, and they were forced to occupy the country along the Llano and San Saba whenever they were not suffered by the colonists to reside closer in. By the time of the Republic of Texas, they numbered but a few hundred.[82] Their enmity with the Comanches was proverbial, and periods of peace were interspersed with hostilities.[83] The Lipan, an Apache band, occupied the country along the San Saba, Llano, upper Guadalupe, and Nueces rivers, and occasionally retreated into New Mexico or across the Rio Grande into the north Mexican states. The enmity between this tribe and the Comanches had its beginning far back in the Spanish period, and continued with few interrupting truces down to the time of the reservation system. Along the whole western border of the Comanche country were various other Apache bands, among which may be named the Mescalero and Faraon, generally found along the lower Rio Grande, and the Jicarilla on the upper Rio Grande and the mountains to the east. These bands were all implacable foes of the Comanches, and warfare prevailed between the two tribes almost all of the time from early in the eighteenth century to 1875. On the plains, the Comanche generally was the victor, but in the hills and mountains, the Apache was able to resist successfully all efforts of his Indian adversaries either to conquer or displace him in any manner.[84]

As regards the tribes that inhabited the different borders of the *Comanchería*, it may be said that those whose country was suited to agricultural pursuits generally maintained a semi-sedentary existence, raising some corn and vegetables, while those who lived in regions not adapted to agriculture did very little farming. Although the country of the Comanches was suited in part for agricultural pursuits, it seems that neither these Indians nor their allies, the Kiowas, ever planted seed of any kind. Once when John W. Whitefield, Indian agent for the Arkansas and Platte tribes, explained to Little Mountain, the Kiowa chief, that the "Great Father" was going to teach the Indians how to farm, the chief replied that he was glad to hear it and that he hoped while the "Great Father" was so generous he would send the Indians some land that would grow corn, since they had none suited for that purpose.[85]

CHAPTER TWO

First Relations with the White Men

The Comanches were among the last Indians to be subdued, but they were not by any means the last natives the Caucasians became acquainted with. Early in the eighteenth century the Spaniards in New Mexico came in touch with them, and fifty years later they were causing the Spanish officials in Texas considerable annoyance. Meanwhile, a few French explorers and traders from the Louisiana settlements had visited them. And finally, during the first third of the nineteenth century, the Anglo-Americans touched the *Comanchería* along its eastern and southern borders, and a few of the most daring penetrated it.

MEETING THE SPANIARDS IN NEW MEXICO

It is said that the Comanches were first seen in New Mexico in 1705, and that they were brought there by their kinsmen, the Utes. In 1716 they joined the Utes in an attack on Taos and vicinity and carried away a number of captives. Captain Serna was sent against them, and at the Cerro de San Antonio, thirty leagues north of Santa Fé, he defeated them badly and recovered the captives. But they soon renewed their raids, and thence for more than half a century the people of New Mexico regarded them as enemies or uncertain friends.[1]

Soon some of the Apache bands of New Mexico began to feel the terrible blows struck by these virile, intruding warriors.[2] The Comanches were notified that the Jicarilla Apaches were Christians and were for that reason entitled to the special protection of the Spanish arms. But the sign of the cross did not stop the wicked Comanches. They attacked the Jicarilla village, burned it, and carried away many women and children.[3] Then, about 1733, a friar at the Jicarilla mission suggested that it would be ethical to use these Christian Indians in war against the heathen Comanches. In carrying out this idea, the Spaniards located the Jicarillas in the pass formed by the Jicarilla river, about twenty leagues from Taos, expecting that they would keep out the Comanches. But the men of the mountains proved to be no match for the warriors of the plains. The "gentile Comanches" came and "despoiled" the Christian Indians, and the few Jicarillas that were left betook themselves to the pueblos of Taos and Pecos, there to secure protection from the very enemy they had been expected to overcome.[4] But the poor Christian Indians were not safe behind the walls of the pueblos, for the Comanches continued to harass them, killing one hundred fifty residents of Pecos alone, and forcing the Spanish to establish garrisons at both villages.[5]

From time to time the Spaniards chased the Comanches from the settlements, but they always returned, and their destructive power was not lessened by the defeats the military claimed to have administered to them. War with them had not proved advantageous for New Mexico; perhaps to make peace with them would be the more sensible course. The white people needed the skins, meats, and horses which the Indians offered for trade, and the Comanches certainly needed the Christian influence which legitimate trade would bring. No doubt illegal trade was being carried on anyway. At any rate, the Spanish officials admitted them to the Taos fair in 1748 or 1749, and they became, in theory at least, a part of Spain's great Indian family.[6] But this trade did not improve conditions, for in less than three years the governor was fighting them again.

Sometimes the Spanish officers on the frontier lost patience with the savages and thus brought upon themselves stern rebukes from their superiors. In 1761 nine or ten chiefs or leading Comanche braves came in to negotiate for the sale of captives, some of whom had been taken in a raid on Taos a few months before. It happened that the provisional governor was at Taos at that time, and this dignitary flew into a rage at the insolence of the savages. He imprisoned the chiefs and ordered an attack on their camp. The attack was made and the Spaniards claimed to have killed more than three hundred warriors and to have made captive over four hundred women and children—probably an exaggeration, since the Indian camp contained only sixty lodges. The attack was made in spite of the fact that a chief "came out with a holy cross in his hand . . . knelt down and begged for peace and promised, if they would only leave them their lives, they would pay with their horses, their children, and their wives. . ." Meanwhile the chiefs, who had been left under a small Spanish guard, offered resistance, and they were slain also. This decisive and ruthless act of the provisional governor did not win him favor with his superiors. These officials contended that instead of attacking the Indians when they came with the Spanish captives, he should have seized the opportunity to make peace with them and recover the prisoners.[7]

No doubt the disposition of the general government to be long-suffering towards the Comanches was due in part to the fear of French and English intrusion. The *Comanchería* as a barrier was worth more to Spain than all the troops she had in New Mexico. The Spaniards themselves never did penetrate it to any great extent. To go from Santa Fé to San Antonio called for a circuitous journey into Chihuahua and Coahuila in order to avoid the plains country and its inhabitants.[8] Likewise these Indians, nearly or quite as much as the semi-arid, treeless country they occupied, prevented the French from threatening seriously the Spanish position in New Mexico. Moreover, since the Comanches were nearly always at war with the tribes around them, it was difficult for Frenchmen to reach the Comanche country even if they dared to trust themselves to these wild Indians of the plains.

But, shortly before the middle of the eighteenth century, the French position was appreciably strengthened and France became a greater menace to the integrity of Spain's empire. The Comanches had generally opposed the coming of French traders to the plains because such traders might furnish the Apaches with arms and munitions. Now the Apaches had been driven from the plains, and with their ancient enemies out of the way, the Comanches were glad enough to welcome the Frenchmen and trade for the guns they brought with them. In 1746 the French managed to reconcile their Jumano allies with the Comanches, and thus opened a route to New Mexico by way of the Arkansas river.[9] Thereafter the Comanches were even better supplied with French arms. After the cession of Louisiana to Spain in 1762, the danger of French aggression was removed. But England was advancing from Canada and the thirteen colonies. Also, in order better to protect her frontier settlements from Indian raids as well as to prevent English encroachments on her empire, Spain found it necessary to reorganize the system of defense in her northern provinces. Such a reorganization called for peace with the Comanches.

Pursuant to instructions, Governor Mendinueta made a treaty with one or more Comanche bands in 1771, but the wars went on.[10] The Spaniards persisted, however, in their determination to win the friendship of the savage plainsmen. The Marqués de Rubí, who had inspected the northern frontier to work out a more satisfactory plan of defense for the northern provinces after Spain took over Louisiana, urged that peace be established with the Comanches and other northern tribes in order that they might be turned against the Apaches. Likewise El Cavallero de Croix, commander-general of the Interior Provinces (a post established in 1776 for the better defense of the northern provinces), urged a Spanish-Comanche alliance.[11] The Apaches were hopeless and must be decimated or exterminated. Spain might make something worthwhile of the Comanches. As Spanish allies they could assist in destroying the Apaches and, at the same time, could guard the empire against the approach of the English from the north and east.

The man who put this policy into execution was Governor Don Juan Bautista de Anza, frontiersman superb and a soldier after the king's heart. Anza was one of the very few white men who ever comprehended the real nature of the Comanche problem. To begin with, in August and September, 1779, he introduced himself to them in a way that must have seemed altogether out of keeping with Spanish tactics. His predecessors in office generally had waited for the Indians to attack and had then pursued them; Anza determined to attack first, hoping to find the savages divided and unprepared. He went to the Comanche country by a new route so that "I shall not suffer what has always happened so often, that is, to be discovered long before reaching the country in which the enemy lives. . ."[12]

His plan was executed with marvelous directness and success. While the great chief Cuerno Verde (Green Horn) was away raiding the Spanish settlements, Anza attacked the chief's people near the present Wigwam, Colorado, and put them to flight. Then he turned back on the trail of Cuerno Verde and met the great chief returning from his attack on Taos—an attack which, thanks to Anza's improvement in the defense of the pueblo, had not proved very destructive. Near Greenhorn Peak, south of the Arkansas river, he defeated the Indians and killed Cuerno Verde, together with the chief's eldest son and a number of leading men, among them "a medicine man who preached that he was immortal."[13]

This victory did not bring peace at once. Spain soon entered the war of the American Revolution, and the slender resources of her empire were drawn on heavily by expeditions against the English. Meanwhile, the war against the Comanches and other savages who were harassing the northern provinces was not pursued vigorously. But in 1783–1784 the Spaniards became more aggressive in their campaigns against both the Comanches and Apaches, and the Comanches soon came to see that peace with the Spaniards would be to their advantage. In July, 1785, over four hundred of those Indians nearest the New Mexico settlements sought amnesty at Taos,[14] and others came in later. Although Anza was willing to regard these particular Comanches as friends henceforth, he wisely refused to make a formal treaty until the outlying bands were ready to enter into it also. The seasoned Spanish official knew, what others destined to deal with these savages in the years to come never seemed to realize, that the Comanches were composed of many divisions aggregating scores of *rancherías*, and that to make peace with a few hundred warriors at one point would be worse than useless unless the others could be brought into the agreement also. His policy was, first, to encourage those Indians pacifically inclined to spread the gospel of peace among their more bellicose neighbors and, second, to build up among the Comanches a general tribal government under one chief backed by the authority of the Spanish government.

The response of the Indians after the council at Taos was encouraging. Shortly after this they held a council in the region of La Casa de Palo, on the Napestle (Arkansas) river, attended by chiefs of the Cuchanec (Kotsoteka) division and representatives of the Yupes (Gente de Palo) and Yamparikas.[15] In the name of the more than six hundred *rancherías* which they claimed to represent, they chose Ecueracapa or Cota de Malla,[16] the Cuchanec chief, as their leader to treat with the white men.

Ecueracapa acted promptly. Several other councils were held, and Ecueracapa himself visited the governor in Santa Fé where he asked for peace and protection for his people, the privilege of settling and subsisting near the settlements, and free trade with Pecos. He assured the governor that the Comanches would be loyal to the king and fight the Apaches. Already chief Toroblanco, who opposed making peace with the Spaniards, had been killed by members of the peace party, and Ecueracapa himself had slain the leader of a marauding band of Toroblanco's followers because he had killed a Pecos Indian. In the presence of the governor, peace was made with the Ute chiefs, the members of each tribe mutually exchanging clothes as a token of good will.

Ecueracapa's mission had now been performed, but Anza was determined to use this influential chief in carrying out the second part of his Comanche policy, that is to say, making Ecueracapa the great chief and leader of all the Comanches. Naturally the chief himself was ready enough to cooperate in such a program. So, late in February, 1786, the governor accompanied the Indians to Pecos where, in the presence of the leading braves, he granted Ecueracapa's petition and accepted his offer to aid Spain against the Apaches. To seal the pledge he had made in the name of his government (subject in some respects to the approval of the commander-general), Anza delivered to Ecueracapa his sabre and banner, and the Comanches responded by "making in the soil a hole which they refilled with various attendant ceremonies."[17] The staff, or insignia of authority which Anza had presented to Ecueracapa, was transferred to Tosacondata, a popular Cuchanec chief, with instructions that he display it in those *rancherías* not represented at the peace council as notice to all Comanches of the pact which had been made with the whites.

As a boon to the Comanches, the peace was celebrated by a fair at Pecos where the Comanches exchanged "more than six hundred hides, many loads of meat and tallow, fifteen riding beasts, and [quite significant] three guns."[18]

The correspondence of the next few months following the peace at Pecos bears evidence of the enthusiasm of the Spaniards and the sincerity of their Indian wards. The Comanches engaged in the war against the Apaches with unusual vigor. Ecueracapa's authority was strengthened and broadened so that by midsummer the great chief reported that he was recognized by all the people of his nation except the larger part of the Yamparikas, with whom he had not treated since they were so far away.[19] Some of the Indians were anxious to learn the Spanish language, but Ugarte, the commander-general, suggested that only the children should be schooled.[20] Ugarte urged that Ecueracapa's authority be strengthened by the appointment of a "lieutenant-general" among the Yupes and Yamparikas, and perhaps another among the eastern *rancherías* of the Cuchanec group, each to be paid a salary of one hundred pesos a year and furnished with a commission from the commander-general. Interpreters were to be maintained among the Comanches, and they should be induced to organize themselves in settlements and cultivate the land.

Concerning the colonization proposal, Anza acted with his accustomed energy. Chief Paranuarimuco of the Jupe division, he who evidently had been commissioned as Ecueracapa's "lieutenant-general," agreed that his people should be the first Comanches to take the white man's road. On the Arkansas river, near the present Pueblo, the village of San Carlos de los Jupes was constructed for this band.[21] The Spaniards spent nearly seven hundred pesos on the project. Artisans built houses, farmers were sent to teach the Indians to farm, and the village of San Carlos provoked the envy of all the other Indians in that region. In fact, the Utes insisted that they must have a village also, and embarrassed the white people by occupying lands already being used.[22]

But pueblos for nomadic Indians did not long remain in style. The Indians abandoned San Carlos almost before it was completed. When a certain woman who was highly esteemed by chief Paranuarimuco died at the village, the chief and his people, according to their custom, abandoned the place immediately and betook themselves to a new location a great way off.[23]

Anza had left New Mexico before the settlement project failed, but he would have been as helpless in preventing it as was his successor. The eagle will not nest in the martin's house, nor the antelope thrive in a pen. Anza's superb tact and ability to fraternize with the barbarians and maintain, withal, their confidence and respect, was worth more than a regiment of soldiers, but he could not make Pueblo Indians of them. Chiefs like Ecueracapa and the Jupe with the unpronounceable name might carry their staffs of authority and wear the king's medals, demanding for the time obedience from all Comanches; but a comprehensive and permanent political system such as Anza contemplated could not exist among these nomadic plainsmen.

It must be said, nevertheless, that this governor succeeded in building up among the Comanches an organization that approached more nearly a general tribal government than any political system that had existed before or was destined to prevail later. Furthermore, he secured for New Mexico a peace with the Comanches that lasted for a generation. In fact, until they were compelled to give up their nomadic existence and come in to the reservation, the Comanches were, with a few exceptions, comparatively friendly towards New Mexico.[24]

The Comanches continued to make war on the Apaches, and at times furnished contingents in the Spanish expeditions that were sent out. They were sometimes useful in ferreting out the foe from his mountain haunts; but they were fickle allies, and the Spaniards complained that they would consume all their rations during the first few days of a campaign and then either withdraw, or beg morsels of food from their white companions.[25] As late as 1810 Cordero, a Texas Kotsoteka, came over to join his kinsmen of the New Mexico border and their Spanish allies against the hated mountain Indians.[26]

WAR AND PEACE IN THE PROVINCE OF TEXAS

In 1718 the Spanish founded San Antonio, Texas. The isolated settlement had many experiences with Indians, but during the first forty years of its existence little or nothing was heard of the Comanches. Then, in order more effectively to carry the gospel to the Apache bands, a mission and a small presidio were established about a hundred miles to the north on the San Saba river, near the present Menard. The Apaches never could find time to attend the mission and be converted; but they were very glad to have the padres and soldiers, particularly the soldiers, in their country, for they had long been engaged in a losing struggle with the fierce Comanches. Now the Spaniards would help them resist these terrible intruders. At any rate, this was the way the Apaches interpreted the coming of the white men, and subsequent events verified their conclusion.

The Comanches did not long delay paying the newcomers a visit. In setting up a mission and fort in the Apache country the Spaniards had become allies of those Indians and enemies of the Comanches. In March, 1758, the Comanches and their allies attacked the mission and killed several persons. It was reported that at least two thousand warriors participated in the attack, all mounted and many of them carrying French firearms.[27] To avenge this insult against the arms of Spain, Colonel Diego Ortiz Parilla moved against the Indians in the following year and attacked them in their entrenched position at the Tawehash villages on Red river, near present Ringgold, Texas.[28] But Spanish pride and arms suffered a severe blow. The allied Indian forces drove the Spaniards away in spite of the latter's swivel guns and a force of six hundred men. Parilla was obliged to abandon his cannon, and was pursued most of the way back to San Saba.[29] Incidentally, a few years later, the courageous Athanase de Mézières, a Frenchman in the Spanish service, recovered single-handed the guns that Parilla lost.

After the attack on the San Saba mission and the Parilla expedition that turned out so poorly for the Spaniards, Comanche attacks on the Spanish settlements became almost a matter of regular routine. Although the frequency and intensity of their raids varied considerably from time to time, the documents in the Bexar Archives indicate that henceforth, until the end of the Mexican régime in Texas, the settlements were never for long free from Comanche attacks. Furthermore, the savages extended their operations to the country along the lower stretches of the Rio Grande, and even south of that stream.

Just as the Spanish policy in New Mexico called for peace with the Comanches whenever it was at all practicable, so likewise did the officials in Texas do everything possible to win over the warlike plainsmen. In 1774, a Frenchman named Gaignard, in the Spanish service, made a treaty with the Yamparikas or "western Comanches" whom he referred to as Naytane. The treaty was made at the Taovayas or Tawehash village, where Parilla had met such ignominious defeat in 1759. Gaignard explained that "the Naytane are a good nation and are not cruel." Also, he added that "the commerce of the Naytane consists in slaves and cattle [buffalo] hides, which they exchange for tobacco, knives, axes, and glass beads."[30]

The great Naytane chief took the flag which Gaignard gave him and promised to place it above the door of his lodge that all Comanches might see it and know that henceforth they must not harm a Spaniard. But the agreement was worth little or nothing to Texas. Gaignard had been dealing with western or northern Comanches, the Yamparikas of Colorado, Kansas, and New Mexico; the southern bands of Kotsotekas and Penatekas continued their attacks on Bexar and other points in Texas. Shortly after this treaty, de Mézières suggested that the Spaniards in Texas try the plan which later proved quite successful in New Mexico, of using the Comanches and their allies against the Apaches. But the death of de Mézières and Spain's participation in the war of the American Revolution prevented the trying out of this idea. However, in 1790, Juan de Ugalde, *comandante* of the Eastern[31] Interior Provinces, did unite the Comanches, Tawehash, Wichitas, and Tawakonies, and use them as allies in his defeat of the Apaches at the Cañon de Ugalde or Uvalde.[32]

First Relations with the White Men

But the depredations of the Comanches became more and more alarming. They stole the horses from the presidial herds at Bexar and La Bahia, they attacked the outpost at Santa Cruz, they drove away the herds from the villages of Rio Grande and Laredo, and left behind them bloody trails across the Rio Grande in Nuevo Santander and Coahuila.

Finally, in 1785, the Spaniards obtained a little relief by drawing some of the leading chiefs of the Comanches *Orientales*, that is, the Kotsotekas and Penatekas,[33] into a formal treaty of peace. In this treaty both sides agreed to bury the hatchet and "treat each other as brothers and good friends," the Indians were to bring in all Spanish captives "in order that they may be redeemed;" they were not to allow foreigners in their villages, and the Spaniards were to send among them traders with goods, and give presents to the chiefs and head-men each year.[34]

Evidently the Indians took the treaty seriously, at least that part that pertained to the presents; for soon Governor Domingo Cabello, half delighted and half alarmed, was sending to his superiors bills for presents, stated that "All [the Comanches] wish to come to learn for sure the consequences of the peace which has been established and the character of those they call their brothers."[35] This matter of presents occasionally became a burden of no little consequence on the impecunious Spanish administration in the northern provinces. Tobacco in large quantities, cloth of many colors, vermillion, needles, knives, awls, various articles of wearing apparel, and beads, which the Indians loved so dearly, made up the principal part of these expenditures. In 1809 the Spanish officials spent on presents for the eastern Comanches and the "Indians of the north" (the latter a somewhat elastic term, which included many tribes), five thousand pesos.[36] Apparently the Spaniards were loathe to give the Indians the one thing they most desired, firearms, with the result that they secured these from American traders, much to the injury of the peace and order of the province. Furthermore, the Texas or eastern Comanches, whose villages were usually found along the upper Colorado, Brazos, and Red rivers, would take horses from the Spaniards and trade them to the western or New Mexico Comanches, who in turn would trade them to the Kansas Indians and other tribes of the north for guns, powder, bullets, spears, cloth, and knives. Thus a certain amount of arms and ammunition came into Texas by this Indian chain, which likewise accounted for the disappearance of many a Spanish horse from herds even as far south as Nuevo Santander.[37]

Evidently the treaty gave the province some relief, but considerable thieving and occasional violence continued. When the responsible chiefs were reprimanded by the white men, they generally laid these depredations on to irresponsible warriors, "crazy boys," whom they could not control; or, when this excuse had been worn threadbare, they might say that they heard that the

Spanish were going to attack their village, or that war had been declared. Sometimes the situation became intolerable, and the Spaniards retaliated with punitive expeditions. But these campaigns did not often result in serious injury to the savages. Then emissaries would be sent out, or the chiefs would hold councils and declare for "peace" and send messengers to Bexar to ask that everything be forgotten and forgiven.[38] The hardpressed Spanish officers could generally not refuse such offers, and the slate would be wiped clean and a new cycle begun. Soon the Comanches would be reported at Bexar in large numbers asking for presents and making much ado about their plans to go and fight the Lipans.[39] In fact, on one occasion, chief Chihuahua came to Bexar and insisted that the governor dress thirty of his braves in uniforms of Spanish soldiers, which the governor did at a cost of 172 pesos. The explanation of this unusual proceeding is that these thirty warriors were to act as a kind of police force to enforce treaty obligations and keep the recalcitrant braves in line.[40] There is no evidence to indicate that these Spanish uniforms helped the cause of peace in any permanent way.

Early in the nineteenth century a new problem arose to add to the vexation of the harassed Spanish officials in Texas. Anglo-Americans began to enter the Comanche villages to trade. The Spaniards were naturally jealous of the Americans, and probably would have looked with suspicion on these intruders even if the latter had not had any relations with the Indians. But the presence of these traders in the Indian villages represented a serious threat to the peace and order of the province. They furnished the savages with arms and munitions and other goods, so that they were no longer dependent on the Spanish for these things. Furthermore, they traded for the Indians' horses, and whenever the Comanche found a horse market, he would supply it by fair means or foul.[41]

Naturally, when the American filibusters moved into Texas in 1812, the Spanish became very uneasy about the attitude of the Comanches, and watched them closely.[42] The Comanche-American horse trade was renewed and carried on more extensively than ever by some of the filibusters who settled in Louisiana after their defeat west of San Antonio.[43] During this period and the years immediately following, the Comanches became more openly hostile, and at times communication between Texas and the rest of New Spain was cut off because messengers could not travel the roads.[44] The Spaniards occasionally sent out expeditions to punish the marauders the results of which were generally insignificant. From time to time the officials talked and wrote of a formidable expedition against the Comanches, powerful enough to destroy the insolence of the strongest bands; but for one reason or another such an expedition was never set on foot.

At the time of the coming of the Anglo-American settlers to Texas, that province and much of the territory adjacent to it was in a pitiable plight. An account, written in 1824, described towns along the Rio Grande as mere skeletons of their former selves, "where widows and orphans weep for dear ones slain," and weep equally for "sons and daughters carried into captivity by these savages to their villages that are over two hundred leagues away, where Christian girls are married to these barbarous people and some sold as slaves to other peoples more remote."[45] By this time the different communities were practically without military protection, there being only fifty-nine soldiers in Texas in 1825. The Indians made raids right up to Bexar, and sometimes into the town. On July 5, 1825, a band of Comanches consisting of 226 men, 104 women, and 44 children, visited San Antonio, remained six days, and in that time committed many depredations. They entered private homes, "insulting and threatening the owners with arms if they did not acquiesce or if they did not permit the Indians to take whatever they desired."[46]

The expanding Spanish empire stopped short when it reached the Great Plains. The San Saba mission project, which was the only effort of consequence made to encroach on the *Comanchería*, failed and had to be abandoned. The Spaniards were not even able to protect their settlements founded within reach of the Comanches, much less to subdue the Indians themselves. Comparative peace prevailed in New Mexico because the Indians found it profitable to trade with these settlements while they preyed on those farther south. The end of a century of conflict found the Indians victors in every respect. Their country had been enlarged, and the Indians they had displaced had been hurled back on the settlements to add to the problems of the white people. The savages not only held the South Plains, but made life and property unsafe in communities hundreds of miles south and west of the Rio Grande.

The Comanches rather than the Spaniards had come to be the aggressors. Their raids extended farther and farther into the north Mexican settlements, and were more destructive than when they were first begun. For every warrior lost in battle, the Indians probably had secured more than one scalp and more than one prisoner. To cope successfully with these fierce warriors of the plains called for more money, more men, and greater resourcefulness than that associated with the Spanish effort during the last three or four decades of the empire. The efforts of the New Mexican government were not one whit more effective.

During their century of contact with the Spaniards and Mexicans, the Comanches acquired many bad habits. They learned to expect presents and regarded them as a reward for keeping the peace during those times when they found it expedient not to make war. The leading chiefs, who received most of the presents, evidently preferred peace and did what they could in the way of admonition and threats to their turbulent followers to keep the agreements with Spain. But the nomadic habits of the tribe and the disposition to break up into small parties prevented the chiefs from accomplishing this end. The different isolated Spanish settlements could not hope for much protection from the local or general governments, and each community was tempted to treat with the savages independently and make with them such agreements as might offer a little protection. Thus, the conception that the white people were located in tribes and that each community was an independent unit became fixed in the savages' minds.

It was an Indian schooled in intercourse of this fashion that the Anglo-Americans were destined to meet in the region of the South Plains. The Americans did not know anything about Indian relations on such a basis, and they naturally would not accept such a condition of affairs. Bold, aggressive, intolerant, and with little understanding of the Indians or sympathy for them, the Anglo-American often treated them with no more consideration than he gave to the dog that trotted at his heels. That violent clashes would result and that war would become almost the normal state of relationship between the two races was inevitable.

THE COMING OF INDIANS AND WHITE MEN FROM THE EAST

It has already been observed that along the Spanish-American border of their country the Comanches, rather than the white men, were the aggressors. Not until after the middle of the nineteenth century were the Indians bothered with invaders from the west. But the story of the eastern border is very different. Here the Comanche country was more inviting to white men as well as to the Indians of the east who were being dispossessed of their lands. Thousands of these red men from east of the Mississippi were located near the Comanche country during the period between 1825 and 1840.[47] These Indians penetrated the Comanche hunting grounds and killed the game which the plains Indians needed.

Up until about 1820 there was very little contact between the Comanches and the Anglo-Americans. Pike looked for them but failed to find them;[48] Major Long, in 1820, met a few Comanches near the Great Bend of the Arkansas, but their demeanor was doubtful, and Long had as little to do with them as possible.[49] Some traders of that day made more progress than the army officers in the matter of cultivating Comanche friendship. Jacob Fowler spent some time in and near the Comanche camps on the upper Arkansas river in 1820;[50] the next year Thomas James and a small party of Missouri traders

A NOTE ON THE PHOTOGRAPHS

The eleven photographs in this book were made between 1869 and 1874 by William S. Soule (1836-1908) while he was post photographer at Fort Sill in the Indian Territory. Taken during his spare time, the negatives were sent to his brother John in Boston, who not only sold individual prints but also gathered together albums of the photographs. One of these albums, in its original blind stamped leather binding, is at the Barker Texas History Center at the University of Texas at Austin. The photos are used here with their permission. The album has a manuscript title-page and captions in manuscript for each of the images. Several tribes are represented in the album; the selection for the present volume includes all of the portraits of Comanches, depicted at the end of their long struggle against submission to life on the reservations.

Tabaloso Comanche

sojourned awhile in the Comanche camps and found some of the tribe friendly and others treacherous.[51] Then, about 1824, there came to the upper Arkansas country William Bent, who henceforth regarded that country as his home. At a site on the north bank of the Arkansas river, some distance above the mouth of Sand Creek, Bent, in 1829, began the construction of an adobe fort which for more than twenty years was the rendezvous of Indians, trappers, and adventurers. To this place goods were brought from the Missouri markets and traded to the Indians and trappers for their pelts and horses. Bent established sub-posts at different points, and his traders and trappers, together with other white men who drifted into the country, soon made the acquaintance of the different Indian tribes of the region.[52]

Meanwhile William Becknell of Missouri thought he saw great possibilities for gain in the Comanche trade; but on learning of the independence of Mexico, he changed his plans and went to Santa Fé in the late autumn of 1821 to trade there on a larger scale. Becknell and his associates proved that it was practicable to go by wagon from Independence, Missouri, or vicinity to Santa Fé, and the famous Santa Fé trail came into existence.[53] This road traversed the battle ground for all the tribes of the South Plains. From the east and northeast the Pawnees, Kansas, and Osages had an open approach and might well claim the right to hunt along the route. On the north and northwest were the Cheyennes and Arapahoes who could claim the right to range along a considerable part of the route, while on the upper Canadian and the tributaries of the Rio Grande various Apache bands were at home. Naturally, the Kiowas and northern Comanches frequented this vicinity. Traders and freighters along the Santa Fé trail were obliged to deal more or less with these various savage divisions, and they sometimes learned more about the Indians than they cared to know. Some attacks were made on the caravans, but the great majority of them went through unscathed.[54] The large caravans were too formidable to be attacked, and the savages were generally satisfied with exacting tolls of the smaller ones.

THE FIRST TREATY WITH THE ANGLO-AMERICANS

While the first American adventurers along the Arkansas river were learning of the Comanches and other Indians of the western plains, others in Indian Territory and Texas were also coming in touch with them. The treatment of affairs in Texas is reserved for another chapter, but the contact along the frontier north of Red river is more intimately related to that on the Santa Fé trail and will be given notice at this time.

About 1832 war and confusion seemed to be increasing in the country west of Indian Territory between the Arkansas and Red rivers. The plains tribes were fighting the one with the other,[55] intruding Indians from the east were going into the prairies and antagonizing the native Indians by killing their game, and the Great Plains country was anything but safe for the few white persons who dared to enter it.[56] These disturbed conditions made it necessary that the United States government restrain the South Plains tribes either by treaty agreements or military force. The government determined to seek a treaty while making at the same time a show of force. To this end combined diplomatic and military expeditions were sent into the prairies of what is now Oklahoma in 1832 and 1833.[57] Neither effort was successful; the Indians kept their distance and no councils were held.

But an expedition launched at Fort Gibson, in June, 1834, resulted in some substantial accomplishments in the direction of friendly relations. The eight companies of dragoons, commanded by Brigadier-general Henry Leavenworth and (after General Leavenworth became incapacitated through illness) by Colonel Henry Dodge, made the most imposing force the United States had ever sent into the plains. The artist, George Catlin, whose pencil sketches of the different Indians and scenes make an invaluable contribution to the history of the plains tribes, accompanied the party.[58]

The expedition (that part of the command not disabled by sickness) went far into the Indian country and visited both the Comanches and Wichitas in their villages, located north of Red river.[59]

The Comanche camp which was visited contained about two hundred skin lodges. About three thousand horses were being herded nearby.[60] As the expedition approached the Comanche village, the Indians naturally became alarmed; but they accepted without reservation Dodge's message (sent in by a Comanche runner) to the effect that the white men came in peace, and a hundred or more warriors rode out, unarmed, to meet the party. After some preliminary ceremonies, which consisted mainly in the two columns of Indians and soldiers respectively gazing at each other for half an hour or more, the head-chief of the band

> ... came galloping up to Colonel Dodge, and having shaken him by the hand, he passed on to the other officers in turn, and then rode alongside of the different columns, shaking hands with every dragoon in the regiment; he was followed in this by his principal chiefs and braves, which altogether took up nearly an hour longer ... .[61]

The white men were shown a place to camp near a spring about a mile from the Indian village. Later the soldiers visited the Indian camp and did considerable trading, a butcher-knife or blanket being considered a fair price for a horse. The men of the party who were still able to travel,[62] 183 in number, went on to the Wichita village on the north fork of Red river. Here councils were held with the Wichitas and also with the Comanche chiefs who gathered at the village. Traveling Wolf,[63] the head-chief of the Comanches, was a mild mannered man of good address who impressed the visitors as being an Indian of character and stamina. The second Comanche chief was a huge fellow named Sun Eagle,[64] who made himself out to be a good Indian, boasting that he had never killed a white man.

While the council with the Comanches and Wichitas was in progress, a band of Kiowas came up and almost provoked a general panic by their rashness and threatening demeanor. Some of their enemies, the Osages, were in the camp of the white men, and this caused the Kiowas to question the friendship of the whole expedition. Fortunately a Kiowa girl, who had been captured by the Osages, was brought along to be restored to her people, and this act of kindness won the friendship of the impulsive plainsmen. The great Kiowa chief, Little Mountain, pledged his friendship to the Americans, and the father of the restored girl wept for joy and gave Colonel Dodge many a hearty hug.

Dodge explained to the Indians that he had come on a friendly visit in the name of the president to urge them to live at peace with each other and to make a firm and lasting peace with the United States. In order to bring this about, he invited and urged the different tribes to select delegations to accompany him on his return to Fort Gibson, where another general council would be held. The other tribes agreed, but the Comanches held back. Finally a small party started with the expedition, but dropped out before reaching Fort Gibson, giving as their excuse the illness of one of their squaws.

The other Indians went on to Fort Gibson, but the failure of the Comanches to attend prevented the making of a satisfactory general treaty. Any agreement without their approval would have been worthless. The Indians who had attended were given flags and presents and sent away, after promising to attend a general council in the "buffalo country" during the summer of the next year, where permanent treaties should be made.[65]

Finally the Indian agents and Coffee's traders[66] gathered the Indians at Camp Holmes, in the Cross Timbers on the Canadian.[67] Governor Montford Stokes from North Carolina, General Matthew Arbuckle (who had succeeded General Leavenworth) and Major F. W. Armstrong were appointed to represent the United States.[68] Some of the Comanches, the Wichitas, and certain border tribes participated in the agreement.[69] The treaty was little more than a pledge of amity and friendship. The savages agreed to share with the border Indians their hunting grounds in the "Great Prairie west of the Cross Timber, to the western limits of the United States;" citizens of the United States were permitted to "pass and repass through their settlements or hunting ground without molestation or injury on their way to any of the provinces of the Republic of Mexico;" and if the Indians stole property from such persons or these travelers took property from the Indians unlawfully, restitution should be made.[70] Since the Indians had little, if any, tribal property, and since the agreement did not call for government annuities, there was no way for the indemnity promise to be enforced against them. Furthermore, the promise of the plains tribes to treat white men and border Indians in a kind and friendly way whenever they found them in their hunting range would be quite as difficult to enforce. White men were already passing through their hunting range, and border Indians had for many years been killing their game. The only change the treaty brought about was that henceforth these practices would be lawful from the white man's point of view. The agreement accomplished but little for either good or evil. Apparently the Indians soon forgot about it since there were no annuity goods to remind them each year of its sacredness, and the government likewise forgot it except when it seemed convenient to invoke it in the interest of the white people.

Furthermore, only a part of the Comanches were represented at the treaty of Camp Holmes. To attempt to state how many of the different divisions of the tribe were represented would be nothing more than conjecture; but the nomadic habits of these Indians and their disposition to range in such widely scattered groups would indicate that several of the main bands were not affected by the treaty. Evidently the band visited by Colonel Dodge in 1834 was there, since the names of Traveling Wolf (Ishacoly) and Sun Eagle (Tabaquena) are found among the signers, but it is likely that a majority of the tribe never heard of the agreement.

In February, 1837, came a report that "She-co-ney" (Ēs-ă-kō'-nēē, Traveling Wolf) had become angry and torn up his treaty when he learned that it permitted the border Indians to hunt in his country and kill his game. Colonel A. P. Chouteau was commissioned to visit this chief and other plains Indians and endeavor to bring about a reconciliation. Chouteau went into the prairies, effected a treaty with the Kiowas, Kiowa-Apache, and Tawakonies[71] and probably brought the Comanches to a better state of mind. At any rate the Comanches brought into Camp Holmes in May, following, three white women and children to be delivered up, and traders were able to purchase others.[72]

Henceforth, until after the middle of the century, accounts of Comanche relations along the Indian Territory frontier are vague and colorless. The scant information available indicates that both white and Indian traders sometimes visited these Indians and that the border tribes continued to annoy them by hunting in their country. The barrier of Indian settlements along the eastern fringe of the Comanche country kept the Comanches out of the Arkansas settlements; they found it dangerous and unprofitable to attack these more advanced and better-armed Indians, and were willing enough to turn their raiding operations against the Texan and north Mexican frontiers. All that they asked of the United States government was to be left alone, and they were not disturbed. At times efforts were made by the Creeks (traditional friend of the Comanches) and by Governor Butler, Cherokee agent, to establish more intimate relations with them, but the Comanches failed to respond to these overtures, and little was accomplished in this direction.[73]

CONDITION OF THE INDIANS

The account of relations between the United States and Indians of the South Plains during the thirties of the nineteenth century would be incomplete without some consideration of the descriptions of the savages made by those who observed them. In 1836 Major P. L. Chouteau,[74] in a report to Governor Stokes and General Arbuckle, on authority of information received from A. LeGrand, representative of the Texas government to the Comanches, estimated the number of Comanche warriors at 4,500; the Kiowas at 1,500; the Kiowa Apaches at 300; and the Wichitas, Wacoes, Tawakonies, and Kichaies collectively, at less than a thousand.[75] Probably this estimate is too high, especially that for the Comanches, but it is in keeping with other estimates and conjectures made at that time. Chouteau made note of the kind and hospitable treatment accorded him by these Indians. He stated that the Kiowas and Comanches had a firm alliance of friendship which both sides adhered to rigidly, and that the Kiowas ranged at will throughout the Comanche country. These wandering tribes traded extensively with the Wichita and neighboring agricultural bands, who raised corn and vegetables. Catlin and Wheelock of the Dodge expedition of 1834 were impressed with the large herds of horses the Comanches possessed. On inspection these did not prove to be the "splendid *Arabian horses*" they had expected to see, but they did find some "tolerable nags amongst this medley group of all colors and all shapes . . ."[76]

They found the plains Indians armed principally with bows and lances, with very few guns. They had just been trading with the "Spaniards" (Mexican traders from New Mexico, generally called *Comanchéros*), a party of whom had left the Wichita village but a short time before Dodge arrived. The Comanche women were always decently clad in deer skins, and Wheelock observed that they were "good looking women." Wheelock described the Comanche men as "fine looking," generally naked, although some of them wore blankets, and added that the "appearance of a Comanche fully equipped on horseback, with his lance and quiver and shield by his side, is beautifully classic."[77] Sergeant Hugh Evans, the personal orderly of Colonel Dodge, was particularly impressed with the fine appearance of the Comanches and their mounts, stating that they "ride gracefully and are excellent horsemen."[78] Wheelock's comparison of the different tribes is so forceful and expressive as to warrant quoting. He writes:

> The Comanche squaws are very troublesome, they steal everything that they can secrete. The Toyash [Wichita] women are infinitely more respectable; the difference in these three tribes seems to be somewhat thus: the Comanche is an arrogant, jealous, savage Don; the Toyash a savage farmer; whilst the Kiowa, more chivalric, impulsive and daring than either, reminds one of the bold clannish Highlander, whose very crimes are made, by the poet, captivating . . .[79]

These soldiers and white adventurers saw the Indians of the plains before there had been anything but brief and casual intercourse with Anglo-Americans, and before the Indians from east of the Mississippi had made inroads of consequence on their hunting grounds. It is significant that all accounts, including Catlin's sketches, give evidence of the absence of want and hunger, and indicate beyond a doubt that in their savage simplicity these Indians as yet knew nothing of that poverty which later drove them to desperation.

CHAPTER THREE

New White People in Texas

BECOMING ACQUAINTED WITH THE ANGLO-AMERICANS

A brief account of the Comanches in Texas during the Spanish era was given in a preceding chapter. In that connection it was observed that the Spaniards sought persistently to win and retain the friendship of these Indians, but that treaties made were soon broken, so that war became almost the normal condition in the province of Texas.

On the other hand, the first Anglo-Americans were not seriously troubled by the Comanches. The colonies of the empresarios Austin, DeWitt, and DeLeon were located mainly outside the territory claimed by the Comanches, and the savages generally saw fit to direct their raids against the Mexican settlements rather than against the homes of the newcomers. Most of them professed friendship for the colonists. On one occasion Stephen F. Austin was captured by a party of Comanches and for a few moments feared for his life, but when the chief learned that he was an "American," he released him and ordered his goods restored. A few articles, including the empresario's Spanish grammar, were not returned, but for this the chief was not to blame.[1] The savages continued to take horses from the Mexican settlements and sell them to American traders, and the advantages of these transactions tended to keep them friendly toward the white men of the east.[2]

During the Texas revolution the Anglo-Americans watched the Comanches with misgivings, fearing that they would join the Mexican invaders in an orgy of rapine and plunder. Although some savage marauders attacked parties of fleeing colonists and plundered a few abandoned cabins, most of the southern bands did not take advantage of the opportunity for destructive forays which the panic in the settlements presented. The northern bands were not so considerate of the Texans, however. In May, 1836, they joined their Kiowa allies in one of the most destructive raids ever made along the Texas frontier. This attack was directed against Parker's Fort, near the present town of Groesbeck, in Limestone county. Some thirty-four persons, about half of them children and mostly descendants or relatives of Elder John Parker, were living at the "fort" or stockade, which was situated in the very van of the frontier.

Only five or six men were at the stockade when, on the morning of May 19, several hundred Comanche and Kiowa Indians appeared on the prairie nearby. They sent under a white flag two messengers to the building, who stated that they were friendly and had come to make a treaty with the white people. When these messengers, who were evidently spies, returned to the main band and reported the small number of persons at the place, the Indians attacked it and killed several of the inhabitants, although a number escaped. The Indians took away five captives, namely, Mrs. Rachel Plummer, Mrs. Elizabeth Kellogg, James Pratt Plummer, the eighteen-months-old son of Mrs. Plummer, and Cynthia Ann and John Parker, who were children of Silas Parker. All of the prisoners were finally ransomed or captured and returned to their people, but Mrs. Plummer and Mrs. Kellogg suffered immeasurably from exposure and cruel treatment, and the story of their experiences, when finally told, added to the bitter hatred the frontier people had for all Indians.[3] Cynthia Ann Parker had lived with the Indians twenty-four years at the time of her capture, and her story is one of the most widely known in all the saga of the Texas frontier.[4]

COUNCILS AND TREATIES

The summer and autumn passed in Texas without depredations of great consequence, a condition to be accounted for largely by the decisive victory of the Texans at San Jacinto. News traveled rapidly among Indians, and it may be presumed that the Texas bands soon learned of the severe Mexican defeat and were not anxious to antagonize the victors over Santa Anna.[5] In the spring of 1837 the Cherokee chief, Bowl, was commissioned to visit the different Comanche divisions. The Cherokee found those Comanches nearest the Texas settlements quite friendly, but they warned him that it would not be safe to go to the villages of their northern kinsmen. In spite of their admonition Bowl went ahead and visited the different Comanche groups on the upper Brazos, Wichita, and Red rivers. He found sixteen villages which he described as "those who trade with Coffee." In this vicinity he found parties returning from both the Texas and Mexican frontiers with large droves of horses and mules, and numbers of women and children prisoners. He felt that the treatment accorded him by the northern Comanches was insulting, and he was ready to go to war against them with a band of Texans and eastern Indians.[6]

Meanwhile, President David G. Burnet, who had lived with the Comanches and understood something of their loose tribal organization, appointed Major A. LeGrand[7] to visit the northern bands and negotiate a treaty. LeGrand proceeded to Fort Gibson, and thence into the prairies, where he got in touch with the Indians.[8] But he was obliged to report that his hopes of a treaty had not been realized. To LeGrand's proposal, Chief Traveling Wolf replied that

> so long as he continued to see the gradual approach of the whites and their habitations to the hunting grounds of the Comanches, so long would he believe to be true what the Mexicans had told him, *viz.*, that the ultimate intention of the white man was to deprive them of their country; and so long would he continue to be the enemy of the white race.[9]

Evidently the southern Comanches were not so bellicose. But Indian affairs in Texas failed to improve during 1837, and by the fall of that year the congress of the republic had come to consider seriously the Comanche problem and to doubt the possibility of ever establishing satisfactory relations with these Indians without first paying the price of an armed conflict with them. On November 1, the house committee on Indian Affairs recommended that "the Comanches on the northwest frontier should be acted against offensively, always having in view, the seizure of the first opportunity to make with them a lasting peace."[10] The northern bands and their allies, the Kiowas, were the Indians principally engaged in these marauding expeditions; but the Texans failed to make any distinction between the different divisions, and regarded all Comanches as alike guilty.

Meanwhile, President Houston was more hopeful of the situation than congress, and urged a system of regulated trade as the best means of solving the Indian problem in Texas generally, as well as bringing about better relations with the "great Comanche tribe." Congress took little interest in the president's proposal, but instead continued to enact measures for the public defense.[11]

Thus, during the first two years of its existence, the government of the Republic of Texas was neither at peace nor at war with the Comanches. Open war had been avoided, but irregular conflicts had continued, and the attitude of these Indians was always uncertain. In the spring of 1838 it seemed, however, that the president's pacific policy would be successful, at least with the southern or Penateka division of the tribe. On February 4, a party of one hundred fifty warriors made their appearance at San Antonio, representing that several of their principal chiefs were encamped north of that place some 250 miles, and requesting that a party of citizens go out with them to their camps and make a treaty of peace. The citizens responded to their overtures and a party, among whom was Mosely Baker, member of congress, accompanied the Indians to their main camping place.[12]

The Texans were received kindly by the leading men of the band, and they held a council with about fifteen head-men and chiefs. In this council it developed that the Indians were anxious to secure a treaty of peace, but insisted that a definite boundary agreement was a *sine qua non*. In fact, they said that they would not listen to any terms unless the government would guarantee to them "full and undisputed possession of the country north of the Guadalupe mountains."[13] This would necessitate the surrender of one of the richest portions of the state, and such regions as Bastrop county in the valley of the Colorado would have been very close to the line of division. The white men were much disturbed at finding that Mexican emissaries had been tampering with the Comanches, trying to persuade them to take up arms against the Texans and assuring them that the Texans were planning to take all of their lands and drive them out of the republic. Likewise, certain Shawnee Indians from north of the Red river had been giving the Comanches bad advice, inspired probably by their desire to hold the trade which they would lose if these Indians became too friendly with the Texans.

The whole situation was complicated by the rapid expansion of the Texas settlements at this time. In fact, it was probably this advance of the white men that had inspired the natives to make their peace overtures. The land offices of the republic had been opened,[14] people from the United States were coming by the thousands,[15] and the Comanche country, hitherto comparatively free from the intrusion of surveying parties, was disturbed all along its eastern and southern fringe by daring men who carried instruments that "stole the land."

In the informal council at the Comanche village, the Texans would not discuss the boundary question, but promised to take it up with their government. It was agreed that a general council for the purpose of negotiating a treaty should be held at San Antonio in April.

The Comanches were late as usual, but they finally arrived about the first of May under the leadership of their chiefs, Isowacony and Isomania. General Albert Sidney Johnston[16] conducted the negotiations for the government, although Colonel Henry W. Karnes and others probably participated in the "talk." In keeping with his instructions,[17] Johnston refused to consider binding his government by a definite boundary agreement. While he tried to discuss the great advantages of peace with the whites and the benefits to be derived from trade between the two races, the Indians persisted in claiming some interest in the land they had occupied for nearly a century, and told him plainly that they did not want trading posts in their country. Thus did the Texas government refuse to concede that the Indians had any possessory rights to their ancestral hunting grounds, thereby preventing any formal peace agreement. Johnston then tried to get the chiefs to visit the president at Houston; but each chief held back and politely insisted that the other make the journey, with the result that neither of them ever went. The Indians were given presents and left the council in a friendly state of mind. But the encroachment by the white people on Comanche territory continued apace, and the Indians would not long endure this intrusion.

|However, this peace agreement proved to be of little value by way of improving Comanche relations in Texas. There was no formal treaty, and the promise which the Indians made to keep the peace was conditioned on the cessation of encroachment by the white people on Comanche territory. There was no cessation and the Government could not compel it, notwithstanding the orders from the land office. |

While negotiations were going on with the Comanches about San Antonio, another band, located along the Colorado not far from the present site of Austin, made overtures for peace and friendship. According to Noah Smithwick, who belonged to a ranger force operating from Fort Coleman, a few miles down the Colorado from where Austin is now located, two chiefs, the Eagle and Puestia,[18] came to the post and asked for peace. Since both Smithwick and the Indians could speak a little Spanish, Smithwick took the leading part in the negotiation. The Indians asked that a commissioner go with them to their village and talk over the terms of a treaty with their leading chiefs; so, with some misgivings as to his safety, Smithwick went along with them and spent some three months in their camp.[19] The Indians treated him kindly, and his stay with them was not unpleasant. He finally persuaded the savages to go with him to Houston and make a treaty with the government. A Mr. V. R. Palmer, a merchant of Bastrop, also accompanied them.

The treaty did not contain any provisions of consequence other than a promise that an agent would be appointed to protect the Indians and supervise the trade with them.[20] A. P. Miles was appointed agent, or resident commissioner, following the signing of the treaty, and the trading arrangement was left to Palmer, who was to establish a trading house at Tumlinson's Block House on Brushy creek. It seems that the treaty was never ratified by the senate,[21] Palmer did not establish the trading post, and Miles did not keep in touch with the Indians. Such failures made it appear to the savages that the government was not keeping faith with them.[22] Furthermore, the absence of a definite boundary provision in the treaty would have made it almost useless even if the other agreements had been carried out. When the Indians raised the boundary question, the president is reported to have said: "If I could build a wall from the Red river to the Rio Grande, so high that no Indian could scale it, the white people would go crazy trying to devise means to get beyond it."[23] Encroachment continued, however, and this made a state of active war inevitable.

President Houston's plan for a system of trading houses and field agents has much to commend it, and if it had been given a fair trial, it might have improved conditions. But trading houses built, to be followed close upon by the white man's clearing and cabin, would have had no value whatever. The people of Texas were not willing to limit their territory for the benefit of the savages, and that fact alone made all other arrangements, or proposed arrangements, futile. Furthermore, the Comanches had for many years depended in a great measure on raids against the Mexican settlements to secure horses, blankets, and other items essential to their preservation. It was to be expected that they would transfer these plundering operations to the settlements of their Anglo-American neighbors whenever the occasion was offered under conditions that promised impunity. As the white people pressed into the Comanche region, they exposed themselves to attacks more and more, and the temptation for the Indians became greater each year. Thus, both the Indians and the white frontiersmen provoked hostilities. Lamar, who succeeded Houston as president, did not try to prevent war, and Houston could not have prevented it if he had been president during the years that followed his first administration. Vigorous, aggressive, white frontiersmen on the one hand, and irresponsible Indian raiders on the other made war the natural condition on the Texas frontier. Before beginning the account of these wars, let us give some consideration to the appearance, habits, and customs of these Texas Comanches and the impression they made on the Indian-hating Americans.

THE COMANCHES OF TEXAS

It seems that all the Comanches the Americans came to know in Texas with any degree of intimacy belonged to the Penateka or southern division of the tribe. The different northern divisions seldom visited the Texas settlements. At least two bands, or Penateka sub-divisions, can be somewhat definitely located, and doubtless there were several more. The group with which Smithwick was associated was that of Muguara, which was making its headquarters along the Colorado north of Bastrop. In their village of fifty lodges were three American and three Mexican prisoners. Only one of these, a Mexican woman, cared to leave; the others, having been taken in early childhood, were perfectly satisfied. The Eagle had out of kindness adopted a little Waco boy, whom he treated as though he had been his own child.[24] This band, being the most easterly of the Comanche groups, was in close touch with the Wacoes, fighting them and holding peace councils alternately. For a while, during 1838, these Indians carried on an extensive trade with the people of Bastrop, coming in on one occasion 150 strong, bringing a large amount of peltry.[25]

Almost without exception the Anglo-Americans were impressed with the squalor and degradation of these Indians, and held them in contempt.[26] When the party visited Houston to make the treaty, the people of the town were disappointed to find that instead of the fine, athletic, dashing fellows they had expected to see, they were "diminutive, squalid, half-naked, poverty-stricken savages, armed with bows and arrows and mounted on wretched horses and mules." Major LeGrand explained to the editor of the *Telegraph and Texas Register* that these Indians were "Comanches of the woods," that they were a "poor, abject race, and hardly bear any resemblance to the Comanches of the prairies."[27]

The other band that stands out somewhat distinctly at this time is that of the chiefs Isowacony and Isomania, which ranged north of San Antonio, on the Blanco river. Persons who visited their village estimated it at four hundred or five hundred lodges, containing a thousand Indians—too small a number if the lodges were correctly estimated. Perhaps the words of one of these white men can best express the contempt in which they held these Indians. This writer stated, to quote his exact expression in part:

> We had heard much of the nobility of this race, and expected to meet the noble savages in all the pride and lofty bearing which we had heard imputed to them by travellers from the far west. Judge of our disappointment then, when we found the village of the *Principal Chief* to be filled with naked, half-starved savages; and of the very lowest order of the human species. They appeared to be but one removed from the brute creation and infinitely inferior to any other nation of Indians which has come within our knowledge. | On the fourth day after our arrival, Isowacony [Ēs-ă Wäk'-kä-nў, Wolf-Turtle] attended by six of his principal chiefs, made their appearance. They received us with many demonstrations of pleasure for the honor we had done them by our visit. We learned from them that the Nation consisted of about 20,000 souls, and could raise about 5,000 warriors. They never cultivate any ground, and depend entirely on hunting for a support. Consequently, they cannot live except in small parties. This would render inefficient a much more formidable people than themselves. Without commissaries, a body of

1,000 Indians cannot be kept together for one week. They range over a country of more than one thousand miles in extent, principally in small parties; and we were assured the company on the Rio Blanco would soon have to be divided, on account of the impossibility of so large a party's securing sustenance. | They were badly armed—not having more than six or eight guns in the village, and were but indifferent marksmen. It was a general impression that our company of thirteen might have whipped the whole village.

After stating that this band had about five hundred horses and mules, some of which were of very good quality, and commenting on some of their customs and habits, the writer stated that "The women are destitute of even the semblance of virtue, and the men as corrupt as the females are degraded."[28]

Evidently the Comanches of the south were not faring so well as their kinsmen north of the Red river. Apparently the many decades of contact with the Spanish and with the Anglo-American colonists in recent years had proved to be demoralizing. They were approaching a condition of hunger and want, and the difficulties of securing a living were destined to increase as the Americans pushed farther and farther into their territory. No doubt the contempt in which the Americans held these savages was partly responsible for the difficulties that soon developed between the two races. The Texans were correct in their conclusion that a band of Comanche warriors was no match for an equal number of white frontiersmen on the field of battle; but they failed to take into account how elusive these warriors of the plains could be. Up to this time the Indian enemy the American frontiersmen had known had been, for the most part, braves who fought on foot and who lived in fixed and permanent villages. Such Indians could be struck *en masse* and defeated, and their villages could be reached and destroyed. Not so with the Comanche; he had no permanent abode, and on a few minutes' notice he could pack up all his belongings and flee with his family. Once in motion, it was generally impossible to overtake him; for his tough ponies and mules may have seemed scrubby in comparison with Kentucky thoroughbreds, but for the use to which they were put, they were the best to be had. Furthermore, the Comanche was a master in the art of getting the maximum amount of service out of a horse. It is likewise true that the Texans did not count the destructive power of these Indians when divided up into small raiding parties. Six warriors could destroy a home and murder its occupants as effectively as six hundred, if they could catch the white people unaware. Thus a few score braves could harry a long stretch of the frontier at the same time, and generally escape with impunity. And so it came about that these "diminutive, squalid, half-naked" savages brought terror to the

Texas frontier repeatedly for more than a third of a century. When the Texans later came to know them better, they may have continued to hate them, but they did not make the mistake of regarding them as of such little consequence.

| These peace agreements of 1838 were of little value in preventing hostilities. It has already been pointed out that they could not have settled the Comanche problem even if they had been carried out for the reason that they did not provide for a boundary between the white and Indian country. |

WARS WITH THE TEXANS

The peace councils of 1838 had scarcely closed before complaints were made that the Comanches were again committing hostile acts. It was alleged that they even took scalps within the town of San Antonio, and they were charged with the murder of fifteen traders who had left for the Indians' camps on May 25 and were never seen by white men thereafter.[29] In August they attacked Colonel Karnes and his rangers at the Arroyo Seco, and in October several citizens of San Antonio were "butchered" within three miles of the town.

The commissioner of Indian Affairs berated the Indians and charged them with treachery. They may have been guilty of treachery, but it cannot be charged that they were responsible for the hostilities that followed. In all their peace promises (and the Comanches of the west had never entered into a formal treaty with the Republic of Texas), they had conditioned their friendly treatment of the white people on a boundary agreement that would secure to them their country. This had not been granted them; the surveyors continued to steal their land, and white intruders to mistreat them. Thus, their resistance was perfectly natural.

President Mirabeau B. Lamar, who succeeded Houston in December, 1838, was an avowed exponent of the war policy, and in his message to congress of December 20 he stated in substance that Houston's practice of exhibiting mercy without showing strength had proved a failure. He thought that the government should carry on a vigorous and aggressive war against the savages until their warriors had been decimated and their military strength broken. He favored the establishment of a line of military posts along the frontier, and the maintenance in the field of a "regular, permanent and efficient force."[30] Lamar's opinion that war represented the only solution to the Texas Indian problem was shared by George W. Bonnell, commissioner of Indian Affairs under Houston, and Albert Sidney Johnston, Lamar's secretary of war.[31] The fact is that the Lamar administration had no choice as to peace or war with the Comanches. It found the war already existing; the only question was the energy and resources that were to be put into fighting it. Congress promptly responded to the president's proposals, and by acts of December,

1838, and January, 1839, provided for a system of frontier forts, authorized the placing of over a thousand men in the field, and appropriated a million dollars to be used in the defense of the country.[32]

Naturally the frontier people were not averse to this war policy, and when reports came to the settlements on the upper Colorado that a large band of Comanches was encamped to the north of them, a company of men from Bastrop under Noah Smithwick joined the La Grange company under Captain W. M. Eastland, and the two companies under the command of Colonel John H. Moore marched into the Comanche country late in January, 1839. The entire force was made up of volunteers, and no regular troops participated.

On the morning of February 15 the party, which consisted of sixty-three white men and sixteen Lipan Indians under their chief, Flacco, attacked a large Comanche village at Spring creek near the mouth of the San Saba. The attackers took the Indian camp by surprise, and killed a number of its inhabitants, but they were soon set upon by a large force of warriors, and were glad to withdraw without serious loss. Then the Indians proposed a parley, sending out one of their number with a white flag, the same one that had been presented to them in May, 1838, at their treaty with President Houston. This was to request an exchange of prisoners; for they stated that they held five white captives, among them being a mature white woman and a girl, Matilda Lockhart, who had been captured a few months before on the Guadalupe, and whose father, Andrew Lockhart, was in Moore's party. Unfortunately, Moore's Lipan allies had slain all the Comanche prisoners the party had taken,[33] and the white prisoners could not be rescued. The white flag in their possession leads to the conclusion that this was Muguara's band, which had been joined by other Comanches.

Other depredations by the Indians were followed by attacks on the savages by bands of citizens. In some of these engagements the white men were worsted.[34] Notwithstanding their superior organization and equipment, the white men of the Texas frontier were finding the Comanches a formidable enemy.

During the year 1839 a great part of the efforts of the Texans was spent in driving the Cherokees out of the republic[35] and in participating in the revolutionary conflicts in Mexico. The Indians for the most part stayed away from the frontier, and there was not much fighting during the summer and fall of that year.

Once again, in the winter of 1839–1840, the Comanches asked for peace. Although they had not suffered serious defeat, the responsible chiefs realized that war with the Texans would finally lead to their destruction. Accordingly, about January 10, 1840, three Indians appeared at San Antonio and repre-

Comanche brave

Comanche squaw

sented to Colonel Karnes that they had been commissioned by their tribesmen in general council to ask for peace on any conditions the white people might name. Karnes replied that before the government would cease its war against them, they must give up their white captives, restore to its owners all stolen property in their possession, and give guarantees to keep the peace in the future. This the representatives said the council had decided to do. Karnes doubted their sincerity, but gave them presents and agreed that they should go tell their chiefs to come in for a council. Karnes suggested procedure that was later followed by the Texans in his statement that their number was "too inconsiderable to think of retaining them as hostages;"[36] and suggested that there should be sent to San Antonio along with the commissioners to treat with the Indians "a force sufficient to justify our seizing and retaining those who may come in, as hostages for the delivery of such American captives as may at this time be among them."

On receipt of Karnes's message, Johnston instructed Colonel William S. Fisher, commander of the first regiment of infantry, to repair to San Antonio with three companies of his regiment and be prepared to seize the Indians when they came, in case they should fail to deliver up the captives. It was stated to Fisher that the Indians must be made to understand that Texas citizens might, under sanction of the law, occupy any vacant lands of the government, and that the Indians must keep away from the settlements. Thus, the Lamar government not only would not consider any matter pertaining to the recognition of an "Indian country," but proposed to bring up in the most objectionable way its theory that the Indians were tenants at will and might be pushed aside whenever white men saw fit to enter their territory. Furthermore, the practice of giving presents to the Indians was to be entirely discontinued, it was planned by the authorities.[37]

Colonel Hugh McLeod, adjutant-general, and Colonel William G. Cooke, quartermaster-general, were appointed commissioners, and went to San Antonio. The Indians came on the morning of March 19, to the number of sixty-five women, children, and men all told. They brought along a number of ponies and a considerable quantity of peltry for trading. At San Antonio they must have felt at home; for their old men could remember when they held pow-wows there and received presents from the Spanish dons; and the younger people could remember how in later years they had swaggered about the old town to the annoyance and even the terror of its Mexican inhabitants. They had often been insolent, and their unwilling hosts had given them many a rebuff, but treachery they had never known in San Antonio. There was no uneasiness or fear, and as the men gathered in the court house for the council, the women and children remained in the yard near by where the boys entertained a small audience by shooting at pieces of money put up as targets for their arrows by some of the assembled white people.[38]

In the council, "Mukewarrah" (Muguara), Noah Smithwick's friend and one of the signers of the treaty at Houston, was the spokesman for the Indians. They had brought along but one prisoner, Matilda Lockhart, who told the commissioners that there were others, that she had seen them a few days before at the main camp. She stated that the savages had planned to get as high a price for her as possible and, if such tactics proved successful, they would bring in the others one at a time and secure large prices for them likewise. On receiving this information, the commissioners ordered the troops brought up to the council house and preparations were made to seize and hold the Indians.

The chiefs were called together and a demand made that they bring in the other prisoners. To this Muguara replied that they had brought the only prisoner they had, that the others were with other tribes. This answer is plausible and likely true if, for the word "tribe," band is substituted. That is, Muguara, who never had a large following, probably brought in the only prisoner he had, although there were several others with the different Penateka bands. At this a pause ensued and the chief, observing the pause, made inquiry; "How do you like the answer?" The account is from McLeod's report:

> The order was now given to march one company into the council room, and the other in the rear of the building, where the warriors were assembled. During the execution of this order, the talk was reopened, and the terms of a treaty directed by your excellency to be made with them in the case the prisoners were restored, were discussed, and they were told the treaty would be made when they brought in the prisoners. They acknowledged that they had violated all their previous treaties, and yet tauntingly demanded that new confidence should be reposed in another promise to bring in the prisoners.
>
> The troops being now posted, the chiefs and captains were told that they were *our* prisoners and would be kept as hostages for the safety of our people, then in their hands, and they might send the young men to the tribe, and as soon as our friends were restored they should be liberated.
>
> Capt. Howard, whose company was stationed in the council house, posted sentinels at the doors and drew up his men across the room. We told the chiefs that the soldiers they saw were their guards, and descended from the platform. The chiefs immediately followed. One sprang to the back door and attempted to pass the sentinel, who presented his musket, when the chief drew his knife and stabbed him . . .

At this, a general melee began which resulted in the killing of seven white persons, the wounding of eight, and the killing of thirty-five Indians, including three women and two children. Twenty-seven Indian women and children and two old men were captured.

At the request of the prisoners, a squaw was sent to the Comanches to inform them that their people were being held for exchange for white prisoners whenever they should bring them in. But only two or three prisoners were obtained in exchange, for when the news of the tragedy that had befallen their people reached the Comanches, they took their white captives, thirteen in number, and put them to death with great torture, sparing only a boy and a little girl both of whom had been adopted into the tribe.[39] Most of the Comanche prisoners were kept for some time, but the vigilance of the guard was relaxed and one by one they escaped and again took up their abode with their own people.

Just nine days after the council house affair, chief Isomania led between two hundred fifty and three hundred of his warriors to the edge of San Antonio, left his men there under arms and, in the company of another warrior, rode about the town swearing at the Americans and challenging them for a combat. Later he led his warriors to the mission San José, where the troops were quartered, and repeated the challenge. However, the Texans had on March 20, the day after the fight, made a twelve-day truce with the Comanches, and the citizens and soldiers alike refused to fight the enraged chief. Thus the Indians were obliged to be content with heaping abuse on the people they felt had betrayed them in such a foul manner.[40]

The ethics of a policy whereby the enemy who comes on an invitation to treat for peace is seized and held as a hostage may well be brought into question. However, the horrors of Indian warfare had caused the Americans to hate the red men so bitterly that we cannot be other than tolerant towards them. The disfigured face of Matilda Lockhart alone must have been sufficient to make the frontiersmen who saw her want to kill every Comanche from the Platte to Durango.[41]

But, laying aside all ethical considerations and viewing the matter wholly on practical grounds, the council house fight was a great blunder. In his report McLeod states that there were twelve chiefs in the party, and leaves the impression that these were the principal men of the Comanche tribe. But it is highly improbable that twelve chiefs would have come into San Antonio with only a handful of warriors and a few women and children. Muguara was not the head-chief of the southern Comanches. We know from Smithwick's account that his village consisted of only fifty lodges. Isomania, the worst of the depredating chiefs and far more powerful than Muguara, was not in the band.

Ēs-ă-wäk′-kä-nў who claimed to be the principal chief of the southern Comanches, is not mentioned in the report. He was well known at San Antonio, and surely he would have been mentioned if he had been in the group. Furthermore, there must have been at least two thousand Penatekas or southern Comanches at this time (the Texans thought there were more), and the killing of some three score of them could not have materially reduced the fighting strength of the tribe. The tragedy provoked severe retaliatory raids by the Indians, and destroyed whatever confidence the Comanches had in the integrity and honesty of the Texas government. In fact, ever after this affair, the southern Comanches, naturally wild and ready to distrust the motives of white men, would, at the slightest gesture from the military forces scatter and run to cover like frightened quail.

As was to be expected, the Indians determined to make a retaliatory raid. Early in August a party of four or five hundred warriors came out of the mountains and passed down the prairie between the Colorado and Guadalupe rivers.[42] They attacked Victoria, but were prevented from entering the town. Then they crossed the Guadalupe and moved on to Linnville on the coast, which they attacked on August 8. Here they took the village unaware, and would have murdered all the inhabitants if they had not fled to boats in the harbor. The fact that the Indians moved so swiftly and directly towards this obscure coastal landing point caused the Texan officials to conclude that they had been prompted by certain Arkansas traders to attack it at this time, they thinking that the warehouse would be a rich prize.[43] On their way down the Indians left behind them a trail of blood, and killed altogether more than twenty people.

News of the raid spread rapidly, and the militia from Austin, Bastrop, and Gonzales under Ben McCulloch, Matthew Caldwell, Felix Huston, and Edward Burleson gathered to cut off their retreat. At the forks of Plum creek near the present town of Lockhart, the white men attacked, put the Indians to rout, and chased them as far north as the San Antonio road. In the running fight the Indians lost much of their plunder, and killed or abandoned their prisoners. Their defeat at the hands of the militia was decisive; they lost fifty or more warriors.[44]

The people of Texas felt that the defeat at Plum creek had not been sufficient punishment for the Comanches, and it was determined to follow up the victory by sending an expedition into their country and attacking them wherever they might be found. Accordingly, Colonel John H. Moore sent out circulars calling for volunteers, and about the first of October a force of about ninety white men and twelve Lipan Indians under their chief, Castro, set out under Moore's command. The white men were mostly from the Fayette and Bastrop communities, which had been exposed to Indian attacks.

The command marched to a point which may have been as far north as Colorado, Texas, where the Lipans stalked the enemy in a village which was estimated at sixty families with one hundred twenty-five warriors. In a night attack the white men rushed on the sleeping Indian camp with such fury that only a few of the warriors made their escape. It is said that the party left one hundred thirty Indians dead on the field, and took away as captives thirty-four squaws and children. They also brought back a *caballada* of five hundred horses, and recovered some of the goods plundered at Linnville during the preceding summer.[45] This was the severest defeat the Comanches in Texas had ever suffered at the hands of white men. No doubt the great distance of their village from the frontier settlements gave the Indians a false sense of security. Also, the fact that Moore had to march nearly three hundred miles northwest of Austin to find a Comanche village indicates that the hostile policy of the Texas government was driving the Indians back. Apparently the savages were losing their taste for war with the white people; for the country was comparatively free from Comanche raids during the winter that followed. Obviously the severe policy had been effective in reducing the frequency and destructiveness of the raids of this tribe. The country was not free from Comanche troubles during 1841, but hostilities were confined largely to the country around San Antonio.[46] Also, during the next year, there was serious Indian trouble, but most of it was laid to other tribes.

CHAPTER FOUR

Sam Houston and Peace

The Texans had been merciless and persistent in these Indian wars and in order to save themselves, the savages had withdrawn into the prairies, far away from the frontier. Except for the brief reports of the ranger and militia officers recounting occasional encounters or describing some raid, little is heard of the Comanches for nearly two years following the council house affair. They knew the Texans as enemies only, and their communication with them was negligible until Sam Houston became president again in December, 1841. In his message to congress of December 20, the president indicated that the Texas government would return to the pacific policy he had always advocated, and that an effort would be made to bring about friendly relations with the Indians again.[1]

INVITATIONS TO THE PEACE COUNCILS

To restore the Indians' confidence in the Texas government, it was necessary to hold councils and make treaties with all Texas Indians, and to that task Houston directed his efforts early in 1842. Scouts were sent to find the different tribes and bands and inform them that the present "Chief" of the Texans was the friend of all red men and wished to make with them a lasting peace. But progress in this direction was slow. The more docile bands responded readily; the Comanches, the dominant tribe of all Texas Indians, persistently remained away from the councils. Finally the president laid upon Colonel J. C. Eldredge,[2] his general superintendent of Indian Affairs, the arduous and dangerous task of finding the bellicose plainsmen and winning their friendship and confidence. Hamilton P. Bee and the experienced Indian trader Thomas Torrey accompanied Eldredge. The Delaware scouts John Conner and Jim Shaw guided the party, and Delaware hunters, four Indian children prisoners, and a few supernumeraries completed the personnel of the expedition. A-cah-quash, or Acer-quash, a friendly Waco chief, later joined the expedition.

The purpose of the journey was to find the Comanche Indians in general, and the great Penateka chief, Päh'-häh-yō'-kō,[3] in particular, and bring them into a council to be held at Bird's Fort on the Trinity.

The commissioners joined their escort of Indian guides and trappers at the council ground near the present Waco. Jim Shaw thought Päh'-häh-yō'-kō was on the headwaters of the Brazos, and the party set out in that direction, May 15, 1843. Later information revealed the fact that the great chief was still farther to the north, and not until August 3 did Eldredge find these Indians at a place in what is now Oklahoma, some distance west of Lawton. Päh'-häh-yō'-kō was away when they reached his village, but they were cordially received by his wives, and the second chief did all he could to entertain them. However, the white men and their Indian associates soon realized that their situation was precarious. Evidently the Indians were divided in opinion as to the proper attitude toward their guests, and while the second chief treated them kindly, he warned them at the same time not to go far away from his lodge, which was at one end of the village. Then Eldredge described the return of Päh'-häh-yō'-kō to the village and the events that followed:

> On the 7th the runner returned and reported that the chief would shortly arrive. About 10 o'clock he made his appearance, escorted by three more wives and a party of warriors. Second-Eye and Harry also returned with them. A-cah-quash, as usual on such occasions, introduced us with great dignity. The chief received us with a great deal of kindness and appeared pleased to see us. Upon learning that I had brought two prisoners, he expressed great anxiety to see them. I sent for them and after having shook them cordially by the hand, he motioned them back to the tent. In personal appearance the chief is large and portly weighing I should suppose upwards of two hundred pounds, with a pleasing expression of countenance, full of good humor and joviality. After our reception he threw himself on a buffalo skin, and his wives proceeded to strip him of his moccasins, leggings, and hunting shirt, after which he went into council with his chiefs and warriors and remained in earnest debate until nearly sunset. The council tent was but a short distance from mine, and I was enabled to see and hear all that passed. Many of the

warriors in their speeches were much excited and violent in their gesticulations and manner. I learned from an interpreter that these had relations slain at San Antonio when their chiefs went in to make a treaty, and were strongly advocating a retaliation upon us, after which they were willing to listen to terms of peace. This was argued against by A-cah-quash in a long and animated speech in which, as I afterwards learned, he laid particular stress upon the fact that our head-chief was not the same chief who ruled in Texas at the time of the massacre, but was the friend of the red man . . .[4]

Eldredge goes on to state that Päh'-häh-yō'-kō favored a policy of peace, but that at the close of the council it seemed that he was going to be overridden by his warriors. To add to the predicament of the party, two villainous Indians, a Wichita and a Tawakoni, arrived at the camp with a tale to the effect that the white men had poisoned some of their people when they were at their villages. In this matter nothing but the testimony of their faithful Waco companion, A-cah-quash, saved the white men. As night approached Päh'-häh-yō'-kō rode through the village giving commands in a stentorian voice that the visitors must not be harmed. They were not molested that night, but they faced the morrow with misgivings.

On the following day the white men were brought before the council. Päh'-häh-yō'-kō addressed the warriors, admonishing them to listen attentively, and Eldredge was permitted to speak, knowing that he was speaking for his life. He explained the purpose of his mission; apologized for the ruthless acts of the Lamar administration; explained that Houston, who had always been the Indians' friend, was now chief; set forth the benefits to be derived from a policy of peace and the curse that war brought; and then presented the two prisoners he had brought along. Finally, he invited the Indians to a great council to be held on the Trinity, distributed the few presents he had brought with him, and closed by reading and presenting Houston's letter on which the great seal of the republic had been affixed.

After this council closed, Eldredge felt more secure, but he still detected considerable division among the Comanche braves. On the following day the chief made his answer, stating:

> My brother, I have heard your talk and listened to the words your great chief Houston sent me. They are good. I have long desired peace. The children of my people which your chief sent me has made our hearts glad. We know your chief speaks the truth and I am willing to assist him to make the great white path between our different people.[5]

The great chief of the Penatekas was now reconciled to the Texans, but even he maintained direct control over but a small part of the southern bands. It was now too late to get in touch with the numerous and widely separated Comanche groups and hold a council that year. Hence, all that the Eldredge party brought with them on their return to Washington, Texas, was an informal peace agreement with Päh'-häh-yō'-kō[6] and that chief's promise to attend a council at a later date. In September the Waco, Caddo, and other small tribes met at the council grounds on Tehuacana creek and entered into a treaty of peace and friendship.[7] But at this council all Comanches were conspicuous by their absence, and any treaty that did not include them could not greatly improve Indian affairs in Texas. Houston understood the situation thoroughly, and did not slacken his efforts to bring the plainsmen into council. In December he sent the Indian agent Daniel G. Watson and John Conner, the Delaware, to invite Päh'-häh-yō'-kō to come to Tehuacana creek in April, 1844. They did not find the great chief, but did come across some chiefs on the upper Colorado who told them that Päh'-häh-yō'-kō was not in that vicinity but had gone with his band far north to the Salt Plains of the Arkansas.[8] The chiefs which the emissaries met proved to be friendly and affable. One of them, Old Owl, will appear again and again in the narrative of the Texas Comanches that is to follow.

The Indian council was convened at Tehuacana creek in April, as the government had planned;[9] but without the Comanches little could be accomplished other than the giving of advice to some of the lesser tribes, and the taking to task of certain renegades charged with horse stealing and plundering.

It was fitting that the emissaries who actually succeeded in bringing in these elusive men of the prairie were the Delaware scouts John Conner and Jim Shaw. They finally found Old Owl and a "young chief," Buffalo Hump, high up on the Clear Fork of the Brazos. Old Owl was ready to keep his promise to go with them to the council; but Buffalo Hump, "who was rather put at the head of affairs with them," appeared to be very indifferent. He said that the Comanches were not yet ready to go. If the president would get everything in readiness and be at the council grounds himself and then send for them, they would come; but they did not care to be put out about the matter. It may be observed that the insolence of Buffalo Hump, which on this occasion first comes to our attention, was just as pronounced as the faithfulness and affability of Old Owl.

The Delawares spent several days in the Comanche village, and explained to the Indians that this was the last time the government of Texas was going to send after them. Finally Old Owl and his followers set out with the scouts, leaving Buffalo Hump behind. However, the young war chief changed his mind and overtook the others on the second day of their journey to the council; but it seems that he came along without a considerable party of his warriors, who went their way to Mexico.[10]

IN COUNCIL AT LAST

The Comanches came on to Tehuacana creek, where President Houston and his commissioners met them in council. The smaller tribes were also well represented and were delighted that at last their powerful neighbors were in the council grove. President Houston addressed the gathering in his inimitable style explaining that the peace he had made with the Comanches six years before had been broken[11] by the "bad chief" who succeeded him as head of the Texas government. That chief had made war on the Comanches at San Antonio and this had "to be mended."[12] Following the president's address, talks were made by several chiefs of the lesser tribes, and on the second day Buffalo Hump spoke. He stated:

> The Great Spirit above is looking down and sees and hears my talk; the ground is my mother, and sees and hears that I tell the truth. When I first heard the words of your chief I felt glad; and I was uneasy until I struck the white path and came here to see him. That is all I want to say. What I came here for was to hear the words of peace. I have heard them and all is right; peace is peace; I have no more to say.[13]

But the chief had more to say before the council was over. On the third day the treaty which Houston had drawn up was read. In it the president had designated a line of division setting off the Comanche country from that of the whites. It provided that the line should run along the upper Cross Timbers to Comanche Peak,[14] thence to the old Spanish fort of San Saba and in a southwest direction to the Rio Grande. In this matter the president was following with a fair degree of accuracy the line proposed by Old Owl during the preceding spring.[15] But Buffalo Hump would not accept this arrangement and voiced an emphatic opposition to it. The dialogue between this chief and Houston is a forceful example of the mental alertness of the Indian. For all of his training in statecraft, the president had no advantage over the savage in this argument. Buffalo Hump knew what he wanted and why he wanted it. Furthermore, he knew the topography of the country to perfection and knew the name and location of the towns and settlements all along the frontier. He evidently had a fairly good conception of the terms *mile* and *league*, although he naturally preferred to speak of distance in terms of days' journey. His argument was that the buffalo, in their annual migration, frequently went below the San

Saba, and he insisted that his people ought to be allowed to follow them. Hence, he wanted the line to run from the mouth of Sandy creek on the Brazos to a point far below the mouth of the San Saba, thence along the mountains north of Austin and San Antonio and on west along the San Antonio-Presidio or Rio Grande road. When the president explained that the government proposed to establish trading posts along the frontier line, the chief replied that he did not want them there. They were already high enough up to suit the Comanches. Buffalo Hump knew full well what trading houses signified; he knew that white hunters and trappers accompanied the traders and, before long, permanent settlers would come there.

"I want the line to run as I have said," Buffalo Hump continued. "It is a good country and has good grass, and I want to live by the white people." Thus the president was forced either to accept the chief's boundary proposal, let the treaty fail, or leave out the matter of boundary agreement. He chose the last course, and the original document, now in custody of the state librarian, shows articles two and three, pertaining to the boundary, crossed out.[16] Thus the treaty was saved by Houston's decisive action; but the boundary line, the object the Indians had so long sought and were to continue to ask for, was not realized because of the opposition of the red men themselves. This is not a matter of great concern, except that it shows that for once, at least, the chief executive of Texas recognized that the Indians had some right to the land other than that of tenants at will. Boundaries did not mean much to the Texas frontiersmen or the Comanches either.

The treaty was signed by the chiefs of the Comanche and several of the smaller tribes, "Po-cha-ka-hip" (Kō'-chō-näw-quoip or Buffalo Hump), "Mome-po-chu-co-pe" (Mō'pe-tschō'-kō-päh or Old Owl), and "Chom-o-pand-u-a"[17] signing for the Comanches. In addition to a mutual pledge of peace and friendship, the agreement provided for official trading houses and Indian agents "who will speak truth to the Indians and hear their talks . . ." The Indians were not to steal any more horses, and were to punish any of their tribesmen who did so; they were not to trade with any other people but the Texans, provided they could get such goods as they needed at the trading houses; they were to permit such persons as the president might send among them to work mines that might be found in their country. Some interesting provisions of the treaty pertain to the method of carrying on war. If the Indians should go to war in the future, they were not to take women and children prisoners, kill them or harm them in any way; and they would always respect a white flag. They promised to attend a general council to be held once a year. In consideration of these promises the government agreed to give them presents from time to time as the president might deem proper. When a general peace should be secured, the Indians were to be supplied with powder, lead, guns, spears, and other arms to enable them to kill game and live in plenty.

Perhaps the treaty was the best that could have been made under the conditions. The very nature of the two opposing forces involved prevented anything in the way of permanent peace. Even if a boundary line had been agreed upon, it would have soon become necessary to move it. Already contractors had engaged to locate families in some of the disputed territory.[18] This expansion was destined to continue, and the Texas government was not strong enough to have stopped it even if it had been determined to do so. On the other hand, the Comanches would not have been satisfied with anything less than a complete cessation of frontier extension. Even then the old Indian difficulty would have remained—that of preventing raids against the settlements by irresponsible warriors.

Thus, after nearly three years of effort the government had at last made a treaty with the Comanches. Because of the unfortunate occurrences of the preceding administration, the making of any treaty proved to be a difficult task, the accomplishment of which is a credit to the Houston administration. On the other hand, it was easy for the people of the republic to expect too much of the agreement. In addition to the failure to include a boundary settlement, its scope was much more limited than most Texans realized. It bound only the Penatekas, or southern Comanches, and but a part of this band. Two of their influential chiefs, Päh'-häh-yō'-kō and Santa Anna, were not present at the council. In the case of Päh'-häh-yō'-kō it should be said, however, that he considered himself to be bound by his agreement with Eldredge, and came a few months later to Torrey's trading house near the council grounds, bringing a white prisoner to exchange for a Comanche, and confirming his promise to walk steadfastly in the path of peace.[19] Santa Anna's attitude was more doubtful. His whereabouts at the time of the treaty cannot be determined, but it would be more than a guess to state that he was leading his warriors in a raid against the Mexican frontier.[20]

| It should be observed that Buffalo Hump in this Council disabused Houston's mind about the number and nature of the different Comanche bands. The fact has already been noted that the Texans had been dealing with the Penatekas only although they persisted in referring to the "Comanche tribe" and "Comanche nation" as though all of the great Comanche divisions had been represented in the negotiations. Houston himself had labored under the impression that chiefs like Old Owl and Päh'-häh-yō'-kō could easily control the other Comanches and also the Kiowas. When the matter was raised Buffalo Hump explained that these northern bands were, in fact, separate tribes, that they were more powerful than the Comanches (Penatekas), that he would do

what he could to keep them from attacking the Texans but that he could not be responsible for their conduct. |

A PEACE FRAUGHT WITH DIFFICULTIES

From the information available, it seems that the Texas Comanches conducted themselves well during the rest of the year 1844, and that the great chiefs took the treaty seriously. Some hostilities were reported from the vicinity of the Upper Guadalupe in May and early June; but it is likely that this was done by Yamparika Comanches from far up on the Canadian—one of the bands Buffalo Hump had said the southern Comanches could not control.[21] In fact, when some Wacoes and Tawakonies, who had been stealing horses, took fright and fled to the Comanches, these Indians would not receive them. Furthermore, Päh'-häh-yō'-kō came in to Torrey's with Old Owl early in January, 1845, bringing along some horses to be returned to their owners and also a white boy named Simpson and a run-away negro.[22]

Päh'-häh-yō'-kō made his visit the occasion for giving admonition to both his Indian followers and the white men. He told the Indians that "this man" (Benjamin Sloat) had been sent to make peace with all the red men, and admonished them to listen to his words. Then he told the white men to be fair with the Indians and give them plenty of presents when they came to make peace. Furthermore, he stated that the Indians would likely wish to visit the settlements in the vicinity of San Antonio in the spring, and the agents should notify the people not to molest them if they carried a white flag, as they promised to do.

Thus did the greatest chief of the Penatekas announce his intention to follow the white path of peace. He had also brought along his war chief, The-Bear-with-a-Short-Tail, to learn of the ways of peace.[23]

But during the year 1845 the Indians gave the pacific policy of the Texas government a severe test. Indeed, one wonders if this policy would not have broken down completely during the years immediately following if it had not been for annexation to the United States and the coming in of large military forces incident to the Mexican War.

To begin with, reports of peace with the Texans, together with a scarcity of buffalo[24] on the northern ranges and a plentiful supply near the Texas settlements, caused the Indians to come much farther south than they had been accustomed to lodge for many years. In the spring a great village of a thousand lodges was located on Little river,[25] small parties visited Austin and other frontier towns, and some even went to San Antonio, the chiefs expressing their gratification that "the blood of their kindred, slaughtered a few years since, had been washed away from the walls of Bexar by the water of peace."[26] Notwithstanding these friendly manifestations, trouble was certain to ensue.

Strained relations developed about as follows: in the spring of 1845 a band of renegade Delawares murdered three Comanches on the San Marcos river, and when the Comanches heard of it they swore that they would wreak vengeance on all Indians friendly to the white people. Päh'-häh-yō'-kō sent word that his warriors were so angry and excited it would not be safe for any white man or Delaware to go near his villages until the matter had been atoned for.[27] This information was discouraging to the Texans; for, as T. G. Western, superintendent of Indian Affairs, wrote at the time, the Delawares were regarded as "the connecting link between us and the Comanches," and a breach between these tribes was a matter of serious concern.[28] Then, possibly in retaliation, but more likely as a matter of natural lawlessness, a party of Comanches and Wacoes killed two young men named Hornsby and Atkinson eight miles below Austin early in June.[29] The Comanches were also charged with an attack on a ranch near Seguin, the murder of a Mexican citizen there, and the stealing of horses at the new German settlement at Comal.[30]

These and other depredations led Western to dispatch Agent Benjamin Sloat and Jim Shaw to the Comanche villages to insist that the chiefs control their warriors better. After the emissaries had delivered their "talks" to the different chiefs, they were to conduct the Indians to the council ground early during the month of September.

It is not likely that the assigning of this task to Sloat provoked any envy among his colleagues. A more dangerous feat can scarcely be imagined. Nothing whatever had been done to appease the wrath of the Comanches, and the blood of their slain kinsmen had not yet been avenged. Furthermore, Sloat's companion and guide was a Delaware. The agent's reports of his hazardous progress into the Comanche country are written in crude style, but for all of that, his achievements are classic examples of the courage and resourcefulness of Texas Indian agents.

With Jim Shaw and two other men, Sloat arrived at Old Owl's village on the San Saba, July 16. The Indians were friendly, but the village was in great confusion over some difficulties among themselves which had already resulted in the death of three men and the wounding of others. The trouble had begun over the efforts of some of the tribe to enforce the treaty made with the Texans. A young warrior who had led in the depredations against the settlements[31] was gathering another party to carry on his bloody work. A chief named Cut-Arm learned of this, and warned the villain that he must desist and conform to the treaty made with the white people; whereupon the young renegade killed he chief. This started a fray that resulted in the killing of the young murderer, tand his father, and the wounding of some of Cut-Arm's party.[32] Naturally these tragedies excited the Indians, and several days later Sloat wrote: "i can not say how this will tirminate they air still fusing about it."[33]

The account of the agent's predicament in the quasi-hostile camp is best told in his own words. "That Night thay but a gard over us for to preve[nt] our escape." he wrote, and added that "we layed Down with our guns By our side with the Determination if thay made an atemped to kill us we would have some of them." Then, to add to the alarm of the white man and his Delaware companions, Buffalo Hump came in from his camp on the Clear Fork of the Brazos bringing his people with him. That chief's presence in any camp was not calculated to promote harmony. Sloat continues with his narrative thus:

> then another Council was held which the Difaculty betwen them and the Delawares was counciled over thin the hed men toled us that the relations of the three Comanches that the Delawares had killed last winter was hear and if we Did not make them some presents thay might kill us all that thay would crawl on us in the night and kill us Before thay [we] would know abought it my self and Shaw Counzulted each other about the matter some time before we gave them eny satisfaction about the truble [at] which thay got very imptient when we agreed to make the[m] some presents if that would setle it for ever which they agred it would the nex mornin the men was sent for thay com thir being four in number it was explained to them that they should never say eny more abought it and we gave the presents.[34]

The troubles of Sloat and his party were not yet over. Before they could get away from the Comanche camp, Buffalo Hump decided to lead a war party against the Mexican border. He had received a message from Captain Hays, in command of the Texas ranger forces, that caused him to believe, or to pretend to believe, that Hays would accompany him in the campaign. Thus, in spite of the protests of the white men and their efforts to persuade the chief that he had misunderstood Hays's proposal and that it would be better to go to the Indian council on the Brazos than to Mexico, they were compelled to accompany the Indians to the vicinity of San Antonio. The chief realized that in the party of agents and scouts he had an excellent escort to help him get beyond the Texas settlements unharmed, and he was shrewd enough to take full advantage of the situation. Upon arrival at a place near the town, the main party of the Comanches were left behind while Buffalo Hump and a few of his warriors, escorted by Sloat, went in and talked with Hays. The ranger captain and Colonel Kinney, a prominent citizen of the Corpus Christi country, tried to persuade the chief to give up his plans, but to no avail. At the head of some 730 warriors he rode off for the Rio Grande.[35]

Now some notice must be taken of the annual council to which Sloat and his comrades were to lead the Indians. They had not only failed to persuade the Comanches to attend council, but had been obliged to assist Buffalo Hump in leading off a majority of the Peneteka warriors in a raid against the Mexicans. The president had expressed the hope that Santa Anna, the only important southern Comanche chief who had not entered into a treaty with Texas, would attend the council, but he too was away, probably in Mexico.[36] Likewise Päh'-häh-yō'-kō was absent, but he sent word, as excuse for his failure to attend, the fact that he had not understood when the council was to be held.[37] None of the great chiefs were in attendance except Old Owl, and the only substantial accomplishment was that the Lipan and Tonkawa tribes made peace with the Comanches, and an arrangement was worked out whereby they agreed and were permitted to move into the Comanche country.

In November Santa Anna, who had returned from his raid against the Mexican frontier, was brought to the treaty grounds by Old Owl, where he entered into a council with L. H. Williams, Texas Indian agent. After Old Owl had made a talk on the benefits of peace and the importance of maintaining it, Santa Anna stated that he did not "talk," but that he wanted to have "peace with the whites as long as the sun continued to give light." He asked but one favor, namely, a pass that would permit him to go through the western settlements of Texas on his raids against the Mexican frontier. Williams agreed to try to get the pass for him.[38]

Williams's official report of this council does not suggest anything out of the ordinary. However, in a letter to the commissioner of Indian Affairs, the agent describes in a graphic way the tense situation that threatened to become desperate. He states, to quote his letter in part:

> ... On the day set apart for the council, seats were prepared and the Indians came up from camp armed with Knifes, guns & Bows. It was their wish that all white men present should attend council but I deemed it imprudent, from the hostile appearance of the Comanches, to have them, and thought it best to have four or five stationed in the different houses. Jim Shaw informed them that it was rather a singular proceeding to bring their arms to council; they replied with the rather lame excuse, "that they was afraid they would be stolen if they left them in camp."
>
> Every man and woman that were not in council lay under the bluff apparently ready for any emergency and judging from appearances and some remarks which J. S. interpreted I accompanied by Messrs. Eldredge, Torrey & Cogswell went into council with but little show apparently of getting out of the scrap with safety ... .[39]

Williams had just stated that they gave the Comanche party more presents than it had been planned to give them "inasmuch as they had seen the presents you distributed to the other Indians and their actions but too plainly showed that we must please them or they would take the necessary measures to please themselves." He added that Päh'-häh-yō'-kō was expected at the trading house soon, and he felt that if the government did not send presents for him or a body of troops for the protection of the trading post, there would be serious trouble. And he closed his letter with the comment that "The whites located here seem to think that should they be similarly situated again they would like the Georgia Major be troubled with a slight lameness, and retreat before the enemy appear."

However, the council closed without any incident of serious consequence, the Indians were given their presents[40] and went away in peace, apparently satisfied. | It may be that the uneasiness of the Indians and the tense atmosphere of the council can be explained because of memories of the Council House affair; but it is more likely that recent events had helped more to produce it. The Indians knew that some of their people had committed depredations during the year that had passed and they were uneasy lest the white people retaliate. |

Thus was the last of the great Penateka chiefs brought into treaty relations with the Texans. Päh'-häh-yō'-kō, Old Owl, Buffalo Hump, and Santa Anna were now each and all obligated to follow the straight white path and lead their people aright. The program begun and so persistently pursued by Houston had been completed, at least nominally, under the administration of his successor, Anson Jones. But Houston's dream of a frontier of peace had not been realized. The Comanches attended council whenever it suited their convenience, and they expected presents whenever they came. The warriors were suspicious and insolent, and the chiefs exacting and grasping. For the most part they were giving vent to their passion for war by fighting the Mexicans, but when Indians acquire the war habit, they are not particular about the nationality of their enemy. On these forays they had to pass through or near the Texas settlements, and some depredations along their trails were sure to be committed. They were suspicious of the white people and dared not trust them far; and as they saw the frontiersmen invade their hunting grounds and kill their game in such wasteful fashion, they were moved by hatreds and passions stronger than any pledges of peace.

Houston's pacific policy accomplished some things worth while, but it did not solve the Comanche problem even for the time being.

CHAPTER FIVE

The Period of the Mexican War

A NEW TREATY AND A NEW MASTER IN TEXAS

On February 16, 1846, President Anson Jones yielded the executive office to Governor J. Pinckney Henderson, and Texas became a state in the American union.[1] The state kept its public lands, but passed its Indian problem on to the United States, and was given guarantees that its frontiers would be protected.[2] Thus the state, relieved of the responsibility for the Indians, retained the only asset with which the Indian problem could be solved—the public lands which were the ancestral home of many of the tribes and the only place where the others could live in peace.

And yet, the people of Texas felt that annexation would soon bring an end to their Indian problems, if certain comments of that day represented public opinion. One editorial ran thus:

> The commissioners appointed to treat with the Indians at Torrey's trading house we understand have returned to the settlements. We have not learned whether they have been any more successful in forming treaties with the tribes assembled there than their predecessors. It is a matter of little importance, however, whether they have been successful or not, as the giant arms of the United States will soon sweep the few bands of hostile Indians from our borders.[3]

A short while before, the same editor had written concerning the Comanches that "The military power of this tribe has long since been broken, and it is a matter of but little consequence whether they remain at peace or at war with our government."[4]

Contrary to these views and hopes, annexation did not bring about permanent peace on the frontier. The Texans should have known by this time that the Comanches could be quite as troublesome in small bands as they had been when they made their forays in larger bodies. Furthermore, their strength had not been reduced as much as the white people seemed to think, nor were the United States forces as efficient in dealing with them as certain enthusiastic Texans had expected them to be.

Since the Comanches, as well as some of the smaller tribes, had ranged in both countries—Texas and the United States—and both nations had made treaties with them, the taking over by the United States of relations in Texas appeared to offer an opportunity for the establishment of a consistent and uniform policy toward the plains tribes. Accordingly, in September, 1845, the commissioner of Indian Affairs of the United States took steps to renew the treaty with the Comanches in such a way as to pacify all bands of that tribe and secure peace along the Indian Territory and Texas frontiers. Governor P. M. Butler[5] and Colonel M. G. Lewis were appointed to carry out the plan.

With a party of some sixty civilized Indians and white frontiersmen, the commissioners set out from Indian Territory in January, 1846. Runners were sent to the Comanches to meet in council at Comanche Peak, in what is now Hood county, Texas. Indian traders, fearing that if the Comanches secured goods from the government they would not continue to make purchases from private individuals, used their influence to prevent the council, and spread disturbing rumors among the Indians. For instance, one Pecan, a Kickapoo Indian, told Old Owl that the white people had three methods planned to destroy the Comanches—spread smallpox among them, give them poison, or cut their throats when they were asleep. Buffalo Hump and Old Owl, with a few of their people, met the commissioners at Comanche Peak, but the attendance was so slim that it was agreed that another council should be held at Tehuacana creek on the appearance of the second new moon in the month of April.[6]

Although they were, as usual, late in arriving, the Comanches gathered in large numbers at Tehuacana creek, or Council Springs. Buffalo Hump with four of his wives was first to come, but Old Owl, Päh'-häh-yō'-kō, Santa Anna, and another influential chief, Yellow Wolf, were there for the council. The Waco, Wichita, and Caddo bands were likewise represented. Jesse Chisholm, Luis Sanches, John Conner, and Jim Shaw served as interpreters,[7] and among the white men present were John H. Rollins and Robert S. Neighbors, both destined to attain positions of prominence in the United States Indian service in Texas. After Hicks, the Cherokee, stated the purposes and plans of the United States government, Päh'-häh-yō'-kō spoke for the Comanches, and assured the council that his people would continue to follow the paths of peace. The treaty was then read and explained and signed by the commissioners and chiefs.[8]

The Indians agreed to accept the exclusive jurisdiction of the United States, to trade with licensed traders only, to give up their white and negro prisoners, to surrender murderers and robbers on demand, to restore all horses that might be stolen in the future, and to cooperate with agents of the United States in suppressing the liquor trade. One provision of significance was that no white person should be permitted to go among the Indians except by authority of a pass from the president. Obviously the United States government had no constitutional right so to restrict the citizens of the state, and it had not the force sufficient to compel obedience to such a regulation even if it had been constitutional. The senate struck out this article and also another which would have permitted the Indians to send representatives to Washington whenever they might think their interests required it.[9] The government was to establish trading houses and agencies along the frontier, and furnish blacksmiths to repair the Indians' arms and utensils. At the council, to be held at some time in the future, the United States was to give the savages presents to the value of ten thousand dollars.

In reference to giving up prisoners, all that was achieved was a promise on the part of the Indians that they would give up their captives.[10]

The council held by Butler and Lewis was beyond a doubt the most representative gathering of Penatekas ever held up to that time.[11] In their report, the commissioners not only gave an account of their proceedings leading up to the council and the events associated with that meeting, but dealt somewhat in detail with the range, habits, characteristics, and significance of the different Comanche bands, naming and locating with some precision six of the great Comanche divisions.[12] In one respect the report is misleading, however. One might read it and the treaty which was negotiated, and gather the impression that all of the Comanche bands were present when, as a matter of fact, only the Penateka or southernmost division of the tribe was represented. In spite of its limitations, the treaty had some constructive value. All the Penateka chiefs of power and influence were now personally obligated to the United States government, and the smaller bands like the Caddoes, Wichitas, and Lipans were likewise in a state of mind calculated to lessen strife and warfare. The United States had built on the foundation of peace and good will laid by the Houston and Jones administrations in Texas.

In order to augment the force of the treaty by showing the Indians something of the power and wealth of the United States, Butler and Lewis selected and escorted to Washington a number of chiefs. Buffalo Hump and Santa Anna were selected to represent the Comanches, but the former refused to go. Santa Anna made the journey and thereafter, until his death, urged the Indians to keep at peace with the whites and learn their life.

ROBERT S. NEIGHBORS AND THE PENATEKA CHIEFS

About the time that the United States commissioners were treating with the Texas Indians on the Brazos, General Taylor was engaging the Mexican forces along the Rio Grande in the opening battles of the Mexican War. The commissioners exerted their utmost efforts toward securing a satisfactory and permanent agreement with the Indians[13] in order that the government might concentrate all its attention on Mexico. Although the period of the war was one of comparative peace along the whole Comanche frontier, the intrusion of settlers into the Indian country and the disturbed conditions incident to the war threatened the peaceful relations on a number of occasions. Not long after the treaty, Buffalo Hump made trouble in the vicinity of Bryant's on Little river; but L. H. Williams, who had been left by the commissioners as acting resident agent, managed to prevent an outbreak.[14] Furthermore, the four companies of rangers which General Taylor authorized to be raised to protect the Texas frontier[15] may have intimidated the chief and his band so that they decided it would be best to keep the peace.

Serious trouble was feared when it was learned that, because of the late arrival of the commissioners at Washington, the senate had adjourned without ratifying the treaty and that no appropriation was available for the purchase of presents. Robert S. Neighbors, who had been the Texas agent to the Tonkawas and Lipans, was assigned the embarrassing task of meeting the Indians and explaining to them why the government had failed to meet its promise.[16] However, Neighbors was spared this ordeal through the initiative of Torrey and Brother, who furnished the goods and took chances on getting their pay after the senate had ratified the treaty.[17] And many presents were needed; for the chiefs who had visited Washington returned to the prairies so highly pleased with their trip that they sent word to Indian friends as far away, almost, as Santa Fé, inviting them down for a great pow-wow and their share of the presents.[18] Torrey reported that between 2,500 and 3,000 Indians, composed of representatives of all the tribes, were present. The Indians were met in council by J. C. Neill, T. J. Smith, L. H. Williams, and Robert S. Neighbors. They were given presents, and departed in fine spirits.[19] Päh'-häh-yō'-kō could not attend the council because of illness,[20] and Buffalo Hump was conspicuously absent, being away on a "very successful expedition against the

Mexicans" in which he captured over 1,000 head of horses, and took a considerable number of prisoners, some money, and miscellaneous plunder. However, the plundering operations of the wily chief, carried on with one hand, did not prevent his receiving presents with the other, for he sent word that he would be on hand at the trading house ready to receive his presents as soon as his horses had rested enough to enable him to make the journey!

During the year 1847 a series of events along the Texas frontier threatened peaceful relations. Several thousand Indians from beyond the Rio Grande moved into Texas and located in the heart of the Comanche country along the upper Colorado.[21] Large bands of northern Comanches came down far into Texas, spending part of the year on the Colorado and San Saba. Mexican spies tampered with the Indians, surveyors penetrated their country, and traders from Indian Territory and Arkansas cheated them and spread disturbing rumors.

But the most serious problem arose in connection with the introduction of German colonists into the Comanche country. The *Adelsverein* or Society of German Noblemen interested in guiding German emigrants to Texas, secured the Miller and Fisher contracts which called for over three million acres of land lying between the Llano and Colorado rivers.[22] Baron von Meusebach, the representative of the German association, took steps to occupy the country, and it was seen that unless an agreement between the Germans and Indians could be reached, war would surely follow. Governor Henderson called on Robert S. Neighbors to use his efforts to avoid trouble, and Neighbors, aided by the tact and good sense of the Germans, settled the immediate difficulty.[23] A treaty between the colonists and Indians was agreed upon on March 2, and later ratified at Fredericksburg. Old Owl, Santa Anna, and Buffalo Hump represented the Comanches at this council. For presents worth $3,000 the Indians agreed to permit the Germans to occupy the country.

Dr. Ferdinand Roemer, a German scientist who was traveling in America at this time, was present at the council held on the San Saba river about twenty-five miles above its mouth. Since the scholarly German gives one of the most vivid descriptions of a Comanche village ever recorded, it seems well to quote from him somewhat at length. His words may be translated as follows:

> After breakfast we made a visit in the camp or tent village; it was considerably larger than the one we had seen earlier. It consisted of about 150 tepees of different sizes, which were scattered at random along the edge of the forest. A few of these belonging to the chiefs or intended for public parleys were conspicuous on account of their size and stateli-

ness. Near several, supported on stakes, were the war paraphernalia of some warriors, consisting of a shield, of a green headdress of buffalo hide, with the horns of a buffalo on it, and a lance. These weapons exposed to view in this way are *medicine*, that is holy, or suitable for religious mysteries and no one is permitted to touch them. As soon as we drew near a tent we were always greeted by the sullen yelping of a number of ugly, skinny dogs, which slunk away as soon as we went straight up to them. Everywhere we saw the industrious squaws busy with domestic tasks. A few were twisting ropes of horse hair, to be used for tying horses; others were plaiting leather thongs or lassos from small strips of horse hide; again others were preparing the hard buffalo hides for use, as with a heel-shaped, shorthandled tool they were scraping the fleshy and fatty particles from the inside; still others were cleaning on the inside hides that had become dirty, by smearing them with a white clay. Farther on we saw a squaw with a pack horse that was loaded down with deer meat, coming home and unloading the meat in front of the tepee. The men, of course, just killed the game and then sent the women on to bring in the meat. In another place we found a number of women busy pulling down tepees and packing them on mules. A mule with a thick bundle of twelve-foot poles trailing on the ground and packed on the back with skins presented a strange spectacle. The marks which the poles, dragging on the ground, leave behind are always the most important signs by which one determines the direction of an Indian train.[24]

We are also indebted to Roemer for a precise description of three great Comanche chiefs as he observed them in council. He states:

Towards noon the pre-arranged council with the chiefs took place. Before our tents buffalo hides were spread out on the ground in a large circle, and on these the chiefs and the most respected warriors sat down on the one side while on the other, facing them, sat Mr. von Meusebach with the interpreter Jim Shaw, Mr. Neighbors, and a few others of our company. The chiefs, who are at the head of all the bands of Comanche Indians who roam on the frontiers of the settled portion of Texas, sat very serene and dignified. In appearance, however, each was very different from the others. Old Owl, the political chief, was a little old man who looked very insignificant in his dirty little cotton jacket, but was characterized by a cunning, diplomatic face. Quite different from him appeared the war chief, Santa Anna, a large, fine-looking man with an affable and lively countenance. The third chief, Buffalo Hump, was the pure unadulterated picture of a North American Indian, who, unlike the rest of his tribe, scorned every form of European dress. His body naked, a buffalo robe around his loins, brass rings on his arms, a string of beads around his neck, and with his long, coarse black hair hanging down, he sat there with the serious facial expression of the North American Indian which seems so apathetic to the European. He attracted our special attention because he had distinguished himself through great daring and bravery in expeditions against the Texas frontier which he had engaged in times past.[25]

| Although this treaty did not altogether prevent difficulties between the two races subsequent events show that the Southern Comanches generally tried to live up to it. |

Notwithstanding these various disturbing elements, the Texas frontier east of San Antonio enjoyed comparative peace during the year 1847.[26] For this peace much credit is due the great chiefs, Santa Anna, Old Owl, Päh′-häh-yō′-kō, and their agent, Robert S. Neighbors.

Neighbors was appointed special agent for the Indians of Texas on March 20, 1847.[27] A better man could not have been found; in courage, energy, and initiative he set a standard worthy of emulation by those who came after him. He acted on the theory that the business of an Indian agent was to keep in touch with his charges wherever they might go. He visited and counseled them in their camps far from the frontier. No matter where they went he followed them up, praised them for their fidelity or took them to task for their lawless acts, and faithfully reported his proceedings to his superiors. For the first time in the history of relations with the plains tribes this plan, which may be termed the field agent policy, was given a fair trial in the work of Neighbors, and the results obtained were gratifying in spite of the many demoralizing forces he had to contend with. Since the history of the Comanches in Texas from 1847 to April or May, 1849, is so closely associated with this man, and since his reports furnish most of the accurate information we have concerning them during this period, it seems fitting to review in some detail the account of his experiences.

Neighbors's part in the treaty between the German colonists and the Indians in February and early March has already been related. In May he made a journey to the principal Comanche village of some 150 lodges, situated about one hundred miles above Austin. Here he met with Old Owl, Päh′-häh-yō′-kō, and Buffalo Hump. He read and had interpreted and explained to them the treaty made the year before, as amended by the senate. The amendment striking out the third article, which would have made it unlawful for white persons to enter the Indian country without special authorization, did not please the chiefs. Buffalo Hump said:

> I cannot agree that the 3rd article in the treaty shall be stricken out, for that article was put in at my request. For a long time a great many people have been passing through my country; they kill all the game, and burn the country, and trouble me very much, the commissioners of our great father promised to keep these people out of our country. I believe our white brothers do not wish to run a line between us, because they wish to settle in this country. I object to any more settlements. I want this country to hunt in.[28]

| Neighbors reported that he found them "violently opposed to my extension of our settlements, and much annoyed by and very suspicious of any persons that visit their country." They were anxious to discuss the question of a boundary line, and it was with great difficulty that he kept them off of that subject. He assured them that this and other matters pertaining to their interests would "be settled by the government in good time, and to their entire satisfaction." | Finally, the chiefs agreed to accept the treaty and to do all in their power to compel their men to observe it, but Neighbors complained that unless something was done to prevent or regulate the intrusion of surveying parties, hostilities would likely develop. He stated that he found Santa Anna much more reasonable about these matters than the other chiefs, and that Santa Anna was anxious that another delegation of chiefs be sent to Washington where they might learn more about the whites and the aims and purposes of the government of the United States.[29] The agent was of the opinion that this ought to be done.

After his visit with the Comanches, Neighbors went to the villages of friendly and docile Caddoes and Anadarkoes, situated at that time on the Brazos, forty-five miles above Torrey's trading house. From here, accompanied by six Delawares and seven Anadarkoes (Captain Howe, commandant of that frontier, refused to furnish him an escort), he visited the murderous and thieving bands of Wichita, Waco, and Tawakoni Indians several days' journey up the river. Undaunted by the odds and the bad character of the Indians, the plucky agent, backed by his little band of friendly Indians and a few Kichaies who lived near by, boldly charged the Indians with theft and recovered over fifty head of horses.[30]

In July, Major Neighbors was informed in a message from Captain John C. (Jack) Hays, that a party of surveyors under the direction of Robert Hays, the ranger's brother, had been attacked while at work on the Llano and four of them killed or captured by the Indians—either Wacoes or Comanches.[31] The agent went to the vicinity and investigated the murder. At first it seemed that the Comanches were guilty, since they had fled with all of their people and gone north far away from the settlements. However, Neighbors later became convinced that the Waco Indians had committed the murder, and that the Comanches had fled lest they be charged with the offense and attacked by the troops. He finally managed to allay the fears of the Comanches.[32]

In September the annual Indian council was held near Torrey's trading house. All the great Comanche chiefs were in attendance except Buffalo Hump, who was away with a large number of men "at war" with the Mexicans.[33] Presents were given the Indians, the treaty was read and explained again, and various matters pertaining to the "welfare" of the red men were discussed. Again the Comanches expressed their desire to secure some agreement in regard to the boundary, and again the agent was obliged to put them off with the promise that this matter would receive attention in the future. Neighbors observed considerable want on the part of the Indians, and he doubted that it would be possible for them to subsist and refrain from depredations much longer unless the government made some provision for giving them annuity goods or taught them to farm.

In the late winter and spring of 1848 Neighbors succeeded in establishing contact with some of the northern Comanche bands.[34] This meeting with the wild bands was the result of a journey far up the Salt Fork of the Brazos to Old Owl's camp where some other Comanche bands were spending the winter.[35] | The reason for this extraordinary journey was that depredations had been committed by the Comanches and there was considerable excitement along the frontier. The Old Owl gave as usual a plausible explanation of the conduct of his people. Certain members of the Northern Comanche bands had been making raids into the settlements and the Penatekas, finding themselves unable to restrain their kinsmen and fearing that they would be held accountable for these acts of violence, left their range and went far to the north away from the frontier. |

Neighbors held a council with the chiefs of the Penatekas, and since some renegade Tenawas, who had lost kinsmen in raids against the frontier, were threatening his life, the Old Owl sent messengers to Päh'-häh-yō'-kō and the chiefs of the northern bands to come and restrain them.[36] Soon the great Penateka with five Tenawa, one Nokoni, and one Kotsoteka chiefs arrived at the village. With much ceremony Päh'-häh-yō'-kō introduced his northern friends to Neighbors, and he, together with the Old Owl and other friendly chiefs, did everything possible to establish cordial relations generally. After an evening spent with these chiefs in Old Owl's lodge, Neighbors wrote: "I found them to be a very jovial set, and the evening was spent in eating and smoking, and the discussion of the usual themes among the prairie bands, *viz*: 'war and women,' finding myself, in the end, upon a good understanding with them."[37]

In this council the chiefs again complained at the fact that white people were taking their country while they could not cross the line set up arbitrarily by the rangers. Old Owl stated his case with pathos:

> You told me that the troops were placed there for *our* protection, as well as the whites; *that* I know is not so. You told me, also, that if I wished to go below the line, if I would go to the captains of the stations, they would give me permission to go down below to hunt. Soon after the council, I wanted to go down below the station, on the Colorado, as I heard that there were some buffalo down in the lower prairies. I applied to Captain McCulloch, with a party of eight old men and their women and children; he would not let me go down. I told him that I did not wish to go to the settlements; had no warriors with me; but merely wanted to hunt where there were no houses, and kill some meat for my women and children, as there were no buffalo near, above his station. He said he would not permit me, under any circumstances, to go down. This made me angry, and I quarreled with him. I told him that I was an old man, and had hunted in these prairies before he was born, and before there was any white man for a long way below . . . We have been at peace for a long time, and I do not see why you keep so many soldiers on the line, if you still wish to keep peace.[38]

Thus did the ranger stations form a boundary line, but a line that was to be applied to the Indians only. White men might cross it into the Indian country whenever they pleased, and settle if they cared to, but the Indians could not cross it for even a week's sojourn in their ancestral hunting grounds. Naturally, the savages would accept such a condition only when there was a formidable military force in their way.

In September and October of this year, 1848, Neighbors again visited the Penatekas at the head of the Clear Fork. Here again he found a few of the northern Comanches. On this occasion Captain S. P. Ross, with a force of fifty Texas rangers, accompanied him, not so much to give the agent protection as to give the Indians a better acquaintance with the rangers. The Comanches were friendly, but Neighbors rebuked them for attacks made on the ranger forces in the country west of San Antonio. The Indians replied by placing the responsibility for the hostilities on the rangers. They stated that they had never made peace with Mexico, and that they frequently made raids against the Mexican frontier. On these raids the rangers frequently attacked them, and there was nothing they could do except resist the white men. The agent could think of no better solution of the problem than to advise them to cross the Rio Grande at some point higher up, or, in case they desired to follow the old trails through Texas, to visit the posts first and obtain a pass, though, as the Indians knew, passes were always denied them.[39] Indeed, under the terms of the treaty of Guadalupe Hidalgo, all American military forces were under obligations to keep them back from the Mexican frontier.[40]

In June, 1849, Neighbors received an order from the commissioner of Indian Affairs directing him to report to Washington to help the department work out a more satisfactory Indian policy for Texas.[41] In Washington, however, he learned that his service with the government had been brought to an end by the appointment of John H. Rollins to succeed him as Indian agent for Texas. The commissioner stated that Neighbors's services had been satisfactory. Evidently he had not supported the Whig ticket in the preceding presidential election, and was removed for political reasons. Thus did the Texas Indian service lose its most efficient employee through the vagaries of the spoils system.[42]

Neighbors's experience of more than two years with the Texas Indians proves the efficiency of the resident or field agent system. It is true that there were outrages and disturbances, but for all of these the period was one of comparative peace. There were difficulties inherent in the Texas Indian situation which no man could have overcome, but Neighbors demonstrated the power of control which the right kind of an agent could exercise over the savages. That he had the support of an efficient ranger force[43] must be considered in evaluating his work, but it is easy to give too much emphasis to the work of the military. The period was one of comparative peace along most of the Texas frontier solely because the Comanches almost completely refrained from depredations east of San Antonio. | That the Comanche raids into the lower Rio Grande region and the Mexican country contributed to the security of the Texas frontier east of San Antonio is true. In these attacks the warriors were led out of the Texas country and given opportunity to supply their wants and satiate their passion for blood. | If the friendship of the great chiefs had not been retained by the tireless efforts of a patient and tactful agent, there can be little doubt that the savages would have soon turned on the Texas frontier. Although the Comanche bands were already giving evidence of disintegration, the chiefs still had a modicum of control over their warriors, and the tribal policy of friendship towards the Americans could be maintained. Furthermore, the friendliness of these southern bands tended to restrain the Kiowas and the Comanches of the north.

The Period of the Mexican War

Even if Robert S. Neighbors had never rendered any other public service, he merits the gratitude of Texas for his work in restraining the Comanche warriors during this period, and credit is due also to the worthy old chiefs, Päh'-häh-yō'-kō, Old Owl, and Santa Anna.[44] They always threw their influence on the side of peace, and when disturbances provoked by Indians over whom they had no control threatened to draw their people into a war with the Texas frontiersmen, they promptly left the vicinity of the settlements and took their followers far away where clashes could be avoided. For them it can be justly said that they tried to keep their agreements, and if they sometimes failed, it was because of forces they could not control.

CHAPTER SIX

Increasing Confusion

THE DECLINE OF TRIBAL AUTHORITY

The years immediately following the Mexican War witnessed the most serious disturbances and crises that the southern Comanches had ever experienced. During 1848 they had suffered severely from smallpox, and shortly after Major Neighbors left them in 1849 a scourge of cholera carried away three hundred souls within a few weeks' time. The faithful Old Owl and the intelligent Santa Anna were numbered with the dead. These losses demoralized the southern branch of the tribe, and henceforth disintegration worked rapidly. Päh'-häh-yō'-kō was still living, but he never spent much time in the southern ranges after 1849, and the southern bands were without a leader.

As soon as they recovered from the cholera scourge, the Penatekas held a general council and tried to select a head-chief to succeed Old Owl. One account says a chief named Sanaco was chosen, but Buffalo Hump and Kătŭm'sē, another chief, visited Fredericksburg to report that the honor had gone to Buffalo Hump.[1] The title was an empty one, for from this time on the Penatekas themselves agreed that they had no common leader. Along with Buffalo Hump and Yellow Wolf, the most questionable characters among the chiefs referred to in the preceding discussion, new chiefs such as Sanaco, Toshua, and Kătŭm'sē assumed leadership. Among these Kătŭm'sē[2] was destined to prove one of the most dependable leaders in the history of Comanche relations, but so much cannot be said for the others. There was no one among them who could take the places of Santa Anna and Old Owl, and Buffalo Hump's disposition did not improve with age.

After selecting their head-chief, the Comanches considered in a council of ten days' duration the policy they should pursue towards the whites. The decision reached was that it would be foolish to make war against the United States. They had fought the Texans when there were but few white men to be reckoned with, and had gained nothing by their wars. Now that Texas was a part of the great United States, a war with the white people would mean the destruction of the Indians. The chiefs then came to Fredericksburg to report their decision and to assure the army officers that the Indians were friendly. Buffalo Hump stated that they might not be able to stop the thieving of small parties "at once," but that he was determined to have peace, and he hoped the white people would not consider these attacks of small thieving bands as cause for war.[3] Buffalo Hump had promised to restrain the warriors, but there was no one to restrain Buffalo Hump. | It is interesting that the chiefs reported their affairs to the army officer at Fredericksburg rather than to Colonel Williams, acting Indian agent, now at Barnard's trading house, near Comanche Peak.[4] |

Another cause of the dissolution of the southern bands was the attitude of Judge John H. Rollins who succeeded Neighbors as Texas Indian agent in the summer of 1849. Rollins was an elderly man in poor health and was not disposed to adopt the field agent policy which his predecessor had followed so successfully. Congress had not provided funds to purchase presents for the Indians, and Rollins felt that it was as well to leave them alone as to meet them and be obliged to disappoint them in the matter of annuities. Thus, while the agent remained at his home at San Antonio, the Indian situation in Texas drifted from bad to worse. Rollins also made the mistake of assuming an antagonistic attitude towards George and Charles Barnard who had established a trading house on the Brazos river near the old Kichai village in 1849.[5] These men had been associated with the Torreys in the Indian trade, and wielded a powerful influence over the natives. Congress tardily came to the agent's relief, and in November, 1850, two special agents were commissioned to assist him; but these men knew little of the Comanches and the Texas Indian problem.

When Rollins finally got in touch with the Indians, in September, 1850, he found chiefs Kātŭm'sē, Little Wolf (or Yellow Wolf), Buffalo Hump, and Sanaco on the Brazos, 125 miles from Fort Graham. As usual, the chiefs denied that they had had anything to do with certain recent depredations, and laid this deviltry to irresponsible young men who had gone into the western settlements against the admonition of their chiefs. The Indians stoutly maintained, however, that they had never agreed to give up the practice of raiding the Mexican frontier.[6] Furthermore, since Mexicans lived in the settlements east of the Rio Grande, the savages found it difficult to see why a river should be the basis of such nice distinctions. Mexicans lived on both sides of the stream, and to the Comanches where Mexicans lived was Mexico.

Rollins thought another treaty would improve matters, and in December, 1850, he persuaded the savages to pledge themselves to a new agreement which was, in most respects, simply an enlargement or a duplication of their former promises. In one respect they did make a substantial concession in that they agreed not to go south of the Llano river without the special assent of an army officer. Buffalo Hump, who had persistently refused to be bound by such a line in the days of the Texas republic, signed the instrument, as did Kātŭm'sē and Yellow Wolf. Sanaco and Toshua were not present and only about half of the Penateka people were at the gathering.[7] It must not be understood that this was the kind of a boundary agreement the savages had been seeking. It was entirely unilateral and in no way prevented white persons from entering the country of the red men. The only consideration the Indians received for their promises was a vague assertion that the government would establish trading houses and agencies for them, give them presents, and later negotiate with them on the matter of a permanent boundary for their country. Since Texas owned the soil, the United States could not fulfill this promise to frame a treaty that would guarantee the Indians permanent rights to their lands, and failure to do this would seem to the Indians just one more example of broken faith. The old chiefs who taught peace and honest dealing must have found broken promises exceedingly embarrassing when they tried to restrain their warriors.

The treaty did not improve the Indian situation permanently, but it did result in the surrender of a number of captives, chiefly Mexicans. The Indians promised to give up their "white" prisoners, but neither Rollins nor the savages understood that this included the Mexicans. But backed by Lieutenant-colonel W. J. Hardee's military force, the agent, somewhat reluctantly it seems, moved against the Indians to compel them to surrender their Mexican prisoners.[8] Then, in October, 1851, Agent John A. Rogers negotiated another agreement with Kātŭm'sē, and soon thereafter the Comanches and Lipans gave up twenty-seven prisoners.[9] When the wild Comanches of the north heard that Kātŭm'sē was giving up these prisoners without ransom, they were very angry with the chief and threatened his life.[10]

In fact, these northern bands troubled their Penateka kinsmen by stealing their horses, and harried the Texas communities as well. In an effort to establish more friendly relations with them, Jesse Stem, of the federal Indian service in Texas, established an agency in the valley of the Clear Fork of the Brazos at the crossing of the road from Fort Phantom Hill to Fort Belknap.[11] In the winter of 1852-1853 a number of these northern chiefs as well as Päh'-häh-yō'-kō and other Penatekas visited this post. Prominent "Ta-na-was," Nokonies, and Yamparikas came to take the few presents the agent could spare them, grumbling that they were not given more,[12] and protesting because Fort Phantom Hill had been built in the heart of their winter range.

WHITE TRESPASSERS

The middle years of the nineteenth century witnessed the appearance of many disturbing forces with which the Comanches had to contend, one of consequence being the penetration of their country by white adventurers and emigrants. The Santa Fé trail continued to be used, and often the travelers were neither considerate of their own safety nor of the Indians' rights.[13] | Even if they did nothing more they disturbed the game along the road. In general, however, the white people followed one or two main trails and beyond the narrow zone of travel they did not often disturb the Indians.[14] | Then, when the great migration of 1849 came on, the emigrants broke through at many points, making new routes or following old ones known but rarely used up to that time. In that year some three thousand persons crossed into New Mexico or Colorado by the Canadian river route,[15] making a trail through the finest part of the Comanche range. In the southern end of the range the "upper road" to El Paso came into use, the emigrants going from San Antonio or Austin to Fredericksburg, thence north to the head of the main Concho, westward to the Pecos, and from there to El Paso and on to California.[16] But all the emigrants did not follow these well-established trails; many argonauts traveled different routes from Dallas to El Paso,[17] and if the whole story were known, it would appear, no doubt, that the Comanche country was bisected in many places.

Then in 1859 came the rush to the Colorado gold regions, when over sixty thousand persons, according to W. W. Bent, traversed the plains across the "center belt" within one year.[18] Bancroft[19] estimates that one hundred fifty thousand entered the plains on their way to Colorado. This mysterious and irresistible movement along many trails aroused distrust and fear in the hearts of the Indians.[20] In fact, as early as 1858 some of the Comanche bands became so hostile that even Jesse Chisholm would not take the responsibility of accompanying emigrant parties through their country.[21]

Meanwhile, the army had built forts in or near the Comanche range; Fort Arbuckle in the valley of the Canadian in 1851; Fort Mann and later Fort Atkinson,[22] far out on the Arkansas; and Forts Belknap, Phantom Hill, and Chadbourne across the southern range in Texas. Only small garrisons were kept at these forts or camps; but there were always some troops, and the lines of communication between them and the scouts sent out from them caused the Indians much annoyance.

North of Texas there was little or no occupation of the Comanche country by white persons before the Civil War; but such was not the case in Texas. In this state the expansion of the settlements between 1845 and 1860 took away from the Comanches some of their best territory. At first Agent Neighbors protested at the encroachment and tried to keep the white people away from the indefinite boundary between the white and the Indian countries. Acting under the authority of an old Indian intercourse act passed by the Republic of Texas in 1843, the agent forcibly removed certain settlers who had located above the treaty grounds on the Brazos.[23]

Governor Henderson agreed to support Neighbors, but it does not seem that he ever took any steps to do so. In 1848 the agent of the Texas Emigration and Land Company notified Neighbors that he intended to extend his surveying operations to a point approximately one hundred fifty miles west of Dallas, and inquired what action the Indian service proposed to take concerning the matter. Neighbors could do nothing more than state that he would advise with his superiors on the subject.[24] Nothing was done to restrain the surveyors because the federal government had no control over Texas lands, and the state was encouraging occupation and settlement. The Indians and the Indian problem were federal matters, but the land belonged to the state. If the citizens of the state proposed to occupy the lands, and if the Indians objected, it was the duty of the United States either to remove the Indians or keep them from harassing the settlers. Meanwhile the frontier people exaggerated every offense of the savages, and added rumor to rumor until it became impossible to determine what the actual state of affairs was. There was foundation for their complaints, but the fable of the youth who cried "wolf" too often is applicable in their case. If the United States had placed ten thousand troops along the frontier they could not have prevented all the raids (acting on the defensive as they did), neither could they have stopped the complaints of the white people. In the days of the republic, when the burden of defense was upon their own government, some of the Texans at least maintained a conciliatory attitude towards the Indians. But now that the responsibility for frontier defense was a federal liability, it was easy and natural for the people of the state to complain about Indian dangers and to become all the more vexed because the United States government insisted on maintaining a conciliatory attitude toward the savages. The Indians were troublesome, said the Texans, and the federal forces ought to make war on them; they shed the blood of helpless women and children, and should be punished; they were in the way of expansion, and should be pushed back; really they had no right to remain in Texas, and the United States should remove them just as it had removed other Indians from Florida and Georgia. With the people in this state of mind, and the savages becoming more and more exasperated and desperate each year, it was not to be expected that the Indian problem in that state would improve. The people of Texas loved peace, but they loved land more.

INTRUDING INDIAN BANDS

While white settlers and adventurers were causing the Indians of the plains great annoyance, a more serious source of trouble was that of intruding Indian bands who entered the Comanche country mainly from the east. These newcomers killed and frightened away the game, fought and alarmed the plains Indians, committed depredations on white frontier settlements, and represented a demoralizing force generally. Some of these Indians, such as the Wichitas, Wacoes, Tawakonies, Tonkawas, and Lipan Apaches were ancient neighbors of the Comanches. As the white men pressed against them and white men surveyed their villages and hunting grounds, there was nothing for them to do but withdraw and seek new homes in the Comanche range to the west of them.

The Wichitas were the most arrant horse thieves on all the border.[25] Unscrupulous white traders offered a ready market for such horses as they cared to sell; and the Texas supply never failed them. It seems that the Wacoes and Tawakonies were nearly as bad as the Wichitas. The merciless pressure from white settlers finally forced these last two bands to seek a home with their Wichita kinsmen north of Red river, from which point they continued to raid the Texas border.[26] The officials of Indian Territory disclaimed responsibility for their conduct, and apparently paid little attention to them. After a visit to Indian Territory, Horace Capron, special agent for Texas Indians, stated that the associated bands of Wacoes, Wichitas, Tawakonies, and Kichaies were more troublesome than all other Indians put together. They invaded the settlements mostly on foot, avoided the military posts, and drove off hundreds of animals from various communities along the entire stretch of the frontier.[27]

The Comanches sometimes took steps to restrain these Indians. Old Owl on one occasion took some horses and a prisoner away from a band of Wacoes and brought them to Torrey's trading house; Sanaco, a Comanche chief, brought a band of thieving Wichitas he had apprehended to Jesse Stem, the agent, and chief Kătŭm'sē volunteered a good "talk" and some excellent advice to this band.[28] But these chiefs were about as helpless as the white men in the matter of trying to reform their Indian friends.[29] Furthermore, the Comanche chiefs had more than enough to do in the matter of restraining their own men, some of whom were chronic plunderers. These bands of the lesser tribes naturally inspired deviltry in their wild neighbors. Also, the Comanches knew that the sins of the renegades were likely to be charged to them; since they would bear the blame, why should they not have a part in the thefts? On the other hand, there was always opportunity to charge their own depredations to the smaller tribes.

A more serious problem still was the coming of the partly civilized eastern Indians such as the Delawares, Shawnees, Seminoles, Cherokees, and Kickapoos. These were tribes which the United States, in its consolidation policy, had removed from their homes east of the Mississippi to new lands along the eastern border of the Great Plains. Certain divisions of these tribes did not see fit to settle on the lands awarded them, but became instead inveterate wanderers. Among the worst of such Indians were the Seminoles. It was charged that they frequently made misrepresentations to the Comanches, and told them so many disturbing lies that the plainsmen were kept in constant fear and excitement.[30] There are accounts of such Seminole parties as that of chief Wild Cat going into the plains country on hunting and trading expeditions, but always ready to fight the people of the plains if offense should be offered.[31] Worse even than the Seminoles were the Kickapoos. A party of these Indians left their home on the Missouri about 1837 or 1838 and moved south to the Canadian. Like most border Indians, they were an agricultural people, but this particular band devoted itself exclusively to hunting.[32] They caused the Texans annoyance as early as 1841, and from 1844 on, references to them are common. At times they visited the Comanches for trade, and on other occasions they made war on them. They carried the best arms that could be furnished by the Arkansas river traders of that day, against which the arrows and spears of the plains tribes were no match.[33] The Comanches hated them as they hated all intruding bands of hunters, but they did not often dare to molest them. | On one occasion the Delaware scout, John Conner, stated that the Comanches and Lipan were afraid of the Kickapoos and were "dodging about from place to place" trying to avoid them.[34] |

Sometimes the plains Indians united against these eastern intruders. On one particular occasion a great party estimated at 1,500 warriors composed of Cheyennes, Osages, Prairie Apaches, Arapahoes, Kiowas, and Comanches was formed at the crossing of the Santa Fé road on the Pawnee fork of the Arkansas, and went forth to "wipe out" all frontier Indians found on the plains. Even some Penatekas from Texas are stated to have been in this unusual Indian army. At some place near the Kansas river they met about a hundred Sauk and Fox Indians, and the latter, much frightened, took refuge in a ravine. But the little band of intruders was armed with rifles, while the plains Indians had very few firearms and most of those of inferior quality. In the conflict that followed the great plains force was so badly beaten that they withdrew and left their dead on the field—evidence of defeat of the severest and most humiliating kind. The Sauk and Fox lost but six killed and those by bullets from a very few good rifles the Osages had.[35] | The results of the battle substantiate the statement of a Commissioner of Indian Affairs to the effect that when the Comanches met the Mississippi Indians the Comanches invariably were defeated.[36] |

THE FAILING BUFFALO SUPPLY

The effects of these encroachments on the country of the plains tribes soon began to be felt in a vital way. The buffalo, on which the Indians depended for food and even for shelter, became more and more difficult to find and kill. Although great herds of these animals were still to be found on the plains at a much later date, the period between 1830 and 1860 witnessed such destruction among them that the hunters of various tribes began to find it exceedingly difficult to kill a sufficient number to sustain their families. At times and in certain places large herds could be found and plentiful "kills" could be made. But the herds were often so harassed by hunters that they moved on rapidly, and often large bands of Comanches could not secure this meat, which was practically their only means of subsistence. They were nomads by habit, and followed the herds to some extent; but they could not leave entirely their accustomed range and take their families along to wander without ceasing in the wake of the great beasts. Also, there were always other tribes following the herd, and clashes might result. Apparently it was difficult to hunt and to fight at the same time. If the game was to be of benefit to the women and children, the families had to be near when it was killed, and even nomadic people could not spend all their time on the move.

As early as 1833 explorers and adventurers had begun to observe that the range of the buffalo along the Arkansas and Canadian rivers and the country between was rapidly growing narrower. In 1833 Latrobe's party had to go one hundred miles beyond the Arkansas boundary to find any buffalo, although at this point and further west they found them in numbers that the writer regarded as "undiminished and undiminishable."[37] At the same time, another writer made substantially the same statement, and commented on the rapidity with which that animal receded before the approach of civilization. He stated:

> Ten years since, they abounded in the vicinity of Fort Gibson; and in the summer of 1822, the writer of this, with Major Mason of the army, and a party of keen sportsmen, killed a number of them near Fort Smith, about forty miles east of us. They have receded, it would seem, one hundred miles westward in the last ten years; and it may be safely assured that thirty or forty years hence, they will not be found nearer to us than the spurs of the Rocky mountains, unless numerous bands of hunters of the Choctaw, Chickasaw, Cherokee, and Creek tribes, established in this country, should relinquish the chase for the arts of civilized life.[38]

In 1841 the Osage agent wrote that the buffalo had receded so far west since the emigration of tribes from east of the Mississippi that each year his

Indians had to extend their hunting operations farther into the plains to obtain even a scant supply. He added that this extension into the plains region increased the likelihood of their having difficulties with the wild tribes who depended solely on the buffalo for a living.[39]

A little later it was observed that they were likewise receding eastward from the Rocky mountains and the western portion of the plains. In this connection Ruxton stated:

> It is a singular fact that within the last two years the prairies, extending from the mountains to a hundred miles or more down the Arkansas, have been entirely abandoned by the buffalo . . .
> With the exception of the Bayou Salado, one of their favorite pastures, they are now rarely met with in large bands on the upper waters of the Arkansas . . .[40]

A strong demand for their hides had arisen, and they were used in Canada and the United States as wrappers or lap robes in traveling, and in Spanish America as beds or carpet.[41] In 1846 it was estimated that 100,000 buffalo cow hides made their way into the Canadian and American markets annually. The bull hides were then regarded as worthless, being so tough that they were never dressed.[42] In 1846 the Torreys were getting at Houston three dollars each for ordinary, and eight dollars for choice hides. It is difficult to determine how extensively professional white hunters operated during the period preceding the Civil War, but this price would seem to have been high enough to invite white men into hunting as a business. Furthermore, it appears that trading concerns like those maintained by Coffee, Warren, and others employed men who combined hunting along with the principal business of trading with the Indians.

During the colonial period and the days of the republic, buffaloes were numerous in Texas, being seen sometimes as far south as the vicinity of Harrisburg,[43] near the present city of Houston. As late as 1845 a hunting party found "immense herds" on the San Gabriel. But by 1852 a "solitary buffalo" seen near the Cross Timbers between Fort Worth and Fort Belknap, attracted considerable interest and the writer who reported the incident added that with this exception none had been seen in that country for some time. In the year preceding, the post surgeon at Fort Phantom Hill wrote that but very few buffalo had been seen as far south as that place since the establishment of the post in 1851;[44] and in 1857, the appearance of herds on the prairies north of the Brazos Indian reservation was regarded as an unusual occurrence and created much excitement.[45] When some Texas Comanches fled from the reservation in 1855, they came very near starving to death because war with the Osages cut them off from the buffalo ranges.[46] This would indicate that the Penatekas would generally be obliged to go north, probably as far as the Canadian, if they hoped to secure buffalo. Evidently the range of the animals changed somewhat, for during the years of the "great kill" of the seventies, Fort Griffin, in Shackelford country, became an outfitting point for numbers of hunters who slew tens of thousands of the great beasts as far south as the present location of the Texas and Pacific Railroad.

| Evidently the trade in buffalo hides grew rapidly. In 1853, Alfred D. Vaughn, Indian agent at Fort Pierre in the Upper Missouri Agency, wrote that he had made the most careful investigation practicable and had learned that the two companies licensed to trade in the superintendency had shipped during the year preceding not less than 100,000 buffalo robes. He also estimated that in his superintendency 150,000 buffaloes were killed annually in addition to the number that accounted for the hides that got into the hands of the traders. Of those killed he did not think that more than a small proportion of the flesh was consumed. Also, he stated that many of the animals were drowned while crossing and re-crossing the Missouri, and in the great snow drifts many frozen carcasses could be found. He thought that, all told, approximately 400,000 of these animals were destroyed annually within the confines of his superintendency. Estimates applicable to the country south of the Arkansas are not available, but slaughter of the animals in this section must have been nearly as great.[47] |

The narrowing range and the smaller herds drew the neighboring bands into the Comanche country, the only region where buffalo could be found from the Arkansas valley south after about 1850, and the presence of so many interlopers worked a hardship on all tribes concerned. In 1857, Little Raven, chief of the Arapahoes, said that his people must either learn to work or starve. Already they had been obliged to leave their homes in the mountains and hills and go into the plains to find any buffalo at all.[48] The next year the Cheyennes made the same complaint.[49]

The deplorable situation of the Indians and the evil consequences of their starved condition are set forth by an agent in forceful language. In 1855, John W. Whitefield wrote:

> These tribes [Kiowa, Comanche, Apache, Arapaho, and Cheyenne] are now confined to a district of country from which the buffalo has almost entirely disappeared, and the smaller game remaining in it is too shy and too fleet to be killed with bows and arrows. Even with firearms it would be a scant, a precarious, and a constantly diminishing means of subsis-

tence which those sterile wilds could afford. If the hunters of these tribes venture into the region of the buffalo, they are liable at any moment to come into contact with the border Indians, the Osages, Delawares, and others, who claim as their hunting grounds all lands over which the buffalo now roam . . . In the absence of other food, they have fed upon their horses and mules until the numbers of those animals have fallen below their needful supply; and hence their frequent forays into Old and New Mexico for the purpose of replenishing their stock.[50]

| In one respect Whitefield exaggerated the case in his plea for the plainsmen. The Border Indians were not always the victor in these fights over the buffalo range. But the wars reduced the forces of the plains people and made their hunting less effective. | There was not enough game for the border Indians, white hunters, and the plains tribes combined. When the supply failed, the white men and the border tribes had other means of subsistence, but the warriors of the plains had nothing left. They found it necessary either to steal or starve, and as long as it was possible, they stole. For a long time they stole principally from the Mexican frontier states, but as that practice became more hazardous and less lucrative, they did not hesitate to turn their attention to the emigrant trains and the Texas frontier.

CHAPTER SEVEN

Establishing Contact on the Arkansas

Not until 1853 did the United States Indian agents establish regular relations with the Comanches north of Texas. It must be understood, however, that these Indians had been quite intimately associated with American traders for some two decades. The best known of these traders is William Bent, owner and proprietor of the famous Bent's Fort. Bent's locations on the upper Arkansas were on disputed territory, where the different tribes were wont to clash, and the fact that he and his traders kept on good terms with all parties is evidence of extraordinary diplomatic talent.

It has already been stated that the Kiowas, Comanches, and Prairie Apaches fought many battles with the Cheyennes and Arapahoes. The battle of Wolf creek, in 1838, in which the Cheyennes and Arapahoes appear to have worsted their adversaries, is one of the most notable of these engagements.[1] These hostilities tended to keep the southern Indians away from the main trading post, and Bent, in order to secure their trade, sent representatives to the Canadian river and probably located temporary trading posts there during the thirties. Finally, in a great and "strong" peace made on the Arkansas in 1840, these warring tribes settled their differences and the peace they made has never been broken.[2]

Notwithstanding the peace made with the Indians of the north, chief Shaved Head, representing the Comanches, and Little Mountain for the Kiowas, asked Bent to locate a more permanent trading establishment in their country. In compliance with this request, Bent's traders built Fort Adobe, on the Canadian river opposite the mouth of White Deer creek, in 1843 or 1844, and another post, near the town of Canadian, as now located in 1845.³ The posts were soon abandoned, probably because of the plundering disposition of renegade Kiowa and Comanche warriors.

It has already been observed that the Comanches did not confine themselves to the Canadian country, but frequented the Santa Fé trail and visited Bent's main post on the Arkansas as well. In 1843 a trader reported that there were "some thousands" of them in the vicinity of Bent's Fort.⁴ Whenever the chiefs conferred with white men, they generally professed friendship for the Americans, but the Indians at large did not live up to these professions. In 1848 they attacked the wagon train at Pawnee Fork, but were repulsed and lost their leader, Red Arm.⁵ The plains Indians were wild and intractable, and army officers leading reconnaissance expeditions into their country found that the Comanches habitually avoided them.⁶ When Captain R. B. Marcy escorted a party of emigrants over the Canadian route to Santa Fé in 1849, he was instructed to remind the Indians that their "Great Father" still remembered the treaty they agreed to in 1835 at Camp Holmes, and that he was expecting them to adhere to the agreement they had made to let emigrants pass through their country unmolested. However, Marcy did not find many northern Comanches on his route, and the Comanches he talked with probably had never heard of a treaty on the Canadian. The chief of the band that he did find had been trading with Bent, and professed the greatest friendship. Inspired by some presents Marcy gave him, the chief even restored to some emigrants some horses his people had stolen from them.⁷ It is obvious that such brief and incidental contact had but little effect on the Comanches generally.

The material benefits to be derived from a treaty with the United States impressed the northern bands when they observed that their southern kinsmen and their Indian neighbors to the east were given presents under the terms of the treaty with that government. Realizing the advantage that the "Hois" or Penateka had because of their friendly relations with the white people, chiefs of the Tenawa, Nokoni, and Kotsoteka bands expressed to Major Neighbors, in 1848, their desire to enter into a treaty with the United States. Four years later, as has been noted, some of these bands were not in the least averse to receiving presents from Jesse Stem at the agency on the Clear Fork, and were disappointed that he had so little to give them.

| Meanwhile these or other northern groups had begun to make overtures of peace to the Indian agents along the Indian territory frontier. In March, 1849, Oh-he-wek-ku, nephew of Sun Eagle, one of the signers of the treaty of Camp Holmes in 1835, came to the Seminole agency under the guidance of Jesse Chisholm, to report that his people desired to make peace. The brave was kindly received, but nothing of consequence resulted from his visit. |

Thomas Fitzpatrick, United States Indian agent for the upper Platte and Arkansas, acting under the superintendent of Indian Affairs at St. Louis, was the first agent to establish regular communication with the northern Comanches and Kiowas. On his return from Fort Laramie, on the Platte, in the spring of 1850, Fitzpatrick held a council with various Indian bands near the Santa Fé road crossing of the Arkansas—common meeting ground for all the great tribes of the plains and eastern Rocky mountains. The Comanches were not present at this council; but on hearing that they were congregated not far to the south of that place, the agent sent messengers inviting them to come in. Although they sent back messages of friendship and assurances that they would not molest travelers on the different trails, they refused to attend the council because their medicine men had predicted another epidemic of cholera.[8]

In the spring of 1851 Fitzpatrick met the Comanches at Fort Sumner (later called Fort Atkinson), near where Dodge City, Kansas, is now located. The Kiowas, the Plains Apaches, the Arapahoes, and the Cheyennes were there also. The agent expressed the willingness of the "Great Father" to make restitution for the damage the Indians might suffer as a result of Americans traveling through their country, and proposed that a general council be held at Fort Laramie on the Platte river in September following. But the Comanches and their allies, the Plains Apaches and Kiowas, flatly refused to go so far away from their range. They said they had too many good horses and mules to risk on such a journey among such horse thieves as the Sioux and Crow.[9] | They insisted that they were already at peace with the United States but stated that they were willing to sign papers, if that was necessary. In this report Fitzpatrick recommended that an Indian agent for the Comanches and Kiowas be located on the Canadian river. |

| The pressing need for closer supervision of these Indians was also brought to the attention of the government by Lieutenant Henry Heith, commanding at Fort Atkinson, in a letter to his military superiors. Heith stated that the Indians who visited his post were friendly towards him, but that they had many prisoners, some of them white persons evidently taken in Texas. He wrote that they seemed to think it was perfectly legitimate to raid and steal in Texas, for they did not regard Texas as a part of the United States and did not regard the Texans as American people. He felt that chastisement by a strong military force offered the only means of stopping this lawlessness.[10] |

THE TREATY OF FORT ATKINSON

In 1852 many of the Comanches and Kiowas hovered about Fort Atkinson in the hopes of securing a treaty and more abundant presents. This probably accounts for the fact that they conducted themselves better than usual.[11] By an act of August 30, 1852, congress appropriated $20,000 for presents for these and other Indians on the Arkansas river frontier, and to enable the president to negotiate a treaty with them.[12] In July of the year following, Fitzpatrick negotiated the treaty. The difficulties he encountered are set forth in his report. He wrote:

> But little intercourse had ever existed between them and the white race, and that usually of the most unfriendly character ... they were ignorant of the proposals to be made to them, suffering from a scarcity of game, and consequently impatient, watchful, jealous, reserved, and haughty. There were no trappers or traders amongst them who could facilitate an interview; no one who could speak a syllable of the English tongue; none present in whom mutual confidence could be reposed; and the "sign language," that common to all the wild tribes of the west, while it might answer the purpose of barter, could not be relied upon in matters of so much importance and delicacy.[13]

At last some Mexican prisoners were brought forth and they, together with an Arapaho brave who had been living with the Comanches, managed to establish a chain of communication.

By the terms of the treaty, the United States agreed to give the Indians annually goods to the value of eighteen thousand dollars for a period of ten years, and for five years additional, if the president thought advisable. On their part, the Indians agreed that the government might lay out roads through their country and establish military posts. They promised to discontinue their raids into Mexico but "positively and distinctly" refused to entertain any proposal that would require them to give up their Mexican prisoners.[14] Six Comanche, six Kiowa, and four Kiowa-Apache chiefs signed the agreement. The agent's lack of acquaintance with the organization of the different Comanche bands probably accounts for his failure to make any comment on the groups or divisions which were represented. The head-chief, Shaved Head, was the most powerful personality among the Indians of the Arkansas[15] and wrought constantly and well in the interest of peace. Both he and his associate, White Eagle, are described by writers as Indians who frequented the Arkansas in the vicinity of Fort Atkinson, which indicates that they were Yamparikas. Ten Bears, another signer, became very influential during the period immediately following the Civil War. He also was a Yamparika. In fact, it seems that all the Comanche signers were Yamparikas except one, named "One who rides the Clouds," and described as "Chief of the Southern Comanches."

Among the Kiowa signers were the illustrious Little Mountain and Sett'aiñte, or Sitting Bear, commonly called Satanta.

RESULTS OF THE TREATY

The treaty of Fort Atkinson did not improve the Indian situation along the Arkansas river frontier, except for a short period. For a year or two the Comanches conducted themselves quite well; but by the summer of 1855 the agent reported that in spite of his admonition he supposed the next emigrant train would have to do as those that had preceded it had done—pay toll in the form of sugar, coffee, etc., before it would be permitted to proceed along the Santa Fé trail. He said the Indians thought the presents given them by the government were in payment for their friendship, and added that it was impossible to buy their good will.[16] It was impossible to punish the Indians for their insolence for the reason that there was but one post with a mere garrison on the upper Arkansas river, and this was very soon abandoned.[17]

In one respect the treaty augmented the disturbed conditions that already prevailed in the northern part of the Comanche country; that is, it led to a renewal of hostilities between the Comanches and the Osages.

About 1843 these ancient enemies had decided to bury the hatchet, and thereafter for some time trading took the place of fighting at the annual meeting on the plains. This trade grew to large proportions.[18] The position of the Osages, which made for easy and frequent intercourse with the white traders, enabled them to trade guns, munitions, and various products of civilization to the Comanches for horses, mules, and sometimes American and Mexican prisoners. John M. Richardson, the Osage agent, wrote that in 1847 his tribe purchased from the Comanches 1,500 head of mules worth from fifty to seventy-five dollars each, paying for them with tobacco, lead, powder, blankets, blue cloth, strouding, and firearms—the last named article representing the smallest item. It seems that the Osages secured these goods from a trader at their agency.[19] No doubt many of these animals furnished by the Comanches had been stolen from Texas and Mexico. For one blanket or a few pounds of sugar or coffee, the Osages could purchase a mule worth from eighty to a hundred dollars.

But after the treaty with the United States, the demands of the Comanches for these products of civilization were met in a large measure by the annuity goods they received, and the Osage near-monopoly was broken. The angry Osages then tried to persuade the Comanches not to use the annuity goods by telling them that they had "bad medicine" in them.[20] Obviously the most unsophisticated plains savage would soon detect this kind of fraud. Failing in this, the Osages made war on the Comanches, and their firearms made them more than a match for their adversaries, who had to fight mainly with bow and arrow and lance.[21] This Osage war cut off or made dangerous for the Comanches the northern buffalo ranges, and these bands, in their desperation, sought sustenance by means of more frequent and extensive forays into Texas.[22] This pressure from the north which the Comanches received during the middle fifties, together with their separation from the best buffalo ranges, was a matter of serious consequence for Texas and the north Mexican states.

Evidently the Osages finally came to realize that, notwithstanding their superior equipment which enabled them to defeat the Comanches, peace with that nation would be better than war; and in 1858 they made peace overtures. However, the Comanches would not treat, but instead attacked an Osage hunting party and killed one of their number. Then the Osages retaliated by killing four Comanches, and the war went on.[23]

It may serve our purpose in this connection to take some notice of the effect of the Fort Atkinson treaty along the other Comanche frontiers.

With the eastern settlements of New Mexico, as already observed, the Comanches generally remained at peace, although they harried the other north Mexican states. It should be stated, however, that relations between these Indians and the federal representatives in New Mexico had not been satisfactory by any means. James S. Calhoun, governor of the territory, invited the Comanches to send representatives to Santa Fé in 1851 for a friendly conference. Eagle Feathers, a chief, and a small party came, but were frightened and stole away one night because of statements made by certain designing persons that the Americans were planning to kill them.[24] This rascality of the white persons prevented the governor from arriving at any satisfactory understanding with the Indians, though it does not seem that the savages committed many serious depredations on this frontier during the fifties. Neither the Indian agents nor the United States army officers trusted them; on the contrary, complaints were made that they sometimes stole horses and killed cattle.[25] Furthermore, it was charged that the relations between the northern Comanches and Kiowas on the one hand, and the Indians of New Mexico on the other was of a decidedly evil tendency. The Indians of the plains received the plunder which the New Mexico Indians stole, and the Indians of New Mexico (and possibly some white men also) kept them informed as to when to expect a caravan on the road from Santa Fé to Independence.[26] It may be said that the situation on the New Mexico frontier was not materially affected by the treaty of Fort Atkinson.

Nor did this treaty improve conditions on the Texas frontier. Now that a treaty had been made and the savages were assured of annuity goods to be delivered each year from some point on the Santa Fé trail, the Indians naturally felt more independent in regard to Texas. The fact that people of that state belonged to the same government that was distributing goods to them did not in any way check them.[27] The Comanche thought in terms of localities, and his hates and passions took shape accordingly. Furthermore, he was an opportunist. It is a long ways from Lampasas county, Texas, to Fort Atkinson on the Arkansas river. How could sins committed in one place ever find him out in the other? The agent and few army officers along the Santa Fé road might admonish him not to disturb the Texas frontier, but they had no way whatever of seeing to it that their admonition was heeded. Furthermore, why should the savages trouble themselves to cultivate friendly relations in a country where there was no hope of reward? They could easily steal horses in Texas in June, and still be on hand at the Arkansas crossing in July to receive their goods; and since the presents were always forthcoming, regardless of their waywardness, there was no occasion for them to cease their remunerative activities in Texas.

In the early spring of 1854, less than a year after the treaty of Fort Atkinson, Major Neighbors learned from some of the southern bands that their northern kinsmen had declared to them that they did not desire to be friendly with Texas any more, and that they had gone north to get their presents. In fact, the northern Indians sent word to Major Sibley, commanding at Fort Phantom Hill, that as soon as the grass was good they were coming down and whip his soldiers and destroy his post.[28]

This treaty, which tended to make the Texas Indian situation all the more hopeless, brought protests from the people of that state and from the Indian agents and army officers stationed there as well. In 1857, Major Neighbors wrote:

> Our frontier still presents the anomaly of peace with a small portion of a tribe of Indians,[29] and continued hostility with the balance of the same people, and during the last year very serious depredations have been traced to them, and there have been several encounters between them and the troops on our frontier, in which a number of both soldiers and Indians have been killed. The strangest feature of this state of affairs, and one that demands your serious attention, is the fact that, at the same time that those bands of Comanches, Kioways, etc., are depredating on our citizens, waylaying our roads, destroying our mails to El Paso, etc., an agent of your department is distributing to them a large annuity of goods, arms, and ammunition on the Arkansas river, which is arming them, and giving them the means more effectually to carry out their hostile foray.[30]

Furthermore, as has already been observed, the treaty probably did not apply to several of the northern bands, and these bands, together with renegades from the southern Comanches, caused Texas the most trouble during the years immediately following the treaty.[31] These groups were made all the more formidable because traders from the Indian Territory, notably Jesse Chisholm, provided them with rifles and ammunition. During one season at least seventy-five rifles were secured by these Indians from this source.[32]

Thus did the federal Indian officers add to the peril they were trying to remove. Now the northern Comanches and their Kiowa associates were independent of the hated Texans. No longer would their chiefs be obliged to look with covetous eyes on the beads and gewgaws which "Washington" gave to their southern kinsmen; no longer would they have to hang around the agency on the Clear Fork to beg a blanket, butcher knife, a plug of tobacco. These things were now furnished them at their own headquarters in their own country. For fear that they should find it too difficult to shoot the buffalo and antelope with bow and arrow, the "Great Father" at Washington was furnishing them also with rifles and munitions, a thing those stingy men in the south had never done; and if "Washington's" supply of rifles and powder and lead was not enough, there were traders in the Comanche range ready to exchange these items for buffalo pelts or horses.

The northern agents were ideal guardians—from the Indians' point of view. They did not trouble themselves to follow up the savages in order to restrain them and chide them for their crimes. They attended strictly to their business, namely, the purchasing, assembling, and transporting to the place of rendezvous the annuity presents. These agents were acquainted with but few of the Indians, and knew very little about the Comanche and Kiowa tribes. It is true that there were a few soldiers in striking distance of the northern ranges, but most of these were infantrymen and hence were impotent to punish the Indians, while the few cavalry units never caused trouble unless the savages became generally hostile. Such conditions could not long exist, but while they did prevail, the great Comanche range north of the Red river continued to be a place of refuge for an increasing number of young warriors who found robbery an interesting and profitable business and made murder a profession.

CHAPTER EIGHT

War Trails Beyond the Rio Grande

RAIDS AGAINST THE MEXICANS

One provision of the treaty of Fort Atkinson calls for an extended treatment. That is the statement in Article 5 that the Indians should in the future refrain from all war incursions into the Mexican states, and should restore all Mexican captives who might be taken thereafter.[1]

It has already been stated that the practice of raiding along the Rio Grande and in the country to the west and south of that stream had come to be well fixed during the eighteenth century. Then when the United States, between 1825 and 1840, transferred thousands of eastern Indians to the territory west of the Mississippi, the disposition of the Comanches and Kiowas to commit depredations in Mexico was augmented. Game became scarcer in the Comanche range, and the border Indians and intruding white frontiersmen offered a good market for the horses and goods which the tribesmen of the plains could secure in Coahuila, Chihuahua, and Nuevo Leon. Thus it came about that in the decade from 1830 to 1840 the raids increased both in frequency and in destructiveness. The information concerning these depredations is fragmentary and incomplete, but there is extant sufficient evidence to indicate that these raids represent a prolonged and gigantic tragedy, one of the most horrible ever enacted on the North American continent. Its significance in the history of the Comanche tribe and of the Mexican and Anglo-American peoples is so great that it must be told in part, at least, even at the risk of provoking in the reader disgust and nausea by its horrible details.

In 1840 the Comanches extended their raids as far as the state of Zacatecas, into a region hitherto exempt from their depredations.[2] It was reported that in 1842 they harried parts of the state of Coahuila almost to the streets of Saltillo, while in the vicinity of Chihuahua they killed a number of men and took captive one hundred fifty women and children. From this raid they took to Bent, at his post on the Arkansas, many mules and horses, which he refused to purchase because he believed they intended to steal them again.[3] In 1844 Thomas G. Western, Texas superintendent of Indian Affairs, explained that Päh'-häh-yō'-kō was "prosecuting vigorous hostilities against Chihuahua."[4] In the fall of this year Daniel G. Watson, Texas Indian agent and scout, saw a party of braves from the camp of Old Owl and Buffalo Hump ride away for the Mexican border at about the same time that the chiefs themselves started for the council on the Brazos.[5] The Comanche elders might find time to attend an occasional council and talk peace, but the young men entertained themselves another way.

In February, 1845, a Comanche band passed San Antonio, killed three Mexicans in that vicinity, and moved on toward the Rio Grande. It was probably the same band that was reported a few days later to have passed near Corpus Christi. These Indians, numbering six hundred warriors, were led by Santa Anna. The Mexican settlements along the lower Rio Grande were the objects of this raid, and they suffered severely from it.[6]

If the Texas government did not encourage these raids, it certainly made no effort to stop them. During May, 1845, a band of a thousand lodges was reported to be encamped on Little river, a tributary of the Brazos, preparing to make a raid into the country beyond the Rio Grande. A party from this village arrived at the trading house on the Brazos and requested that they be furnished with supplies for the trip and with a pass that would permit them to get beyond the Texas settlements unmolested. In compliance with this request, Western asked Lieutenant Coleman, commanding the Travis county rangers, to permit them to pass unmolested and to furnish them with supplies if they should call on him on their way out,[7] and he gave similar instructions to Robert S. Neighbors, of the Texas Indian service.[8] In his letter to Coleman, Western explained that the Comanches had recently made an "unfortunate" expedition into the Mexican country and were returning to take revenge. It seems that in this particular case they got their "revenge," for in July Benjamin Sloat, of the Texas Indian service, wrote that the Comanche party that he and Lieutenant Coleman had furnished with a pass, had returned with a large herd of horses which they had taken from the Mexicans near Laredo.[9] And so it went. If one raid into Mexico was successful, it naturally prompted another; if it was not successful, the Indians felt obliged to make another in order to take revenge.

However, the Indians were not always victorious. In June of 1845 Neighbors found thirty Comanches under chief Bear's Tail crestfallen and footsore at the Lipan camp some fifty miles south of San Antonio. They explained that they had been defeated by the Mexicans near Matamoros. But at the Lipan camp they had secured new mounts and were ready to raid again.[10] During this same year another party under Buffalo Hump suffered defeat, possibly in the same engagement with the party of Bear's Tail. But Buffalo Hump avenged this defeat in a swift and terrible way. The story of this expedition has already been partly told—how the chief compelled Sloat and Jim Shaw to accompany him to San Antonio, how Hays and Colonel Kinney were unable to dissuade him from his plans, and how with more than six hundred warriors he set out for Laredo. The writer has not seen an account of the results of this expedition, but with such a large Indian force the havoc wrought must have been considerable. Whatever the results of this last expedition may have been, it is certain that Buffalo Hump was not sufficiently avenged, for in 1846 he made another foray and brought back a thousand head of horses and mules besides a number of prisoners, a quantity of money, and different kinds of plunder.[11]

Leading war parties into Mexico came to be Buffalo Hump's regular summer amusement. In August, 1847, with six or eight hundred warriors, he crossed the Rio Grande near the mouth of the Pecos. The chief knew the country to perfection, and talked about his proposed raid much as a tourist discusses his itinerary. He proposed to visit Chihuahua, Parras, and the surrounding country, and on his return, to attack San Fernando or places in its vicinity.[12] It is true that the invasion of Mexico by the United States army at this time invited more than the usual amount of Indian depredations; but the American forces probably offered better protection to the Mexican settlements near them than did the Mexican forces, which they superseded.[13] There is grim humor in the reason the southern Comanches gave for this unusually formidable expedition in the summer and fall of 1847. They were going to take revenge for a defeat suffered near Parras a few months before—a defeat which had been administered not by the Mexican people or the Mexican soldiers, but by the Missouri volunteers of the United States army.[14] As usual, the Comanches returned from this expedition with a large number of horses, mules, and some captives.[15]

Soon after the close of the Mexican War, clashes began to occur more frequently between the troops of the United States and the Indians along the "war trails" leading to the Mexican frontier. Neighbors's report that the Indians disclaimed any hostile intentions towards the troops has already been referred to. Under these conditions, all that the agent felt that he could do was to advise them to avoid the country between San Antonio and the Rio Grande and the region below that, and to make their ingress into Mexico at points above the Rio Frio over routes not guarded by the troops. That this was a violation of the letter and spirit of the treaty of Guadalupe Hidalgo, made between the United States and Mexico, 1848, cannot be denied. In defense of Neighbors it may be said, however, that he realized that the treaty with Mexico imposed upon him obligations he could not meet. The habit of plundering could not be broken by the decree of any one man no matter how courageous he might be or how influential with the Indians. On numerous occasions the chiefs of the southern Comanches insisted that their right to invade Mexico ought to be recognized, contending, and rightly so, that they had never agreed to discontinue the practice.[16]

In its report, the Mexican commission of 1873 gives in detail an account of Indian depredations in several of the north Mexican states for each year from 1848 on.[17] Though all this violence should not be charged to the Comanches, accounts indicate that the Mexicans correctly blamed them for much of it. In addition to the Comanches and their Kiowa allies, various Apache bands in Texas, New Mexico, Chihuahua, and Coahuila, acting independently, were a terror to the Mexican people. All bands, whether Comanche, Kiowa, or Apache were joined by individual adventurers and renegades from other tribes.

The promise of the United States in the treaty of Guadalupe Hidalgo, 1848, to restrain the Indians, proved to be of little benefit to the Mexican people. The raids became even more frequent and destructive, and the Indians extended their operations farther into the interior than ever before. Likewise, the promise of the Indians in the treaty at Fort Atkinson, 1853, to discontinue their attacks on the Mexicans brought no relief. The next year the savages denied that they had ever agreed to stay out of Mexico; and within a few weeks after receiving their annuity goods from the agent on the Arkansas, several hundred warriors went their way to Mexico.[18] According to data compiled by the Mexican commission, 652 persons were killed, wounded, or captured in the state of Nuevo Leon from 1847 to 1857 inclusive. They contend that this destruction is to be charged almost wholly to Comanches from the United States. Likewise, the states of San Luis, Zacatecas, Durango, Chihuahua, Tamaulipas, and Coahuila suffered, although not so seriously as Nuevo Leon.[19]

From time to time during the years of destruction, the Mexican local, state, and national governments took notice of conditions in the Indian-infested area, and made efforts to punish the savages and protect the country. In 1852 several of the northern states formed a "coalition" to defend themselves; the states as well as the different communities put troops in the field,[20] but the savages generally went unpunished. These efforts to protect the country did not strike foreign observers who visited Mexico at the time as being either effective or sincere.[21] In their desperation, the Mexican officials sometimes hired Indians and white adventurers to help them overcome this deluge of northern Indians. These Indian fighters were paid by the scalps they presented to the state officials. Since the scalp of an honest, peaceful Indian could be used quite as effectively as that of a marauder, these savage white men soon began the practice of killing friendly Indians for their scalps, and the scalp hunters had to be discharged.[22] The government also tried employing the Comanches in hunting down and killing the hostile Apaches, with results just as unsatisfactory.[23]

The havoc wrought in the north Mexican states by these raids made a profound impression on all observers. In 1846 Ruxton, the English traveler and adventurer, wrote:

> They are now [September] overrunning the whole department of Durango and Chihuahua, have cut off all communication, and defeated, in two pitched battles, the regular troops sent against them. Upward of ten thousand head of horses and mules have already been carried off, and scarcely has a hacienda or ranch on the frontier been unvisited, and the people have been killed or captured. The roads are impassable, all traffic is stopped, the ranchos barricaded, and the inhabitants afraid to venture out of their doors. The posts and expresses travel at night, avoiding the roads, and intelligence is brought daily of massacres and harryings.[24]

On his journey from Durango to Chihuahua, Ruxton saw on every hand evidences of depredations. He passed through a region termed the "Desert of the Frontier," a section of country which had been abandoned by the inhabitants because of the frequency of Comanche raids. At El Real de Mapimi, a town of more than two thousand inhabitants, he learned that the Comanches had recently entered the place and driven off the herd of mules. From Mapimi to Chihuahua he passed through the *Traversia*, a large tract of country which once possessed several thriving towns, which he found deserted and in ruins.

Conditions had not improved when Bartlett traversed the country in 1851. Comanches had attacked the town of Sancillo, in the Conchos valley, an hour before his party arrived, and had attempted to drive off the cattle. He saw the people bringing in the dead body of one of their townsmen who had been unfortunate enough to be caught by the savages outside of the village. He learned that the Bolson de Mapimi, a wild plateau north of Durango, was completely given over to the Lipans and Comanches, and he traveled three days' journey out of the way to avoid it.[25] The German traveler, Julius Froebel, found conditions just as bad when he spent the winter of 1852-1853 in Chihuahua, and pages of his narrative might be quoted setting forth the condition of terror under which the people lived.[26] In fact, it may be said that for a decade or more preceding 1855, the settlements in a considerable part of northern Mexico were actually receding before the onslaughts of these Indians from the United States.

In 1857 the raids showed a marked decline in number, and by 1860 they were comparatively infrequent.[27] The Mexicans credited this diminution to better defensive means adopted by their government, but a considerable part of the credit certainly must be given to the efforts of the government of the United States to keep the Indians out of Mexico. As early as 1852 Kătŭm'sē for the southern Comanches, and Chiquito for the Lipans, complained to Agent Howard that the troops in Texas not only frightened away the game, but prevented the Indians from going to Mexico and getting horses and mules "as they had always done."[28] As the troops interfered with their ancient "war trails" to Mexico, the savages made new trails farther west and north out of reach of the military forces. | In August, 1853, the southern Comanches told Neighbors that they had many young men away in Mexico at that time. When the agent rebuked them for permitting the raiding practice, they replied that they should be glad to discontinue it if they could find any other means of subsistence. Efforts of the United States to keep the Indians out of Mexico were not inspired altogether from a sense of obligation under international law. Warriors were always loathe to return empty handed; and if by chance they suffered the loss of their loot at the hands of the Mexican or United States soldiers they were likely to attempt to recoup from the American frontier as they returned home.[29] Hence it was necessary that they not be allowed to start on the raids. | Therefore, in order to head off these attacking parties, several new posts were established and garrisoned during the fifties, more troops were sent to the western part of Texas, state troops were used on several occasions, and decisive efforts made to keep the savages out of Mexico and the Texas settlements as well.[30] Their success in attaining this end is reflected in the decline of Indian depredations south and west of the Rio Grande.

The reaction of the savages to this more effective policing of western and southern Texas redounded, however, to the serious injury of another part of the state. When raiding in Mexico became too hazardous, the Indians naturally turned towards another frontier closer to home; and the decline of raiding in northern Mexico and its increase along the north Texas frontier synchronize perfectly. If the Indians could not go to Mexico for their horses, mules, and plunder "as they had always done," they must needs supply these wants elsewhere, and they turned to the north Texas frontier, a region that had been comparatively free from Comanche attacks up until 1855.

MEXICAN PRISONERS

The greatest tragedies incident to these raids, worse perhaps than the killing of many Mexican people, were the large number of women and children carried away into captivity. Evidence of this practice is to be found on every hand, but it is difficult to give an estimate of the number of such persons that would be more than a guess. There is scarcely a contemporary account of the Comanches and Kiowas that does not mention the large number of Mexican captives to be seen among them.

When, in 1851, the United States Indian agents in Texas, backed by the army, insisted that the Comanches and Lipans give up their Mexican prisoners, thirteen were taken at one time from the Comanches and fourteen from the Lipans,[31] and it seems that eleven others were secured in 1852 and turned over to the officer in command of the military colony at Guerrero.[32] It is certain that those liberated represented but a small portion of the prisoners held by the southern Comanche bands, for Kătŭm'sē appears to have been the only chief who honestly tried to cooperate with the agent. In 1853 Neighbors gave credence to the estimate of an old Mexican, who had lived for many years among them, that the number would not fall far short of 300, "principally Mexicans, but some few Americans and Germans," held by the Comanches generally.[33]

In 1856, after a portion of the southern Comanches had been on the reservation for more than a year, they were reported to have still twenty Mexican prisoners of both sexes and various ages.[34] Since the Indians must have expected that on taking up their abode on the reservation they would be required to give up their prisoners, it may be assumed that they had disposed of many of them before coming in. Hence this cannot be taken as a fair average for the entire tribe. Furthermore, since captive Mexican children and sometimes older persons became Comanches in every respect except in their physical characteristics, it must have been difficult for an observer to pick out the prisoners.

The treatment that prisoners received varied according to the age and sex of the prisoner and the disposition of his owner. It was the general policy of the Comanche and Kiowa tribes (if we may speak of a general policy among a people where each individual warrior did about as he pleased) to conserve the lives of women and children. The women and girls were taken by some chief or warrior for wives. Thus were forces of the tribes augmented sufficiently to offset in part the heavy losses from wars and diseases incident to the struggle for existence | the plains tribes underwent during the nineteenth century. Many prisoners evidently mingled with their captors on terms of perfect equality. In this connection Thomas Fitzpatrick, who negotiated the treaty of Fort Atkinson, wrote:

In fact, so intermingled amongst these tribes have the most of the Mexican captives become, that it is somewhat difficult to distinguish them. They sit in council with them, and partake of their perils and their profits, and but a few have any desire to leave them. Upon this account the chiefs of the nations refused positively and distinctly to entertain any proposal, or make any treaties, having in view the delivery up of these captives now dwelling amongst them. They stated very briefly that they had become part of the tribe; that they were identified with them in all their modes of life; that they were the husbands of their daughters and the mothers of their children, and they would never consent to a separation; nor could any persuasion or inducement move them to abate this position.[35]

But in his eagerness to defend the treaty he had negotiated Fitzpatrick overstated the case. Naturally the Indians would have kept in the background those captives who were dissatisfied with their lot and of these some were to be found with almost every Comanche and Kiowa band. | That a girl or woman, taken even from the lowliest Mexican hovel to be made a slave amongst nomadic savages, would suffer every conceivable kind of mental anguish, if not physical torture, goes without saying. The plight of these unfortunate people often touched the hearts of the border Indians and seasoned frontier white men. One case will illustrate what was evidently happening in the lives of dozens of other captives, most of whom were not so fortunate as the boy purchased by John R. Baylor, Comanche agent.

The agents observed that the Comanche chief, Sanaco (who was not on the reservation), had a secretary of unusual intelligence. For some two years he wrote letters for the chief from time to time, and finally when he came to the reservation, it turned out that he was a mere child. He plead with the agent to purchase him from the chief and send him back to his people. In a beautiful hand he wrote in laconic style the story of his capture for the archives of the United States Indian Office.

Comanche Agency, May 14, 1856

The name of my father was Don Julian Rivera. My mother was named Doña Josefa Herrera. My father came from Del Oro and my mother was from Santiago Pasasquiaro and we lived at Topia, in the State of Durango, of Mexican Spain. On May 7, 1853, the Comanches took me away together with five mule drivers and our mules, which were loaded with corn. We had sixteen mules and the horse which I was riding.

Tito Rivera

Naturally, many captives never survived the cruelties imposed upon them and the hardships incident to life with the Indians. Rosalie Tavores, an intelligent woman captured by the Comanches and Apaches near Monclova in 1849, informed John S. Calhoun, Indian agent at Santa Fé, that eight other persons in her community were taken about the same time, but that all died or were killed within a few weeks after their capture. She said the Indians killed all the men that were captured. Calhoun stated that trading in Indian captives had been going on so long in New Mexico that it was thought to be a legitimate business, and even Indians at peace with the government would not give up captives except on the payment of adequate ransom.[36]

Neighbors reported that the presence of these slaves at the Comanche reservation in Texas had a demoralizing effect on their masters, since the Indians looked to them to do all of the work. He also stated that the condition in which these people were obliged to live and the treatment accorded them was "worse than death" to a civilized people.[37] Accordingly, these prisoners were taken away and restored to their people in Mexico, but little or nothing was done in the way of securing the release of those unfortunate creatures held by the wild prairie bands.

CHAPTER NINE

The Texas Reservation

The necessity of giving the Indians of Texas a permanent location that they could consider as their home was brought to the attention of the government of the United States at the time it assumed control of Texas Indian affairs.[1] But nothing was done then, and as the Indians raised the question from time to time, they were put off with the promise "that all matters appertaining to that subject should be adjusted by the government of the United States at a proper time and to their entire satisfaction."[2] For several years after annexation, those who championed the interests of the Texas Indians generally advocated a plan whereby the United States should quiet any claims the Indians had to that portion of the Texas public domain which the state might require for use in the near future, while the Indians should be guaranteed exclusive rights to the remainder for a given period of time. By such a plan, white intruders could have been kept out of the Indian country, or, at least, there would have been legal sanction for keeping them out. Neighbors suggested that the territory north and west of a line drawn from the intersection of the one hundredth meridian and Red river to some point on the Rio Grande be given over to the Indians, to be used for a given number of years under government supervision and a system of annuities. In fact, in 1847 and 1848, the governor of Texas had proposed that the state sell the general government a portion of its public lands, stating among other reasons, that such an act would enable the United States to control the Texas Indians more satisfactorily.[3] John H. Rollins, who succeeded Neighbors as Texas Indian agent, advocated substantially the same thing, and the commissioner of Indian Affairs recommended that a commission be appointed to treat with the Texas government concerning the matter.[4]

No definite action resulted, however, and the state consistently maintained that neither the Indians nor the United States had any property rights in the public lands of Texas. Thus, the Indian agents found it impossible to locate their wards in the state or to protect them against the aggression of the settlers.

Meanwhile, the misery and poverty of the Indians increased from year to year, and the problem of restraining them grew proportionately greater. | In 1850, chief Kātŭm'sē complained to Rollins that his people were starving. The game was gone, he stated, and there was no hope for the Indians in trying to learn to farm like the white men when the settlers could come along and drive them away from the place they had chosen to make their home.[5] The next year the same chief said that the Comanches had "been driven about for the last seven years," and now they wanted a home where they could learn to raise crops.[6] Still later he said that the soldiers' tents dotted the prairies and where you did not find soldiers there were houses. If the "Great Father" would just give his people a home and teach them to farm, they would live at peace with all men. Mention has already been made of the establishment of forts in the upper Nueces country and along the Rio Grande. These forts made it more difficult and hazardous for the Indians to reach the Mexican settlements. Also they cut them off from the mustang country in the lower Nueces and Rio Grande valleys and thus stopped a supply of food that helped to sustain them and to offset in a measure the failing supply of deer and buffalo.[7] | Near Camp Johnson, on the Concho, in 1852, Horace Capron found some seven hundred Comanches under Kātŭm'sē, Sanaco, and other chiefs, "suffering with extreme hunger bordering on starvation." In forceful language the chiefs stated their plight. He quoted them as saying:

> What encouragement have we to attempt the cultivation of the soil, or raising of cattle, so long as we have no permanent home, and in every attempt we have ever made to raise a crop, we have been driven from them before they could mature by the encroachment of the white man.
>
> Over this vast country, where for centuries our ancestors roamed in undisputed possession, free and happy, what have we left? The game, our main dependence, is killed and driven off, and we are forced into the most sterile and barren portions of it to starve. We see nothing but extermination left for us, and we await the result with stolid indifference. Give us a country we can call our own, where we may bury our people in quiet.[8]

The chiefs also complained that their young men were debauched by liquor, sold to them by unscrupulous white men whom neither they nor their agents could keep out of the Indian country. For a tribe traditionally noted for its sobriety, this was indeed evidence of depravity.[9]

The plight of the Caddoes, Anadarkoes, Kichaies, Hainaies, Tawakonies, and other small bands along the Brazos valley was even more pathetic than that of the Comanches, whose home on the prairies farther west had not been settled. As early as 1848, José María, the Anadarko chief, feared that his people would be driven away from their growing crops.[10] The next year he complained that his village had been surveyed, and he could not feel sure that the fine crops of corn his people were raising would ever be gathered by them.[11] These small tribes, or remnants of tribes, were crowded out from time to time and forced to seek new locations higher up the river.[12] The Tonkawas, who generally lived on the Colorado below the Comanche country, and the Lipans, on the head of the Nueces, were in just as precarious a condition.[13]

ESTABLISHING THE RESERVATION

Finally, after one or more "location bills" had failed, the legislature of Texas, by an act of February 6, 1854, authorized the federal government to select not more than twelve leagues of land to be located in not more than three different tracts for Indian reservation purposes.[14] This was a parsimonious grant when thought of in terms of the vast area the Comanches had once claimed as their home. Yet, the state contended that the Indian problem was a federal and not a state matter. The cession was regarded as a gift, and the legislature was not in a liberal humor.

Captain Randolph B. Marcy, of the United States army, and Robert S. Neighbors, representing the Indian office, were appointed to locate and survey the lands to be used. Before their departure from Fort Belknap, they procured a map from the state land office. It is significant that they found that "a great share of the land bordering the principal streams was noted as disposed of to companies and individuals." They stated that this land represented "a great portion of the most desirable localities in the country."[15]

After an extensive reconnaissance of the country along the upper Big Wichita and Brazos rivers during the summer of 1854, two tracts were selected, one of eight leagues on the main Brazos near the mouth of the Clear Fork, and the other on the Clear Fork along what has since become the boundary of Haskell and Throckmorton counties. The reservation on the Brazos, containing eight leagues, was to be used by the various smaller tribes; and that on the Clear Fork of four leagues was to be used by the Comanches exclusively.[16]

A vivid description of the Indians is given by W. B. Parker, who accompanied Marcy and Neighbors.[17] These people were principally members of Sanaco's band, and they must have been as prosperous as any of the southern Comanches; yet squalor and misery were in evidence everywhere. They had come into possession of various trappings of civilization, and the combination of these with articles of their own manufacture produced a ludicrous appearance. Two chiefs rode in bareheaded with umbrellas raised to protect them from the sun; others combined cotton shirts with more substantial buckskin leggings. Apparently most of the warriors of consequence had come into possession of looking glasses, and these, together with tweezers purchased from some trader, and vermillion, enabled them to make their toilet—which they did with much care and deliberation. Evidence of the growing tendency towards drunkenness was shown in the case of two chiefs who offered a good portion of their entire belongings for a quart of whiskey. The Indians generally did not own many horses, and those they owned were of poor quality. One young dandy wore on his shield a bear's claw, a mule's tail, and a human scalp, indicating that he was a great hunter, a successful horse thief, and a mighty warrior.

One interesting and rather remarkable woman, the widow of the great Penateka chief, Santa Anna, is described. Although her husband had been dead five years she still mourned his loss, going out from camp and wailing every evening. She had gathered about her six other widows, and the seven mourned together. She was described as a fine-looking woman, a veritable "Amazon," and was one of the best hunters in the tribe. She owned a good herd of horses and, according to Comanche standards, was therefore quite wealthy.

There were a few traders along with the party, but the Comanches had so little to trade that there was no opportunity for them to derive any profit from their venture.

Pride, independence, and self-respect were virtues the savages were losing. Both the chiefs and their followers did not hesitate to beg, and even Kātŭm'sē stayed behind after the others had left to beg corn and meat.

When Neighbors returned in November to establish the reservation, he found nearby "the whole southern band" of Comanches (Penatekas), which he estimated at from one thousand to twelve hundred souls. In other camps close by the various smaller tribes were congregated. Another council was held, and the Indians urged that the government hurry the preparations for the reservation since they were in a starving condition.[18]

But before the Indians had been located on their reservation, an incident occurred prophetic of the difficulties the government was destined to encounter in its efforts to civilize these wild people. In January, 1855, a small party of Sanaco's band went to Fort Chadbourne, about sixty miles southwest of the reservation, for the purpose of trading. While there, an unofficial trader told them that a military force was coming to kill them all, and that they must hurry to Sanaco's camp and inform him of the fact in order that the Comanches might avoid the wrath of the soldiers. "Do not eat, sleep, or rest until you give him this talk from his friend," said the trader.[19]

At the time of this occurrence at Fort Chadbourne, Sanaco and Kătŭm'sē were helping Major E. Steen of the army recover some horses which a frontier citizen claimed the Comanches had stolen from him. Steen left the chiefs altogether friendly and manifesting every disposition to remain at peace with all white men, but before he reached Fort Belknap, Kātŭm'sē overtook him with the news that Sanaco and Buffalo Hump had fled precipitately with all their bands and a portion of his own people towards the country of the northern Comanches. Some eight hundred souls fled with the chiefs,[20] the most of whom were never persuaded to return to the reservation. Only about a hundred eighty Indians were left with Kātŭm'sē, and these were settled for the time on the lower, or Brazos reservation.[21]

As soon as the frontier was clear of troops and the agents could assure the Indians that they would not be molested if they would return to the reservation, runners were sent from Kātŭm'sē's band to invite the run-aways to come back. The refugees had broken up into several small parties, however, and some of them could not be reached. Some had joined the Nokonies and Tanimas along Red river, some had gone farther north where, it was reported, the Osages were harassing and killing them, some had gone to New Mexico, and others were drifting about over northern Texas in a poverty-stricken and desperate condition.[22] A few returned, however, and by June 10, 1855, the Comanches under the control of the agent numbered 249, with others reported to be coming in. The agents found it difficult to get the Comanches to work, and it was thought that they would do better on their own reservation on the Clear Fork.[23] They were removed to that place in May or June, 1855.

RAISING WHEAT AND CORN

The reservation had been established, but only a minority of the Penatekas were there to receive its benefits. This poor beginning was prophetic of more serious difficulties that were to be encountered later. Under the conditions that prevailed, the reservation system could not be made to solve the Texas Indian problem. If the lower estimate of the southern Comanches, i.e., one thousand souls, be accepted as approximately correct, it will be seen that less than a third of these Indians were on the reservation at or near the time it was established. The two most influential chiefs, Buffalo Hump, a chronic disturber, and Sanaco, destined to be quite as troublesome, were still at large. The hurried flight had forced these Indians to leave behind their scanty stock of goods, which meant that they must commit theft and perhaps murder in order to get new equipment. Furthermore, in this poor condition the bands disintegrated, and what remained of tribal organization broke down. The military strength of these roving bands was no longer a matter of consequence, but their power and disposition to steal had been augmented.

Along Red river were the Nokoni, Tenawa, and Tanima bands, bands that had never been brought into treaty relations with the United States. Although they were no longer very numerous, there were still enough warriors left to make them a powerful factor in the matter of committing theft and attacking isolated farms. Furthermore, the Yamparika, Kotsoteka, and other northern bands together with the Kiowa still frequented northern Texas at certain seasons and still raided the states of northern Mexico. It is true that other Indians came to the agency so that on one occasion there were as many as 557 people, but 350 or 400 would represent a fair average over the whole period of the reservation's history.[24] It may be assumed that those who did come in were the mildest and least disposed to make trouble. Chief Kătŭm'sē, to whom a portion of the credit must be given for any success attained by the experiment, was the only chief of influence to live on the reservation continuously. Sanaco and Buffalo Hump occasionally came in, but they never stayed long, and were soon off again, much to the annoyance of the agents and Kătŭm'sē.[25]

Naturally the going and coming of these wild Indians, and their occasional presence at or near the reservation made it all the more difficult for the agents to control the Indians on the reservation. An affair that occurred during the first summer is worth relating because it illustrates the sympathy that existed between the wards of the agents and their roving kinsmen. About the middle of July a large party of reservation Comanches appeared at the Lower or Brazos reservation where the agent, S. P. Ross, treated them kindly but advised them to return home at once. They left immediately; and nothing of consequence occurred until about a week later, when a frightened runner appeared at Ross's headquarters and stated that a large war party of Comanches was at the Tonkawa village a few miles away. A second runner soon appeared with word that the women and children of the Tonkawa, Waco, and Tawakoni town had taken flight, and a fight had commenced at the Caddo and Anadarko settlement.

The report of the fight, happily, proved to be untrue. The facts were that Kătŭm'sē and Buffalo Hump at the head of seventy-five Comanche warriors (evidently about all there were of the reserve Comanches), had approached José María's village in a very threatening manner. But the veteran Anadarko chief was expecting trouble, and proved to be equal to the occasion. He had his men drawn up in battle line awaiting the Comanches, and informed them that if they wanted a fight he was ready to accommodate them. Kătŭm'sē then stated that they had not come to fight, but to talk, and through the intervention of Ross, who had hurried with Jim Shaw to the scene of confusion, a council was held. When called upon to explain their extraordinary conduct, the Comanches, evidently embarrassed at the turn the affair had taken, said that all was well, but that they wished to ask just one question: "Were the Caddoes going to continue to act as guides for the troops?"[26]

This question explains the whole affair. No doubt Buffalo Hump, using the milder Kătŭm'sē as a tool, had hoped to frighten the smaller bands into withholding the valuable aid they had been rendering to the troops as scouts and guides. Although these Comanches were wards of the government, their sympathy for their wild and marauding kinsmen was stronger than that for any government agent or soldier, and they resented the fact that the smaller tribes were taking such an active part in the interest of law and order. Also, it may be that Buffalo Hump himself had had occasion to suffer because of aid given the troops by the more civilized Indians. It should be added that the warriors of the smaller tribes continued to act as guides and scouts for the troops.

Each reservation was maintained under the control of a resident agent who lived at the agency, located on the reservation. The resident agent was subject to the direction of the supervising agent for the Indians of Texas. John R. Baylor was resident agent for the Comanches until May, 1857, when he was succeeded by Mathew Leeper,[27] who remained at that post until the reservation was abandoned, in 1859. Robert S. Neighbors was supervising agent for all Texas Indians during the whole period. An interpreter, a farmer, and, during part of the time, a teacher, were retained for the Comanches. The Indians were allowed a daily ration of two pounds of beef, three-fourths of a pound of flour or corn meal, and four quarts of salt for each hundred rations.[28] The daily ration was lessened when the Indians' crops or cattle enabled them to sustain themselves in part.

The difficulties with which the agents had to contend were almost sufficient to have made the hope of success futile, even if the reservation had had a better start. It has already been noted that the renegade Penatekas joined the Tenawas, Nokonies, and other northern bands, and that these renegades managed to keep in touch with their kinsmen on the reservation, ever trying to entice them away. It was easy for the reserve Indians to leave unobserved by night, and small groups frequently did so. Strange Comanches often visited the reservation, and when they left one or more of the agent's wards was likely to leave with them. Sometimes, when the wild Indians could think of no better excuse for visiting the reservation, they would pose as emissaries sent to hold a "talk" and make peace with the Indians and agents located there.[29]

"Dog Eater," Comanche Chief

Comanche, one of twelve raiders into Texas, the only one who returned.

In September, 1857, Neighbors wrote that although a strong military force was kept at the reservation, it was impossible "to resist the influence of the outside bands of Comanches, or to prevent the young men from quitting the reserve to join in the continued forays made by them both upon our frontier and that of Mexico." Then he added: "I can perceive but little difference between the condition of the Comanches now and at the date of my last annual report."[30] In this connection it may be observed that the Indians did not depend entirely on the troops for protection. They established patrols and not only managed to protect themselves, but made it uncomfortable for renegades who tried to loiter about their camps.[31] However, sometimes the visiting Indians had influential friends among those at the reservation, and in such cases the chief found it difficult to oust the intruders. This protracted annoyance from outside Indians, together with the hostility of white frontiersmen, finally forced the inhabitants of the reservation to refrain from hunting and to discontinue the practice of grazing their stock at points away from their homes. This meant that they had to keep their horses in pens and feed them much of the time.

The protection afforded by the troops was often so inadequate that the savages were in a state of uneasiness. When the Indians were first assembled, there were no troops in that section of Texas except one company of infantry at Fort Belknap, fifty miles away.[32] But about the first of January, 1856, four companies of cavalry were established on the reservation, and for a time the inhabitants enjoyed a sense of security.[33] Then after a few months, ill-feeling developed between the army officers and the agents, each side charging that the other had not manifested a desire to cooperate;[34] and most of the troops were removed.

Without an adequate military force to support them, the agents were not able to discipline refractory savages. This is illustrated by an incident that occurred in August, 1858. A notoriously bad Indian, named Santa Anna, came and put up in Kătŭm'sē's cabin, the only building the Indians had. The chief ordered Santa Anna and his companion, a Nokoni Indian, to leave; but they informed him that they were resting from their arduous journey and did not propose to leave until it suited their convenience. When this was reported to Agent Leeper, he called on the detail of troops at the old post to come at once. It happened that on this occasion the troops were in charge of a commissioned officer, Lieutenant Van Camp. Van Camp came with his detachment of twenty men (all there were at the post),[35] surrounded the house and took steps to seize the renegades. But to the chagrin of the agent and soldiers, fifty or sixty warriors, armed with bows and guns, together with about thirty women and boys, armed with sticks and clubs, closed in around the cabin, and took the side of the visitors so positively that Van Camp saw that a fight was ahead if he forced the issue. He ordered his men to prepare for action and a battle would have followed but for the fact that he discovered that his men had but one round of ammunition each! Thus, the only thing left for the lieutenant to do was to order the two visitors to leave, which they did at once. During this disturbance Kătŭm'sē had tried to exercise his authority and had called on his people to abandon their lawless guests; but very few did so, the main group aligning themselves on the side of rebellion.

On the following day the Indians who had taken an active part in protecting the visitors came to Leeper and explained that they had offered resistance because they thought the soldiers would kill them all, and they were determined to die fighting. Obviously they thought no such thing. Their bad faith in the whole matter was more pronounced in their telling Leeper as they approached him for a "talk" that they expected him to say that their "talk" was "good." In that case everything would be all right, but if he did not say that their "talk" was good, they would kill him and his family.[36]

Naturally the agents and army officers as well were vexed with the Indians over this affair. Notwithstanding the veneer of civilization they had begun to acquire, these people were still savages, and the sanctity of law and authority meant little to them. The visiting savages were evidently fellows of forceful personality, and the reservation Indians had become attached to them and felt that to abandon them to the soldiers while they were their guests would be treachery. Some of the older men and women tearfully begged Kătŭm'sē not to force the issue, urging him to let the men escape.

Soon after this "ridiculous affair," General Twiggs ordered that company D, of the second cavalry be stationed at old Camp Cooper.[37] However, the entire company did not long remain there, for, on November 15, Leeper again complained that he was without protection since the detachment of fifteen men stationed at the buildings of Old Camp Cooper would not be of any use as a protection to the agency.[38] During the crisis in June, 1859, when the frontier citizens were threatening to attack the reservation, an adequate cavalry force was stationed there and remained until the Indians were removed.[39] However, it must be said that during much of the four years that the reservation was in existence, the United States army did not give the protection which even its limited means might have permitted.

The sale and barter of liquor to the Indians was a source of considerable annoyance to the agents. In addition to their right to exclude liquor from the reservation proper, the agents had the benefit of a state law which provided that the federal law against the sale of liquor might be applied in a ten-mile zone extending around the reservation.[40] However, since congress did not take any action to extend the federal law over this ten-mile zone, the authority of the agents to stop the sale of liquor in that area was doubtful.[41] Nevertheless, the agents frequently destroyed liquor stocks on and in the vicinity of the reservation.[42] They reported that it was exceedingly difficult to apprehend persons who carried on this traffic since little or nothing could be learned from the Indians themselves. It was charged that certain soldiers as well as certain civilians were guilty of engaging in the demoralizing business.

The vexations incident to controlling, teaching, and starting on the road towards civilization several hundred nomadic savages just taken from the prairies and confined to a reservation of a few square miles were too numerous to be adequately described. The conduct and practice of the Comanches were enough to have exhausted the patience of a saint, and that they were dealt with so successfully is a credit to the men responsible for the administration of the reservation.

Savage lawlessness and lack of self-restraint provoked clashes between individuals of a tribe where freedom of action had recently been unlimited. In a fit of anger, one of the head-men stabbed his wife, and her brother vowed to avenge her wrong. The husband's friends came to his side, and a general fight seemed imminent. But the guilty Indian came to the agent in a penitent mood, and offered to take any punishment the agent should impose. The agent left it to the other chiefs, and nothing was done. The woman recovered and her brothers apparently became reconciled.[43]

The reservation farmer had his troubles also. The Indians would turn their horses into the cornfield—or turn them loose where it was evident that they would get in the field. They would pull melons no larger than an egg, and were wont to consume all their corn before it had grown to good roasting-ear. In the spring of the second year, they refused for some time to plant their crops until they had been given presents, but finally the agent persuaded them to go to work without the presents.[44]

Sometimes there was violence unto death. A chief or headman had engaged in intrigue with another man's wife. According to custom, the injured man demanded that the chief compensate him to the amount of a horse. When the chief refused or hesitated to do this, he was slain at once by the sons of the injured man. Then the father and his sons and their women and children fled and were not overtaken, although a scout followed them for a hundred fifty miles.[45]

And yet, notwithstanding these evidences of savage crudeness, it must be said that at least some of the Indians were making progress toward a more civilized existence. Settlers near the reservation lived in peace and without fear of the reservation Indians, and the white population in the neighborhood increased rapidly.[46] Under the direction of a reservation farmer, the Indians worked and made fairly good crops. In 1858 the community fields were divided into six divisions in order that each of the six prominent clans might have a separate plot to work. The farmer thought that some of the clans would make enough grain this year to do them.[47]

Some of the children made good progress in the school. In 1858 it was reported that ten boys were in school, and in a later account it was stated that they were learning very rapidly. Thomas T. Hawkins, special agent who was sent to investigate the reservation in 1858, wrote of the Comanches: "I regard them as superior in natural sense and intelligence to any of our full blooded native tribes and I have seen many specimens in Washington, in the west and upon my journey hitherto."[48]

THE DEPREDATIONS CONTINUE

The people of Texas had expected that the reservation would improve and make safer life on the western frontier; but it was a vain hope. The various bands of southern Comanches who refused to settle, together with parties of their northern kinsmen and Kiowas and Lipans, and remnants of other tribes continued to harass the settlements to such an extent as to call forth protest from many sources. Instead of improving, conditions grew worse from year to year, especially after 1856.

The year 1857 saw a marked increase in the depredations reported from Texas. Comanche bands, particularly Nokonies, plundered and killed in a number of communities.[49] A characteristic of the attacks worthy of note is that they were made in a section of country north and east of the region that had suffered most previous to this time. The counties of Palo Pinto, Eastland, Erath, Comanche, Bosque, and Hamilton, lying between the Brazos and Colorado rivers, which had been comparatively free from attacks since they had been settled, began to attract the attention of the Indians.[50] In November, Leeper reported that there had been more depredations in the vicinity of the reservation, and also on Pecan Bayou (Brown county) than ever before. For this reason he was keeping his Indians confined to the reservation.[51] Other Indians, particularly the Kickapoos and Kiowas, were charged with being equally responsible with the Nokoni Comanches for these murders and thefts. In December, Neighbors estimated that five hundred horses, worth fifty thousand dollars, had been stolen recently from citizens along the Brazos and Colorado valleys, and reported that three citizens had been killed.[52]

It has already been observed that the shift in the points of attack in Texas to the more eastern and northern frontier communities occurred at about the same time that the attacks against the Mexican frontier began to decline. No doubt the large number of military posts and the aggressive action of the cavalry in the country south and west of the Colorado cut off the routes into Mexico or made them more dangerous for the Indians. The savages accordingly found it more profitable and less hazardous to steal the better horses nearer home. Furthermore, during at least a portion of this year, Fort Belknap, the post best situated to serve as a base for troops protecting these counties, was garrisoned by infantry only.[53]

During the year 1858 portions of the Texas frontier were harried as never before. Apparently the main aim of the savages was to steal horses, but they would attack and kill any small party of white persons that happened to cross their path.[54] Reports of murders charged to the Indians came from counties as far east as Denton and as far south as Lampasas; and along with these reports would come accounts of "general alarm" and statements that the people were "forting up."[55]

The people of Texas had hoped that the reservation policy would bring a measure of peace and quiet to their frontier, and they had been disappointed. They were not in a humor to investigate the reasons for this failure. They had come to charge the thefts and murders to the reservation Indians, and the clamor against the reservations had become violent by the close of 1858. | The people could see but small relief in the removal of the Indians. | They did not propose to let this shedding of blood go unavenged, and their attitude towards all Indians became hostile and aggressive. The war must be transferred from the frontier settlements to the villages of the Indians wherever they might be found. This aggressive and hostile policy was also adopted by the United States army in Texas, and the army and the militant citizens together made a series of expeditions against the Comanches—the first serious military movements made against these Indians since the administration of President Lamar of the Republic of Texas.[56] If the white people could not stop the raids, they could at least punish the marauders, and they clamored for war.

CHAPTER TEN

Enemies on Every Border

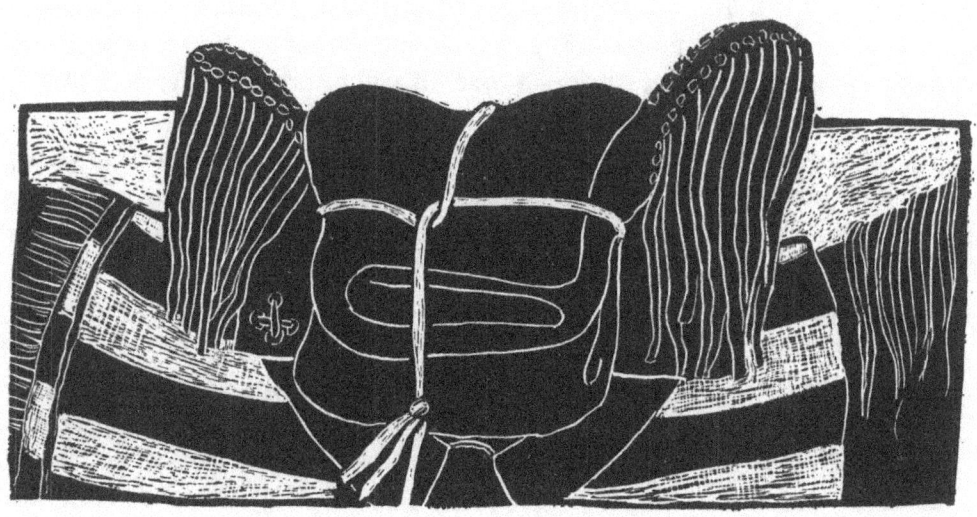

THE WRATH OF THE TEXANS

The aggressive and hostile Indian policy adopted in Texas in 1858 was promoted by all factions concerned, i.e., the United States Indian agents, the reservation Indians, the frontier citizens acting independently or under authority of the state government, and the United States army. The Texas Indian agents as well as the chiefs on the reservation realized that if the peaceful Indians were to remain in Texas, the raids from the northern bands would have to be stopped. In January, 1858, Neighbors wrote General Twiggs urging a campaign against the northern Indians in the spring. He would furnish guides from the friendly tribes, and the army could carry the war to the very villages of the northern Comanches and Kiowas.[1]

Neighbors had long endeavored to get the government to place these northern bands on a reservation, and in these efforts he had been joined by the Indian agents of the Arkansas river frontier.[2] Finally, a strip of territory west of the ninety-eighth meridian was set aside for them.[3] But it was one thing to legislate the wild Comanches and Kiowas into a state of settled existence, and quite another matter actually to place them on a reservation and keep them there.[4] While the Great Plains region was still unsettled and a few buffalo and deer were still to be found to supplement the food and plunder obtained by theft, the small army force on the frontier was altogether inadequate for such a task. Hence Neighbors, General Twiggs, and the people of Texas were united in the conviction that these bands would have to be crushed by an effective military force before they ever could be brought to accept the dull life on a reservation.

The change in the policy of the army is reflected in a communication written by General Twiggs to the assistant adjutant-general. He stated:

> I would respectfully recommend a change of policy with the Indians. For the last ten years we have been on the defensive. I would suggest that it would be better not to detach the regiment [the second cavalry] to the posts as formerly, but send two detachments into the Indians' country, and follow them up winter and summer, thus giving the Indians something to do at home in taking care of their families, and they might possibly let Texas alone. I think the experiment worth making . . .[5]

But before the army launched its campaign, the militia, together with some warriors of the Brazos reservation, struck the severest blow the Comanches had felt since the days of the Republic of Texas. These more civilized Indians on the Brazos made excellent scouts and were numerous enough to muster a considerable force of excellent fighting men.[6] By permission of their agent, these Indians had on a number of occasions sent out scouts to pursue the marauders and recover stolen property. Naturally Captain John S. Ford was glad to augment his little force of one hundred two rangers by a picked band of these Indians under the command of their agent, S. P. Ross. The two forces together totaled about two hundred fifteen men; and with this command Ford and Ross marched in the direction of the Comanche country determined to attack the Comanches wherever they might find them.

The expedition moved north to Red river, striking it some distance below the junction of the two main forks, and moved up that stream to a point above its intersection with the ninety-eighth meridian. Thence they went to the valley of the Washita, where they discovered Indians with horses loaded with buffalo meat going towards the Canadian. Following the trail of these Indian hunters, the rangers, on the morning of May 12, 1858, found and attacked a Comanche village of seventy lodges north of the Canadian on Little Robe creek. The village was taken by surprise, and the Comanches thoroughly beaten. An armed Indian party that endeavored to come to the rescue of the village was also defeated. Seventy-six Comanches were killed that day, and eighteen, mostly women and children, were made prisoners.[7] Among the slain Comanches was the chief, "Pohebits Quasho"[8] (Iron Jacket), widely known because of his coat of mail which was supposed to have made him invulnerable to rifle fire. Although, according to their report, the Texans were confronted with a total of about three hundred warriors in the two engagements, they lost only two men killed and three wounded.

There were other Comanche forces in the vicinity, apparently under the direction of Buffalo Hump; but the Texans did not see fit to force another engagement. They took up the march for Camp Runnels[9] and arrived there May 21, having been away no more than thirty days.

The village which was destroyed was that of a band of Kotsoteka or Buffalo-eater Comanches.[10] The fact that there were no "American" horses among the three hundred or more head which Ford and Ross took from the village indicates that this Comanche band had not recently committed depredations on the Texas settlements. Ford does not state the number of women and children among the seventy-six Indians slain, for that was a matter of no great concern to the Texas people. They were tired of a conciliatory Indian policy, and the fact that these hostilities resulted in the death of Indian women and children did not, as they thought, detract from the propriety or justice of the war. The attack broke up one of the Kotsoteka bands, and in the autumn following the remnant of the group went to the reservation and asked permission to settle there.[11]

A singular characteristic of the Ford-Ross campaign is that it was carried out by Texas forces, acting on state authority only, yet operating and fighting a battle outside of the state. In their report, the officers take no notice of the fact that the battle with the Indians was not fought on Texas soil, and the boundary line evidently was a matter of little concern to them.[12] The Indians had been defeated; the place of the engagement and the means used were items of little consequence. As one enthusiastic citizen wrote the president: "The rangers, with the assistance of the friendly Indians, killed seventy wild Indians. When did the soldiers ever do as much?"[13]

Lieutenant Allison Nelson drew the most significant conclusion from the results of the campaign.

> The beneficial results [he stated] do not stop with the signal punishment inflicted. It demonstrates the practicability of following the enemy with white men, well provided with subsistence transported by wagons to the fastnesses from which they have hitherto sallied forth to rob and murder on our frontier with impunity.[14]

That the Comanche villages could be reached by military expeditions was evident, and that a small, well organized force could wreak havoc among the savages when it attacked them in their homes had been well demonstrated. However, that by such expeditions the Indians really guilty, that is, the small squads of marauding warriors, could be reached was an entirely different question. Such attacks might help to solve the Indian problem by the process of extermination, but that they would bring any immediate relief was not to be expected. As bands like this one were decimated and broken up, the old men and women and children might come into the reservation and ask to be given a home. But many of the young warriors would not do this. They would attach themselves to other large divisions, or form small bands of their own companions. Then, without any of the restraining influences of organized tribal society, they became much more dangerous. Utterly irresponsible and thirsting for revenge, they would be all the more ready to harass the people they charged with the responsibility for their desperate plight.

During the year 1858, the Comanches received another severe blow from "the people of the south." Major Earl Van Dorn, at the head of a cavalry force, moved against them that fall. His orders were to scout thoroughly the country between Red river and the north fork of the Canadian lying between 100 and 104 degrees of longitude. General Twiggs, who ordered the expedition, was more particular than the rangers had been, and secured permission from the war department to authorize Van Dorn to follow any Indian trails that might be discovered without reference to department limits. He was to take four companies from the second cavalry and fifty troops from the first infantry.[15]

Van Dorn moved north in September and set up a depot on Otter creek near the ninety-ninth meridian.[16] He was about to move his main force on to the Canadian when the information reached him that a large party of Comanches was camped near the Wichita village, about ninety miles to the east.[17] He set out at once for that place, reached the Indian village thirty-six hours later, and attacked the Indians at once. More than a hundred Texas Indians, under L. S. Ross,[18] aided Van Dorn's cavalry. The Comanche village of about 120 lodges was burned, fifty-six warriors and two squaws were killed, and over three hundred animals were captured. Two Wichita Indians, who happened to be in the Comanche camp, were killed also. The victory cost the troops the life of Lieutenant Cornelius Van Camp, one sergeant, and three privates. Several men were seriously wounded, including Van Dorn and Ross.[19]

In a special order commemorating this engagement, General Twiggs, with more enthusiasm than accuracy, had his adjutant write that it was "a victory more decisive and complete than any recorded in the history of our Indian warfare."[20] The attack of the cavalry took the Indians by surprise just as the rangers had done. Both commands struck blindly, without regard for the guilt or innocence of the savages attacked.

The remarkable and even astounding fact about this attack at the Wichita village is that it occurred while the Comanches were acting on the advice of a United States army officer, and while the chiefs were probably on their way to Fort Arbuckle to treat with the government.

This blunder had come about by a series of events growing out of the attack of the Texans in the spring preceding. Among the Indians in Ford's attacking party was a Kichai, whom the Comanches recognized as a man who had once lived with the Wichitas. This led them to believe that the Wichitas had betrayed them to the Texans, and they set about to retaliate by stealing horses from those Indians. When they were convinced of their error, they sent captains to the Wichita camp to make amends. The Wichitas called in Lieutenant Powell from Fort Arbuckle, and he advised the Comanches to go back and tell Buffalo Hump and his three leading chiefs to come in to Fort Arbuckle and talk with the commanding officer.[21] Thus the Comanches were on a friendly and peaceful visit to the Wichitas. They had brought back to restore to their owners some of the horses that they had stolen,[22] and had followed the advice of Lieutenant Powell to the letter, except that they had not yet visited Fort Arbuckle. They had planned to hold a council with the Chickasaws and Choctaws, and expected to settle all differences that might exist between them and all the tribes of Indian Territory; and at their camp at the Wichita village they had every reason to think that they were perfectly safe and at peace with everybody.

Van Dorn was not aware of these facts, but if he had learned of them, he probably would not have changed his plan. He was responsible for the protection of the Texas frontier, these Comanches were avowed enemies of the Texans, and in attacking their village wherever he found it, he was acting according to the spirit and letter of his orders.[23] It must be said that the Indians were quite logical in their conclusion that Texas was not a part of the United States. Surely it is too much to expect of the savage mind that it could grasp the idea that the Texans and the Americans were really the same people when military expeditions from the Texas frontier attacked the Indians at the very time that army officers in Indian Territory were inviting them to friendly councils, and while still further north another representative of the same government gave them presents each year.

The accounts are too meager to enable one to determine with certainty what band or bands suffered from this attack; but it is likely that it was made up of renegade Penatekas, together with additions from various other Comanche divisions. The fact that Buffalo Hump was head-chief is significant in that it indicates that the traditional bands were disintegrating and new alignments being made. It will be remembered that Buffalo Hump was a Penateka, but his following from his own band had grown very slim, and it evidently had been augmented by other Indians. Although many of his people were killed, Buffalo Hump escaped uninjured. It is reported that the doughty old renegade made his escape early in the engagement.[24]

The policy of the army was to continue to punish the Indians, and Van Dorn accordingly spent several months in the Indian country. From his camp on Otter creek (Camp Radziminski), he sent out a number of expeditions, but the Comanches managed to keep out of his reach for some time.[25] However, spurred on by the protests of Governor Runnels, who persisted in his contention that the Indians had not yet been punished enough, and by the Texas congressmen and senators, General Twiggs, in March, 1859, issued orders for another general campaign against the Comanches and Kiowas.[26]

Major Van Dorn had advocated a combined attack against the Comanches in which forces from the Indian Territory, Arkansas, and New Mexico frontier should cooperate with him in a movement calculated to break the strength of all the wild tribes south of the Arkansas; but this plan never received the approval of the war department.[27] Notwithstanding the failure of the war department to approve this plan for a united attack, Van Dorn moved from Camp Radziminski April 30, and marched north. On May 13, 1859, on or near "a small creek fifteen miles south of Old Fort Atkinson," he killed, wounded or captured nearly all of a band of about ninety or a hundred Comanches. These were Buffalo Hump's people, part of the same band that he had defeated so severely in October preceding.[28] Fifty Indians from the Brazos reservation under Jack Harry and Shawnee Jim aided Van Dorn in this attack. Among the cavalrymen who were wounded was Lieutenant Fitzhugh Lee. On the day before this battle Van Dorn came to a large abandoned Comanche village which he thought had been occupied by at least two thousand Indians—the bands of Ola Mocohopie and Mu-la-que-top. Apparently these bands had received warning and kept out of the way of the troops, but Buffalo Hump was either not so fortunate or not so alert. No doubt his position, within a few miles of the Arkansas river and near the northern border of the Comanche range, made him careless. Although the Indians were greatly outnumbered, they evidently fought desperately; for some twelve of Van Dorn's men were wounded besides Lieutenant Lee, and one was killed.[29]

In autumn of 1859 the cavalry made another expedition, marching from Camp Cooper to the Cimarron river; but no Indians were seen.[30] Evidently the Comanches were becoming more alert, and well they might, for they were no longer safe in the heart of their own country.

FRONTIER HYSTERIA

The vigorous offensive policy of the cavalry and rangers gave little relief to the frontier. In September, 1858, thefts and murders were reported in Denton, Montague, and Jack counties.[31] In late October, Brown and Lampasas counties suffered; in February following, citizens near the Brazos agency lost horses, and eighty head were taken from the Caddoes and Anadarkoes—"about the last" of the five hundred head that these Indians had possessed three months before. It was reported that a party of reservation Indians gave chase to the marauding band that stole their horses, but gave up the trail when they realized that the force they were pursuing was too strong for them.[32] People along the Llano had to leave their homes, and citizens of Lampasas declared that the savages were coming almost into the town.[33]

The number of horses stolen by Indians along the north Texas frontier during 1858 and 1859 would probably total several thousand, which represented a serious loss for the frontier stockmen. But the murders the Indians committed were incidental to their thieving operations, and if the number of persons actually killed by the savages could be positively determined, it would certainly not be large. Probably nearly as high a percentage of the population of those counties in our own times meet death by accident or violence as were killed by the Indians in the late fifties. However, it was not the damage actually done but the condition of panic which was created that made the raids a matter of such serious consequence. No physical condition of modern times can be compared with the terror produced by Indian raids. Notwithstanding the fact that they were living on the frontier, very few of the settlers in these counties were seasoned frontiersmen. They had recently come from the older states or from eastern Texas, where Indian raids had come to be nothing more than memories. They knew little or nothing of the habits or characteristics of the savages, and consequently they could neither cultivate the friendship of peaceful Indians nor protect themselves very effectively against the marauders.

| Furthermore, they were confronted with the most difficult Indian problem that any people could face. It was not a matter of meeting the enemy in pitched engagements. Supremacy in such a conflict would have been an easy thing for the white man to attain. But small bands of Indian robbers struck their settlements decisive blows and were away with all the speed that the swiftest mounts would permit and could not be overtaken by the pursuing citizens. The many wars and the merciless pressure from the white intruders had broken up the tribes into numerous small bands, none large enough to represent any military strength of consequence, but each just as destructive as a larger party would have been. |

Also, it must be stated again that the white people were largely the victims of their own rumors. Every report of a raid, whether founded on facts or not, was sure to be exaggerated and told in so many different ways that it would soon develop into several distinct accounts, each apparently about a different incident, but all growing out of the same report which probably had been an exaggeration to begin with. "Indian rumors are generally spread by riders who come into town and depart all by night," one writer complained.[34]

However, the people of Texas had good cause for complaint; and by the spring of 1859 the frontier citizens were in an ugly humor. The reservations had not brought peace to the frontier country, the offensive policy of the army and rangers had helped but little, and now sentiment, which had been taking shape for some time, demanded that the Texas reservations should be broken up. The people were laying the responsibility for the attacks to the reservation Indians, and the faithfulness and valor that some of these tribes had manifested in trying to protect their own property and that of the white men from the marauding bands was forgotten in the mad clamor that Texas must expel all Indians, whether friendly or wild.

THE END OF THE TEXAS RESERVATION

It would not be in keeping with the purpose of this book to present here a complete account of the Texas "reservation war" in which certain bands of citizens compelled the government to remove the Texas Indians from the reservations into the leased district of Indian Territory.[35] However, the story of the Comanches requires that some attention be given to the series of events that brought to an end the efforts of the government to colonize these people in Texas.

From the very beginning of the Comanche reservation, the agents had found it difficult to restrain their warriors from joining bands of Indians from the north bound for Mexico or the Texas frontier. The various accounts indicate that many parties thus came and went somewhat promiscuously, notwithstanding the efforts of the agents to prevent it. In fact, the different census reports show so much fluctuation in the population of the reservation that it is evident that many transient bands put up there for but short periods of time.[36]

Thus, for very good reasons, some of the frontiersmen had come to regard the reservation as the source of much mischief. Ranchmen frequently came there to hunt their lost or stolen stock. They were extended every aid and courtesy by the agent and Kātŭm'sē, but they rarely ever found their property there, and when they did, it was readily given up.[37] But this fact did not clear the reservation Indians in the minds of the frontiersmen; for they believed the Indians left the reservation, stole horses from the settlements, and then made their way to join their wild friends to the north. It must be said that the large number of desertions evidenced by the census returns furnish considerable foundation for this contention.

Then, late in 1857, petitions signed by Texas citizens were sent to the secretary of the interior asking that Neighbors be removed from office. They alleged that the reserve Indians had been stealing horses all along, although Neighbors kept denying it in spite of proof to the contrary.[38] Soon many complaints were made, some by persons near the reservation. At Clear Fork, a few miles away, a communication to General Twiggs, endorsed by Captain N. C. Givens of the United States army, was signed by several citizens who alleged that they had proof that the reservation Indians were stealing. They claimed that in pursuing a band of marauders, they had captured the complete equipment of a reservation Indian.[39] In January, 1858, a select committee of the state senate criticized severely the United States Indian policy in the state. They referred to the fact that only a fraction of the Comanche Indians was located on the reservation, and that friendly Indians were in the habit of passing and repassing into the settlements, so that wild Indians were mistaken for friendly ones and the white people were thus placed at the mercy of marauding bands. In addition to recommendations for better military protection, the committee stated that the agents should not permit the Indians to leave the reservations.[40] Still, the agents stoutly denied that their Indians had been guilty of any theft or any other unlawful act.[41]

If these charges should be accepted at their face value, they would represent within themselves rather convincing proof against the reservation Indians, but the records show that the whole issue was so completely shot through with bias and personal animosity that one is unable to know what to accept or reject. That some of the citizens were sincere cannot be doubted, but that the great majority of them were misinformed and under the persuasion of a few designing men is highly probable.

In the case of the protests and threats of the citizens at Clear Fork, the element of prejudice and personal hatred can be established with certainty. At one time or another Neighbors had antagonized a number of army officers along the frontier. Once he had protested that Captain Stoneman, at Camp Cooper, would not cooperate with him, and had asked that Stoneman be transferred from that post.[42] Stoneman's fellow army officers took his part, and the evidence indicates that they never lost an opportunity to annoy the Indian agents. Furthermore, John R. Baylor, who had been Neighbors's subordinate in the Indian service, hated his former superior bitterly. Baylor's service as resident agent had not been satisfactory to Neighbors, and on at least one occasion, Neighbors reported him to the Indian office.[43] The reason for Baylor's dismissal from the Indian service does not appear in the records of the time, but he was probably dismissed at Neighbors's recommendation.[44] At any rate, Baylor never missed an opportunity to criticize Neighbors and bring discredit on his administration of Indian affairs in Texas.

The excellent scouting service of the Brazos Indians—their work in taking and restoring to their owners horses stolen by the wild Indians, and their part in Ford's victory over the Comanches in May—caused some favorable reaction in the sentiment of the frontier people in the spring of 1858. But Baylor and a few others kept up their attacks against the reservations, and the press carried numerous articles of charges by Baylor, replies and counter-charges by Neighbors, and replies by Baylor. Baylor, together with General E. H. Tarrant[45] and others made speeches in towns near the frontier and called on the people to drive the Comanches from their reservation.

The complaints against the agents and the reservation Indians led to the sending of a special agent to investigate the administration of affairs. This representative, Thomas T. Hawkins, stayed at Camp Cooper for five weeks, and every opportunity was given the complainants to make their appearance and testify as to their charges, but very few did so, and nothing of consequence was submitted.[46] Hawkins's report commended the agents and the administration of the reservations very highly. It may be urged that the critics of Neighbors and his administration felt that the investigation was *ex parte* and that the whole matter would end in a "whitewash" of the Indian administration in Texas; but we should have more sympathy with their cause if they had gone through with their part of the program and had submitted whatever evidence they had.

Perhaps the strongest testimony in behalf of the Comanches is that of John S. Ford and E. N. Burleson, of the ranger forces. In the spring of 1858 they watched the Comanches closely, and sent out many details to secure information as to the movement of the Indians, but nothing occurred that gave any foundation to their suspicions.[47] It is significant that many persons, if not a majority of those living near the reservation, never believed that the Indians were guilty.[48] But all the reports of special agents from Washington and officers of the Texas militia did not satisfy the agitators in the least, and they continued their work of sowing the seeds of hatred against the savages and their agents. Naturally so much excitement and ill will inspired cruelty. In May, 1858, an inoffensive old Comanche with his wife and two children left the reserve for the purpose of visiting the lower reservation. He camped one night near the residence of a man named King, where four men from Lampasas county happened to be spending the night. King heard the men remark that the old Indian had some good horses and that it would be well to kill him and take them. In spite of King's protests, they waylaid the Indian down the road the next day and killed him and took his horses, although his wife and children managed to escape. When the Indian's relatives asked for a military guard to accompany them in order that they might go get the body and bury it, Captain

Evans refused, stating that he had no authority to protect Indians off of the reservation.[49]

Late December of that year saw the beginning of the end of both Texas reservations. A little party of friendly Indians from the Brazos reservation, known as Choctaw Tom's party, was attacked in camp at night and several men and women killed. They had left the reservation by permission of their agent in order to secure better grazing for their horses down the Brazos in the neighborhood of Golconda (now Palo Pinto). The party that attacked them was citizens of Erath and neighboring counties further down the Brazos valley. They alleged that they were after a band of Indian marauders, and that the trail they were following led to this camp.[50] However, it was brought out that they were part of a posse of forty or fifty men who had met at Jamison's Peak, on the headwaters of the Bosque, to consider the matter of punishing Indian thieves. They decided to kill any and all Indians found to the south of Cedar creek, a tributary of the Brazos which flows into it from the west. The unfortunate Indians were encamped to the south of this "dead line" which the frontiersmen had established, and that, after all, is about the only reason that can be given for the attack.

The people of Palo Pinto were very much offended at the conduct of the visiting party[51] of white men. In fact, Choctaw Tom had already returned to the reservation, but had left his party in order that they might accept an invitation of some citizens of the community to stay a little longer and hunt bear with them.[52]

The killing of these Indians created general excitement along the frontier because of the fear that their tribesmen would retaliate. A few days later two hundred citizens gathered near Palo Pinto to ward off an attack, but through the influence of the Indian agents and the chiefs at the agency, the reserve Indians were restrained and no clash occurred.[53] However the men who made the unwarranted attack on the Indian camp were never arrested, although in a special proclamation the governor called for their arrest.[54]

The grand jury of Palo Pinto county not only did not indict the men, but instead, indicted the Anadarko chief, José María, for horse-stealing, and their report stated that the reservations were nuisances and that the people ought to take up arms against the Indians.[55] Obviously the enemies of the reservation were too strong to be coped with, and henceforth they continued their activities without any fear of restraint from the county or state governments. In fact, Baylor, Nelson, R. W. Pollard, Peter Garland, "Buck" Barry, and other prominent men of the frontier communities inaugurated a movement to drive the Indians from both reservations, and set March 20 as the day for the attack.[56] However, the attack was not made because of the firm attitude main-

Comanche braves

Kwahadi Comanche camp

tained by Captain King, who was guarding the reservation. Also, the citizens of Young county had held a mass meeting and adopted resolutions opposed to the policy of violence.[57]

The immediate objective of these threatening movements was the lower or Brazos reservation. This was not because the frontier people regarded these Indians as the most culpable, for there were many men who appreciated the faithful service they had rendered in campaigns against the wild Indians. The fact was that they felt that both reservations must be destroyed, and the lower Indians being the more numerous and powerful, were regarded as the chief obstacle in the way of this program. Furthermore, the correspondence shows that these Indians persisted in leaving their reservation, even after the white people had become openly hostile; and in their efforts to gather up their stock and save a little of their property, they brought upon themselves charges of horse-stealing.

Long before this crisis came, Neighbors had realized that the Indians should be removed from Texas[58] and had urged the matter upon the Indian office. After the attack on Choctaw Tom's party, he became more emphatic about the matter,[59] and after the demonstration made by the frontiersmen in March, 1859, he wrote that unless the Indians were removed or given better military protection, they would leave. Furthermore, he insisted that he be given some instructions as to what course to pursue. The Texans would certainly renew their demonstrations soon, a clash would likely occur, and the agent felt that it was not fair that he alone should shoulder all the responsibility of the government in the matter of resisting them.[60] On March 30, the commissioner of Indian Affairs, Charles E. Mix, wrote Neighbors that the Indians would have to be moved, and instructed him that this was to be done early in the fall or winter. These instructions did not satisfy the agent, and on April 11 he wrote that he and his associates "had stood their ground" so far, but he wanted his superiors to share with them the responsibility for determining what should be done in the next crisis when it came, as it certainly would come.[61] On this subject "Washington" maintained a discreet silence.

The announcement that the Indians were to be removed in the fall or winter did not allay the fury of the frontiersmen. More Indian raids excited the people. In April came a resolution signed by a hundred fifty men demanding that Neighbors and the resident agents resign.[62] But the lion-hearted superintendent and his associates stood their ground in spite of a hundred threats of violence and the snarling denunciations of their fellow frontiersmen. In May, an army officer acted in very indiscreet fashion by leading a large party of Brazos reservation Indians into the town of Jacksboro, whither they had gone in search of a party who had killed in brutal fashion an Indian named Fox.[63]

This incident furnished the radical party an excellent torch with which they now set the whole frontier aflame with excitement. "Gatherings" took place again. A citizen of Jacksboro commented on the affair as follows:

> The news of our crowning outrage spread like wild-fire through our neighboring counties, and removed from the minds of even the most timid and prudent men the last lingering scruple as to the proper course to pursue; and they left their ripening harvests in the fields, and flew by hundreds to our relief. On coming here and learning the full particulars, and seeing our actually distressed condition, there was, and is, but one voice in the assemblage—"these Indians *must* be removed—necessity knows no law."[64]

The citizens organized into "ranger companies" and surrounded both reservations, threatening the Indians and their agents day and night, and preventing the Indians from gathering up their stock.[65] Edward J. Gurley, who had tried to prosecute the citizens who attacked Choctaw Tom's party, wrote on May 5:

> These leaders make it their business to watch closely the public sentiment from one extent of the frontier to the other, and immediately following any pacific demonstration, they take steps to counteract it and to increase the excitement and animosity against the reservations. George B. Erath has just returned from a tour upon the frontier. Wherever he went he addressed the people, and in some of the counties he succeeded in restoring reason and judgment. But he no sooner left than his influence was counteracted by firebrands of some kind from these designing men. Col. M. T. Johnson has also been amongst them, and advised pacific policy. He succeeded in one or two counties, but in others they threatened to stake him to a limb, and compelled him to desist. Judge Gregg and several of our attys. and citizens have just returned from the courts in the upper Brazos country and have startled me by their positive assurances . . . that what we know and hear of is but a drop in the bucket.[66]

On May 23, Baylor at the head of about 250 men came into the Brazos reservation, but the army officers offered such determined resistance that the citizens withdrew, not, however, until they had picked a fight with some of the Indians. The Indians pursued them for some distance and a skirmish took place.[67] The settlers declared that they would raise a thousand men and take the reservation by storm.[68] But sufficient forces were not forthcoming, and the "army of defense" disbanded for a time. The governor appointed a board of commissioners to visit the camp of the citizens, and endeavor to work out a peaceful method of attaining their ends.[69]

Still, Baylor and his party kept up the agitation, and in order to prevent another gathering, G. B. Erath, one of the commissioners, called out a special force of a hundred militiamen for McLennan and Bell counties in order to satisfy the citizens that the Indians were being watched.[70]

Meanwhile, Neighbors had been working frantically to secure from Washington authority to remove the Indians at once. The department gave its consent on June 11,[71] and on July 31 the Indians from both reservations, escorted by United States infantry and cavalry, started on their journey to the upper valley of the Washita in the leased district.[72]

The census made at the time the journey was begun showed that 1112 Indians left the Brazos reservation, and that 384 Comanches were escorted away from their reservation. It was estimated that the Comanches took away with them livestock worth $9,550, and that they lost or were forced to leave behind livestock worth $14,922.50.[73]

A sequel to this bitter controversy between the Indians and their agents on the one hand, and the citizens of Texas on the other, was the murder of Robert S. Neighbors on the streets of Belknap by a man named Edward Cornett, presumed to have been an entire stranger to him. Neighbors had seen the Indians safely located in the leased dirtrict, had turned them over to their agent there, and was returning home to make his final report to the government. He stopped at Belknap on matters of business, and was killed as he was preparing to proceed on his way to San Antonio.[74] It seems that the fatal difficulty grew out of some rather free conversations by Neighbors in which he denounced the killing of a reserve Indian some time before. Although he was struck down in his 45th year, Neighbors succeeded in leaving behind him a record of constructive public service that entitles him to a place in the annals of great American pioneers.[75] The courage manifested by the supervising agent and his resident agents, Ross and Leeper, in protecting their Indian wards against the onslaughts of the unreasonable citizens is an inspiring example of selfless devotion to duty.

Thus the first effort of the government to colonize the Comanches was interrupted by a combination of forces over which the Indian agents had no control. Although it appears that the reservation policy, as tried in Texas, was doomed to failure from the very beginning, it did, nevertheless, establish the fact that the Comanches were capable of progress. That even a few of these people could be kept at the reservation working their crops and sending their children to school, when there were so many temptations thrown in their way inviting them to take up again their old nomadic habits, was encouraging, and proved beyond a doubt that the Indian of the plains could be colonized and made at least partly self-sustaining. But in the Texas experiment is to be found proof quite as positive that this colonization could not be brought about without the application of great military force, and then only in connection with a scheme that would reach all of the South Plains Indians. As long as Nokoni young men rode away to war in the spring, Penateka youths would go with them in spite of all the dictates of agents or threats of soldiers. And when the rich, brown grass of the Texas prairies brought the fat buffalo into their old range, the Indian hunters would have stolen away and followed them even if their reservation had been guarded by legions of angry frontiersmen.

EVERY HAND AGAINST THE COMANCHES

Comparatively few of the Indians felt directly the wrath of the Texas soldiers and citizens. The killing of a hundred or so savages out of a tribe of several thousand did not appreciably reduce the number of actual or potential marauders. Smallpox, syphilis,[76] whiskey, and, most of all, hunger were far more effective in the work of decimating the tribe than the bullets of white men. But indirectly this aggressive policy of "the people of the south" affected the whole Comanche nation as well as the allied Kiowa tribe and many other plains Indians.

Among the first reactions to this pressure from the south was a series of attacks along the Indian Territory frontier, a region where the Comanches had for many years been friendly.[77] The Comanches believed that their old friends the Wichitas had betrayed them to the soldiers, and Van Dorn had scarcely got his horses out of the Wichita corn fields and returned to his post before the Comanches forced these Indians to seek refuge at Fort Arbuckle.[78] The correspondence of the army officers and Indian agents of Indian Territory at this time indicates that if a few more of these "protective forces" from Texas came north of Red river, the whole Indian situation would be demoralized.[79] Since the Texans had been harassed by northern Indians for three decades, it is to be presumed that they felt that turn about was fair play. Having begun the practice of raiding the Wichita country, it was natural for the Comanches to keep it up, and complaints from that section are not uncommon thereafter.[80] In fact, after the Texas Indians were moved into the leased district in 1859, the Comanches and Kiowas harried them so that at times their agent was cut off from communication from the rest of the world.[81]

Fort Cobb was established to protect the leased district, but it does not appear that this served any purpose other than giving protection in its immediate vicinity. These Indians on their new reservation fought the wild Comanches and Kiowas much as they had in Texas, and occasionally brought in scalps as evidence of their prowess.[82]

The attacks from the south soon brought about a hostile attitude among the bands along the Arkansas frontier, the very northernmost point of Comanche contact. Buffalo Hump and other warriors from the south had come among them, and the whole northern portion of the tribe was in an ugly humor. Buffalo Hump's defeat at the hands of the rangers and the Texas reservation Indians had made him a martyr in the eyes of his northern kinsmen, and on one occasion, in 1858, the grizzly old warrior strutted about the annuity train taking a share in the goods distributed and boasting all the while that as soon as the distribution was over, he would lead a band of warriors against the "white man of the south." He was credited by the agent with instigating an attack against a Mexican train and of robbing it of its provisions in the very sight of the agent's camp. Probably unknown among the Comanches outside of Texas and the Red river country until a year or two before, he had now come to exert a "controlling influence" over the Comanches of the north,[83] the only Penateka, with the possible exception of Päh'-häh-yō'-kō, ever to enjoy much influence outside of the southern bands.

The Kiowas were likewise in a bad humor. Little Mountain told the agent that the white chief was a fool to get mad because the Indians took a little sugar and coffee from the trains on the Santa Fé trail. The traders and emigrants were driving away and killing the buffalo, he said, and the Indians had to steal in order to live.

In 1859, Agent Bent reported that the Comanches, as a result of the hostile front opposed to them in Texas, had concentrated in the country between the Arkansas and the Canadian, and that they were likely to remain there perpetually.[84] However, as we have noted, they were not safe from the attacks of the Texans even there. At the mouth of Walnut creek, on September 16, they were collected to the number of 2,500 warriors, and although they expressed a desire for peace, Bent thought that only the presence of a considerable military force could prevent their attacks on emigrant and freight trains.[85] Bent urged the necessity of giving these Indians a home, where the great concourse of emigrants "constantly swelling and incapable of control or restraint by the government" would cease to harass them.

The hostile front offered by the Texans on the south, the intrusions of the civilized Indians on the east, and the host of white emigrants pressing in from the north and northeast caused many Comanches to seek the *Llano Estacado* and the New Mexico frontier. Even in this isolated region, the white men would not leave them alone. The Indian superintendent proposed to make a treaty with them, but when he started into their country with an escort of 180 soldiers, the savages suspected treachery and fled precipitately.[86]

Meanwhile, conditions along the Texas frontier were not improving. Driving the Indians from their reservations in Texas had not helped matters in the least. From almost every county in the northern part of the state came reports of plunder, raping, and murder.[87] The state continued its Indian war policy, and one expedition of frontier citizens went from Texas as far north as southern Kansas, but achieved nothing of consequence.[88] Captain L. S. Ross with a small ranger and cavalry force was more successful, attacking a Comanche village on Pease river in the present Foard county, killing and scattering the band and capturing the celebrated Cynthia Ann Parker.[89]

In summarizing events between 1850 and 1860, it may be said that in general the condition of the Comanches was becoming more desperate. They found it more difficult to invade the Mexican frontier, game was becoming scarcer, and, in order to maintain an existence, they had to break up into smaller thieving and marauding bands. More than ever in the past, small squads of irresponsible warriors carried on their operations without restraint. But most significant of all, the Texans proved to them that their retreat into the heart of the plains country offered no security. Heretofore white men had considered this northern and western region impenetrable, and in its semi-arid fastness the Indians had felt secure. But Ford, Ross, and Van Dorn penetrated to their farthest retreat with military forces large enough to destroy them wherever they set their lodges. Thus it seemed to the Indians that on every frontier they were met by aggressive foes; the hand of every white man was against them. In despair, they huddled their families together near the agency on the Arkansas, and sent their young warriors in small parties to harass the settlements. This state of affairs could not have long continued but for the outbreak of the Civil War and the consequent slackening of the merciless pursuit of the red men by the white men.

CHAPTER ELEVEN

When the White Men Fought Each Other

Secession naturally had its effects on the Indian situation of the South Plains. The Civil War relieved for a time the pressure along the Indian frontier and lessened the encroachments by white men on the hunting grounds of the savages. Furthermore, neither the Federal nor Confederate governments cared to spare the men and money necessary to fight Indian wars; and in order to avert such a military episode, both the North and the South made overtures to the savages, with the result that the Indians also were divided into two hostile camps. The more advanced tribes of the Indian Territory were divided from the very beginning, and furnished their quota to one side or the other in the internecine strife. Likewise the tribes of the plains were affected by the maelstrom, though it cannot be said that they were caught up in it. They found themselves sought after by both governments, and they accepted peace with the one, or the other, or both, much as it suited their convenience.

COMANCHE RELATIONS WITH THE SOUTH

In diplomacy with the nomadic tribes of the South Plains, the Confederate government was the more successful during the first few months of the war, due principally to the efforts of the versatile explorer and poet-lawyer, Albert Pike. On a visit to the plains nearly thirty years before the war, Pike made the acquaintance of some Comanche bands, and learned of their marauding and warlike disposition. Hence, when the war broke out, he felt that the winning of the friendship of these Indians was a matter of vital importance to the Confederacy. He knew of the disposition of the Comanches and Kiowas to plunder the Texas frontier. Now that Texas was a part of the Confederacy, that government was responsible for protecting the Texas frontier. If these Indians could be persuaded to leave Texas alone, troops might be withdrawn from that frontier to be used where more decisive engagements must needs be fought. Also, as allies of the Confederacy, these Indians would represent an impediment to communication between the Missouri frontier and Santa Fé and Colorado.

In May, 1861, Pike was appointed by President Davis as special commissioner to treat with the Indians west of the Arkansas.[1] The special commissioner acted with that decisiveness and vigor in keeping with the liberal powers granted him. The late United States Indian agents who would take the oath of allegiance to his government were taken into the Confederate service and instructed to inform their wards that the Confederate states would take them over on the same terms that they had obtained under the United States.[2] Then Pike went forthwith to the Indian Territory and made treaties with the civilized tribes.[3] Fort Cobb and the Wichita agency had fallen into the hands of the Confederates, and at this place the men of the south had an excellent base from which to establish and maintain contact with the wild bands of the plains. Next, using the Creeks, the traditional friends of the Comanches, as emissaries, Pike got in touch with these Indians and secured their promise to meet him in council at the Wichita agency where, on August 12 and 13, 1861, he negotiated two treaties, one with the Indians of that reservation and the other with the "Comanches of the Prairies and Staked Plain."[4] The treaty with the Indians of the agency included, among others, the Penateka Comanches; and the treaty with the prairie Comanches included four branches of the tribe, the Nokoni, Yamparika, Kotsoteka, and a remnant of the "Ta-ne-i-weh" (Tanima or possibly Tenawa).[5] More than a dozen chiefs signed the treaty on behalf of these wild bands. Some of them were men of importance, such as "Qui-ha-hi-wi" or Drinking Eagle, principal chief of the Nokonies, "Bis-te-va-na" of the Yamparikas, and "Ma-a-we" or Shaking Hand.[6] Every important band but the Kwahadi had a part in these treaties, and it probably was the most representative assembly of Comanches ever gathered together up to that time.

In most matters these treaties did not differ widely from those the United States had made with the Comanches in former years. Each side was to give up the prisoners then held, and the Indians were to be paid for theirs. The Confederate government was to maintain at least one agency in the leased district, with an adequate force of employees and a sufficient quantity of equipment. In one respect, however, the treaty with the wild bands was quite different from any they had ever made with the Anglo-Americans before; that was that the Indians agreed to remain at some point in the leased district, and that "the reserves shall be their own property, like their horses and cattle."

The treaties were quite specific in the matter of promises to furnish the Indians with supplies until they should become self-sustaining, as well as with cattle to enable them to start herds. The obligations which the Indians incurred are summarized in the following words taken from the agreement: "The Confederate states ask nothing of the bands of the Neum [Comanches] except that they will settle upon their reserves, become industrious, prepare to support themselves, and live in peace and quietness." In short, nothing was asked of the Comanches except that they should no longer be Comanches, but should almost in the twinkling of an eye become white men. This was too much to expect of the restive lords of the plains. As long as there were buffalo to chase and unprotected ranches to despoil, it would take more than their crude marks on a piece of paper to hold them to such an agreement.

Agent Leeper, who was now in the Confederate service, was instructed to do everything possible to make the reserve inviting to the Indians. Buildings were constructed for the chiefs, and they were told that their presents would soon be on hand. Meanwhile, Pike was exerting every effort to purchase the goods for the Indians and forward them to the agent, and to this end the sum of twenty-five thousand dollars was transmitted to New Orleans to be used for presents for the Comanches and other reserve Indians.[7]

But the wild Comanches and their Kiowa allies (the Kiowas had also been invited) never came except occasionally to trade and to ask for presents. Agent Leeper provided well for the Penateka Comanches who were on the reservation, but the warriors of the prairie did not in any way envy their brethren at the agency. On the contrary, the Confederates were not even able to hold all of the Penatekas on the reservation, and there was an alarming decline in discipline among those who did remain. In this connection, one of Leeper's letters seems worth quoting in part:

> ... The recent friendly relations which have been professed on the part of the Indians and attempted to be cultivated on our part have produced an opposite result upon the Comanche reserve Indians from that which was anticipated, boys who have been partly reared upon the reserve and who hitherto have conducted themselves with the greatest propriety are now unruly and are subject to the most unbridled passions and unheard of improprieties ...

The agent continues his letter by explaining that the boys were shooting down or wounding agency cattle promiscuously, and insulting the employees.

On one occasion H. P. Jones, the interpreter, asked Buffalo Hump to restrain the young men, and in response the old savage sustained his bad reputation by abusing Jones.[8] Obviously the influence of the wild bands on the milder Penatekas was very demoralizing while, at the same time, it does not appear that the savages of the prairie were being civilized one whit by the contact.

Relations between the Confederate government and the wild Comanche bands were broken, never again to be satisfactorily established, by the destruction of the Wichita agency on the night of October 23, 1862. A band of about one hundred Delawares and Shawnees, in sympathy with the United States government, attacked the place and killed four white men, one of them being Matthew Leeper, the agent. Interpreter H. P. Jones barely escaped. They plundered and burned the agency buildings, and on the next morning attacked and decimated a band of unfortunate Tonkawa Indians nearby. On their return to Kansas, the marauders took with them the papers of the agency.[9] The Confederacy was hard pressed and had neglected to protect this important post. The attack produced a general state of alarm, and all fled from the reservation. The Penateka Comanches took up their abode in the Wichita mountains; later they came closer to the settlements, but in the winter of 1862–1863 some of them, together with certain Caddo and Wichita Indians, slipped away to the north and got in touch with the United States agent at Fort Larned.[10] It seems that after the destruction of the Wichita agency, Confederate headquarters for the prairie tribes was at Cherokee Town, northwest of Fort Arbuckle, far to the east of the Comanche country,[11] a location that made communication with the wild bands difficult and infrequent.

Conditions along the Texas frontier during the first eighteen months of the war indicate that Pike's efforts at conciliation were not wholly futile. As compared with the two preceding years, there was a marked decline in raids for this period. A more effective system of frontier defense may explain this fact in part, but evidently the Indian raiders were not so numerous as in former years.[12] Beginning with 1863, however, conditions became much as they had been before the war. Cooke, Denton, Montague, and Wise counties suffered an attack in February, and a party of soldiers which pursued the marauders was repulsed.[13] Parker county was pillaged as usual, the savages raiding within three miles of the town of Weatherford.[14] Defense of the Texas frontier since the beginning of the war had rested mainly on the Texas frontier regiment, a state organization. By 1863 the personnel of the organization had been reduced by one third, the horses were poor, there were no percussion caps along the whole line, and the soldiers were not in condition to do effective fighting.[15]

If there were fewer raids in 1864 than during the preceding year, the savages made up for the difference by striking in larger parties. In October of that year one of the most formidable attacks in the history of the frontier was made by two hundred or more Comanches and Kiowas on a Confederate outpost near "Fort" Murrah, about twelve miles west of Fort Belknap, in Young county. Five troopers were killed, and the remaining fifteen men who belonged to their platoon or detail were chased back into the "fort," being forced to abandon all their camp equipment and clothing, except what they were wearing. The Indians swept through the community and killed eleven citizens and carried into captivity seven women and children. Reinforcements were sent to the beleaguered community; but the Indians escaped with their usual impunity, except for a few warriors they may have lost during their attack on the outpost.[16]

During the last few months of the war, the Indians apparently drew away from the Texas frontier, probably because of attacks from the Union forces or because threats of the United States to send expeditions into their country caused them to turn their attention to the northern part of their range. During the last few weeks of the war they became so vexed with the United States they made another treaty with the South, that tottering government being represented by General J. W. Throckmorton at Camp Napoleon, Indian Territory.[17]

RELATIONS WITH THE FEDERALS

During the early months of the war, while the Confederates were making such rapid progress in Indian diplomacy, the United States government accomplished but little pertaining to the tribes of the South Plains. For two years preceding the outbreak of the Civil War, that government had virtually been at war with the Comanches and Kiowas, and their annuity goods had not been delivered to them.[18] Then, when secession brought on a struggle that was to decide the fate of the nation, the officers of the Arkansas frontier warned the government that the Indian situation was delicate and liable to become dangerous. Again and again they urged their superiors to act, explaining that the Indians did not wish war or a continuation of a state of near-war, but that because of hunger and want it was difficult for them to keep the peace. The wars with the Texans during the two preceding years had forced many southern Indians into the country along the Arkansas, where the game supply was not sufficient to support them. The savages were hanging around the agency and army posts begging food and importuning the officers to make a treaty with them.[19]

Despite these reports, the Washington government appeared indifferent. The confusion increased, the attitude of the savages became threatening, and

Agent A. G. Boone left Fort Wise, where the Indians were assembled, and repaired to Denver where he could not have been of much service either to the government or to the Indians.[20] Meanwhile, numbers of the savages drifted away, but others remained near Fort Wise and other posts on the Santa Fé and Denver trails, threatening caravans, or begging or stealing from them as the occasion made most profitable. Thus, while the Confederates established friendly relations with these Indians, the United States maintained an indecisive attitude, an attitude neither of peace nor war.

Finally, in late August, 1861, Governor Gilpin of Colorado, either on his own initiative or acting on instructions from Washington, sent Boone back to Fort Wise, and a vague and indefinite agreement was made with the Indians. This agreement provided that the United States was to suspend hostilities against the savages (really hostilities with them had never begun), and on or before the first day of September, 1862, a permanent treaty was to be entered into at Fort Larned, Kansas. On the signing of this permanent treaty, the Indians should deliver up 157 head of horses and mules to compensate for those stolen in the vicinity of Denver during the year 1860. The permanent treaty should provide for such annuity goods for the Indians as might be agreed upon. During this "armistice," or until the treaty should be made, the Indians were to cease all hostilities and not molest citizens of the United States traveling to and fro on the highways.[21] The savages had been clamoring for a treaty. They not only did not get one, but they agreed that the United States might put off negotiating one for a year, during which time the Indians would be obligated to behave themselves. However, Boone explains that he gave the Indians food; no doubt this food was given only on condition that they agree to the "treaty," and the savages quite sensibly agreed to any measure that would remove the pinch of hunger. Indeed, the goods the agent released not only restrained those Indians in the vicinity of Fort Wise, but drew in their kinsmen from the south much as honey draws ants.[22] The Confederates had been much more liberal in their promises than had the men of the north, and Pike and Leeper were working manfully to rush their supplies to the frontier and keep faith with the Indians; but a little sugar, coffee, bread, and beef in hand appealed to the Comanche far more than the promise of tons of food and presents.

Among those Comanches who came in from the south was Bis-te-va-na, described as the principal chief of the Yamparika Comanches. This chief brought along and showed to the agent a copy of the treaty made with Pike, and also a "letter of safeguard" which Pike had given him in the name of the Confederate government. Boone wrote that the chief and his followers were "much astonished when I informed them that they had made a treaty with the enemies of our government and their Great Father at Washington."[23] The situation did represent an anomaly that must have puzzled the savage mind. For many years the Comanches had known what seemed to them to be two United States governments; the one along the Arkansas which was, if not always friendly, at least willing to leave them alone; the other a hostile government far to the south that snarled at them when they visited Texas, and even sent out soldiers to kill their women and children. No doubt the chief felt that in making up with this formerly hostile southern government, he was not in any way forfeiting his right to be friendly with that of the north. If good things were to be had at Fort Cobb as well as Fort Wise, why should not the lords of the plains partake of both? However that may be, the chief gave up his copy of the treaty and the "letter of safeguard." Since Boone, on October 26, reported between 500 and 600 lodges of Comanches near Fort Wise, it is evident that a number of Pike's Indians had, like Bis-te-va-na, come north to see what they could get from the United States. Others continued to come in from the south, so that by midwinter, 1861–1862,[24] there were probably as many acknowledging the sovereignty of the United States as there were in touch with the Confederates at Fort Cobb.

Either at the time of his agreement with them, or a little later, Boone distributed to the savages the annuity goods which had for two years been withheld from them, and these goods, together with the food that was evidently given them from time to time, kept them reasonably quiet and peaceful.[25]

While these events were taking place along the Indian Territory and Arkansas frontiers, the Comanches near New Mexico also were brought into an agreement with the United States. At Alamo Gordo, May 13, 1861, they entered into a truce with Superintendent J. L. Collins of New Mexico, and Captain R. A. Wainwright representing the army. The Indians agreed to discontinue depredations upon the property and lives of the people of the United States, of New Mexico, Kansas, and Texas; to punish any of their warriors who might violate the agreement; and to leave the settlements of New Mexico and return only to Fort Union or some other place that might be designated whenever they wanted to trade. It was agreed that at the end of ninety days another meeting should be held, at which a formal and permanent treaty would be made.[26] Neither party kept the truce, no permanent treaty was made, and the temporary agreement turned out to be of little consequence. Before it had expired, the Comanches made a raid on the settlements, and a detachment of troops was sent against them. The savages were defeated and some of their women and children taken captive. It seems that the captives were soon released, but Comanche relations in New Mexico continued to be uncertain and unsatisfactory.[27]

After the tense condition that prevailed during 1861, Indian relations along the Arkansas river improved. Southern Indians continued to come in and report at Fort Larned, where the agent spent a part of his time, and the tribes of that region generally were peaceable during most of 1862 and 1863. In order to strengthen his hold on the savages as well as to settle many questions pending with them, the United States agent, S. G. Colley, obtained permission to take some of the chiefs to Washington. Ten Bears and Prick-in-the-Forehead represented the Comanches, and Yellow Buffalo, Little Hart, Lone Wolf, and White Bull represented the Kiowas. Arapaho, Cheyenne, and Apache chiefs also accompanied the party.[28]

While in Washington, the chiefs agreed to a treaty defining their obligations a little more clearly in the matter of staying away from the Santa Fé road, and making perpetual the treaty signed at Fort Atkinson, July 27, 1853. The amount of annuity goods to be given the associate tribes of Comanches, Kiowas, and Apaches was to be $25,000 per year. The treaty was never ratified,[29] but since the annuity goods were furnished to the Indians anyway, it made but little difference.

On the return of the party from Washington, there was a great Indian gathering to greet the chiefs at Walnut creek, and the general attitude of the savages appeared to be good. A little later medals were given to other prominent chiefs including Over the Buttes, Shaking Hand, and Drinking Eagle.[30] The Indians were generally peaceful, stating that they had made "a strong treaty with their Great Father at Washington" and intended to hold on to it.[31] But they found it difficult to hold on to it.

The year 1864 witnessed widespread Indian disturbances in which the Comanches participated. It is thought that there was formed in the autumn of 1863 an alliance of the Comanche, Kiowa, and Prairie Apache tribes of the south with the Cheyenne, Arapaho, and Sioux of the north looking toward a general Indian war on the plains. Whatever the intentions of the Indians may have been, trouble did develop during 1864. In August of that year numerous attacks were made along the northern route to Denver, and the Overland Mail Company was obliged to abandon the stations along its route for a distance of 400 miles. Emigration was stopped, the ranchmen abandoned their homes, and much of the country was depopulated.[32] This destructive work was done principally by the Cheyennes and their allies, but along the Arkansas river and south of it the Kiowas and Comanches were not guiltless.

Then the war spread to the region south of the Arkansas. On August 19, the savages killed ten men of a wagon train party at Cimarron Springs, on the Santa Fé road, and on the twenty-first over 200 Indians attacked a train of ninety-five wagons at a point sixty miles west of Fort Larned, Kansas. The officer charged with protecting that portion of the route reported that he would have to have more men in order to protect the trains or even to punish the savages when he overtook them.[33] But the west was not dependent on the government at Washington in the matter of defense. Governor John Evans of Colorado raised a regiment to fight the Indians, there was much excitement, and the people of the territory were soon clamoring for an Indian war. Now the Indians, true to their habit of making war in summer and peace in autumn, asked for peace. But Governor Evans had his troops ready for the campaign, and was not interested in their proposals. Instead, on November 29, Colonel J. M. Chivington, at the head of the Colorado cavalry, attacked the Cheyenne band of Black Kettle and White Antelope at Sand creek, near Fort Lyon. The savages, following the instructions of their agents, thought that they were at peace with the whites, and were not expecting trouble. Chivington struck them a terrible blow and slew many men, women, and children. The officer was denounced in the bitterest language by many persons, particularly those far away from the frontier. That some of the savages merited the severest punishment cannot be disputed, but it seems that Black Kettle's band suffered for the sins of others.[34]

It seems that while the Cheyenne war was in progress and as autumn approached, the Kiowas and Comanches slipped away to the south.[35] It has already been observed that in October a large party of them was raiding in Texas. Troubles along the Santa Fé trail increased as summer passed and winter approached. For some time complaints had been made that the Kiowas, joined at times by the Comanches, were committing thefts and levying "blackmail" along this route.[36] Finally, during 1864, the savages grew so insolent along the New Mexico part of the route that General James H. Carleton, commanding the United States forces in that territory, launched a campaign against them.

This punitive expedition was placed in charge of the famous scout Christopher (Kit) Carson, who took along in his command 321 California and New Mexico volunteers and 75 Indians. Carson left Fort Bascom, New Mexico, November 10, 1864, and moved east down the Canadian river. On the twenty-fourth he attacked an Indian camp of 150 lodges at a point above Bent's abandoned adobe "fort." The Indians fled from their camp, but fell back to the adobe building and made a stiff resistance. While this fight was in progress Indians began to appear from another village of 350 lodges about three miles east of the adobe fort, and soon Carson was fighting a thousand warriors.

The savages fought so desperately and harassed the soldiers so effectively by means of grass fires which they started about them that Carson was glad to retreat without having attacked the larger of the two villages. But for his howitzers, his force might have been overwhelmed by the Indians. He flattered himself that "he had taught these Indians a severe lesson;"[37] but the accounts indicate that the Indians might well have flattered themselves that they were still a formidable factor to be reckoned with when attacked in their own villages in the heart of the plains. Carson was unable to destroy the larger Indian village, and the strength of the resistance which the red men made presaged many long and difficult campaigns yet to be fought before these savages were finally subdued.

And yet the achievement of the soldiers in this campaign was another proof that the barrier of the plains was being broken down. There was perhaps no spot in all their range (where game could be found) farther removed from the white settlements and forts than this place on the Canadian river; and still the soldiers found them there and killed their women and children even after winter had set in. The savages might still kill, steal, and burn along the different frontiers and escape without immediate punishment; but when the warriors returned to their villages they never could feel safe from the terrible vengeance of the soldiers.

According to Carson's report, the Indians he attacked were principally Kiowas, with a small number of Comanches, Apaches, and Arapahoes. According to Kiowa tradition, the old chief Little Mountain, was in charge of the village, and many of the young warriors were away on the chase.[38] Carson thought that the Indians lost about sixty in killed and wounded, while his own force suffered a loss of two killed and twenty-one wounded, several mortally. The Indians were well supplied with arms and ammunition, and a large amount of their powder, lead, and caps was destroyed by the troops in the captured Indian village. Evidently the *Comanchéros* had supplied their customers well in spite of the efforts of the military to stop this troublesome traffic.[39]

Carson's expedition and the bristling attitude of the army in New Mexico drove the Comanches and Kiowas eastward. In the late winter they assembled in large numbers on the Cimarron, about 150 miles south and west of Fort Larned, evidently trying to keep as far away from the military forces as conditions would permit.[40] Now at Fort Riley, Kansas, was Colonel J. H. Leavenworth, agent for these Indians, who thought that more could be accomplished in Indian relations by peace than by war. The various campaigns of the last few months and the costly patrols along the overland trails had not brought peace or safety for travel along the roads. Leavenworth believed that these military operations were largely unnecessary, and that more could be accomplished by a little kindness and discretion than by legions of troops. Although there was some truth in his contention, he failed to realize that the very eagerness with which the savages sought for peace was produced in them by the horrors and dangers of war with the soldiers. Leavenworth was determined to secure peace, and he worked doggedly to that end, proving himself a better strategist than were the military men who were almost without exception opposed to him.

From his base at Fort Riley, Leavenworth sent out Indian runners who soon returned with Kiowa, Arapaho, and Apache chiefs and warriors.[41] This was a good start, especially since among the Kiowas was Little Mountain himself. It would be easy to use these Indians as scouts and emissaries to draw in other Kiowas and Comanches to enter into negotiations for which all the plains Indians were evidently eager.

But while Leavenworth was calling the Indians to council, the troops were preparing to chastise them. Then Leavenworth appealed to Washington, pleading that the soldiers be called off. Although his own Indian department was against him, he managed, with the aid of Senator J. R. Doolittle, to win his point, and the Indians went unscathed during that season. A congressional peace commission headed by Senator Doolittle visited the frontier and advised the war department to avoid an Indian war, which they predicted would cost many millions of dollars.[42] Leavenworth had considerable difficulty in gathering up his Indians, but early in August he finally coaxed old Little Mountain and some associate Kiowa and Comanche chiefs to a council at the mouth of the Little Arkansas.[43] Then a few days later Chisholm (a son of old Jesse Chisholm) came in with a number of Comanche chiefs who were anxious to secure terms of peace. The Indians entered into an agreement with General John B. Sanborn and Colonel Leavenworth "to cease all acts of violence or injury to the frontier settlements, and to travelers on the Santa Fé road, or other lines of travel, and to remain at peace." They further agreed to meet in council with commissioners of the United States on October 4. Accordingly, on October 18, the treaty between the Comanches, Kiowas, Apaches, and the United States was signed at the mouth of the Little Arkansas.[44] Thus was the United States once again nominally at peace with the Comanches and their allies.

It cannot be said that the Indians of the South Plains represented a factor of great consequence during the Civil War. They harassed the emigrants on the Santa Fé road and harried the Texas border. They forced the United States to increase its troops and military expenditures on the Arkansas and New Mexico frontiers, and the Confederacy had to maintain a border regiment or two to watch them. They were divided first and last in the matter of their allegiance, and when they joined one side or the other, they were fickle allies. Neither the Confederates nor Federals tried to send these Indians against the enemy, but tried instead to hold them as passive allies and prevent their joining the foe. If either side encouraged them in their marauding operations against the enemy, it was more with the idea of giving them employment for the time and thus to get some temporary relief from their annoyance than with the hope that the savages would accomplish much in beating down the strength of the other side. In slowing up emigration into and across their country, the war gave the Indians a breathing spell, and if they were not more numerous, they were more insolent and desperate at its close than at its beginning, and they still made a formidable barrier to the settlement of their country.

CHAPTER TWELVE

The Last Treaties

THE TREATY AT THE LITTLE ARKANSAS

The council at the mouth of the Little Arkansas river, which had been brought about by Leavenworth's tireless efforts, was an extraordinary Indian gathering. A large number of Cheyennes and their allies, the Arapahoes, were there and entered into a treaty; the Kiowa Apaches severed their alliance with the Kiowas and Comanches, and formed a union with the Cheyennes and Arapahoes; the Kiowas were well represented; and the commissioners reported that there were delegates from "six of the nine bands which compose the Comanches tribe."[1] Among the representatives of the United States government were General John B. Sanborn, Kit Carson, and W. W. Bent.[2]

Like all preceding treaties with the Comanches the agreement was defective in that some of the bands were not represented. The Kotsotekas did not sign except by proxy, and the Kwahadies were not represented at all. The signers do compose a roll of Indian greatness, nevertheless. Ten Bears, Named Sun, Iron Mountain, and Over the Buttes represented the Yamparikas; Drinking Eagle and Horse's Back signed for the Nokonies; Iron Shirt was the champion of the Tanima, or Liver-eater band; and Silver Brooch and Milky Way represented the Penatekas. Likewise, Little Mountain and his warlike Kiowas were there—Big Bow, Satanta, Kicking Bird, Sa-tank, and others.

The purpose of the negotiations was to secure peace with the savages, stop their attacks on overland wagon trains and frontier settlements, secure the release of prisoners they held, and confine them to a narrower range. Insofar as the terms of the treaty were concerned, the United States government attained its ends quite satisfactorily; but in the matter of actual accomplishment, about all that is worthy of mention is the release of at least a part of the captives. Neither the government nor the Indians could keep the agreement.

It may be that the leading chiefs tried to abide by the treaty of the Little Arkansas, but the conduct of their warriors was not improved perceptibly by the agreement. Texas was in the throes of reconstruction, and the federal military officers could not or would not protect the frontier of that state nor would they permit the state government to do so.[3] Finally the United States did station troops along the frontier, but they were men unacquainted with Indian warfare and therefore ineffective—especially during the first year or two of their service. The savages were not slow to learn of the unprotected state of the frontier, and the raids became so bad that some of the counties had to be abandoned.[4] These raids continued with such fury and destructiveness that on August 5, 1867, Governor Throckmorton was obliged to report that since the close of the Civil War 162 persons had been killed, 43 carried away into captivity (29 of whom had been reclaimed), and 24 wounded.[5]

The purpose of the raids by the Indians was primarily to secure horses and sometimes cattle. They did not hesitate to torture and kill white persons, however, when opportunity was offered, and they continued their old practice of taking women and children captive. In former times they had taken prisoners in order to augment their own diminishing numbers, but now their purpose was to secure a reward for the return of the unfortunate white persons. Ordinarily the Indians would not give up a captive without the payment of a reward. The general policy of both the war and Indian departments was to discourage the practice of paying ransoms, but it continued in spite of their nominal opposition.[6] Some of the more responsible chiefs tried to stop this stealing of white women and children. Ten Bears deprecated the practice; Horse's Back brought in many captives, and Milky Way, the Penateka, visited his wild kinsmen occasionally and bought from them or persuaded them to give up captives.[7] But some of the most prominent Comanche chiefs either participated in or condoned this practice of taking captives. Horse's Back's brother owned the prisoner Dot Babb, and Ten Bears had to apologize to Agent Leavenworth because his fellow Yamparika, Named Sun, had a little captive white boy. And Named Sun, or Tăbby-nan-ĭ-käh, headed the list of Indian signers at the treaty of the Little Arkansas.

These captive white children were generally initiated into the tribe by a series of terrifying experiences in which the Indians tried their courage by the most brutal treatment and threats of destruction. They would be tied to the back of a wild horse or yearling buffalo, or perhaps tied to a stake while their savage captors with slashes and menacing gestures, punctuated by the most hideous yells, threatened to cut them to pieces, shoot them or even burn them. No doubt many of these unfortunate children never lived to recount these experiences. Then the captive was made a slave and compelled to do many menial and dangerous tasks.

But if the youth proved his mettle according to Comanche standards, better days would await him. He would likely be adopted as a member of a chief's or warrior's family. Soon he would be permitted and expected to take part in the raids and battles. His childhood experiences would be relegated to the past, his mother tongue almost or quite forgotten, and he would become to all effects and purposes a Comanche warrior. Then, if he should ever be taken and returned to his own people, they would find it a difficult task to direct him back into the paths of civilized existence. These ex-captives generally held a kindly feeling for their guardian savage comrades and some of them even ran away and returned to the Indians.[8]

Although the officers at Washington did not realize the extent of the depredations committed by the Comanches and Kiowas, they did know that affairs in the Indian country were not going in a satisfactory manner. Accordingly, in the autumn of 1866, two special Indian agents were sent to investigate conditions along the Arkansas river frontier.

The report of these men, Special Agents Charles Bogy and W. R. Irwin, shows that the Indian situation in the South Plains region in the autumn of 1866 was grave. A large part of both the Kiowa and Comanche tribes were flagrantly violating the treaty made the year before, and they did not even come in to receive their annuity goods. The Cheyennes were still smarting from the blows struck them in preceding years, particularly the terrible Sand Creek massacre. They were suspicious and afraid, and their presence in the Comanche-Kiowa range added to the uncertainty of conditions.

The commissioners found that the goods furnished the Indians were of inferior quality, even for the prices paid.[9] The army as well as the Indian service came in for criticism, and it was charged that the officers in command showed "by their acts an utter ignorance of the Indian character and of the proper method of dealing with Indians."[10] The report emphasized the need of permanent agency headquarters with adequate buildings for residences, offices, and storehouses, and suggested that some place near old Fort Cobb, in the leased district, would be suitable for the Comanche and Kiowa tribes.

During the winter of 1866-1867, conditions failed to improve. To the north of the Arkansas the Cheyenne and Sioux tribes were at war against the government, and great fear was felt that the disturbance would spread to the tribes of the south. A factor that complicated matters and made the Indian far more formidable was the issue to them of arms and ammunition. These were furnished both by the Indian agents and the traders who exchanged these commodities for buffalo robes and horses.[11] In defense of this policy of supplying the Indians with arms, Agent Leavenworth explained that the buffaloes were disappearing, small game was becoming scarcer, and the Indians could no longer secure a living from the chase without the use of firearms. Indeed, the government was confronted with a dilemma for which there was no solution. Without rifles and ammunition the Indians must starve, unless their agents could furnish them with a quantity of goods much greater than congress had provided; on the other hand, if firearms were supplied them, the savages might become formidable enemies.[12] The commander of the division of the Missouri, General Sherman, issued orders calculated to restrict this traffic; but the trade continued notwithstanding, and henceforth troops confronting hostile Indians might find an enemy better armed than themselves.

THE TREATY OF MEDICINE LODGE CREEK

As the spring of 1867 approached, there was much talk of war along the Indian Territory and Arkansas river frontier. Captain Smith, at Fort Arbuckle, reported that Shaking Hand's Kotsotekas were committing raids, and asked for ten additional companies to reinforce his post.[13] In the summer General Sherman ordered that the annual goods for the Cheyennes, Arapahoes, Kiowas, and Comanches, which had already been delayed, be withheld from them as they were in "open hostility." "And I doubt the wisdom," he added, "of their ever again having annuity goods till they are punished for their late acts."[14] On the other hand, Leavenworth insisted that "the Indians of my agency . . . at the present time, were never more friendly." He added that he spoke of them "as tribes," and admitted that there were some "bad men," but that the tribes could and would control them.[15]

Sherman seemed determined to order a campaign against the savages when a peace commission interfered and saved them from the wrath of the military. The costly Indian wars of the preceding eighteen months had so provoked the people of the nation that congress felt impelled once again to take a hand in the matter.[16] Accordingly, by an act passed June 20, 1867, another peace commission, composed of four civilians including the commissioner of Indian Affairs, and three generals of the army, was authorized. General Sherman accepted a place on the commission, although he evidently had misgivings about the efficacy of any peace program until the Indians had been punished.[17] It was expected that the commission would secure a lasting peace. To that end the existing causes of complaint on the part of the savages were to be corrected, and the projected railway routes and other lines of travel were to be made safe and free from Indian attack. This necessarily meant the segregation of the Indians at points remote from the settlements and lines of travel.

The commission visited the Arkansas river frontier in October, and at Medicine Lodge Creek, seventy miles south of Fort Larned, the council with the tribes of the South Plains was held. The Cheyennes, Arapahoes, Kiowas, Comanches, and the remnant of Prairie Apaches were there. The treaty was the last ever made with these tribes, and one of the last old-fashioned Indian gatherings in which they were represented. Savage brazenness and gaudiness met Caucasian suavity and diplomacy amidst the primitive setting of a country not yet marred by the axe and plow. Noted frontiersmen were there, among them Black Beaver, the Delaware scout, Jesse Chisholm, and George Bent.[18] Several leading newspapers sent reporters. A large wagon train and fifteen or twenty ambulances were necessary to transport the commission and those attached to it.

As the commission, under the escort of five hundred regular soldiers, approached the great Indian encampment near the treaty grounds, the troops, the howitzers, and the train were arranged so as to make the most formidable appearance possible for the benefit of any of the red men who might possibly wish to match strength with them. But the Indians likewise believed in the efficacy of display, and their maneuvers are described by an observer as follows:

> By this time, thousands of mounted warriors could be seen concentrating and forming themselves into a wedge-shaped mass, the edge of the wedge pointing toward us. In this sort of mass formation, with all their war paraphernalia, their horses striped with war paint, the riders bedecked with war bonnets and their faces painted red, came charging in full speed toward our columns . . .
>
> . . . When within a mile of the head of our procession, the wedge, without hitch or break, quickly threw itself into the shape of a huge ring or wheel without hub or spokes, whose rim consisted of five distinct lines of these wild, untutored, yet inimitable, horsemen. This ring, winding around and around with the regularity and precision of fresh-oiled machinery approached nearer and nearer to us with every revolution. Reaching within a hundred yards of us at breakneck speed, the giant wheel or ring ceased to turn and suddenly came to a standstill.[19]

The writer continues by stating that an opening was made in the circle and the commission and its secretaries admitted—all this being "a test of the good faith of the 'white man.'" These scenes had often been enacted in the history of the American frontier, but the actors and their setting were passing rapidly; the era of such performances was soon to end.

Senator Henderson opened the council with an explanation to the effect that reports had come that the Indians had been violating their treaties and making war on the whites; and these reports, he stated, made "the hearts of our people very sad."[20] Then the Indians were urged to state their side of the case and to tell the whole truth. If they had been wronged by the white men, the commissioners wished to know it, and if they themselves had committed depredations, they were to say so in a blunt and honest manner.

As usual, the voluble Kiowas were first to speak, being represented by Satanta,[21] who seemed willing enough to assume the responsibility of speaking for the tribe. He represented himself as a man of peace, but he wanted it understood that all the country south of the Arkansas belonged to the Kiowas and their allies, and they did not want it disfigured by soldiers' camps and "medicine houses." In a later speech, the chief emphasized his position on this matter, when he stated as follows:

> This building homes for us is all nonsense; we don't want you to build any for us. We would all die. Look at the Pennektatus [Penateka Comanches]. Formerly they were powerful, but now they are weak and poor. I want all my land even from the Arkansas south to the Red river. My country is small enough already. If you build us houses, the land will be smaller. Why do you insist on this? What good can come of it? I don't understand your reason. Time enough to build us houses when the buffalo are all gone; but do you tell the Great Father that there is plenty of buffalo yet, and when the buffalo are all gone I will tell him. This trusting to the agents for my food I don't believe in.[22]

For the main band of Comanches as well as for their allies, Ten Bears, the Yamparika, spoke. Since his speech is one of the finest examples of Indian oratory that has been preserved, and since it presents the Indians' case so forcefully, it may well be given in full.

> My heart [said he] is filled with joy when I see you here, as the brooks fill with water when the snows melt in the spring; and I feel glad as the ponies do when the fresh grass starts in the beginning of the year. I heard of your coming when I was many sleeps away, and I made but few camps before I met you. I knew that you had come to do good to me and to my people. I looked for benefits which would last forever, and so my face shines with joy as I look upon you. My people have never first drawn a bow or fired a gun against the whites. There has been trouble on the line between us, and my young men have danced the war dance. But it was

not begun by us. It was you who sent out the first soldier and we who sent out the second. Two years ago, I came up upon this road, following the buffalo, that my wives and children might have their cheeks plump and their bodies warm. But the soldiers fired on us, and since that time there has been a noise like that of a thunder storm, and we have not known which way to go. So it was upon the Canadian. Nor have we been made to cry once alone. The blue-dressed soldiers and the Utes came from out of the night when it was dark and still, and for camp-fires they lit our lodges. Instead of hunting game they killed my braves, and the warriors of the tribe cut short their hair for the dead. So it was in Texas. They made sorrow come in our camps, and we went out like the buffalo bulls when the cows are attacked. When we found them we killed them, and their scalps hang in our lodges. The Comanches are not weak and blind, like the pups of a dog when seven sleeps old. They are strong and far-sighted, like grown horses. We took their road and we went on it. The white women cried and our women laughed.

But there are things which you have said to me which I did not like. They were not sweet like sugar, but bitter like gourds. You said that you wanted to put us upon a reservation, to build us houses and make us medicine lodges. I do not want them. I was born upon the prairie, where the wind blew free and there was nothing to break the light of the sun. I was born where there were no enclosures and where everything drew a free breath. I want to die there and not within walls. I know every stream and every wood between the Rio Grande and the Arkansas. I have hunted and lived over that country. I lived like my fathers before me and like them I lived happily.

When I was at Washington the Great Father told me that all the Comanche land was ours, and that no one should hinder us in living upon it. So, why do you ask us to leave the rivers, and the sun, and the wind, and live in houses? Do not ask us to give up the buffalo for the sheep. The young men have heard talk of this, and it has made them sad and angry. Do not speak of it more. I love to carry out the talk I get from the Great Father. When I get goods and presents I and my people feel glad, since it shows that he holds us in his eye.

If the Texans had kept out of my country, there might have been peace. But that which you now say we must live on is too small. The Texans have taken away the places where the grass grew the thickest and the timber was the best. Had we kept that, we might have done the things you ask. But it is too late. The white man has the country which we loved, and we only wish to wander on the prairie until we die. Any good thing you say to me shall not be forgotten. I shall carry it as near to my heart as my children, and it shall be as often on my tongue as the name of the Great Father. I want no blood upon my land to stain the grass. I want it all clear and pure, and I wish it so that all who go through among my people may find peace when they come in and leave it when they go out.

There is nothing in the record to indicate that the savages were ever convinced that it was best for them to cede away any of their lands. Probably they signed the treaty because they realized that they must either do so or go without their annuity goods and fight the soldiers besides. They had no intention of staying on the comparatively small reservation which would remain to them, and it was to be expected that they would insist to the last on the right guaranteed in the treaty of hunting in their old range.

The treaty provided for the very things that the Indians had said emphatically they did not want—houses, farms, agricultural implements, instruction in farming, physician and military posts. While they were saying unequivocally that they did not wish to become civilized, they were agreeing to terms that would permit the United States to compel them to become so. They asked simply to be let alone and to be permitted to live as their fathers had lived. To this the United States could not assent. It was the old story: the Indians were interfering with the streams of American expansion. But now the story could not have the ending which had always been worked out in former times. These Indians could not be removed or driven away to a new country. There was no new country, no "west" beyond the frontier to which they could be sent, and thereby put momentarily out of the way. They were in the very heart of the last frontier. Through their country ran the great railway and overland transportation routes, and it was necessary to brush them away from these. Also, it was no longer true that they acted merely as impediments to those who wished to cross their range; their country itself was sought after and must be opened up to settlement. The savages must either be pushed aside or crushed, they must either be confined on small reservations or annihilated, and this fact seems to justify any compulsion the commissioners may have used in negotiating the treaty.

The treaty of Medicine Lodge Creek did not in any sense settle the Indian problem of the South Plains. It simply legalized the steps the army would have to take during the next few years in compelling the savages to stay away from the settlements and routes of travel. Like the former treaties with these tribes, it made unlawful wrongs against the person or property of the Indians, but no provision was made for enforcing such regulations. Like the preceding treaties, it obligated the savages to give up to their agents or the military any

Indians guilty of acts of violence against white persons; and this provision was quite as worthless as those in the past had been. The savages would not and could not live up to such agreements. The Indians agreed to stop their raiding practices in much the same language that had been used to pledge them in former years. They relinquished the right to occupy permanently territory outside of their reservation, but they might hunt anywhere within their old country south of the Arkansas river, and white settlements were not to be allowed in this territory for a period of three years. They would not oppose the construction of wagon roads or railroads across their territory.

The confederated Kiowa, Comanche, and Apache tribes were allowed to retain a reservation in southwestern Oklahoma, which later surveys showed to contain 5,546 square miles. This was not a liberal grant of territory, but it would be sufficient to sustain the Indians after they had learned to farm and raise stock.[23] Also, the land turned out to be of greater value than it was thought to be at that time.

The treaty provided that the head of each family could secure exclusive possession of acreage not in excess of a half-section, and any Indian over eighteen years of age not the head of a family might secure exclusive possession of not more than eighty acres whenever he was ready and disposed to commence separate and independent farming operations. If it should be necessary, additional lands should be granted for this purpose. Seeds and agricultural implements to a limited amount were to be furnished each Indian during the first three years of his farming efforts. Congress was to appropriate twenty-five thousand dollars each year for a period of thirty years "to be used . . . in the purchase of such articles . . . as from time to time the condition and necessities of the Indians may indicate to be proper . . ." In addition to this expenditure, certain articles of clothing which were enumerated were to be furnished each person. Teachers, an instructor in farming, a physician, and one or more blacksmiths were provided for.

In a special treaty between the United States and the Kiowa, Comanche, and Apache Indians, the Apaches gave up their affiliation with the Cheyennes and Arapahoes, and were confederated with their old allies, the Kiowas and Comanches.[24]

Ten chiefs from each of the Kiowa and Comanche tribes signed the main treaty. Among the Kiowas, the name of the influential Lone Wolf is missing, and among the Comanches, the Kotsotekas, if represented at all, were represented by obscure chiefs.[25] Ten Bears, probably the most influential Comanche chief, headed the list of signers from that tribe, but under Comanche custom he could not bind any one outside of his own band, the Yamparikas. Painted Lips and Iron Mountain, also Yamparikas, signed with him, giving that branch of the tribe liberal representation. Horse's Back, another influential chief, signed for the Nokonies, which seems to indicate that Drinking Eagle, formerly their most influential chief, was now dead. Shaking Hand, the Kotsoteka, was absent, and there were no Kwahadies whatever. Probably a third of the Comanche tribe was not represented at all.

THE KWAHADIES

Since the Kwahadies, the Comanches of the *Llano Estacado*, were not directly associated with the other Comanches, it is necessary to give a brief, separate account of this powerful band, the last of the tribe to become reconciled to life on the reservation. For more than a century they had been living in the plains country of Texas and New Mexico,[26] escaping for the most part both the influence resulting from contact with Anglo-Americans and the punitive expeditions that had so often brought wailing and self-torture to the other Comanche camps. Reference has been made to the insolence of these bands during the Civil War, and how they escaped punishment except for Carson's expedition in 1864 (which fell mainly on the Kiowas), and some fighting by Carleton in New Mexico. In 1866 they were visited by Superintendent A. B. Norton, who reported that they were engaged extensively in stealing stock from the people of Texas and Arkansas, and exchanging it for goods, particularly ammunition and whiskey, supplied by the *Comanchéros*, or traders, from New Mexico.[27]

In 1867 Norton sent Lorenzo Labadi, an Indian agent in New Mexico, to visit the Kwahadies and demand the release of a captive boy, Rudolph Fischer. In company with six men, Labadi made the journey into the Comanche country. He held council with some of their chiefs at "a place called Qutaque [Quitaque], near the state of Texas, east of New Mexico,"[28] where he learned that eighteen different parties were then out on raids against the Texas frontier, and several prominent chiefs had gone with about 300 warriors to attack the Navajoes at the Bosque Redondo reservation. These Indians were described as being "rich," having about 15,000 horses and 300 or 400 mules. Labadi stated that they raised their own stock, and had over 1,000 cows, and Texas cattle without number. Buffalo was abundant in their range, and their country was large and fruitful.

The trade in Texas cattle which Labadi mentions should be given further notice. This barter had been going on for many decades, but it does not seem that cattle became the chief commodity until about the time of the Civil War. During the early years of the century, the Comanches had given buffalo robes and occasionally horses or Mexican captives for the ammunition, knives, calico, and gewgaws which the *Comanchéros* supplied. But as soon as cattle came to have some value in New Mexico, the Indians had a commodity that was easily procured and transported, and could be supplied in almost limitless quantities. Regular meeting places, probably the ones used from time immemorial,[29] were agreed upon and here the Mexicans delivered their cartloads of commodities for cattle which the Indians had taken from the frontier ranchmen. As the business became more profitable, wealthy Anglo-Americans entered it, supplying the capital to their impecunious Mexican neighbors, who dealt directly with the Indians. The trails made by the carts of these Mexican traders were to be seen on the plains for years after the country had been occupied by Anglo-American cattlemen, "almost as big and plain as the roads of today."[30]

In 1867, Superintendent Norton stated that the territory of New Mexico was "filled with Texas cattle"[31] and at a later time, he added: "When no cattle or horses are found in the Comanche camp by the Mexican traders, they lend the Indians their pistols and horses and remain at camp until the Comanches have time to go to Texas and return, and get the stock they desire."[32] It is difficult to make any satisfactory estimate of the number of Texas cattle thus stolen. In 1867, Charles Goodnight found 600 head of his cattle on Gallinas Creek in New Mexico—cattle which had been stolen some time before from his range near old Fort Belknap, and traded to the Mexicans. He not only failed to recover his stock by legal proceedings at Las Vegas, but lost seventy-five dollars in court costs. He was firmly convinced that at least 300,000 head of Texas cattle had been stolen and sold or traded to New Mexicans during the Civil War.[33] John Hitson, another Texas ranchman, writing in 1873, was more conservative, estimating the loss of Texas cattle during the two preceding decades at 100,000 head.[34]

Norton tried to stop this wholesale theft by revoking the permits of the *Comanchéros*, but it may well be doubted that this was in any way efficacious. These Mexicans, or their forbearers, had engaged in this business long before such a thing as a permit was known, and the lack of license was not calculated to deter them. Mackenzie gave them a fright in 1872 when he followed their trail into the New Mexican settlements, near Alamo Gordo. When the broad and well-marked trail began to break up into many smaller traces, he made an effort to find the guilty parties. However, he was obliged to report that he could not apprehend them, and that they had probably left the country to escape capture by a party of citizens who were arresting cattle thieves and taking possession of stolen cattle.[35] Apparently the trade in stolen cattle abated somewhat after 1872, but the *Comanchéros* continued to trade with the Comanches, furnishing them whiskey, tobacco, hardtack, sugar, coffee, arrow and spear points. Clinton Smith, the Kwahadi captive, describes this trade thus:

... and such trading that took place! Those fool Indians would let the Mexicans pick their mules for a keg of whiskey; ten pounds of coffee was accepted for a pack horse, five pounds of tobacco would get a mule, and a buffalo robe would be exchanged for little or nothing. The traders stayed with us two or three weeks. The only way the Indians would let them come into camp was with packs loaded down on jacks, but they would let them take back [away] what they had traded to them.[36]

This trade was not altogether discontinued until the Indians had been gathered together and were all located permanently on the reservation.

A SEASON OF DISCONTENT

The chiefs and old men might engage in councils and sign treaties, but the restive Comanche and Kiowa warriors continued to plunder the settlements. The winter of 1867-1868 was one of the worst the frontier people of the Indian Territory and Texas ever experienced. Instead of recounting in detail these murders, it seems a little less tiresome and revolting to quote Philip McCusker, a special scout or agent sent by the commissioner of Indian Affairs to keep in touch with the Indians and report on their conduct and movements. He stated that "the Comanches and Kiowas are going to Texas to steal horses continually, and if they get them without any trouble, they do so, but if in order to get them it is necessary to kill a family or two, they do so."[37] When he berated the responsible chiefs like Ten Bears and Painted Lips for not controlling their warriors better, the chiefs "felt bad about it," but declared quite truthfully no doubt, that they were unable to do anything to stop it.

It was provided in the treaty of Medicine Lodge Creek that the Comanches, Kiowas, and Apaches should assemble on the lands assigned to them and make that region their home. Accordingly, Agent J. H. Leavenworth repaired to the vicinity of old Fort Cobb, and in March or April set up agency headquarters at a place called Eureka valley.[38] Unfortunately, the place selected was in the territory of the Wichitas and associate tribes.[39] The Indians soon came in larger numbers, finding to their disgust that no arrangement had been made to provide subsistence for them. In the treaty of October preceding they had reluctantly agreed to accept life on the reservation; now they had come, and the government was not ready to receive them. Washington had spoken with a forked tongue; his agents were cheats and liars, thought the red men. It must be said that in this, the most critical hour in the history of Indian relations on the South Plains, the United States Indian service proved unequal to the task. Likewise, the army had failed either because of its own limitations or because of a disinclination to cooperate with the Indian agents. There were no troops to protect the agency, although at no place on all the frontier from Texas to Canada were they needed more. The problem of controlling the Indians soon became serious.[40] Hundreds and thousands of wild "Staked Plains Comanches" gathered near the agency and demanded food and presents.

Troubles for the agents multiplied rapidly. In May, Henry Shanklin, agent for the Wichitas and associate tribes, reported that because of the presence of these wild Comanches and Kiowas, his own Indian wards had been compelled to stop their work in the fields in order to guard their stock by day and night. Also, he added that a war party of eighty Comanches had paid him a visit on its way to raid in Texas and, "in Plains parlance completely cleaned me out of all my personal supplies, leaving myself and help without food of any description." He stated that this was the second raid on his agency, and that John Shirley's trading house had also been robbed by them. Philip McCusker and Shanklin, by distributing presents, persuaded about fifty of these Comanches to turn back, but the remainder went on to Texas,[41] there to carry on their work of destruction and leave behind them the mangled bodies of helpless frontier people and the smoking ruins of the isolated cabins that lay in their path. A week later Shanklin wrote that he had been compelled to move his agency to Cottonwood Grove, fifteen miles to the east, where he would be obliged to remain until the wild Indians left the country or the troops came and gave protection. Shanklin added that some of his Indians had already left their cabins and lodges to seek other locations, and he feared that others would feel obliged to do so unless protection was given.[42]

But the Comanches did not stop with driving away the agent of the Wichitas. Early in June a party of Yamparikas burned one of the agency buildings with its contents, consisting of pine flooring, doors, windows, farm implements, and other articles so badly needed by the sedentary tribes who were trying to learn how to live like the white man. The Indians gave as their excuse for this outrage the allegation that Dr. Palmer, who had been living with Shanklin in the building, was a "bad medicine man" and they did not propose to be bewitched by his presence in the community. They did not do Shanklin any personal violence, but they forced him to take down the agency flag, and forbade him to build any more houses or cut any more timber "until they would see further about it."[43]

An interesting and somewhat significant matter is the change in the attitude of Colonel J. H. Leavenworth towards the Indians, which took place during this memorable winter and spring of Indian discontent. It will be recalled that Leavenworth had always been one of the foremost champions of the peace policy. He had felt that a tactful agent could do more with the Indians than a regiment of soldiers, and he generally deprecated any war talk. But during the spring of 1868 he reversed his position on this matter and began to send to his superiors many damaging statements concerning his wards. He reported that both the Kiowa and Comanche tribes had committed many outrages, and even then had many stolen horses and prisoners. | He charged that the Yamparikas, Nokonies, and Penatekas were especially guilty and that Little Crow, son of the great Yamparika chief, Ten Bears, and a certain Penateka brave, the son of Silver Brooch were among the worst offenders. | Concerning the other Comanches, he said "they have all, without an exception, as bands, been engaged in acts of violence and outrages in Texas, and should be dealt with severely."[44] He reported that he had recently recovered four captives from the Comanches. He had been in council with the Kwahadies from the Staked Plains, who had a number of captives; but he could not secure these without distributing many presents. The Kiowas had been equally guilty in the matter of depredations, and they still held five prisoners. Then he closed his letter with the statement:

> The other Kiowas holding captives are well known to me, and as the whole tribe is more or less implicated in these cruel acts, I recommend that their annuities, as well as the Comanches, be stopped, and all confiscated for the benefit of the orphans they have made; the guilty demanded—according to our treaties with them—for punishment; and if not delivered up, then let them be turned over to the military, supported by the Navajoes and civilized Indians, to make short and sharp work with them, until they can see, hear, and feel the strong arm of the government.[45]

It may be observed that the raids on the Texas frontier were not a great deal worse than they had been during most all of the preceding decade. The fact of the matter is that Leavenworth had never seen their destructive work in all its horror until he moved into the region adjacent to Texas. Furthermore, he had never comprehended the ugliness of savage insolence until he tried to control a thousand disappointed warriors, many of them strangers to him, without the support of troops. While this anarchy prevailed at the agency, Colonel Leavenworth left affairs in charge of S. T. Walkley, acting agent, and never returned.[46]

Walkley stayed at his post, notwithstanding the fact that very soon after Leavenworth left there was "a general stampede of the traders and whites from this immediate vicinity." He managed to protect what little public property there was left at Eureka valley, but he could not control the Indians since he had neither food nor presents to give, nor soldiers to enforce his orders.[47] Hence, from May to October of 1868, the affairs at the Comanche-Kiowa Indian agency received no attention whatever from the United States government, and the property custodian, the only white person at the agency, could do no more than chronicle the raids into Texas and count the scalps which the young warriors brought in.[48] To this state of affairs had come the first efforts of the United States Indian service to collect these nomadic tribes and carry out the treaty of 1867. The Kiowa-Comanche reservation had been launched for a poor start.

| The events in the vicinity of old Fort Cobb during the spring and summer of 1868 demonstrate forcefully that the nomadic Indians of the plains could not be controlled without the presence of troops. Adequate supplies for the savages might have improved matters, but sooner or later the agents would have been compelled to back up their decisions by force. Among the Kiowas and Comanches tribal authority had become practically negligible. Try as hard as they might, the chiefs could not even control their own sons. For all practical purposes the tribes had become mere fictions. The United States government was having to deal not with organized groups of people but with hundreds of individual savages, many of whom proposed to do just as they pleased regardless of treaties or tribal custom and law. Faithful chiefs like Ten Bears, Shaking Hand and Horse's Back might occasionally restrain the young men, but they could not in justice be held accountable for the sins of these youths.[49] |

Now, in the absence of their duly authorized agent, failing to receive the presents and subsistence which they had expected, some of the Comanches, including the Yamparikas and a large body of the Kiowas, left the reservation and moved to their old haunts along the upper Arkansas river. According to General Sheridan, their arrival there marked the beginning of disturbances. They assumed a threatening attitude, and the general felt obliged to increase his garrison at Fort Larned and issue rations to them in order to avoid war.[50] Sheridan became very uneasy about the situation a few weeks later when the Cheyennes, joined by some Arapahoes and Sioux, began an Indian war. It was felt that the Kiowas and Comanches were liable to join these hostiles, and to prevent such a union, Sheridan met the southern Indians in council and tried to induce them to return south to their reservation. It was finally agreed between the army officers and the chiefs that General Hazen should conduct the Indians to their reservation, subsist them while on the way, feed them during the ensuing winter, and issue to them their annuities.[51] To enable him to carry out this plan, Hazen was supplied with funds by the army, and in order to expedite the work of getting the Indians back to their reservation and out of the proximity of the warring Cheyennes and Sioux, the secretary of the interior virtually turned these tribes over to the army and instructed all officers of the Indian service to cooperate with the military in every way possible.[52]

It was understood that General Hazen was to meet the Indians near Fort Larned and escort them to their reservation. Meanwhile, General Sheridan was to launch a campaign to punish the hostile Indians. Thus the army was to play the part both of an escort for the friendly Indians and a scourge for the hostiles. While Hazen led away his Kiowas, Comanches, and Prairie Apaches, Sheridan was to take the field against the troublesome Cheyennes and other Indians that might align themselves with the hostiles.

The Kiowas and Comanches, who had probably been tampered with by meddlesome white men, suspected treachery, and failed to meet General Hazen; but most of them later went on to the agency.[53] There they held councils with Captain Henry E. Alvord and later with General Hazen, and convinced them that they had been friendly all along. In fact, Hazen became much alarmed lest General Sheridan, who was still under the impression that the Kiowas and Comanches were hostile, should attack them before they could be gathered in at Fort Cobb, and to prevent this he sent out swift runners to inform the Indians of the situation.

The attack that Hazen had feared was made, although it fell to the lot of the Cheyennes to bear the brunt of Sheridan's blows. An advance column under General George A. Custer moved into the valley of the upper Washita in December, 1868, destroyed the village of the Cheyenne chief, Black Kettle, and fought a large party of Kiowa and Comanche warriors who came to the aid of their Cheyenne friends.[54] Sheridan then led his force (the most formidable that had ever been sent against Indians on the South Plains) down the valley of the Washita, and forced the Indians to take refuge at Fort Cobb. A little later he moved south to the Wichita mountains and established Fort Sill on Cache creek.[55] The Indians were required to accompany the troops, and henceforth this post, or the agency that was established near it, was headquarters for the Comanches, Kiowas, and Kiowa Apaches.

Meanwhile, Lieutenant Colonel A. W. Evans, who had moved into the Comanche country from New Mexico with a strong detachment of troops, came upon and defeated on December 25 a party of Comanches on Red river, west of the Wichita mountains. He captured and burned their village, destroyed much Indian property, and thought that he killed about twenty-five Indians and wounded many others. Verily, when such destructive work could be carried on in the very heart of the Comanche range, in the dead of winter with the mercury sometimes as low as twenty degrees below zero, the Indians could never hope to find a safe retreat. Sheridan's experimental winter campaign was a success to the extent that it showed the practicability of punishing the Indians at any season. Some of these Staked Plains Comanches were so hard-pressed and frightened that a delegation of head-men went over to Fort

Bascom, New Mexico, to arrange for terms of surrender. There they were arrested and imprisoned; but were later sent to Fort Leavenworth, Kansas, and finally to their reservation on the promise that they would also have their people come to the reservation and stay there. Their people came to the reservation, but it is not likely that they long remained there.[56]

It must not be understood that the Comanches had come to the reservation to stay. On June 30, 1869, General Hazen reported 916 Comanches on the reservation, and estimated that those not there would number 1500. He reported 1000 Kiowas on the reservation and, while he does not estimate the number not present, there certainly must have been several hundred Indians of this tribe still roaming over the prairies.[57]

The conduct of the United States Indian service and military forces on the South Plains during the year 1868 was such as to puzzle the savage mind. To begin with, in compliance with the treaty of the preceding year, many of them came to their reservation and agency headquarters. Here they found things in confusion: supplies were inadequate, there were no troops to maintain order, and neither life nor property was safe in that vicinity. Their agent, either because of fear or disgust, deserted them, and the agency was practically abandoned. Naturally they drifted away, those who had in times past frequented the region of the Arkansas river returning to their old haunts, while the more independent "Staked Plains" bands took to the *Llano Estacado*. Then the Cheyenne war broke out along the Arkansas and to the north of that stream, and these Kiowas, Comanches, and Apaches were urged to return to their own reservation. This they did, although they did not accompany Hazen to that place as Sheridan had planned. They settled down near their agency, although some of them may not have been actually on their own lands. The more independent Comanches of the plains remained farther out to the west; but at least part of them, like Shaking Hand, assured Hazen of their friendliness and agreed to come in whenever the goods and presents arrived. There was no game for the Indians to subsist upon near the agency.

Then, as they waited, the troops struck them with the swiftness and fury of a Texas norther. That there were murderers and cut-throats in every band is true; but it is likewise true that the great majority of the savages were at that time trying to obey the instructions of their white guardians. They had repaired to the vicinity of Fort Cobb as they had been told to do,[58] and as they waited there for food and presents, and while the soldiers there treated them kindly, other soldiers came by night to slay and burn. Although (with the exception of the Cheyennes and one band of Comanches) they avoided serious punishment, they must have, nevertheless regarded these acts as the work of a mad and vacillating government that did not know its own mind.

CHAPTER THIRTEEN

The Quakers in Charge

CHANGES IN THE INDIAN POLICY

The Indian peace commission of 1867 hurled scathing criticisms against the federal Indian administration. Among other allegations they stated:

> ... The records are abundant to show that agents have pocketed the funds appropriated by the government and driven the Indian to starvation. It cannot be doubted that Indian wars have originated from this cause. The Sioux war, in Minnesota, is supposed to have been produced in this way. For a long time these officers have been selected from partisan ranks, not so much on account of honesty and qualification as for devotion to party interests and their willingness to apply the money of the Indian to promote the selfish schemes of local politicians ...[1]

Such denunciations were repeated by members of Congress, with the result that the Indian office almost lost the confidence of the House of Representatives. Indeed, the administration found it difficult to get the house to adopt measures essential to the carrying out of the treaties of 1867. Hence, in order to give new tone to Indian affairs and to restore in a measure the lost prestige, congress, through the appropriations act of April, 1869, authorized the president to organize a board of Indian commissioners, who were to "exercise joint control with the secretary of interior over the disbursement of the appropriations made by this act."[2]

This provision represents both an expression of the lack of confidence in the

Indian administration and a determination to correct some of the abuses charged against it. The board was organized in June, 1869, and is still in existence, though from time to time its powers have been enlarged or modified. Among its duties during the first few years of existence were the supervising of the purchase and transportation of annuity goods, and the audit of the accounts of the Indian service.[3] Members of the commission visited the different agencies and held councils with the Indian chiefs; occasionally escorted parties of Indians on visits to the great cities of the north and east; investigated, reported on, and gave publicity to cruelties committed by white persons against Indians; made recommendations as to needed changes and improvements in the service; and acted as the champion of Indian rights generally.[4] They served without pay, and seem to have been men "eminent for their intelligence and philanthropy," as the act required. The body became at once a dominant force in determining the Indian policy of the government.

Along with the establishment of the board of Indian commissioners came another important change in Indian administration. This was President Grant's peace policy or "Quaker policy." Shortly after his election, Grant was waited on by a committee representing all of the "yearly meetings" of the Orthodox Friends in the United States. The committee suggested that the president appoint religious men as Indian agents and employees, believing that such persons would have a more wholesome influence over the savages than that which had often been exercised. The president either thought he saw in the proposal a partial solution for the vexing Indian problem or, if not that, a means of shifting the responsibility for failure to solve it. "Gentlemen, your advice is good," he said. "I accept it. Now give me the names of some Friends for Indian agents and I will appoint them. If you can make Quakers out of the Indians, it will take the fight out of them. Let us have Peace."[5]

Thus it came about that the Quakers assumed control of the wild tribes in Indian Territory and the agencies in Kansas. The Friends selected an "executive committee" to represent them in all Indian affairs and to recommend for appointment men considered to be worthy. For Indian superintendents and agents not on the reservations, Grant proposed to use principally army officers, selecting those who could be spared from regular military duty. Early in his administration, however, congress prohibited the employment of an officer of the army in any civil capacity, and the president, in order to beat the "politicians," enlarged his original plan and invited other denominations to participate in the Indian work.[6] The result was that in a short time most of the Indian agents, teachers, and the principal employees at the agencies were the nominees of some church or religious society. It seems that the church organizations were given a free hand in selecting these agents and employees. In some cases they even supplemented the salary of the agents in order to secure men of integrity and adequate ability. Furthermore, the churches sent missionaries and teachers among the Indians to supplement the work carried on by the government employees. Evidently the church people and the new board of Indian commissioners worked hand-and-glove and there was harmony, at least in the beginning.[7]

The Orthodox Friends were given ten agencies, including the upper Arkansas (located on the Canadian rather than the Arkansas), which was headquarters for the Arapaho and Cheyenne tribes, and the Kiowa and Comanche agency, which was located at Fort Sill. Thus, the fiercest and most daring Indians of all the South Plains fell to the Quakers. On July 1, 1869, Lawrie Tatum, an unimaginative but courageous and sensible Quaker, took up his duties as the agent of the Comanches, Kiowas, and Prairie Apaches.

"I knew little," wrote Tatum years after, "of the duties and responsibilities devolving upon an Indian agent. But after considering the subject as best I could in the fear of God, and wishing to be obedient to Him, it seemed right to accept the appointment."[8] An index of his attitude toward the work and the policy which he and other fellow Quaker agents adopted may be found in the following expression:

> The agents were encouraged to use every effort to Christianize and civilize the Indians on the peaceable principles of the gospel, and to deal with them honestly, firmly, and lovingly, and so far as practicable to procure religious employees, and to look to God for a blessing on their labors. This, I believe, was the wish and intent of every agent.[9]

Tatum was a Quaker; his neighbor agents were Quakers; Enoch Hoag, his superintendent at Lawrence, Kansas, was a Quaker; Hoag's chief clerk, Cyrus Beede, was a Quaker; and henceforth Quaker grammar, simplicity of style, and quaint expressions characterize the outgoing correspondence pertaining to the Indians of this section.

The Friends believed that kindness and honesty would solve the Indian problem. William Penn's generous and equitable conduct had been successful in colonial days, and they felt that the same tactics would enable them to subdue the wild savages of the plains. But there were forces at work which the Quakers could not remove or control. They could not blot out of the savage heart the traditional hatred for Texas and Texans, neither could they overcome the disposition to raid, fixed in habits of the savages through generations of practice. Wrongs committed against the Indians, their acts of retaliation (which had generally gone unpunished), and decades of lawlessness and confusion had produced in the Cheyennes, Kiowas, and Comanches a state of mind such as William Penn had not been obliged to reckon with. Of course these Indians, like all human beings, generally responded to kindness, but they could not yet be controlled without the persistent show of force and its occasional application.

ESTABLISHING THE AGENCIES

General W. B. Hazen, who was in charge of the Indians in the vicinity of Fort Sill until succeeded by Lawrie Tatum, July 1, 1869, had worked with great energy to establish permanent homes for his wards. There were to be three agencies within the limits of his "sphere of duties," the Wichita, Cheyenne and Arapaho, and Kiowa-Comanche. Hazen placed Philip McCusker[10] in charge of the Wichita and affiliated bands on the Washita near old Fort Cobb,[11] with instructions to start the Indians off in their farming operations. However, these bands, although located north of the Washita more than thirty miles away, were attached to the Kiowa and Comanche agency until 1870. In July, 1870, Jonathan Richards was chosen by the executive committee of Friends to act as sub-agent for these Indians.[12] About forty miles north of the Wichita agency, on the north bank of the north Canadian river, the so-called upper Arkansas agency was located for the Cheyennes and Arapahoes. Meanwhile, Hazen himself remained at Fort Sill, where he set up agency headquarters for the Comanches, Kiowas, and Apaches, and directed the breaking of land for making a crop.[13] | When writing on June 30, 1869, and summarizing his accomplishments Hazen stated:

> ... I have twelve hundred acres broken, with contracts for fencing it all; have three hundred acres planted in corn; over a hundred patches, from a few rods to ten acres each, started for Indians as gardens, tended by their own hands, and as cleanly kept as the best gardens in Ohio; have built a few substantial houses for chiefs, and have full established confidence in the good intentions of the government; have secured the interest of all in farming, while very many actually take hold with their hands. The season is proving the most auspicious possible, the gardens are certainly wonderful for Indians just beginning, and they come to the post with marketing every day ... |

Hazen complained of the lack of funds, but he managed to supply with adequate rations all Indians who came to the reservation.[14] He warned his successors of the danger in failing to feed them satisfactorily. "The ration to them is not merely subsistence," he wrote, "but a kind of subsidy, given in lieu of the ample supply they can get by the chase . . ." He added that they especially prized sugar and coffee, and if they should fail to get it, trouble would result. If the Indian administration had been willing and able to follow Hazen's advice more literally, serious troubles might have been avoided more than once.

THE QUAKERS TAKE CHARGE

General Hazen and his associates had worked faithfully and well, but they bequeathed to Friend Tatum a task difficult enough indeed. First, several hundred Kiowas and some two-thirds of the Comanches were not on the reservation and had never been there, except possibly for a few days at certain times. Of course, the Penatekas, the remnant of the old southern Comanches, with their chiefs, Silver Brooch and Milky Way, were at hand;[15] but their young men were neither too lazy nor too good to join their friends of the prairie in an occasional raid. The Nokonies were at the agency, headed by Horse's Back, who was trying hard to lead his people aright; and many of the Yamparikas, under the veterans Ten Bears and Iron Mountain, were there. But Shaking Hand's Kotsotekas and the wild Kwahadies under He Bear, Named Sun, and the young war chief, Quanah Parker, were away. Obviously the reservation idea could not be put into practice if the Indians were not on the reservation. Hazen had well stated the reservation plan when he said it was to place the Indian "on reservations, where white men, except servants of the government, cannot come; where he shall be taught and supported as a ward of the government, required to remain there, and war made upon him if he goes away."[16]

A second and more serious difficulty confronted Tatum in that he could not adequately feed those Indians that were on the reservation. In midsummer of 1869, soon after he had taken charge, he wrote that he did not have enough meat, the meal issued was musty and made the Indians sick, and coffee and sugar had been stricken from the ration. Chief "Cutscrip"[17] (Quĕrts-quĭp) told the agent that he knew the Indian's road was bad but that he could see no other for his people; for they were not getting enough to eat. Silver Brooch wanted to talk with "Washington," for he thought the agent was lying to him about the rations.[18] Tatum became genuinely alarmed when he heard that "several thousand" other Indians were headed for the agency expecting to be clothed and fed. Fortunately for the safety of the agent, these Indians never came.

The farming operations of the Indians did not turn out well. It is true that the Comanches were reported as having grown seventy-two acres of good corn and vegetables, but it is likely that most of this was done by the Penatekas who had, in Texas, learned a little about farming. Fifty-five acres of corn had been planted for the Kiowas and Apaches. These Indians took but little interest in their crops, permitted their horses to run in the fields, and when their corn was gone, expected the Comanches to divide with them.[19]

Before the end of the summer Tatum was manifesting considerable discouragement in regard to his wards, especially the Kiowas. "They appear," said he, "to have no higher wish than to roam unmolested on the plains, and occasionally make a raid into Texas to get some horses, mules, and such other things as they find and want."[20] Satanta, for the Kiowas, explained that his people found the white man's road hard. There was nothing on it but a little corn which hurt the Indians' teeth; there was no sugar and no coffee. He said that the Indians wanted ammunition; this was part of the white man's road.

Even at that time the Indians were becoming ill because, it was thought, of the bad condition of the meal they were eating. Supplies were on the way, but delays in transportation caused by the ravages of the Texas cattle fever among the freighters' oxen was given as the excuse for their failure to arrive.[21]

The conditions during the summer of 1869 were not peculiar to that season, but illustrate what frequently happened during the first few years of the reservation period. At this critical time, when it was so imperative that the Indians be instilled with confidence in the agent and the Indian administration, that organization proved to be unequal to the task.

As the spring of 1870 advanced, the zealous Friends renewed their efforts to impress upon the minds of the Indians the merits of the "white man's road." In this connection President Grant and J. D. Cox, the secretary of the interior, were enthusiastic supporters of the churchmen, and a council of the Indians of the South Plains was determined upon "for the purpose of more thoroughly inaugurating a system of industrial labor, and of advancing them in peace and civilization."[22] It was held at the Cheyenne and Arapaho agency, but few Indians from other places attended except the "white" Indians, *i.e.*, those who had long been associated with white people and were at least attempting to adopt the civilization of the whites. Perhaps the Caddoes, Wichitas, and others needed this advice, but they were not the Indians the Quakers were chiefly concerned with, and they did not represent the most serious obstacle in the way of the peace policy.[23] Those Indians who did attend spent most of their time grumbling that the government was doing so little to help them on their road to civilization, while the Friends, on the other hand, insisted that the Indians ought to be thankful that the "Great Father" had done so much for them. Hoag explained that the white man's road was a road of self-respect and initiative, and that if the Indians were to make progress along this road, they must not wait for the "Great Father" to do everything for them.

Since the Friends had been unable to induce the Kiowas, Comanches, and Apaches to come to the council on the Canadian, some of the committee went to Fort Sill to confer with members of those tribes. They got in touch with several prominent Kiowa chiefs, but Shaking Hand was the only Comanche chief of importance they mentioned in their report. Lone Wolf told them that the Indians liked to roam about, but that they meant no harm by it.[24]

Concerning these councils, Superintendent Enoch Hoag wrote:

> These several councils, resulted, I think, to the satisfaction and encouragement of all in attendance, and I am satisfied that our government will receive no more trouble from the Indians of this Superintendency if it faithfully and promptly carries into execution its treaty stipulations, and if its employees faithfully perform their respective duties.[25]

It is difficult not to doubt Friend Hoag's sincerity in the matter of his enthusiasm about the results of the council. He must have known that the troublesome Indians had not been reached, that a majority of the Comanches and Kiowas were not staying on their reservation, that their old habit of raiding was being renewed, that they were not satisfied with their rations or life in any aspect on the reservation, and that they were sure to give much trouble in the near future. The most charitable conclusion that can be drawn is that he was so obsessed with the peace policy and with his exaggerated idea of the power of kindness over the savages that he would not let himself believe there was anything fundamentally wrong. He did not even visit the Kiowas and Comanches, although he did make a journey up the Canadian to meet with the Cheyennes, who, like the Kiowas and most of the Comanches, had not attended the council at the agency headquarters. A more thoroughgoing investigation of the situation and a complete presentation of all the facts to the Indian administration at Washington at this time might have prevented untold difficulties later on.

THE AGENT'S WORRIES

Superintendent Hoag's optimistic report and prediction to the contrary notwithstanding, there were forces at work that threatened the peace policy and even the whole reservation system, and the integrity of the agents was not sufficient to offset these forces, especially since the government was not always able to carry into execution its treaty stipulations. First, the fact that but few of the Indians remained on the reservation was a matter of serious possibilities; for when they were out there was no telling what they were doing. Many of those Indians who had come in good faith, intending, no doubt, to remain, moved away during the first year because of the unusual amount of sickness

The Quakers in Charge

and the number of deaths that visited them in their new homes. Tatum explained that this scourge had been caused in part by the wet season, which "in new countries is apt to cause malaria and bilious complaints," and also by eating green watermelons, corn and other vegetables. He told the Indians that this diet would make them sick, but they gave no heed to his admonition. On the other hand the Indians, more in accord with the teachings of modern authorities on sanitation, laid their troubles to the locality in which they lived, and insisted on leaving it.[26] No doubt the ancient Comanche habit of fleeing from any place where death had visited their group saved many a band from extinction by an epidemic. Apparently most of the Indians returned near the agency for the winter, but they would not remain there during the summer of 1870 and neither would they make any attempt at farming that year.

However, the chief difficulty with which the agent had to contend was the policy of the Indian administration of punishing its wards for good conduct and awarding viciousness. This anomalous situation is stated by Tatum thus:

> At the close of a war with them, after they have committed many barbarous murders and stolen a large number of horses and mules, a treaty has been made, and it was understood by the Indians that they were to retain all the horses and mules stolen previous to that time, and have a large amount of goods, but they were not to steal any more. If they behaved reasonably well in the future they did not get many goods.[27]

Most of their annuity money for 1869 had been taken to pay depredation claims, that is, to atone for old sins which the Indians thought had been forgiven them.[28] Thus, the savages became convinced that good conduct did not pay, and determined not to err in that direction any more. As Tatum expressed it for them, they thought that the easiest way to get a large amount of goods was "to go on the warpath awhile, kill a few white people, steal a good many horses and mules, and then make a treaty, and they would get a large amount of presents and a liberal supply of goods for that fall."[29] Even some of the Penateka Comanches concluded that raiding was more profitable than farming and consequently joined the disaffected bands.

Hence, it came about that during 1870 the Indians were especially insolent and defiant. Furthermore, they did not always take the trouble to go to Kansas or Texas. In May, twenty or thirty Comanches, accompanied by a few Cheyennes, raided the agency, chased the laborers out of the corn fields, killed one man, and stole some twenty head of horses and mules.[30] Then, in June, eight Kiowas stole seventy-three mules from the quartermaster's corral at Fort Sill; a little later a small party of the same tribe attacked and wounded an employee almost within sight of the agency buildings, after which they rode to the butcher-pen and killed a man there.[31] Cattle were killed, herders were attacked, and life made unsafe generally in the Indian country.

Following these disturbances of the spring and early summer, preparations were made for the annual sun dance. This was the tribal ceremony of the Kiowas, and it seems that they alone actually participated in the rites; but other Indians friendly to this tribe, among them the Cheyennes and Comanches, generally attended to watch the proceedings and to sit in council with the Kiowas, for the ceremony of the sun dance had come to have a social and political significance to every tribe in the South Plains.[32] The ceremony was held, as usual, in June, the season when the down appeared on the cottonwoods; the place of the dance for 1870 was the north fork of Red river, about seventy or eighty miles west of Fort Sill.[33] The council at the medicine lodge lasted ten days, and the question of peace or war was discussed at length. Prevailing sentiment was for peace, although some of the chiefs seemed determined to have war. After the council many of the bands remained out, and organized raiding parties which went to harass the Texas frontier.

As reasons and excuses for the hostile actions, the Indians plead that they had been given such a small quantity of annuity goods at the preceding issue, that many of their people had sickened and died at the agency during the preceding summer, that they were not allowed to purchase ammunition, and that the Indian Territory was being divided into reservations while the Indians preferred to possess their country in common.[34] On July 1 Tatum reported that the Kiowas, Apaches, Cheyennes, and about half of the Comanches were camped near the southwest part of the reservation, that in the vicinity of the agency they had shot four men, three of them fatally, and that they were manifestly endeavoring to provoke an attack by Colonel Grierson, commander at Fort Sill. When Tatum and Grierson sent runners out to summon them in, the Indians refused to receive the runners.[35] Finally, some of the more docile Comanches and many of the Kiowas asked permission to return, and were allowed to do so on condition that they deliver up their stolen stock and inform the agent who the leading raiders were.[36] The Indians did not comply with these terms, though many of them evidently returned to the agency during the fall of 1870. Their insolence and raids for that year were not punished. No doubt many of the responsible chiefs deprecated the raids, but it was the old story of inability to control their young men.

The experiences of 1870 proved beyond a doubt that as long as game was plentiful and the Indians could secure arms and ammunition from the traders, they could not be kept on the reservation without the use of force. The people on the Texas frontier continued to suffer, and they complained bitterly that

The Quakers in Charge

they could not recover their stolen stock even when they found it at the agency or in the possession of the Indians.[37] The federal troops in Texas at this time were doing the best they could to protect the people, but posts so widely separated as forts Richardson at Jacksboro, Griffin on the Clear Fork, and Concho where San Angelo is now located, left too many unprotected gaps through which the Indians could enter.[38] Even when the number of troops was increased and sub-posts established between these different forts, the matter was not much improved.

| It seems that danger merely added spice and flavor to the occupation of raiding and made it all the more alluring to the young braves to run the gauntlet into the settlements. As long as the Indians stayed out away from the troops and their own agent some of them would form these wild marauding parties. As they approached the settlements the party would be divided and subdivided so that a few warriors would approach different communities or several homes within the same community simultaneously. Some of these small parties might be driven back by alert troops, rangers or bands of citizens before they had accomplished their purposes, but others would be sure to get through any cordon of outposts that might be established. They traveled at night and so swiftly did they carry on their destructive operations that they could be out of reach of soldiers within a short period of time. |

CHAPTER FOURTEEN

The Quaker Policy Is Modified

A series of events that occurred along the Indian Territory and Texas frontiers during the spring and summer of 1871 represents a peculiar combination of the tragic and the ridiculous, and led to the modification of the Quaker policy. On May 17, at Salt Creek, on the road between Jacksboro and Fort Griffin, the wagon train of "Captain" Henry Warren, a government contractor at Fort Griffin, was attacked by a large raiding party composed principally of Kiowas.[1] The wagonmaster and six men were killed, one of the men being tied to a wagon wheel and burned. Five members of the party managed to escape, at least one of them being wounded. The Indians returned to the agency soon after this horrible butchery and their leader, Satanta, stated in substance to Tatum that he, Satanta, led the party and that any other chief who might claim that distinction was a liar and not to be believed. The agent, with what probably seemed to the Indians a lamentable lack of a sense of humor, called on the military for the arrest of this chief and other leaders connected with the affair.

Now it happened that at the time of this raid William Tecumseh Sherman, who bore the title General of the Army of the United States, and Randolph B. Marcy, inspector-general of the army and a veteran of the plains, were traveling with an escort of seventeen men along the Texas frontier and were at the town of Jacksboro when one of the teamsters who had been fortunate enough to escape staggered into that place and related what had happened. There is grim humor in the possibilities connected with the affair. These officers and their escort had just arrived from Fort Griffin and had on the day before passed over the very spot where the unfortunate freighters met their death a little later. Before an attack of Satanta's well-armed warriors, Sherman and Marcy and their little guard would have been nearly as helpless as the teamsters proved to be, and it is likely that Satanta would have attacked the senior military officer of the United States just as readily as he set upon the obscure teamsters who made up Warren's freight train.

Sherman, after sending a detachment in pursuit of the savages, went on to Fort Sill. The soldiers did not overtake the raiders, but Sherman was present when Tatum asked for the arrest of the chiefs on the basis of statements from their own lips. One of them, Eagle Heart, made his escape; Sa-tank was taken and started on the road to Jacksboro for trial, but as he left Fort Sill he began to chant his death song after he had told some of his people where they would find his dead body. Then a short distance from the fort, he attacked his guard single-handed, and was slain. Satanta and Big Tree were taken and tried on a charge of murder. They were convicted and assessed the death penalty by the jury, but the governor of Texas, E. J. Davis, partly through the influence of Tatum, commuted their sentence to life imprisonment.

The arrest of these chiefs caused great excitement among the Indians, and many of them fled from the agency. However, on the demand of Tatum, who was supported by the military, the Kiowas brought in the mules taken from Warren's train, and made earnest promises of good behavior in the future.[2] The Comanches in the vicinity of the agency seem to have been sobered also by the swift justice meted out to the Kiowa chiefs. In his third annual report, Tatum wrote: "The effect of arresting some of the leading Kiowas and sending them to Texas for trial has been more effectually to subdue them than they have ever been before."[3]

THE ARMY TAKES A HAND

Although Tatum asked for clemency for the Kiowa raiders because he thought such a course would be more effective than more severe punishment, he had become thoroughly convinced that force would have to be used repeatedly against the savages. Early in August he requested of Colonel Grierson and Colonel Mackenzie that they arrest other Kiowa chiefs and forcibly take from those Indians certain stolen animals they were known to possess, unless the Indians should bring them in as promised.[4] It turned out that such procedure against the Kiowas was not at that time necessary, since the Indians brought in the stock in accord with their promise. Tatum reported at the same time that Shaking Hand held a captive child;[5] he had made repeated efforts to secure the release of the boy and had failed; now he asked the military to recover him, if at all practicable. In the same communication Tatum explained that besides Shaking Hand, there were two other chiefs who with their bands had been serious offenders.⁶ He also added that the Kwahadi Comanches, although properly belonging to the agency, had never reported there, and he thought that they were responsible for much of the raiding.

Finally, Tatum wrote Grierson as follows:

> I should be very glad indeed if thee and General MacKenzie could get that little captive and induce Mow-Way [Shaking Hand] and his band to come into the reservation and behave. Mow-Way does not appear likely to bring in that poor little captive child of his own volition. I did not get a definite idea of where Mow-Way is.⁷

These soldiers were glad enough to punish the savages, particularly at the request of a Quaker Indian agent. The army had been sending some expeditions into the region of the Staked Plains, and the country was no longer entirely unknown to them.⁸ To Colonel R. S. Mackenzie was assigned this task, and on August 19 he set out from Fort Richardson to attack the Indians in the canyons that skirt the eastern border of the Staked Plains. The force was reorganized and prepared for field duty at old Camp Cooper, and early in October the command, consisting of about six hundred men, entered the Indian country.⁹

At a camp on the "Fresh Water Fork of the Brazos"¹⁰ the Comanches, in a night attack, surprised Mackenzie, stampeded his stock, and caused him to lose seventy horses. Later an advance column of his forces attacked the savages near the mouth of Blanco Canyon, but the Kwahadi warriors under Quanah Parker fought back the soldiers until the women and children could escape.¹¹ Mackenzie pursued the Indians on up the canyon and the high plains on either side, finding it difficult even with the aid of his Tonkawa scouts, to trail the elusive foe. The savages finally moved out on the plains, but a "norther" with its cold snow and rain forced him to give up the chase.

Thus did this aggressive policy, even when carried out by a veteran Indian fighter, miss its goal almost entirely. Mackenzie did not even seriously punish the Kwahadies, much less drive them into the reservation. Tatum realized this, and he continued to call on his superiors to ask the military either to crush these Indians or bring them to terms. He pointed out that these Comanches persisted in raiding, and also formed a nucleus about which renegade Indians from the reservation continued to gather.¹²

Possibly the arrest, trial, and imprisonment of the Kiowa chiefs tended to restrain both the Kiowa and Comanche warriors on and near the reservation during the summer of 1871 and the autumn and winter following.¹³ But by the spring of 1872 there is little evidence of any restraint whatever. Major John P.

Quinine, Kwahadi Comanche

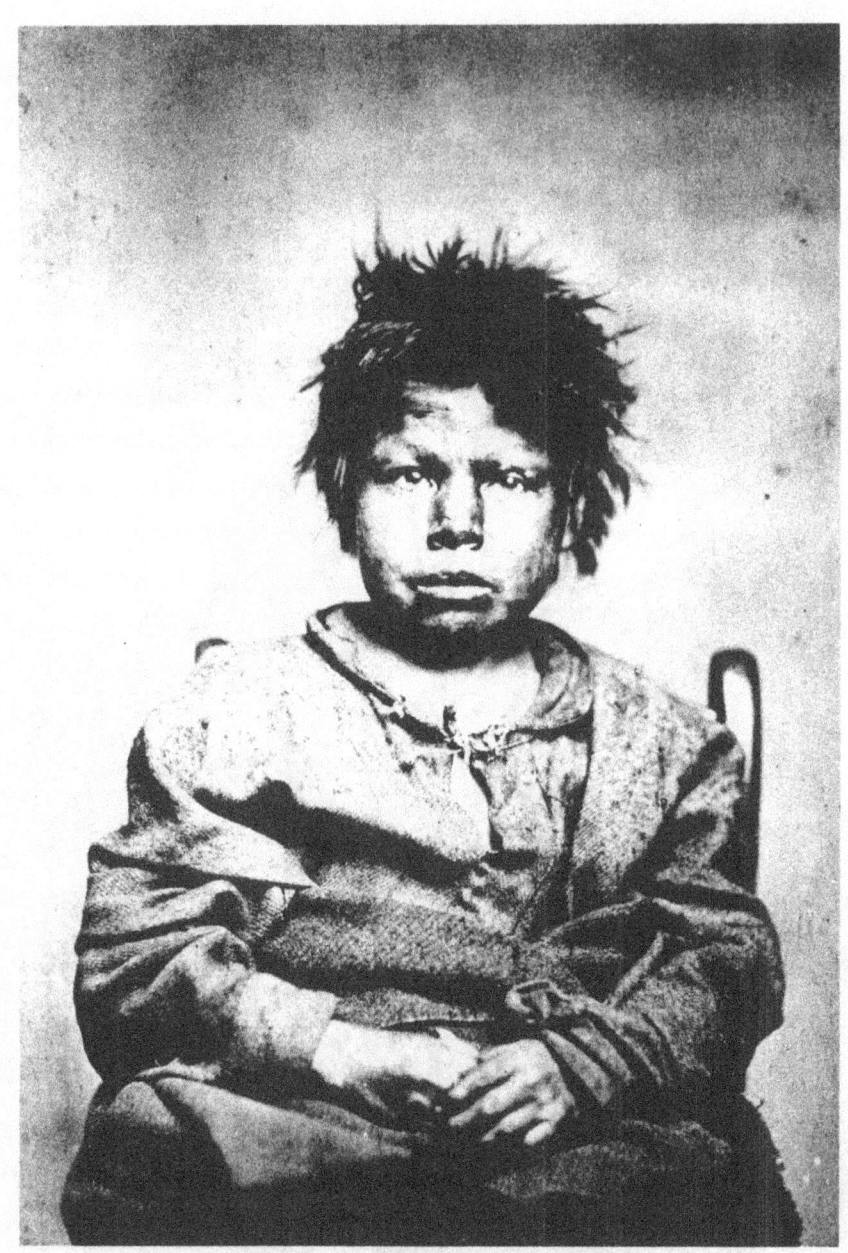

Comanche captive (Mexican boy)

Hatch at Fort Concho, and the veteran Mackenzie at Fort Richardson, declared that the situation was worse than they had ever seen it, and they charged most of the disturbances to the reservation Indians.[14] On April 20, at Howard Wells, in Crockett county, Texas, the Kiowas, and possibly some Comanches, carried out what amounted to another Salt Creek massacre. A wagon train was attacked at that place, and when two companies of troops arrived on the scene a few hours after the attack, they found the charred bodies of sixteen persons in the smouldering ruins of the wagons. The troops attacked the Indians, who were still camped close by, but were not able to inflict any serious punishment on them.[15] After recounting a number of these bloody activities, an army officer at Fort Concho stated: "Can you wonder that there are hundreds of desolate and vacant ranches in the region and that the hardy pioneers are retiring into the interior and severely blaming the government for risking and protecting untamed savages on our borders?"[16] The Indians were impartial and did not confine their operations to the Texas frontier. In June a band, said to have been composed of Kwahadies, stole fifty-one head of horses and mules from the stockade of the quartermaster at Fort Sill.[17]

Notwithstanding Tatum's recommendations that a more severe policy be adopted, and in spite of the reports of numerous outrages, the officials of the Indian office continued to adhere, for the most part, to the peace policy, and insisted that in it was to be found the only humane solution to the Indian problem. It seems that they felt that the raids were exaggerated, and they had a sympathy for the red men which persons on the frontier could not appreciate. By the winter of 1871-1872, Tatum was evidently out of harmony with his brethren in the matter of the peace policy; and well he might have been. His Indians would not try to farm, none of them would send their children to school, and they secured arms and ammunition from lawless traders or from Mexican traders through the Kwahadies.[18] Many of them would not even trade at his agency, but preferred to go to neighboring agencies to trade, and even to draw rations whenever they could beg something from the neighboring agents.[19] They mistreated their neighboring agricultural Indians north of the Washita river, killing their hogs and stealing their ponies. A number of the chiefs hated Tatum, and some even threatened to take his life.[20] The agent was honest and faithful to this trust, but he would not permit insolence and violence on the part of his Indians to go unpunished whenever it came to his attention and he had any way of dealing with it. About all he could do was to reprimand the guilty Indians and withhold all or a part of their rations. Naturally, these disciplinary measures incensed the refractory savages, while Tatum's readiness to call on the military for aid provoked discord between him and his Quaker superiors which finally led to his resignation.[21]

ADVICE THAT IS NOT HEEDED

Superintendent Hoag refused to be discouraged by reports of the vicious conduct of some of his wards, and in June, 1872, he took new hope because of a proposal of the general council of the Indian Territory to call representatives of the wild bands to meet with them in a special council to be held near old Fort Cobb. It was felt that these more docile and advanced Indians of the timber country could have much greater influence over their prairie neighbors than white men could hope to have. Thus the idea of an all-Indian council was carried to fruition in the summer of 1872. Superintendent Hoag approved the council, and designated his chief clerk, Cyrus Beede, as his representative to attend it.[22]

There was plenty of work for the council to do. The Kiowas, in addition to their raids in Texas, had recently stolen 121 mules from Captain Moore's command of four companies of infantry, on Bear Creek, thirty-five miles south of Fort Dodge. Beede found the Cheyennes and Arapahoes friendly, but with the Kiowas in a hostile frame of mind trying to get allies for the war which they contemplated, there was no telling what might develop. On July 25 enough Indians had assembled to begin the formal session. The Cheyennes were present in great numbers, but unfortunately, the Kiowas held back. Since they were the offenders for whose benefit the whole affair had been planned, their absence would have made the proceedings quite futile and meaningless.

The Cherokees, Seminoles, Creeks, Delawares, Comanches, Apaches, Caddoes, Wichitas, Cheyennes, and Arapahoes were represented. In council these Indians were in their natural element.[23] While they were waiting for the Kiowas to come, there was time and opportunity for speeches and numbers of chiefs addressed the gathering. Colonel John Jumper, a "white" Indian, edified the crowd with an oration on the brotherhood of man. In part his speech ran: "When God created man on the earth, he made the *red* and *white* and the *black*, the Creator is *one*, he made all, and if we live in peace He will love all." The aged Black Beaver pleaded with the Indians to watch their conduct so that when Indians "meet white man, he ask what tribe you belong to—we tell him. He say that's mighty good Indians, we like that."

But all of this good advice did not reach the Indians who most needed it, the Kiowas and wild Comanches. And, to add to the difficulties of the situation, Agent Miles and his Cheyenne and Arapaho Indians grew tired of waiting and left the council. Then Agent Tatum decided to leave before the arrival of the Kiowas, "doubting his own safety in the hands of the latter without the protection of the Cheyennes and Arapahoes."[24]

Finally the Kiowas arrived, and now the orators had an audience to whom they could address their pointed remarks on the sins of the nomadic tribes.

Their speechmaking continued; but the reaction of some of the young warriors to this wholesale distribution of admonition can best be presented by quoting again from Beede's journal:

> After adjournment of council this evening, being visited as usual by large numbers of Indians, the following conversation occurred at my tent, between interpreters McCusker and Jones and about a dozen of the most raiding and depredating Comanches of the Yap-pa-rick-ka band. In reply to the proposition of McCusker for them to take the white man's road, quit raiding and depredating and live at peace, their speaker said "we will take the white man's road, and leave the war path, when the white man will drop his paper and books," in reply to the proposition, that the Buffalo will soon be gone and they would have nothing to eat, he said, "there were yet millions of Buffalo, and there was no danger on that hand, but lest they might fail, they, the Comanches had determined to hunt buffalo only next winter, then they would allow them to breed a year or two without molestation and they would rely on Texas cattle for subsistence meantime." In reply to further propositions to go the white man's road, he said, "If the delegates here from the civilized tribes are representative men, we have but little respect for them, they are an old dirty inefficient looking set, hardly capable of managing their own affairs, we don't take much stock in them. We have heard enough of their talk. We would be willing to hear the white folks talk awhile now, but we don't want to hear these *White Indians* any more."

Then the Kiowa chiefs, Lone Wolf and White Horse, recounted their depredations with all of the nonchalance of a sophomore telling about a hazing escapade. The civilized chiefs continued their admonition, and Beede, in a special conference with Lone Wolf, tried to bring him to his senses. Ten Bears of the Comanches spoke, but took an indifferent attitude, and this probably encouraged the Kiowas to persist in their policy of insolence and defiance. Furthermore, the Kiowas were evidently playing for the release of Satanta and Big Tree. The best proposition Lone Wolf ever made was that if the government would bring back Satanta "so we can see his face," the Kiowas would return the white prisoners and mules and go to Washington for a council. The chief never did commit himself or his tribe to any policy that involved a repudiation of their recent acts of violence, and the council adjourned, August 4, without having accomplished anything of consequence toward the settlements of matters. Beede implied that the soldiers would be sent against the tribe, and the future looked dark for these Indians.

Now Kicking Bird, who had remained silent during the council, took the initiative and expressed his regrets at the turn things had taken and asked for a chance to make amends. Likewise Lone Wolf seemed somewhat sobered. A few days later they brought in and delivered up a few captives[25] and manifested some disposition to try to prevent such occurrences in the future. The Indian war that was inevitable was postponed for awhile as a result of the council, but the important points at issue had not been settled. It was to be expected that the raiding would go on.

The savages had scarcely reached their different hunting grounds when word went forth that there was to be another council. Evidently the commissioner of Indian Affairs had little confidence in the efficacy of the all-Indian council that had just closed. While this gathering had been in session, the commissioner appointed Professor Edward Parrish, of Philadelphia, and Captain Henry E. Alvord, who had seen service on the South Plains frontier, to meet with the Indians south of the Arkansas river, try to persuade them to discontinue their marauding, and escort some of the leading chiefs to Washington. Because of illness, Professor Parrish was not able to participate in the council, and he died at the Kiowa-Comanche agency about the time the council adjourned.[26]

On their way out to the agencies, Alvord and Parrish visited the superintendent's office at Lawrence, Kansas, read a part of Beede's report on the council that had just been closed, and there learned that the Kiowas were making a sort of *sine qua non* of their demand that Satanta and Big Tree be released or, at least, brought where the Kiowas could "see their faces." It was with some difficulty that Alvord persuaded Governor Davis to send the chiefs under guard to the Indian country. They did not arrive in time to attend the council; but they were taken to St. Louis and were permitted to spend a few hours with some of their tribesmen who were being escorted to Washington.

Meanwhile Alvord, working through Jones, the interpreter,[27] and Horse's Back, the Comanche, managed to bring together a good representation of the agricultural tribes and the Comanches. The Cheyennes and the Kiowas were not present. The absence of the Kiowas was a matter of great concern, for it was for their benefit that the affair was staged. The revival was being held and the chief sinners were not there to be converted. The council began on September 6, at Leeper's Creek, six miles up the Washita from the Wichita agency. A correspondent of the *New York Herald* has given us a vivid description of the assembly. He writes:

> Fronting the table were the Yam-pa-ri-ko Comanches: Ten Bear, Iron Mountain, Little Crow, Gap-in-the-Woods; and close by them Chewing

The Quaker Policy Is Modified

Elk or Quirto-Quip. To the right of these set, smoking the pipe of peace, the representatives of the Arapahoes: Little Raven, Big Mouth, Yellow Bear, Left Hand, Spotted Wolf, Curley, White Crow, Yellow Horse and Little Neck, and on their extreme left Mrs. Keith, the half-breed, who lives with them and acts as their interpreter . . . Opposite the Arapahoes, on the left of the table and on the outer edge of the circle of chiefs, sat Pacer, chief of the Apaches: Taw-haw, head medicine man, and seven minor dignitaries of that tribe; Horseback, Milky Way, Mowway and Black Horse, of the Comanches; Black Beaver, of the Delawares (an old man, nearly white, and famous as the guide of Audubon), and Wah-Saupie [Guadalupe], second chief of the Caddoes. George Washington, an old shrewd and well-to-do man, of dark complexion and gaudy dress, occupied a log in the right foreground, and near him sat Interpreters Jones and McCluskey [Philip McCusker], Agents Richards and Miles. Your Commissioner sat at the table. This was the position at the moment. Very shortly after the bushes were parted and young warriors galloped up, and dismounting formed a second and third circle; and then a party of Kiowas, under Running Bear (now with the Apaches, having been banished from their tribe for killing a chief in a drunken brawl) strode up and took position under a shady oak. But the audience had not yet arrived; the squaws and papooses were still busy drying beef, but they came later and squatted about fifty yards from the inner circle of chiefs.[28]

Then Captain Alvord opened the council by stating that he came with words directly from the "Great Father," that the good Indians would be well fed and well treated, but the bad Indians would be punished. He referred to the raiding of recent months and the vicious conduct of many of the Indians, and insisted that this must stop. After Alvord had completed his introductory remarks, Milky Way, the Penateka, led out for the Indians, and made some complaints about "Washington's" agents not keeping their word to the Indians; and Red Food[29] endorsed his sentiments. Then Alvord spoke more emphatically declaring that the United States would not tolerate any more lawlessness, and would henceforth punish persons harboring lawless Indians as well as the depredators themselves.

The reply to this speech, made by the Comanche Chief, Named Sun, represents an excellent statement of the attitude of the wild bands:

. . . I have kept out on the plains because the whites were bad. Now you [pointing to Alvord] come here to do good, you say, and yet the first thing you do is to pen us up in a narrow territory. I would rather [with great vehemence] stay out on the plains and eat dung than come in on such conditions. Um! ah! I was on the warpath, but now am not; but I don't want to hear such talk about having me penned up on a reservation.[30]

The chief indicated also that he did not propose to continue to view complacently the repeated encroachments of the white people on the Indians' country. He said that nearly all the tribes present had participated more or less in the raiding, and that it was not fair to lay all the depredations to the Kiowas and the Kwahadi Comanches.

The chiefs of the sedentary bands such as the Caddoes and Wichitas took their turn at pleading with the prairie Indians, and Little Raven of the Arapahoes gave them much good advice. Among the Comanche chiefs who spoke was Black Horse. He was of the "out" bands, and associated with He Bear, who had refused to remain for the council. | The *Herald* correspondent denounced Black Horse in severest terms:

> This is *the most blood-thirsty scoundrel on the plains*. Not very long ago he murdered a man at Fort Cobb while he was asleep in fancied security. He has a small face, narrow forehead and a large sensual mouth. On this occasion he looked hideous. His face—except across the eyes, and that tract of mud was as yellow as a kite's claw—was painted a dark blue, and his long hair looked as if it had been struck by lightning. He wore no shoes or moccasins, but carried a fine silver-mounted six barrelled revolver. |

He would not commit himself, for, he said, he did not know what the other chiefs of the plains wanted to do. Then the elderly Ten Bears spoke, and much to the same end as those who had preceded him. There was a touch of humor in his suggestion that, since the United States had moved the Indians so often with such unsatisfactory results, that government might try moving the Texans. They were the cause of all the trouble. Shaking Hand, the inveterate wanderer, spoke briefly, and added that "when the Indians in here are better treated than we are outside, it will be time enough to come in."

Thus the roving Comanches stated their position, and the Kiowas, if they had been present, would have agreed with them fully. They would not admit that they had been engaged in acts of war and, as was their traditional custom on such occasions, they minimized the depredating that had taken place and laid it to a very few irresponsible young warriors. All had complaints, and were ever alert to score some blow against this or that practice of the United States government and its agents. They had no confessions or apologies to make, and were boastful about the independent and wild life they led. It was plain that they did not wish to become reservation Indians, and they did not propose to eat beef as long as there was plenty of buffalo meat. All that they asked was to be left alone—a condition with which the government could not comply. When urged to name chiefs to accompany the commissioner to Washington, they held back, but finally agreed to send representatives as requested.

The councils adjourned *sine die* without the presence of any prominent Kiowas; but a few days later, on September 16, a company of the principal Kiowa chiefs consisting of Lone Wolf, Woman's Heart, Red Otter, Little Mountain, Son of the Sun, Sleeping Wolf, Stumbling Bear, and Fast Bear, met with Alvord in council. The chiefs were much more interested in presenting their grievances and inquiring about Satanta and Big Tree than in any proposed trip to Washington. Finally Alvord promised them that if they would send delegates to Washington these delegates should see the two prisoners at some point on the road, and some of the chiefs agreed to go.[31] It has already been stated that this promise was kept by taking the prisoners to St. Louis and permitting their tribesmen to spend a few hours with them there as the delegation passed through on its way to Washington. Lone Wolf headed the Kiowa delegation, and Ten Bears the Comanches. Representatives from the Arapaho and Apache tribes and the tribes of the Wichita reservation also went along.

The two Indian gatherings of 1872 would have been more effective if they had been held together as one council. The Indians must have felt that "Washington" was talking too much and doing too little. Nevertheless, the councils helped matters some. They were followed by the surrender of stolen stock and captives and a slight, temporary improvement in the conduct of the Indians. But it would require more than threats to send out soldiers and the escorting of chiefs to Washington to end forever Indian trouble south of the Arkansas.

CHAPTER FIFTEEN

The Last Wars

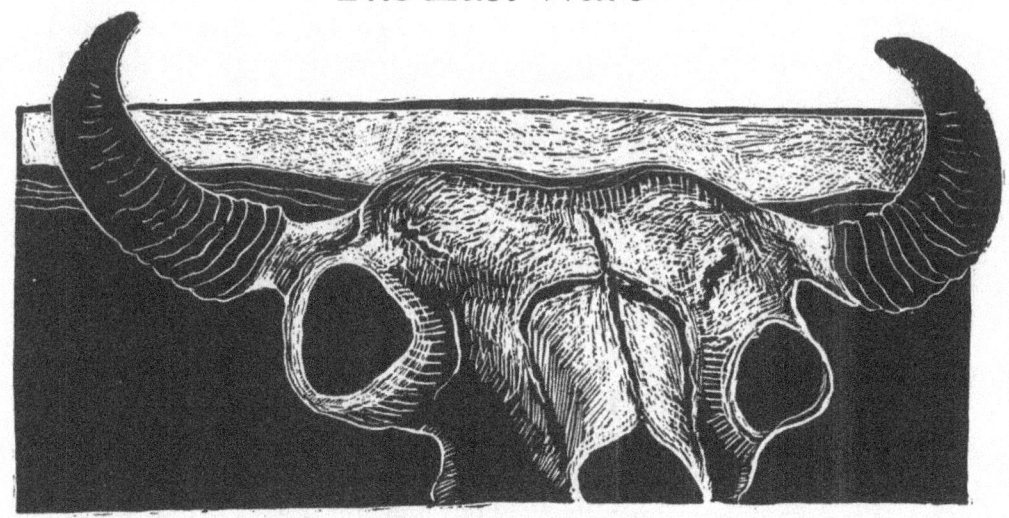

PUNISHED BY MACKENZIE

In the councils of 1872, the "out" Comanches had declared themselves friendly to the United States government, but they had flatly refused to bring their people in and reside on the reservation. Raiding went on, and the military continued to send expeditions out against them, having always the approval and cooperation of the Indian administration at Washington, even though the Quaker officials at the reservation may have sometimes doubted the wisdom and justice of the course pursued. The commissioner of Indian Affairs, Francis J. Walker, stated the point of view of the Indian office as follows:

> In the first announcement made of the reservation system, it was expressly declared that the Indians should be made as comfortable on, and as uncomfortable off, their reservations as it was in the power of the government to make them; that such of them as went right should be protected and fed, and such as went wrong should be harassed and scourged without intermission.[1]

The most effective campaign against these nomadic bands during this year was led again by Colonel R. S. Mackenzie. With two hundred seventy-two men, this officer followed pretty much the route of the preceding autumn by way of Fort Griffin, northwest to the "Fresh Water Fork" of the Brazos river, where he located his supply camp near the mouth of Canyon Blanco.[2] From this point he moved with most of his force to McClellan's creek, a tributary of the north fork of Red river. On the evening of September 29, the command came upon a Comanche village of two hundred sixty-two lodges placed snugly in the valley of the creek about seven miles from its mouth.[3] The Indians were taken by surprise, but evidently fought desperately. The fight lasted about thirty minutes, at the end of which time the village and about one hundred thirty captives were in Mackenzie's hands. Most of these were women and children. More than twenty warriors were killed, but by far the larger part of them escaped in spite of the efforts of a detachment sent to pursue them. Mackenzie lost three men killed, and several wounded.

The lodges were burned, and most of the captured property destroyed. The large Kwahadi horse herd, said to number 3000, was taken; but that night the Indians managed to stampede the herd and recover most of these animals and make way with some that belonged to the soldiers also. Mackenzie's guard, and the Tonkawa scouts who had been permitted to pick for their own use the best mounts out of this Comanche herd, were greatly chagrined at its loss. So expert were the Comanches at stampeding and driving away horses that thereafter Mackenzie never tried to hold another Comanche horse herd, but shot the animals upon capturing them.

This village belonged to Mow-way or Shaking Hand,[4] and though it is spoken of as a Kwahadi village, it evidently contained Comanches from several bands and was a kind of loitering place for renegade Indians from the agency.[5] Horse's Back, a Nokoni chief, had several relatives in the camp, including his mother-in-law, a former wife, and her daughter.[6]

The spirit of this band was broken and, although they did not come into the agency at once, they assumed an attitude of humility. Horse's Back went among them to urge that they come to the agency and promise to sin no more. They were in mourning for their dead braves and captured women and children, and would not do so at that time. But they gave up several captives, among them Clinton Smith. Shaking Hand came in in December with Named Sun and He Bear.[7] Though Mackenzie administered harsh punishment, it is difficult to see how he could have avoided it if he wished to bring the Indians under control. They would never stay at the agency as long as they could find peace and security on the open prairie, and as long as they were out, the raiding would go on.

This severe drubbing at McClellan's creek had a salutary effect on all the Comanches and the Kiowas as well. Other chiefs came in, meek as lambs, and agreed to abide by the regulations. Horse's Back constituted himself special agent for the recovery of captives, and soon brought in a dozen or more Mexican children.[8] In this work of mercy, Kicking Bird, the Kiowa chief, also participated. Besides their prisoners, the Comanches and Kiowas gave up a large part of the horses and mules which they had stolen during the year preceding. In January, 1873, Tatum wrote: "The Indians manifest a more docile and better disposition than they have ever done before, and give strong assurance of friendship."[9]

The Indians were doubtless further sobered by the fact that both tribes had members held as hostages by the whites. Satanta and Big Tree were still in the penitentiary, and more than one hundred Comanche women and children were prisoners at Fort Concho. The warriors knew full well that any raid or other gross misconduct on their part would lessen the chance of their people's being released. The amount of raiding into Texas during the early spring of 1873 was negligible. Most of the prominent chiefs remained close to the agency and begged for the release of their relations. The demeanor of the Indians was so docile and mild that their new agent, J. M. Haworth, who had succeeded Lawrie Tatum on April 1, 1873, removed the military guard from about the agency buildings and left to the Indians themselves the matter of police duty on issue day. Haworth came filled with Quaker idealism, and was enthusiastic about the peace policy.[10]

Superintendent Hoag likewise persisted in his enthusiasm for the peace policy, and in March he sent Cyrus Beede to Fort Sill to inform the Indians that the two Kiowa chiefs and the Comanche women and children would be released about the first of June in case the Indians on the reservation continued to remain quiet and peaceful. The Comanche prisoners were in charge of the United States soldiers at Fort Concho, and could be delivered up whenever the president so ordered. The case of the Kiowa prisoners was a different matter; they were state prisoners, and the governor of Texas found it difficult to make up his mind to release them.

On June 10, the Comanche women and children arrived at Fort Sill, and were released amid great rejoicing and the manifestation of much good feeling. When the Indians told the braves how kindly they had been treated, the warriors came forward to shake hands with or embrace Captain Robert McClermont who had commanded the escort that saw the prisoners safely through from Fort Concho. Many of the leading braves gave assurance that they would never cause the United States any more trouble.[11]

Now the Comanches had their people with them again, but the two Kiowa chiefs were still in confinement, and their braves became exceedingly restless, charging the government with failure to keep its promise made by Beede in March preceding. The Indians managed to prevent any retaliation on the part of irresponsible braves, however. So determined were the leading Kiowas to keep peace and order that they organized their warriors into a battalion of four companies, and marched about in military style.[12] They said that they were resolved to prevent their reckless young warriors from committing acts of violence and thereby injuring the cause of their prisoner chiefs.[13]

No sooner had the women and children been given up than the Comanche warriors began to make destructive forays into Texas. However, a ray of hope and encouragement was to be seen in the fact that the chiefs began to bring in to the agents the horses which their young renegade kinsmen had stolen. The indefatigable Horse's Back did not allow his weakened body to prevent his carrying on his missionary activities among the wild bands. On one occasion, while suffering from hemorrhage of the lungs, he left his bed in order to visit a Kwahadi camp and urge those Indians to surrender their stolen stock.[14] Some of the wildest chiefs like Red Food, Quĕrts-quĭp, Black Beard, and Black Duck brought in and gave up stolen horses and a few prisoners. This wholesome conduct gave Haworth much encouragement, especially, as he said, when "I reflect that it has been brought about without a threat being made, simply kind talk and appeals to their better nature."[15]

This year some of the Comanches even farmed a little, or rather sent their women into the field to represent them there. Haworth thought that the Kiowas had not raided any at all up to August 30, the date of his annual report. Furthermore, these Indians had treated kindly the Quaker teacher, Thomas C. Battey, who had tried to establish a school among them. Battey found it impossible to accomplish anything in the way of maintaining a school among the Kiowas, however, because of the nomadic habits of the Indians and their skepticism about the benefits to be derived from schooling.[16]

But the Kiowa braves and their Comanche allies became very restive during August and September because of the failure of the United States government to redeem its promise by releasing Satanta and Big Tree. Governor Davis was determined to make the most of his control of these noted warriors, and refused to give them up except on conditions which the president could not comply with.[17] Finally Davis brought the chiefs under guard to Fort Sill, where a sort of three-cornered council was held, Davis and the Indians taking opposite positions, while the agent and the commissioner of Indian Affairs worked frantically to bring them to some common understanding. At last the governor agreed to give up the prisoners on the promise that the United States would return them or chiefs of equal rank to him whenever it should appear that the Kiowas had been raiding in Texas; and that the agents would make rollcalls of the Kiowa tribe at such short intervals as would make it impossible for the warriors to go as far away as Texas without detection. It seems that the Kiowas themselves accepted these terms. Thus Satanta and Big Tree were released on parole, and the grievances of the Kiowa tribe were allayed for the time. Subsequent events proved that this was unwise.

The most serious demand pertained to the Comanches. Most of the raids during the preceding summer had been charged to them, and the commissioner had to agree to compel that tribe to surrender five of the leading raiders. When this demand was made known to them, they naturally inquired which five it should be. Would the governor and agents point them out? Naturally neither the commissioner nor the agents nor governor could do this. One Indian in war paint looked very much like any other. An Indian caught raiding never lived to be identified later, while one who escaped left little evidence of guilt.[18]

Though the Comanches would not surrender the raiding Indians, they offered to restore the horses and mules they had stolen, and promised, as was their custom, not to depredate in the future. When the governor refused to be satisfied with this measure, it was agreed that a chief and a party of young men should accompany a cavalry force into Texas in search of marauders. This was done, with results quite as negligible as might have been expected. Probably the savages could not have apprehended the raiders had they wanted to. The old chiefs might berate their warriors about these offenses; but the time had not yet come when they were willing to apprehend them and turn them over to the military for imprisonment, a punishment which to them was worse than death. The Comanche's sense of loyalty was outraged at such a thought. This was not his "road."

If the disposition of the Kiowas was not improved by the release of Satanta and Big Tree, the condition of the Comanches was certainly made no better by the terms imposed upon them. The demand that they give up five raiders alarmed them. There was no way of selecting the five who should be given up, and consequently all the friendly chiefs could do was to hover about the agency and give repeated assurances of their friendliness, while the wilder ones drew away waiting for the government to play its hand. Obviously at the first show of force, they would break camp and flee to the plains.

Agent Haworth was likewise in doubt about what policy he should pursue toward the Comanches. The commissioner of Indian Affairs had held up their annuity goods pending the outcome of the efforts to apprehend the Comanche raiders. Should the agent continue to hold these goods, or should he release them to the Indians on the theory that his wards had done the best they could to comply with the demands? Neither the Indians nor the agent knew what steps the government would next take. Then came instructions from Washington that the agent should withhold not only the annuity goods, but should begin the withholding of rations at the end of ten days unless the five (or some five) raiding warriors had been given up. If at the end of the time allowed, the warriors had not been delivered up, the Indians should be turned over to the military.[19]

The plight of the friendly chiefs was pitiable. Cheevers, who had always maintained a friendly attitude towards the whites and who had led the party that went out in search of the raiders, said, "I have tried very hard to do right, have done everything I can to get my people to do as Washington asked us to, and only a few have done wrong and they are now far out on the plains, we can't catch them, let us try as hard as we may, if the soldiers should kill them, we would not cry or care, but Washington must be crazy to want to kill all the Comanches because a few have done wrong."[20] Horse's Back told Haworth that he was old and sick and could not fight or run. He would stay close to the agency, even if he was going to be attacked and killed.

But now the Quakers took a hand. On hearing of the proposed drastic action, the Washington branch of the executive committee of the Orthodox Friends hastened to the capitol and protested at this proposed action which they considered unjust and unduly harsh. The officials of the Indian administration reconsidered, revoked the order about the goods and rations, and ordered the continuation of rations and the delivery of three-fourths of the annuity goods on condition that the Comanches bring in the stolen stock. Thus the government finally came to accept almost the identical terms which the Indians had proposed at the council in October preceding. "This vacillating on the part of the government," says Battey, "cannot have a very salutary effect on the minds of the Indians. Making a positive demand, refusing any other consideration, and then retreating from it, after threats of extreme measures, when it is seen they will not comply, is construed by them into an act of fear or weakness on the part of the government."[21]

But the reversal of the position came too late to avoid some of its evil consequences. The Indians had become frightened, and all save a few of the most dependable chiefs had fled for some distance from the agency. The Kiowas were also angered and alarmed at what they considered an injustice to their allies. However, as soon as word concerning the reversal of the extreme regulations went out, the Indians gradually became quiet and returned to the vicinity of the agency. Haworth held a council with the Comanches, at which the terms of the new agreement were made clear and the obligations of each side explained. The Indians agreed to give up their stolen horses and mules, a matter that must have seemed to them to be quite a concession in view of the fact that over two hundred head of their own stock had been stolen by white desperadoes since the council in October preceding.[22]

THE WAR PROPHET

During the winter of 1873–1874, the Comanches renewed their raids into Texas. The soldiers and rangers in that state dealt with them severely. One party suffered a loss of some twenty or more killed, losing nine braves and two squaws at the hands of Lieutenant Hudson near Fort Duncan, and later, on their way back to the agency, suffering about the same loss to Lieutenant-colonel Buell, near the Double mountains of the Brazos.[23] Furthermore, as the spring advanced, conditions at the agency grew worse. Torrential rains interfered with the freight service so that once again, at a most critical time, the agent had to apologize for issuing half rations. The Indians at the agency became unruly and began the wanton killing of beeves, and at all the agencies in the South Plains it was necessary that special guards be placed.[24] The Cheyennes also became troublesome. In the early spring depredations were committed along Medicine Lodge creek, in Kansas, with which they were charged,[25] and a little later a party of them moved down into the Comanche country and invited the Comanches and Kiowas to join them in a raid against Texas. Haworth reported that his Indians were well armed with new pistols and guns and a very large amount of ammunition, which had been sold to them in violation of law by the Cheyenne and Wichita traders.[26]

Then, when conditions were already alarming, the Comanches conceived the idea of holding a tribal medicine dance, similar to the annual ceremony of the Kiowas. This was a new thing for the Comanches, and law-abiding chiefs like Horse's Back felt that it portended evil.[27] This new movement was inspired by a young medicine man, named Ĩ'sätaí. This young brave could accomplish wonders. He had at times ascended above the clouds and conversed with the "Great Spirit;" he had raised the dead; he could control the elements and send the lightning and hail upon his enemies. In warfare he was invincible, for he had in the presence of several Comanches belched forth a wagonload of cartridges at one time and had swallowed them again. Also, when this prophet fought in a battle, the bullets of the enemy fell harmlessly from their gun muzzles to the ground. He was both a weather prophet and an astronomer, for he predicted that the comet that was then attracting attention would disappear within five days and that a drought would come during the summer following. In both matters his prophecy did not fail.[28]

Now this was a gospel to appeal to restless young braves who were finding the white man's road monotonous. But the Comanche prophet preached also a social and political gospel even more forceful than this. He explained that the "Great Spirit" had pointed out to him the fact that the Caddoes, Wichitas, and other docile Indians were "going down hill fast" in both goods and population, and becoming more miserable every day. If the Comanches continued to follow this road and adopt the habits of the whites, they too would go the way of these miserable, dependent Indians about the reservation. If they wished to be prosperous and powerful again as they had been in the good old days, they must go to war and kill off all the white people they could. This warlike message was in perfect harmony with the sentiment of the evil-disposed element among the nation, and it was easy to form a war party.[29]

The Last Wars 191

Hence, the call for a Comanche medicine dance and celebration was widely heralded, and when the tribesmen assembled in May at a point on Red river near the agency boundary, every band was represented, several of them by almost one hundred per cent of their people. The Comanches as a tribe had never been united. In historic times there had never been a general tribal council; there had never been a head-chief of all the tribe; each band or division had determined its own policy, and sometimes there was very little unity in the various bands. But now a new force was at work; here was a social and religious gospel that appealed to every Comanche's sense of patriotism. The great chiefs of the past had never been able to bring the scattered threads of the tribe together, but now a youthful warrior was about to accomplish that. The unequal contest with the whites had driven the braves to desperation, but had not entirely broken their spirit. For the time, at least, the forces of coherence were powerful, and it seemed that the whole tribe was about to enter into a war as crusaders under the banner of one who had conversed with the "Great Spirit" and who was strong enough to defeat their hated enemies and save them from dependency on a government they despised.

Even before the ceremonies proper had begun, some of the young men were reported to be riding about the camps in war paint, calling for volunteers.[30] Evidently the council was to be given a martial tone.

Unfortunately, we do not have a satisfactory account of the proceedings at the medicine dance. It is very likely that the ceremonies were adaptations of those used by the Kiowas in their annual ceremony, which the Comanches had so often watched. From the meager reports that came through, brought by Indians who left the celebration, it is evident that the councils were prolonged, and that there was anything but harmony in their deliberations. Early in June a good many of the Indians came back to the agency. They had gone to the gathering out of curiosity, not realizing that the council would be dominated by the war party. One of these, Quĕrts-quĭp, the Yamparika, reported that "they have a great many hearts—would make up their minds at night for one thing and get up in the morning entirely changed . . ." He added that whiskey, furnished by the Mexican traders, was making them drunk and adding to the confusion.[31] The hostile elements did all they could to prevent those peacefully disposed from leaving, even going so far as to kill, or threaten to kill, their horses. Nevertheless, most of the Penatekas, Horse's Back's Nokonies, and many of the Yamparikas, with the more sensible members of the other bands, managed to get away from their mad kinsmen and make their way in to the agency.[32]

It seems that at first the cry of the war party had been to make an attack on the Tonkawa Indians in Texas as the opening campaign of their war. These Indians had acted as scouts and had aided the soldiers in many campaigns in which Comanche blood had been spilled. Even as late as the winter preceding they had aided Lieutenant-colonel Buell at the Double mountains where some ten Comanches had been killed. What could be more fitting than that the war should begin with an attack on these traitors to their own race? But the Tonkawas were located dangerously close to Fort Griffin, and the Comanches may have learned that their plans to attack these Indians had been revealed to the commander of that post. At any rate, they determined to make the opening stroke of their war an attack against an enemy in the opposite direction, an enemy far more destructive than the score or two of Tonkawa braves that maintained a miserable existence gathering crumbs about the military posts in Texas. This other enemy was the buffalo hunters.

It has already been observed that for decades past the plains Indians had suffered from inroads on their game by both white and Indian hunters.[33] But about 1870 the commercial interest in buffalo hides revived remarkably, and for a few years became the major industry of the plains. Hide-buyers from the east came to Hays City, Kansas, and later to Dodge City, Kansas, and Fort Griffin, Texas, and other towns near the buffalo range, and offered tempting prices for the hides of the great shaggy beasts. At first one dollar for cowhides and two dollars for bullhides was the current price, but soon these amounts were doubled. Then commercial hunters, armed with the latest improved long-range rifles, entered the plains and wrought havoc with the Indians' "cattle." Superb marksmen did the killing, and their companions, the "skinners," stripped off the hides and left the carcasses on the plains to rot or be devoured by wolves and vultures. Incidentally, it may be added that the bones of these great beasts were, in many regions, gathered up a decade later and sold to some advantage to the producers of commercial fertilizers. Every day brought its kill and reduced the herds by thousands.[34]

The Indians well understood the significance of this old business which had suddenly revived and taken on such gigantic proportions. Kicking Bird said:

> ... The buffalo was their money their only resource with which to buy what they needed and did not receive from the government. The robes they could prepare and trade. They loved them just as the white man does his money, and just as it made a white man's heart feel to have his money carried away, so it made them feel to see others killing and stealing their buffalo which were their cattle given them by the Great Father above to furnish them meat to eat and means to get things to wear...[35]

Now "Washington" seemed to be doing nothing to stop this destruction, and the Comanches, aided by their allies, the Cheyennes, who had remained near during the medicine ceremonies of the Comanches, determined to try

Medicine Bluffs Pathway, near Fort Sill, Indian Territory

Medicine Bluffs Pathway, near Fort Sill, Indian Territory

their hand at putting an end to it. Here was a wonderful opportunity for their new prophet to demonstrate his power in a cause dear to every plains Indian's heart—protecting their "cattle," which the "Great Spirit" had furnished them.

The country north of the Arkansas soon became depleted of buffalo, and the hunters pushed south into the Panhandle of Texas. The Arkansas river, or at most the Cimarron, had been regarded by the Indians as the "dead line," south of which no hunter should go, and the United States army maintained a feeble patrol to aid the savages in keeping out intruders.[36] However, by the summer of 1874, a number of hunters had entered the Texas Panhandle and had established headquarters near the ruins of Bent's old adobe buildings.[37] Hence, it was towards this new settlement that the Comanches and Cheyennes turned their war ponies. They were led by the young war chief, Quanah, and urged on by the prophet. It has been stated that there were seven hundred warriors in the attacking party[38]—probably an exaggeration. Soon after the engagement, the Indians informed certain white frontiersmen that they had two hundred or two hundred fifty men.[39] The accounts generally state that the party was composed of Comanches, Cheyennes, and Kiowas. But the Kiowas had not yet finished their annual medicine dance, and it is not likely that many of their warriors would have absented themselves from that ceremony.[40]

The Indians attacked the trading post on the morning of June 27, just before daylight. Indian alarms had been spread throughout the Panhandle region, which accounts for the unusually large number of men at the settlement—twenty-eight men and one woman.[41] The white men had no organization, and had not posted a sentry. Most of them had made their beds outside on the ground. Because of some noise in one of the buildings, possibly the cracking of a cottonwood ridge pole, several of the men were aroused, and were up and dressed at the time of the attack.[42] The savages galloped up in a reckless charge, and almost overwhelmed the white men before they could find protection in the buildings and organize for defense. But the Indians lost the fight when they failed to destroy their adversaries in the initial attack. As the fight continued, the long-range buffalo guns in the hands of the hunters took a heavy toll of life; the charges became less frequent, and after each the Indians fell farther and farther back, so that the attack became a poorly-organized siege. Then the Indians, in their efforts to remove their dead and wounded, would come within range occasionally, and their losses continued.

The warriors were directed by bugle calls until their bugler was killed late in the afternoon of the first day's fight. These tactics, which had been copied from the United States army, proved to be unfortunate for the Indians since the calls were understood by the hunters and gave them notice of the maneuver that was coming.[43]

The first day saw most of the fighting, and when the battle had practically ceased by four o'clock, three of the white men had been killed and the bodies of thirteen Indians were left near the buildings.[44] The Indians hung around for several days, but other buffalo hunters continued to come in to the post, and the reds did not dare to make another attack.

The prophet's medicine had failed. His horse had been shot in the encounter, and he was with difficulty rescued by some Cheyenne braves.[45] Some of the braves suggested that he ought to be flogged, but with that superb tolerance Indians could so often exercise, most of the warriors seemed to think that his humiliation was sufficient punishment. But Ĩ'sätaí was not cast down. He had his excuse. He explained that on the way to Adobe Walls a Cheyenne Indian had killed and skinned a skunk, and this indiscretion had broken the charm![46]

The breaking up of the settlement at Adobe Walls resulted only in checking for a short while the killing of the bison. The hunters were soon back in the Texas Panhandle, and the lucrative business went on. The wholesale destruction tended to decimate the herds in the region north of the Canadian river, and the remaining beasts sought safety in the South Plains area and the prairie country to the east. Then for a while Fort Griffin, Texas, vied with Dodge City, Kansas, as a frontier supply and hide-marketing point, and the "great kill" went on. By 1881 the hunting was over, and the bison almost extinct.

The Indians did not stop after their attack on Adobe Walls. Imbued with the war spirit, the bands of the braves plundered and killed in many places. Near Buffalo Springs, about fifty miles north of the Cheyenne agency, a party of Cheyennes and Comanches attacked and burned a train of three wagons, a train that was moving goods to be consumed by the Comanches themselves at their agency. The four men in charge of the train were killed. Early in July the Cheyennes and Comanches raided through the ranch country of southern Colorado and killed a number of persons, estimated at from thirty to sixty.[47] So threatening were the Comanches and Cheyennes in the vicinity of the Cheyenne and Arapaho agency that Agent John D. Miles was "utterly stampeded," and called frantically for help.[48] These Indians then moved against the settlements in the vicinity of Sun City and Medicine Lodge, Kansas, killed several persons, and forced the people of that frontier to "fort up" in approved Texas fashion.[49] The Indians did not neglect the Texas settlements, but continued their destructive raids in that direction.[50]

As reports of these acts of violence came in to Fort Sill, it became evident that the army would have to be used against the recalcitrants. Now once again arose the difficult problem of distinguishing between the hostile and friendly Indians, of separating the sheep from the goats. On July 17, Lieutenant-colonel Davidson, in command at Fort Sill, issued an order to all friendly Indians to place their camps on the east side of Cache creek.[51] On the following day the commissioner of Indian Affairs, Edward P. Smith, issued orders for the governance of the Indians and their agents, which fit hand-in-glove with the policy already launched by the military. Haworth sent word to the different Comanche, Kiowa, and Apache bands that they must move in to the east side of Cache creek which was to be known as a "land of peace and not of trouble." The friendly chiefs like Iron Mountain, Howeah, and Cheevers, as well as some of those more doubtful like He Bear,[52] complied with the order. Most of the Kiowas likewise came in. But some of both tribes became alarmed and refused to come near the agency. Also, the Cheyennes were reported as doing all they could to keep the other tribes from complying, even to the extent of shooting some of their horses.[53] Then the situation was made desperate when someone, probably malicious Indians, burned the grass near the agency so that the friendly Indians could not find subsistence for their stock. Furthermore, the Kiowas, because of their traditional superstition, objected to being enrolled and numbered, and became quite insolent.[54]

Lieutenant-colonel J. W. Davidson set August 3 as the day for closing the rolls, and at that time only 173 Kiowa braves, 108 Apaches, and 83 Comanches had been enrolled. Thus, many Kiowas and a large majority of the Comanches failed to register on time, and the military regarded them henceforth as enemies. Then the army officers drew up a list of the different bands they considered hostile and asked Haworth to approve it. This the agent refused to do.[55] He felt that the failure of Indians to register was caused by ignorance or timidity, while the army officers regarded it as defiance. The traditional lack of harmony between the military and the Indian agents was exemplified anew at a time when it was of vital importance that the white men maintain a uniformly consistent attitude. The military insisted that the Indians comply rigidly with the order requiring them to stay on the east side of Cache creek near the agency, while Haworth declared that their stock would starve if this rule should be enforced.

The premature closing of the rolls left some of the Comanche bands in a serious predicament. They were not willing to go in to Fort Sill and surrender as prisoners of war, and they did not wish to remain out on the prairies where they would be attacked by the troops as hostiles. Red Food, with a band of sixty lodges of Nokonies, was in this group, and in seeking protection he had gone north with his people to the Wichita agency and encamped among the friendly Indians, hoping to avoid arrest or attack from the troops until the storm should blow over. When report of the presence of the band reached Davidson, he took four companies of cavalry and went at once to demand that they surrender as prisoners of war. Red Food, on the advice of the Penatekas, agreed to a number of demands of the soldiers, including that of surrendering his firearms, but balked on the point of surrendering bows and arrows. While the parley was in progress, the chief gave a whoop and dashed away at a gallop.[56] This act was interpreted as an effort to run away. He was fired upon and wounded, but made his escape for the time being. It was issue day at the Wichita agency, and there were many Indians in the vicinity. Davidson's cavalry, assisted by a company of infantry stationed at the agency, attacked the Nokonies and put them to flight. It happened that a number of Kiowas, some of whom had registered at their agency and had left without permission, and others who had not registered, were in the neighborhood. Chief Lone Wolf, now regarded as an outlaw, was their leader.[57] These Kiowas joined the Comanches in resisting the soldiers, and general fighting ensued. The soldiers were seriously handicapped in being unable to tell hostile Indians from friendly ones. The fighting in the vicinity of the reservation lasted two days and did not end until many of the Indians had fled and aligned themselves openly on the side of the hostiles. The conclusion seems justifiable that the fighting at the Wichita agency started as the result of an incident of the moment, and was not premeditated.[58]

When news of the fight at the Wichita agency reached Fort Sill, a general stampede seemed to be unavoidable. Many of the Indians complied with Davidson's terms of surrender, but others joined the wild bands of their kinsmen who had never enrolled or surrendered. Probably one half of the Comanche, Kiowa, and Cheyenne tribes was openly hostile during the early autumn of 1874.[59]

The registration and concentration policy had been adopted to enable the agents and the army to distinguish the Indians genuinely friendly from those doubtful or hostile; as it turned out, the plan made a majority of the savages enemies of the government. The military based their actions on instructions from the commissioner of Indian Affairs, and laid to him the responsibility for the costly war that followed.[60] Concerning the wisdom of the severe policy, the Quakers were divided. William Nicholson, a member of the executive committee of Orthodox Friends, expressed the view which evidently governed the Indian department when he said: "My confidence in our present plan of management is completely shaken—in fact, it never has been strong—I mean so far as the wild Indians are concerned. I believe the proper field for *our work* is amongst Indians that are *located*, and unless the rovers are located, the influences necessary to civilization cannot be brought to bear upon them." On the other hand, Superintendent Hoag and his staff opposed the war, and expressed resentment that their efforts to prevent it or make it less severe were defeated by the military who received their instructions from the commissioner of Indian Affairs. Hoag believed that the Indians were more sinned against than sinning, and excused the savages because of repeated depredations on their stock by Texas thieves and the inroads of whiskey peddlers and buffalo hunters. He thought that some of the renegade warriors would have to be punished, but felt that a general Indian war was not necessary.[61]

No doubt the army men, by their impatience and severity, drove a number of friendly and comparatively law-abiding Indians into the camp of the hostiles; for the United States army was never noted for its gentleness in these matters. On the other hand, Hoag's persistence in refusing to recognize that the Indians would have to be punished and that the Quaker policy, as applied to the roving bands, had been a failure, was either due to ignorance, stupidity, or stubbornness. During the five years the Quakers had been in charge of these Indians, they had utterly failed to check the depredations of the reckless young warriors. The great majority of the red men were peaceful and friendly; but the renegade element had escaped almost entirely the Quaker influence. Many of the warriors were just as lawless, just as ignorant, just as insolent, and just as far from the white man's road as when Tatum succeeded General Hazen as their agent in June, 1869. As long as these warriors were running at large, mixing and mingling with the other Indians, coming and going at will and seducing and making depredators out of the boys as they approached manhood, the tribes as a whole could never make much progress.

THE END OF THE WAR TRAIL

It has already been observed that by mid-summer of 1874, most of the Cheyennes and many of the Comanches and Kiowas were at war. Troops were sent against them early in the season, but the fact that the soldiers could not attack the Indians on their reservations without the consent of the agents prevented effective punishment. However, when the interior department gave its assent in July, and agreed that the troops might attack the Indians on their own territory if necessary, the military began to act in earnest. The Quaker agents winced at this, but the officers of the Indian service at Washington encouraged the soldiers to subdue the Indians wherever they were offering resistance to constituted authority.

From all sides troops poured into the Comanche and Kiowa range like winds rush into an area of low pressure. Colonel Nelson A. Miles moved south from Camp Supply; Major Price moved east from Fort Union; another force watched the Cheyenne and Arapaho agency to punish hostiles who might seek safety there; Davidson operated to the west from Fort Sill; Colonel Buell pushed up Red river; and still farther to the south and west, the veteran Mackenzie operated along his old haunts, the "Fresh Water Fork of the Brazos."[62] The purpose was to kill or punish the savages and drive them in to the reservation.

Never before had the Indians contended with such a foe. The troops were commanded by seasoned plainsmen, and both white and Indian scouts trailed the hostiles and advised the army officers in their difficult undertakings. The campaign was a fitting episode to the close of Indian wars on the South Plains. Both the Indians and the soldiers exerted themselves manfully. There was no rest for either side; and through the stifling heat of August and September on into the season of "northers," when the icy winds chilled the soldiers and their savage foes to the bone, the war was pushed relentlessly.

The details of the campaign or campaigns are difficult to follow. When sketched on a map, the trails of the different commands cross and recross each other like the tracks of many lizards in the sand.[63] Miles struck the Indians on the Washita, pursued them for a week, and on August 30 attacked them near Red river and chased them into Tule Canyon. These were principally Cheyennes, and were reported as numbering 250 warriors. Between the Sweetwater creek of Red river and the Washita, Major Price met and defeated some 150 Indians on September 12. September 24–26 Mackenzie put to flight a large Indian village in the Palo Duro Canyon, capturing and killing a large number of their horses in order that they might not be stampeded and retaken.[64]

The savages did not always fight on the defensive, as the following letter, written by an officer in charge of Miles's supply train, shows:

> In the field near the Washita river
> 3 o'clock p.m., September 10, 1874

Commanding Officer
Camp Supply

Sir: I have the honor to report that I am coralled by the Comanches, two miles north of the Washita, on Gen'l. Miles' trail. We have been engaged since yesterday morning, having moved since the first firing, about 12 miles. I consider it injudicious to attempt to proceed further, in view of the importance of my train, and the broken ground ahead. It was nearly stampeded yesterday. Communication with General Miles is closed. My scout very probably will not return.

Lt. Lewis is dangerously wounded through the knee, and I think will die if he has no medical assistance. The Assistant-wagoner McCoy is mortally wounded I fear. Sergeant DeArmon, Co. 1, 5th Infantry, is killed; a dozen mules [men ?] are disabled.

I think I may properly ask quick aid, especially for Lt. Lewis, a most valuable officer. I have only a small pool of rain water for the men, which will dry up today. I estimate the Indians vaguely at several hundred (as Lieut. Baldwin did) whom we have punished somewhat.

Scout Marshall, who left Camp Supply, I am told, has not reached me.

I have but twelve mounted men. West made a pretty charge with them yesterday.

>Very respectfully, Your obedient servant,
>W. Lyman, Captain, 5th Infantry, Commdg. Train Guard[65]

It may be added that the bearer of this message, William F. Schmalsle, was pursued by the Indians as he dashed through their lines in his endeavor to reach Camp Supply, but by desperate riding, he kept ahead of his pursuers until he ran into a great buffalo herd, which obliterated his horse's tracks. After riding until his horse was exhausted, he managed to reach the post on foot. Aid was sent immediately, and arrived in time to relieve the beleaguered party. The wound resulted in the permanent disability of Lieutenant Lewis.[66]

On the day that the letter quoted above was written, Miles, from his position on McClellan's creek, sent scouts "Billie" Dixon and Amos Chapman, with four enlisted men, to Camp Supply. At sunrise on the second day, as the little party neared a divide between the Washita river and Gageby creek, they were surrounded by a large party of Comanche and Kiowa warriors. The white men managed to make their way to a buffalo wallow where, in spite of the fact that one was mortally and three others seriously wounded, they held off the Indians until relief came on the following day.[67]

Very few Indians were killed in these engagements, and virtually none of the braves were captured. However, their mounts and supplies were so depleted that they could not continue their existence on the plains, and as cold weather approached, the bands straggled in one by one. All were required to surrender unconditionally.

Woman's Heart, Satanta, and Big Tree of the Kiowas came in before cold weather, and surrendered at the Cheyenne agency. They had been outlawed from their own agency, and were returned to it in chains. Satanta was returned to the Texas penitentiary where, like an eagle caged, he wore himself out and committed suicide in 1878.

Of the Comanches, among the first to repent were Named Sun, the Yamparika, a chronic rover and disturber; Red Food, the Tanima, who with his Nokoni followers had started the trouble at the Wichita agency in August; Little Crow, son of the great Yamparika Ten Bears; and White Wolf, the Kotsoteka, one of the worst raiders of them all. Many of the hostiles stayed out during the winter of 1874–1875, but doubtless more from fear than because of any disposition to continue to resist the power of the United States. In February, Lone Wolf and his band of Kiowas came in. In early March a large number of Cheyennes surrendered at their agency. Then Shaking Hand, with 170 followers, was coaxed in to Fort Sill on the promise that he would be granted amnesty;[68] and early in the summer 407 Kwahadies surrendered, having been brought to the agency by Dr. J. J. Sturm, who had been sent to them by General Mackenzie. This last-named band brought in and gave up over fifteen hundred head of stock.[69] The warriors of all these parties were seized and imprisoned, but most of them were soon released. Among the first arrivals were a number of warriors charged with taking an active part in the raids. They included twenty-six Kiowas and nine Comanches, who were arrested and sent away to be confined at Fort Marion, Florida. Here everything possible was done for their training and advancement. They were returned to their people a few years later, and seem to have been cured of their disposition to make trouble. The late arrivals at the reservation, presumably the worst offenders, were not thus punished.

By mid-summer, 1875, a few small parties were still at large, and others occasionally stole away and stayed out for short periods of time; but the damage done by these small groups was negligible. An enrollment made on August 5 showed that there were 1076 Kiowas, 763 of whom were classed as "loyal," that is, had not participated in the wars of the preceding year, and 1597 Comanches, 938 of whom had been hostile during the troubles of 1875.[70] It was estimated that about fifty Comanches were still at large, and those who were sent to Florida were not counted. The total adult male population of the tribes, counting the Comanches still not enrolled, did not much exceed seven hundred. They were not numerous, but they had been able to bring death and terror to a large area. These Indians never again participated in an outbreak, nor was there henceforth any organized effort to defy the authority of the government. Raiding had practically ceased by the close of 1875. The Indians could not stay out in large parties without provoking a renewal of the wretched wars of the year before. The buffalo hunters were making the plains dangerous for them, and hunting there was becoming unprofitable; and if the braves followed their old trails to Texas, the rangers were sure to pounce upon them.[71]

Colonel Mackenzie sold the horses which the Indians gave up, and purchased for them cattle and sheep with the money. The chiefs began to arrest and deliver to the agent Indian offenders, lest the whole tribe be made to suffer for the sins of a few. They placed their children in schools, and the men went to the fields and worked. Verily, though only a remnant, they were now on the white man's road.

The account of the Comanches since their confinement on the reservation is the story of development from the status of "blanket Indians" to that of self-sustaining citizens who live much like their white neighbors.[72] How the braves gave up the lance and rifle for the plow, and the women put away the awl and sinew for the needle and thread, how certain savage customs and taboos were slowly forgotten or left off, how Quanah, He Bear, Named Sun, and others laid aside the war bonnet and taught their people the ways of peace—all this would represent within itself an extensive study and cannot be given in this book.

The year 1875 is one of sharp transition in the history of the Comanches, and marks the end of their influence as a frontier factor of significance. At this point time finished a chapter and turned a page. No longer were these Indians a retarding element; instead of holding back the stream of settlement, they had now become a part of it. For a century and a half they had resisted the efforts of white men to take their country and impose civilization upon them. They were finally defeated in the unequal conflict, but what a magnificent fight they made! When the summer grass made the ponies sleek and frisky, the veterans must have felt a mighty urge to roam again over the sea of grass that was the *Llano Estacado*, or take a few more horses from the San Saba. About the reservation campfires these graduates of the war trail no doubt tempted many a youth with tales of war and plunder done in the heroic days before the Comanches gave up the trail of the buffalo for that of the cow. Mere memories and dreams; times like these could never return. But even yet, if we look by the light of an August moon across a Texas prairie dotted here and there by gnarled mesquite and mottes of scrubby oak, surely we shall see phantom warriors riding as of old—Comanches.

Notes

As in the main text, additional material from the
author's original manuscript is delineated
by single vertical rules.

CHAPTER ONE

1. For information concerning the Comanche language, I am indebted to Mr. Robert L. Boake of Anadarko, Oklahoma. Mr. Boake has traded with the Comanches for many years and is well acquainted with their language. Tah-vah-nah, a Comanche Indian, Anadarko, Oklahoma, kindly gave assistance.

2. James Mooney, "The Ghost-dance Religion and the Sioux outbreak of 1890," in *Fourteenth Annual Report* of the Bureau of American Ethnology, part II, 1043; Mooney, in bulletin 30 of the Bureau of American Ethnology, *Handbook of American Indians North of Mexico*, I, 327. This work, in two volumes, edited by Frederick Webb Hodge, will be cited hereafter as *Handbook of American Indians*, or *Handbook*.

It should be stated, however, that the term Ietan was more commonly applied to the Ute, another Shoshonean tribe. *Handbook*, synonymy.

3. Clark Wissler, *The American Indian*, 309, 409.

4. According to Mooney, who secured his information after the Indians had been on the reservation for a number of years, there were twelve or more of these. They were Detsanayuka or Nokoni; Ditsakana, Widyu, Yapa or Yamparika; Kewatsana; Kotsai; Kotsoteka; Kwahari or Kwahadi; Motsai; Pagatsu; Penateka or Penande; Pohoi (adopted Shoshoni); Tanima; Tenawa or Tenawit; Waaih and possibly others. *Handbook*, I, 328.

5. This dividing for long periods of time, and uniting for occasional short periods, was common among the plains Indians. Wissler, *The American Indian*, 160.

6. Robert H. Lowie, "Dances and Societies of the Plains Shoshone," in *Anthropological Papers of the Museum of Natural History*, XI, part X, 809–812. It is Lowie's conclusion that at a celebration which preceded a war of revenge, *nä'wap-in ä'r* it was called, the Crow dance was used by the Yamparikas, the Colt or Horse dance by the Kwahadies, and the Swift-fox dance by the Nokonies and Penatekas. The Buffalo dance was practiced by all of the divisions, but each band performed it separately.

7. Robert L. Boake to the writer, May 30, 1931.

8. From *pĕ'-näh* (honey or sugar), and *tĕth'-kä* (eater).

9. From *yampa*, a sweet root used for food, and *mäh-rĕth'-kŭn*, to eat.

10. W. P. Clark, *Indian Sign Language*, 118 ff.

The authorities state that the Comanches were driven southward before the advancing Sioux, Cheyenne, and Kiowa Indians. Mooney, "Calendar History of the Kiowa Indians," in *Fourteenth Annual Report* of the Bureau of American Ethnology, part I, 162; George Bird Grinnell, *The Fighting Cheyennes*, I ff., 32 ff.

It is my opinion that the Comanches moved into the South Plains in order to secure a more abundant supply of horses. The horse was introduced in America by the Spaniards, and all accounts indicate that these animals advanced into the Great Plains from the south. Hence, it seems probable that the Comanches came into possession of horses before their northern neighbors, the Kiowas, Cheyennes, and Sioux. It was natural that as soon as some of the warriors secured mounts and had felt the freedom and power that the mastery of the horse gave them, they would move towards a country where horses were more plentiful. Furthermore, there was no country in America better suited for nomadic, mounted Indians than the South Plains. I do not think the Comanches were driven into this country. On the contrary, it seems that they visited it, found that it was well suited to their mode of existence, and proceeded to fight for it and take it.

11. Alfred B. Thomas, "An Eighteenth Century Comanche Document," in *American Anthropologist*, XXXI, 290; and (by the same author) *Forgotten Frontiers, A Study of the Spanish Indian Policy of Don Juan Bautista de Anza*, 294, 295. Through these and other publications, all of which bear evidence of comprehensive and scholarly investigation, Dr. Thomas has made available a great deal of information about the Comanches and the New Mexico frontier.

12. From *kō-chō* (buffalo), and *tĕth'-kă* (eater).

13. James Mooney, "The Ghost-dance Religion and the Sioux outbreak of 1890," *op. cit.*

Robert L. Boake states that he never knew a Comanche to use the word nine. Instead they would use *sā'-er-mĭn* (ten) coupled with *a-wōō'-mĭn-nŏt* (nearly, or just under). Then when a chief, in whose name the word ten appeared, died, many of the older people would no longer use *sā'-er-mĭn*, but used instead *tō'-quet* (enough). So when an old Comanche calls for "enough" of a certain object, the traders know that he wants ten units of it.

14. There were two distinct Comanche bands with names very similar, the Tenawa and Tanima. The divisions were often confused by writers during the nineteenth century, and the names were sometimes written in such a way as to make it impossible to determine which band is referred to. According to the *Handbook of American Indians*, the Tenawas (from *tĕ'-năw*, down stream) were "practically exterminated in a battle with the Mexicans about 1845." It is difficult to reconcile this statement with the fact that references to the Tenawas are frequent after 1845. Some of the variations are Tenawish, Ta-ne-wa, Te-na-wa, Te-ne-mis, De-na-vi, Ta-ne-wah, Tan-nee-wish, Ten-en-e-ree, etc. There were no Tenawas left, however, when the Comanches went on the reservation in 1869, or else the division had been absorbed by other bands. There were a few Tanimas or Liver-eaters living at this time. See *Handbook*, II, 686, 728.

15. It is said that the original name of this band was Qua-he-hu-ke, meaning back-shade, so called because in their treeless country the only way to shade the face was to turn one's back to the sun. Clark, *Indian Sign Language*, 119.

16. The Yupes or Jupes were described as *gente de palo* (people of the timber). I am not able to identify this band positively, although I believe it was the division commonly referred to by Anglo-Americans as "Tenawish" (Tenawa). The Spaniards referred to the Yupes and Yamparikas as "western Comanches" who ranged in or near New Mexico, in contradistinction to the Kotsotekas or "eastern Comanches" who inhabited Texas. The Kotsotekas were well known in New Mexico also, however. In this connection see Report of Pedro de Nava, Chihuahua, July 23, 1799, *Provincias Internas*, tomo 12, *Archivo General y Publico*, Mexico, University of Texas transcripts; Mindinueta in the Junta at Chihuahua, June 6, 1778 (copy), Bexar Archives, University of Texas; Thomas, "An Eighteenth Century Comanche Document," *op. cit.*; Report of Butler and Lewis, August 8, 1846, Office of Indian Affairs, Misc., B 2738, Univ. Tex. photostat copy; "B" (David G. Burnet) in the Cincinnati *Literary Gazette*, May 8, 1824.

Concerning Tenewa and Tanima see footnote 14.

17. Thomas, *Forgotten Frontiers*, 325–327.

| Anza thought each Tipi represented about three warriors and from seven to eight women and children. During this year the Comanches were negotiating and celebrating a treaty of peace with the Spaniards. It is not to be understood that all this host of Indians came to the Spanish settlements at one time. |

18. *Ibid.*, 321–325.

| Besides the eight large *rancherias* Ortiz learned of other smaller ones which he did not visit. It may be, however, that some of those visited belonged to divisions other than the Kotsoteka. Ortiz states that at the smallest village he visited (thirty lodges) could be counted "nine hundred beasts of burden, with the item of five herds of mares, with young up to three years." |

19. W. P. Webb, *The Great Plains*, 68–84.

There is a tradition that many years ago the Comanches and Shoshonis, then belonging to the same tribe, were going north. Somewhere on the Platte river a dispute arose over the division of a bear and other game which had been killed, the Shoshonis refusing to divide according to the custom of the bands when on the march. The Comanches became incensed and turned south again, while the Shoshonis continued north. Hence Shoshoni in sign language is "snake that advanced," while Comanche is "snake that came back."

| 20. However, Dr. Webb (in the Great Plains, as cited) presents a convincing argument that the sign language of the Great Plains was developed not so much to serve as a means of communication between Indians who did not speak the same language as a means of transmitting information at great distances. That is, if all Indians had spoken the same language the sign language would have been developed just the same. |

21. Clark Wissler, *North American Indians of the Plains*, 149.

| Wissler's figures on the height of Indians are as follows:

Cheyenne, 68.7"	Crow, 68.1"	Blackfoot, 67.5"
Arapaho, 68.03"	Kiowa, 67.2"	Plains Ojibway, 67.8"
Dakota, 67.09"	Comanche, 66.06"	

22. For a general account of the characteristics of the plains tribes, see W. P. Webb, *The Great Plains*, 48 ff.; Clark Wissler, *The American Indian*, 218–222; Clark Wissler, *North American Indians of the Plains*.

23. George Bird Grinnell, *The Story of the Indian*, 57–64.

24. Bourgmont's journal is printed in Pierre Margry's *Découvertes et établissements des Français dans l'ouest et dans le sud de l'Amérique Septentrionale*, VI, 398–449.

| Bourgmont explains the absence of colts by the fact that riding the mares so hard in the buffalo chase caused abortions. No doubt they did raise colts at this time, or could have done so if it had been necessary. It was the practice of the Comanches to separate their breeding mares from their riding stock. I am disposed to believe that even at this early date they had these herds of mares and colts but that the Frenchman during his short visit with this Comanche band failed to see any of them. |

25. Clark Wissler, "The Influence of the Horse in the Development of Plains Culture," in *American Anthropologist*, new series, XVI, 1–25.

26. Theodore R. Davis, "The Buffalo Range," in *Harper's Magazine*, XXXVIII, 147 ff.

27. R. B. Marcy, *Exploration of the Red River of Louisiana, in the Year 1852*, 33 cong., I sess., House Ex. Doc. (no number), 98; Burnet, in Cincinnati *Literary Gazette*, May 8, 1824; George Catlin, *North American Indians*, II, sketch 172.

28. R. B. Marcy, *Thirty Years of Army Life on the Border*, 23.

29. R. B. Marcy, *The Exploration of the Red River of Louisiana*, 96, 97.

30. Catlin, *North American Indians*, II, 74; R. B. Marcy, *Thirty Years of Army Life on the Border*, 28.

31. Report of Alex B. Hasson, post surgeon at Fort Phantom Hill, 1852, in the *Texas State Gazette*, March 24, 1857; Henry R. Schoolcraft, *Information Respecting . . . the Indian Tribes of the United States*, I, 234; David G. Burnet, in Cincinnati *Literary Gazette*, May 22, 1824, 162.

32. Catlin, *op. cit.*, II, 83.

33. Schoolcraft, *op. cit.*, 234, 235. For an account of the dress of the plains tribes see Wissler, *Indians of the Plains*, 41–55.

34. Clinton L. Smith and Jeff D. Smith, *The Boy Captives*, 79.

35. *Ibid.*, 56; Thomas C. Battey, *The Life and Adventures of a Quaker Among the Indians*, 323; Herman Lehmann, *Nine Years Among the Indians, 1870–1879*, 206.

36. Marcy, *Exploration of the Red River of Louisiana*, 102.

37. Smith, *The Boy Captives*, 60. For other accounts of the Comanches' food, see Burnet's articles, *op. cit.*; Nelson Lee, *Three Years Among the Comanches*, 120 ff.; T. A. (Dot) Babb, *In the Bosom of the Comanches*, 132.

38. Domingo Cabello to the Commandant General, April 30, 1786 (copy), Bexar Archives. The letter is a report on the Comanche Indians.

39. Marcy, *Thirty Years of Army Life on the Border*, 49; see also Babb, *op. cit.*, 104; Lehmann, *op. cit.*, 177.

40. Thomas, *Forgotten Frontiers*, 313.

41. The practice was common among many plains and plateau tribes. Wissler, *The American Indian*, 77.

42. Report of a council held with the Comanche Indians by Colonel L. H. Williams, at Trading House, post no. 2, November 23, 1845, Republic of Texas Indian Papers, Texas State Library, Austin; L. H. Williams to T. J. Western, June 23, 1845, *ibid.*; Ferdinand Roemer, *Texas*, 326, 327.

| The records show that chiefs Buffalo Hump and Old Owl each lost a wife through desertion, these women apparently running away from the band for no other purpose than to escape their husbands. The German scientist, Roemer, tells of an old Indian in the Penateka camp whose wife ran away with a war party Mexico bound. With tears in his eyes the old Comanche reported his predicament to the chiefs. They thought this is a good joke and laughed heartily, but advised him to take some young men and go in pursuit of his erring spouse and her consort. This the old Indian did. He not only recovered his wife but brought back two mules also which he had taken from him at the time they ran away with his wife. This procedure

suggests that tribal authority was on the old man's side and that his efforts to recover his wife were backed by a little more sanction than his own strength. When Roemer asked him why he did not cut off his wife's nose according to Comanche law and custom he replied in effect that he was so glad to recover her he was no longer angry with her. Ferdinand Roemer, *Texas* (Bonn, 1849) pp. 326, 7. |

43. Noah Smithwick, *The Evolution of a State*, 181. Smithwick dictated his account at ninety, but his book bears evidence of genuineness and accuracy.

44. See pp. 78 ff.

45. The only case I know of is that of Quanah, son of Nokoni and Cynthia Ann Parker. Both Nokoni and Quanah were head-chiefs.

46. A number of chiefs, representing three great Comanche divisions, named Chief Ecueracapa their "attorney general" to make peace with the Spanish in New Mexico in 1786. Thomas, "An Eighteenth Century Comanche Document," *op. cit.*

47. Robert S. Neighbors, in Schoolcraft, *op. cit.*, II, 130.

48. Lowie, *op. cit.*, 810; Roemer, *Texas*, 325; Burnet, in Cincinnati *Literary Gazette*, June 5, 1824, 177; Schoolcraft, *op. cit.*, V, 684.

49. Lowie, *op. cit.*, 812. Lowie's informants mentioned certain "dauntless men." The Comanche captive, Clinton Smith, states that a certain chief "wore the black star on his breast indicating bravery." *The Boy Captives*, 129.

See also Thomas, *Forgotten Frontiers*, 324 and editorial note 117, where a tally sheet is reproduced showing a war party of Comanches arranged apparently according to their status in the military societies of the tribe.

50. *Nine Years with the Indians*, 150, 151. In this connection see also Smith, *The Boy Captives*, 45.

51. *Ibid.*, 48, 126; Lowie, *op. cit.*, 811; Babb, *In the Bosom of the Comanches*, 43.

52. *Ibid.*, 108, 110; Dodge, *Our Wild Indians*, 172; Marcy, *Thirty Years of Army Life on the Border*, 56 ff.; W. B. Parker, *Notes Taken during the Expedition through Unexplored Texas*, 192.

53. E. Lamberg, at San Carlos, September 27, 1851, to the Minister of War and Marine, *Boletin de la Sociedad Mexicana de Geografia y Estadistica*, III, 22; Smithwick, *The Evolution of a State*, 180. This practice of rendering obeisance to the sun was common among the plains tribes. See George Bird Grinnell, *The Cheyenne Indians*, I, 74, 76.

54. Wm. Bollaert, "Observations on the Indian Tribes in Texas," in *Journal* of the Ethnological Society of London, II, 268.

55. Neighbors, "The Na-ü-ni, or Comanches of Texas," in Schoolcraft, *op. cit.*, II, 127. See also W. B. Parker, "Manners, Customs and History of the Indians of Southwestern Texas," in *ibid.*, V, 684, 685.

56. I have not given any consideration to the peyote feasts or celebrations engaged in by the Comanches and neighboring tribes at the present time. During the summer of 1928 I attended one of these celebrations given under the auspices of the Native American Church, near Lawton, Oklahoma. The communicants assemble in a tepee and, by the light of a small fire, partake of the downy center or "button" of a small cactus, *Anhalonium* or *Lophophora* (Coulter), commonly called peyote. Mooney (*Handbook*, II, 237) states that the drug produces "a sort of spiritual exaltation differing entirely from that produced by any other known drug, and apparently without any reaction." Others contend that the drug is destructive in both its physical and moral effects on those who use it. In the ceremony that I observed, there was nothing whatever unseemly or disgusting, the whole affair being one of song, prayer, and quiet contemplation.

It seems to me, however, that the peyote service or celebration cannot be regarded as a part of the Comanche religion proper. It is true that certain Indians in northern Mexico partook of this drug as early as the middle years of the eighteenth century, and it may be that their ancestors had used it from time immemorial. But there is no reference to religious practices of this kind among the Comanche Indians in Texas who were settled on a reservation in that state from 1855 to 1859. Surely, if the Comanches had practiced the cult at this time, some notice would have been taken of the fact, and it seems reasonable to conclude also that if the use of the drug had been common among the Comanches, some of these Penatekas would have used it. The practice first attracted the attention of the Indian agents a short while after the Comanches had been finally confined on their reservation near Fort Sill, Indian Territory, about 1875. I think the Comanches, Kiowas, Cheyennes, and other South Plains Indians acquired the practice from the Indians of Mexico, and that its use among the Comanches and their neighbors is comparatively recent. As practiced among the Indians at the present time, the peyote celebration represents a combination of Christianity and various Indian ceremonies and concepts.

57. Domingo Cabello to the Commandant General (copy), April 30, 1786, Bexar Archives.

| "Some Comanches worship a pet crow—some a deer skin, with the sun and moon pictured on it. The band that I was with, worshipped an eagle's wing."—The Rachel Plummer Narrative (reprint of 1962), p. 111. |

58. Burnet, in Cincinnati *Literary Gazette, op. cit.*, 162.

59. *Ibid.*, 162. On taboos, see also Battey, *A Quaker Among the Indians*, 333; Smith, *The Boy Captives*, 66; E. Lamberg, *op. cit.*

60. Burnet, in Schoolcraft, *op. cit.*, 233.

61. Smith, *op. cit.*, 108. The prickly pear poultice is still a home remedy.

62. Burnet, in Schoolcraft, *op. cit.*, 234; Battey, *op. cit.*, 148, 149.

63. Battey, *op. cit.*, 143.

64. In this connection, see Marcy, *Thirty Years of Army Life on the Border*, 56; Babb, *In the Bosom of the Comanches*, 144; Bollaert, *op. cit.*, 271.

65. Smith, *The Boy Captives*, 132, 162, 170.

66. Dodge, *Our Wild Indians*, 329, 330.

67. *Ibid.*, 341, 342.

| Marcy quotes the celebrated Delaware guide, Black Beaver, to the effect that on one occasion the Kickapoos purchased a fine horse in Missouri, took him out on the plains to win Comanche wealth in races, and were almost completely shorn for their trouble. Beaver himself lost a horse, which the Comanches were kind enough to return to him with the admonition that he never again try to beat the Comanches in a horse race. Beaver passed on this advice to Marcy, warning that horse-racing with the Comanches was a losing game.—*Thirty Years of Army Life on the Border*, 52. |

68. Mooney, "The Ghost-dance Religion," *op. cit.*

| Smithwick states that it was customary for the first fellow who awoke in the morning to announce that fact in song; but he thought this was more a "spontaneous outpouring akin to that of the feathered songsters than a religious rite."—*The Evolution of a State*, 181. |

69. They did occasionally torture captives, however.

70. E. Lamberg, *op. cit.*

71. In this connection see Mooney, "Calendar History of the Kiowa Indians," *op. cit.*, map opps. 140.

72. *Ibid.*, 163.

73. *Ibid.*, 156.

74. In this connection, see the account of James Pursley as related to Zebulon M. Pike in Santa Fé, 1806. Pike, *Expeditions* (ed. Coues), II, 757.

75. Grinnell, *The Fighting Cheyennes*, 32–59. For other accounts pertaining to the Cheyennes in this period, see Grinnell, *The Cheyenne Indians*, I, 39–40, "Calendar History of the Kiowa Indians."

It is evident that as early as 1820 certain bands of Cheyennes and Arapahoes were living along the Arkansas in company with the Kiowas and Comanches. In 1820 Long reports seeing "Kaskaias," "Bad-Hearts" (possibly Wichitas), "Shiennes," "Arrapahoes," "Kiawas," "Bald-heads," and a few "Shoshones or Snakes." Long, *Expedition* (ed. James), in Thwaites, *Early Western Travels*, XVI, 55. In November of the same year the Jacob Fowler party struck some of the same bands higher up on the Arkansas. Fowler, *Journal* (ed. Coues), 55.

76. Hodge, *Handbook of American Indians*, II, 213–216.

77. The Osages were estimated at 5200 souls in 1821. *Handbook of American Indians*, II, 158, quoting Jedidiah Morse.

78. *Ibid.*

79. Charles C. Royce (compiler), *Indian Land Cessions in the United States, Eighteenth Annual Report* of the Bureau of American Ethnology, part II, 708, 709, and map no. 26.

80. "Extracts from the Diary of Major Sibley," in *Chronicles of Oklahoma*, V, 205; Pike, *Expeditions* (ed. Coues), II, 563, 407; Long, *Expedition* (ed. James), in Thwaites, *Early Western Travels*, XVI, 232 ff.; Fowler, *Journal* (ed. Coues), 62; James, *Three Years among the Indians and Mexicans* (ed. Douglas), 114, 115, 224; Pattie, *Personal Narrative* (ed. Flint), in Thwaites, *op. cit.*, XVIII, 69.

81. *Handbook of American Indians*, II, 948, 949. For instance, Ke-chi-ka-ro-que, Tawakoni chief, at the council on Tehuacana creek, Texas, May, 1844, said: "I cannot say that I will make peace with the Tonekewas and Lipans until I see the Comanches, else I may tell a lie. My people do as they do. If these Indians are away, let them stay so until the Comanches come in, and then if they say they will make peace we will do the same." Minutes of the council held at Tahwahkano creek, May 13, 1844, ms., Archives of the

Republic of Texas, State Department, Indian Affairs, in the Texas State Library. This collection will be cited hereafter as Texas Indian Papers.

82. *Handbook of American Indians*, II, 778 ff.

83. (Houston) *Telegraph and Texas Register*, May 12, 1838; J. T. DeShields, *Border Wars of Texas*, 275; minutes of the council at Tahwahkano creek, May 13, 1844, *op. cit.*

84. For an account of the Apaches, see *Handbook*, I, 63, 768, 453, 846; for a general account of the Indians of Texas, see H. E. Bolton, *Athanase de Mézières and the Louisiana-Texas Frontier*, 1768–1780, I, map in *frontispiece*, and 1–123. See also Thomas, *Forgotten Frontiers*, 1, 2.

85. Whitefield to Cumming, Sept. 27, 1854, 33 cong., 2 sess., *Sen. Ex. Doc.* no. 1, part 1, vol. I, 299.

CHAPTER TWO

1. R. E. Twitchell, *Spanish Archives of New Mexico*, II, 269, 184; by the same author, *Leading Facts of New Mexican History*, 1, 430 ff.

2. At the same time the Jumano Indians, allies of the French far to the east, were pushed back by the eastern wing of the Comanche wedge. Thomas, *Forgotten Frontiers*, 57 ff.

3. H. H. Bancroft, *History of Arizona and New Mexico, 1530–1888*, 239, footnote 32.

4. Twitchell, *The Spanish Archives of New Mexico*, 1, 20, 148–151.

5. H. E. Bolton, "French Intrusions into New Mexico, 1749–1752," in H. Morse Stephens and H. E. Bolton, *The Pacific Ocean in History*, 392.

6. Twitchell, *Spanish Archives of New Mexico*, I, 148–151; H. H. Bancroft, *History of Arizona and New Mexico*, 249–250.

7. There are a number of communications concerning this affair in tomo 102, *Provincias Internas, Archivo General*, Mexico. See especially Tomás Velez Cachupin to Marquis of Cruillas, January 16, 1762. I used University of Texas Transcripts.

8. It is true that Spanish explorers such as Pedro (Pierre) Vial (a Frenchman in the Spanish service), and José Mares found more direct routes across the plains (1786–1793), but the Spaniards never made use of these routes to any great extent. See Herbert E. Bolton, *Texas in the Middle Eighteenth Century*, 128–133.

9. In their efforts to extend the Louisiana frontier into the Great Plains and ultimately to enter New Mexico, the French began to try to reach the Comanches as early as 1718. In 1724 Bourgmont visited a Comanche band in western Kansas and made peace between them and the Missouri, Osage, Kansa, Oto, and Iowa. But subsequent conditions prevented the French from following up this westward thrust, and nothing of consequence grew out of it. It seems that the first Frenchmen actually to enter New Mexico from Louisiana were the Mallet brothers and some companions who came by way of the Platte valley in 1739. After the treaty between the Comanches and Jumanos in 1746, Frenchmen could enter the Comanche country guided by Indians from these border tribes. A few other traders, deserters, and adventurers did reach Santa Fé by way of the Great Plains, much to the alarm and vexation of the Spanish officials. Their number and the trade they represented was inconsequential, however. See Pierre Margry, *Découvertes et établissements des Français*, VI, 433 ff.; Bolton, "French Intrusions into New Mexico, 1749–1752," in H. Morse Stephens and Herbert E. Bolton, *The Pacific Ocean in History*, 389 ff.; Bolton, *Athanase de Mézières*, I, 58 ff.

By the middle of the eighteenth century there had grown up a considerable trade between the Comanches and Wichitas, in which the Comanches exchanged Apache slaves and horses and mules for French weapons and Wichita agricultural products. The center of this trade was the Wichita village on Red river. *Ibid.*, 47.

The Jumanos are to be identified with Taguayaces (Tawehash or Taovayas), a tribe of the Wichita confederacy. See *Handbook*, II, 705.

10. Twitchell, *Leading Facts of New Mexican History*, 1, 450; *Mendinueta to Bucareli*, October 20, 1774, *Provincias Internas*, t. 65, *Archivo General* (Univ. Tex. Trns.); *Mendinueta to Bucareli*, March 30, 1775, *ibid.*

11. Thomas, *Forgotten Frontiers*, 61, 65.

12. Anza's diary of this expedition is translated and edited with copious notes by Alfred B. Thomas, in *Forgotten Frontiers*, 121–139. The quotation is taken from page 124.

13. On this campaign Anza had with him 600 men, 259 of whom were Indians. *Ibid.*, 122.

14. *Ibid.*, 72, 73.

15. *Ibid.*, 294, 295. If this gathering was as large as the Spaniards believed, it was one of the most representative assemblies of Comanches known in history.

16. Ecueracapa was "the captain most distinguished as much by his skill and valor in war as by his

adroitness and intelligence in political matters." *Ibid.*, 295. Ecueracapa means Leather Cape, Cota de Malla, Coat of Mail. He was well known both in New Mexico and Texas.

17. *Ibid.*, 305.

| The articles of peace proposed by Ecueracapa and the replies of the governor and resolutions of the commander are given pp. 320-332. |

18. *Ibid.*, 306. Probably the guns had been secured from Louisiana traders.

19. *Ibid.*, 315. Up to that time at least twenty-three chiefs, representing, according to the estimates of the Spaniards, eight or nine thousand persons, had come to Pecos or Santa Fé to trade and signify their approval of the treaty. List of Comanches who came to make peace in New Mexico, 1786, *ibid.*, 325-328.

20. Ugarte to Anza, October 5, 1786, *ibid.*, 332-342.

21. Thomas, in *Forgotten Frontiers*, 386, note 133, locates the settlement at the stream now called San Carlos, near Pueblo. He has given the history of the Comanche pueblo in "San Carlos, A Comanche Pueblo on the Arkansas River, 1787," in the *Colorado Magazine*, VI, May, 1929.

22. The account of the village San Carlos de los Jupes is given in *Expediente sobre la Población de San Carlos de los Jupes en el Nuevo Mexico, Provincias Internas*, t. 65, *Archivo General* (Univ. Tex. Transcripts). See especially Anza to Ugarte y Loyola, October 20, 1787; Ugarte to Manuel Antonio Flores, March 13, 1788, *ibid*.

23. Concha to Ugarte, July 22, 1788, *ibid*.

24. It seems, however, that this was due quite as much to policy as to any sense of treaty obligation. The Indians were disposed to commit depredations against other communities and trade their plunder to the New Mexicans. If trade went on, it was necessary for a measure of friendly relationship to prevail.

25. For instance, see "Diary of a campaign from the villa of Santa Fé, New Mexico, by the order of commandant-inspector, D. Joseph Antonio Rengal," October 21, 1787, *Prov. Internas*, t. 65.

26. Bonavia to Antonio Cordero, August 1, 1810, Bexar Archives. One wonders if the chief did not name himself after the Spanish officer.

27. William E. Dunn, "The Apache Mission on the San Saba River; its founding and its failure," in *Southwestern Historical Quarterly*, XVII, 379-414.

28. The Taovayas or Tawehash Indians had participated with the Comanches and members of other tribes in the attack on the San Saba mission. | At this time there was a well established trade between the Comanche and these Indians, in which the Comanche exchanged Apache slaves and horses and mules for French weapons and Wichita agricultural products. The center of this trade was at the Tawehash village. These Apache slaves ultimately reached the French in Louisiana. |

29. H. E. Bolton, *Texas in the Middle Eighteenth Century*, 90-91. Some of Parilla's men were Indians.

30. Gaignard's journal, ed. Bolton, in *Athanase de Mézières*, II, 83-100.

31. When Spain took over Louisiana from France, she inherited numbers of Indian tribes that had been controlled by the French through the fur-trade. Realizing that it would not be possible to control these powerful and warlike tribes by means of their time-honored mission system, the Spaniards decided to adopt the French plan of control through the fur-trade. To this end they placed the Red river country under the control of Frenchmen who understood the Indians and their problems. See Bolton, *Texas in the Middle Eighteenth Century*, 119-127; Bolton, *Athanase de Mézières and the Louisiana-Texas Frontier, 1768-1780*, I.

32. Bolton, *Texas in the Middle Eighteenth Century*, 123 ff., 127.

33. In their references to these events, the Spaniards do not mention the Penatekas. However, they were at this time located on the southern edge of the *Comanchería*, were comparatively numerous, and the term Comanche, without any modification, evidently was commonly used to refer to them. The Spanish often mention the Kotsotekas, whom they call Cuchanticas, and use the term to include all of the Comanches *Orientales*, or eastern Comanches.

34. Pedro de Nava, at Chihuahua, to the viceroy, July 23, 1799, *Provincias Internas*, tomo 12, *Archivo General*, University of Texas Transcripts. The treaty is published in *Tratados y Convenciones Concludidos y Ratificados por la Republica Mexicana* . . . (1828), 617-619.

35. Cabello to José Antonio Rengal, January —, 1786, Cabello's blotter, Bexar Archives.

36. To be exact, Bonavia reported that he had spent 4999 pesos, four reales and eleven and seven-eights grains. April 21, 1810, Bonavia's blotter, Bexar Archives.

In a communication of June 17, 1789, the governor gave a list of presents which Pedro Vial and Francisco Zavier Chaves took to the Comanches. Copy, Bexar Archives.

37. Domingo Cabello to the commandant-general, April 30, 1786, copy, Bexar Archives.

| Cabello's brief report on the Comanches is the most informative thing to be found in all the bulky

correspondence that pertains to them in the Bexar Archives. He could call the names of several chiefs, among whom were Iron Jacket and Shaved Head—typical Comanche names. He regarded these two men as the most influential of all the Comanches *Orientales*. These two chiefs held their positions by election and were chosen by their fellow tribesmen because of prowess in war. He pointed out that the Comanches were exceedingly sensitive and proud and were quick to resent any insult. It seems that Iron Jacket was the chief so well known in New Mexico as Ecueracapa or Cota de Malla. |

38. A typical case is that reported by the governor of Texas to the commandant-general, November 24, 1802, copy in Bexar Archives.

39. For instance, see Governor Antonio Cordero in a report of March 30, 1803, Cordero's blotter, Bexar Archives.

40. Salcedo to the governor of Texas, June 3, 1805, Bexar Archives.

41. See Dionisio Valle, at Nacogdoches, to Don Juan Bautista Elguezabal, March 22, 1805, and the governor to the commandant-general, September 1, 1809, blotter, Bexar Archives; also, letters of Governor Bonavia, May 14, 1810, and May 16, 1810, blotter, Bexar Archives.

Dr. John Sibley, in charge of United States Indian Affairs at Natchitoches, was charged with courting the favor of the Comanches and other Texas Indians and inciting them against the Spanish. At any rate, these Texas Indians occasionally visited Natchitoches, where they were given presents, and the Spanish were eternally afraid that Sibley was weaving some sinister plot against the peace of Texas. Cordero to Don Francisco Viana, November 3, 1807, Cordero's blotter, Bexar Archives; Salcedo to Cordero, December 1, 1807, *ibid.*; Cordero (?) to Salcedo, February 1, 1805, Cordero's blotter, Bexar Archives.

42. The governor to the officer in command at Nacogdoches, August 3, 1812, copy, Bexar Archives.

43. Austin to Bustamante, May 10, 1822, *The Austin Papers* (ed. Barker), part I, 507 ff.; Ramon Querque's declaration, Bexar, February 13, 1816, Nacogdoches Archives; Jasper López to José Felix Trespalacios, July 9, 1822, Nacogdoches Archives.

44. See, for instance, the report of José Felix Pérez, at his camp on the San Miguel, to Governor D. Venito de Armiñan, August 22, 1814, Bexar Archives.

45. Guiterrez de Lara, governor of Tamaulipas, to the governor of San Luis Potosi, July 19, 1824, enclosing papers intended apparently for the president of Mexico, Bexar Archives.

46. Lester G. Bugbee, "The Texas Frontier, 1820-1825," in *Publications* of the Southern History Association, IV, 118, 119.

47. According to the report of the commissioner of Indian Affairs for 1841, 87,615 eastern Indians had been removed to the west, and the process was not complete. 27 cong., 2 sess., *Sen. Ex. Doc.* no. 1, 268, 269.

For a general account of this Indian policy of the United States, see Anna Heloise Abel, "History of Events Resulting in Indian Consolidation West of the Mississippi River," in the *Annual Report* of the American Historical Association, 1906, I. See also Grant Foreman, *Pioneer Days in the Early Southwest*; Roy Gittinger, *The Formation of the State of Oklahoma*.

48. Pike, *Expeditions* (ed. Coues), II.

49. Long, *Narrative of Expedition* (ed. James), in Thwaites, *Early Western Travels*, XVI, 232 ff.

50. Fowler, *Journal* (ed. Coues), 51 ff.

51. James, *Three Years among the Indians and Mexicans* (ed. Douglas), 98-130.

52. Grinnell, "Bent's Old Fort and its Builders," in *Kansas Historical Collections*, XV, 29 ff.

53. Becknell's journal is given in the *Missouri Historical Review*, IV, 64-84. See also Josiah Gregg, "Commerce of the Prairies," in Thwaites, *Early Western Travels*, XIX, 177-181.

54. An account of the different persons killed or robbed along the route by Kiowas, Comanches, Osages, and other Indians is given in 22 cong., I sess., *Sen. Ex. Doc.* no. 90, 81-86. The Comanches were not nearly so destructive as some other tribes, particularly the Osages. The Comanches were charged with only nine murders or robberies of the 234 persons so dealt with.

55. The Osages and Pawnees fought each other; the Comanches, Kiowas, and Wichitas were at war with the Osages and Pawnees. *The Arkansas Gazette*, May 25, 1831, July 6 and May 23, 1832, February 10, June 7, and April 15, 1829, August 14, 1833; Grant Foreman, as cited 57-70. | See also, the "Report of Isaac McCoy, head of a delegation of Indians to explore the country west of the Mississippi in 1820," *American State Papers*, Vol. 190, p. 22 ff. |

56. See *The Arkansas Gazette*, June 3, 1831, and February 6, 1833; Albert Pike, "Narrative of a Journey in the Prairie," in Arkansas Historical Association *Publications*, IV, 108.

57. For the expedition of October, 1832, see C. J. Latrobe, *The Rambler in North America*, II, 153-232; Washington Irving, *A Tour on the Prairies*. For that of 1833, see *The Arkansas Gazette*, May 15, 1833, March 25, 1834; Foreman, *op. cit.*, 104 ff.

58. George Catlin, *North American Indians*, ii, 51–99. For other accounts of the expedition, see Lieutenant T. B. Wheelock, *Journal*, 23 cong., 2 sess., *House Doc.* no. 2, 70–91; "Journal of Hugh Evans" (ed. Perrine and Foreman), in *Chronicles of Oklahoma*, III, 175–215; Mooney, "Kiowa Calendar," *op. cit.*; Foreman, *op. cit.*

| A number of men who had attained distinction or who were destined to do so went along. Among these were: Lieut. Col. Stephen W. Kearny, Major Richard R. Mason, Captains Edwin V. Sumner and David Hunter, Lieut. Philip St. George Cooke, Lieut. Jefferson Davis, Special Commissioner Montfort Stokes, Col. Auguste P. Chouteau, Major William Armstrong, superintendent of Indian Affairs and agent for the Choctaws, and Captain Nathan Boone, son of Daniel Boone. |

59. Mooney, *op. cit.*, 265, locates the Comanche village on Chandler creek, about ten miles north of the present Fort Sill. The accounts of this time refer to the Wichitas as "Pawnee Picts," after the French *Pani Pique* (tattooed Pawnee). The term Pawnee later came to be applied only to the Pawnees of the Platte. See *Handbook*, II, 213, 947.

60. Wheelock, *op. cit.*, 76. Except where otherwise indicated, I have followed Wheelock's account.

61. Catlin, *North American Indians*, II, 69.

62. Severe illness, which in many cases proved fatal, was decimating the ranks of the soldiers. Colonel Leavenworth had been left at a camp on the Washita river, and died there July 21.

63. Catlin renders his name "Ee-shah-ko-nee (the bow and quiver)." The name is generally written Ishacoly. The correct form is probably ēs'-ă (wolf)-kō-nēē (trip or journey), that is Traveling Wolf.

64. The name is more commonly written Ta-ba-que-na, from tăb-by (sun)-quē-nē (eagle), Sun Eagle.
| Catlin writes the name Ta-wah-que-nah and translates it "the mountain of rocks," which, as is usually the case with Catlin, is incorrect. |

65. Foreman, *Pioneer Days in the Early Southwest*, 154.

66. Holland Coffee's traders helped to collect the various scattered Indian bands. Letter from "A Military Friend" to the editor, *The Gazette*, Little Rock, August 25, 1835.

Coffee operated at Fort Smith with Robert M. French and others under the name of Coffee, Calville, and Company. They located a trading post on Red river as soon as it was learned that Colonel Dodge's expedition to the plains tribes had proved their friendly disposition. Foreman locates the post as established in 1834 at "what was called the old Pawnee village, about twenty miles above the Cross Timbers and seventy-five miles in a direct line above the mouth of the Washita River." Later, in 1837, Coffee's post was located on "Walnut Bayou, which empties into Red River within what is now Love County, Oklahoma. At approximately this location there was subsequently a trading post known as Warren's, which was abandoned in 1848, and located at the mouth of Cache Creek." Foreman, *op. cit.*, 157 and 181 ff.

67. Camp Holmes was located about five miles northwest of the present town of Purcell, Oklahoma. Colonel Auguste Chouteau built a trading house on the same site soon after the council of 1835. It was the site of a Kichai Indian village at about 1850. Mooney, "Kiowa Calendar," 171.

68. Major Armstrong died before the council assembled. Foreman, *op. cit.*, 162.

69. The Kiowas were not a party to this agreement. It seems that they assembled near Camp Holmes, but grew impatient at the delay in the coming of the commissioners and left before the council was held. A treaty with substantially the same provisions was negotiated with them May 26, 1837. Mooney, "Kiowa Calendar," 169.

70. The treaty is printed in Charles J. Kappler, *Indian Affairs, Laws and Treaties*, 57 cong., 1 sess., *Sen. Doc.* no. 452, II, 435–439.

71. See Foreman, *op. cit.*, 229; Report of C. A. Harris, commissioner of Indian Affairs, December 1, 1837, 25 cong., 2 sess., *House Ex. Doc.* no. 1, 567; Kappler, *op. cit.*, II, 489–491.

72. Foreman, *op. cit.*, 227. However, the Comanches still kept a number of prisoners.

73. See Foreman, *op. cit.*, 289 ff.

74. The Chouteaus were a French-American family with a genius for understanding the Indian mind. It has already been stated that Colonel A. P. Chouteau owned a trading establishment at Camp Holmes, on the Canadian. He was born in St. Louis, 1786, son of John Pierre Chouteau who had been prominent in the early history of that place. A. P. Chouteau spent two years or more at West Point, and was commissioned as an ensign in the First United States Infantry in 1806. He resigned in 1809, returned to St. Louis, and engaged in the fur-trade. He probably came to Oklahoma about 1819 or 1820. He engaged in extensive trading operations, and was for some time United States Indian agent for the Osages. He died in the winter of 1838–1839. Thoburn, *Standard History of Oklahoma*, 1, 125, n. 5. Major P. L. Chouteau, brother of A. P. Chouteau and Edward, son of P. L. Chouteau, were also intimately associated with the Comanches.

75. Chouteau to Stokes and Arbuckle, April 20, 1836, published in the *Arkansas Gazette*, July 19, 1836.
76. Catlin, *North American Indians*, II, 69; Wheelock, *op. cit.*, entry for July 16.
77. Wheelock, journal entry for July 14.
78. "The Journal of Hugh Evans," *op. cit.*, 204, 188. | But Evans was not at all enthusiastic about the appearance of the Comanche off of his horse. "Those Commanch Indians," he observed, "are the most homely featured being verry large & corpulent in size not so tall as the Osages but of a heavy square and inelegant proportion . . ." |
79. Wheelock, journal entry for July 24.

CHAPTER THREE

1. E. C. Barker, *The Life of Stephen F. Austin*, 46.
2. Mary Austin Holley, *Texas*, 155–158; Austin to J. E. B. Austin, March 23, 1822, in *The Austin Papers* (ed. Barker), 1, 487.
3. See *The Rachel Plummer Narrative* (ed. Parker).
4. The prisoners were divided soon after leaving Parker's Fort. Mrs. Kellogg was given to the Kichaies (which seems to indicate that this tribe participated in the massacre at Parker's Fort). Some Delawares purchased her and delivered her up, receiving $150 from President Houston for their services. She was a captive only a few months. *The Rachel Plummer Narrative*, 14.

Mrs. Plummer was separated from her little son and later ransomed far north of Santa Fé by the agents of William Donoho, of Santa Fé. She arrived at her home again in February, 1838. According to her *Narrative*, the savages perpetrated against her and her infant that she gave birth to after her capture barbarities too horrible to describe. They killed the child. Her little son, James Pratt Plummer, was ransomed and taken to Fort Gibson by the Delawares in 1842, and a little later John Parker was ransomed and taken to the same post. *Ibid.*, 31.

Cynthia Ann Parker was daughter of Silas Parker and granddaughter of Elder John Parker. She was about nine years old when captured; and, in spite of the persistent and heroic efforts of her uncle, James W. Parker, to secure her release, she lived with the savages until 1860, when Captain L. S. Ross and a band of rangers, United States dragoons and armed citizens, conferred upon her the doubtful favor of restoration to civilized life.

On many occasions the agents of Texas and the United States heard of her, but they never could secure her release. In 1846, Colonel Leonard Williams, acting as agent for the United States, offered goods worth several hundred dollars for her; but she was claimed by a chief, who refused to give her up, and furthermore, she would run away and hide from those who tried to ransom her. Butler and Lewis to Medill, August 8, 1846, O.I.A. Misc., B 2738, University of Texas photostat copies of papers in the United States Indian Office. In November, 1847, Robert S. Neighbors, special Indian agent, reported that she was held by the "Tenawish" (Tenawa?) Comanches, who generally ranged along the headwaters of Red river and with whom the agents of the government had little or no intercourse. He stated that the chiefs of the band kept promising to give her up, but never did so, and that certain friendly chiefs with whom he had talked thought it would require force to secure her release. Neighbors to Medill, Nov. 18, 1847, O.I.A., L.R., Univ. Tex. phot. Her brother once told Captain Marcy that he visited her in her Indian home, but was unable to persuade her to leave the savages. She said that "her husband, children, and all that she held most dear, were with the Indians, and there she should remain." Exploration of the Red river of Louisiana, 33 cong., 1 sess., *House Ex. Doc.* (no number), 103.

Evidently during all the years of her captivity she was with the wild Nokonies, a band that was not often associated with the white people. She became the wife of Nokoni, a chief of that band, and the mother of Quanah, the last great Comanche chief.

5. However, the attack on the Parker place was committed in May following the battle of San Jacinto, which had been fought April 21.
6. The report of Bowl or "Bowles" is given in the *Telegraph and Texas Register*, May 30, 1837.

| Because of the Cherokee revolt against Texas, which Bowl later participated in, he gained ill repute among some Texans. However, his report was evidently accepted at face value by Goyens, Millard, LeGrand and Houston. Houston gave it out for publication and it bears every mark of genuineness and a fair degree of accuracy. |

7. Many stories were told about LeGrand, most of which are probably apocryphal. One of these, told by Mrs. Holley, is to the effect that LeGrand was a Frenchman employed by an English mining company in

New Mexico; that he antagonized the alcalde, who condemned him to clean the streets in chains. After his release, he ingratiated himself with the Comanches, led a party of them to Santa Fé, killed the alcalde, and nearly destroyed the place. Notes made by Mrs. [Mary Austin] Holley in interviews with "Prominent Texans of Early Days," ms., University of Texas Archives. It seems that Mrs. Holley, who was a contemporary of LeGrand's, got the story secondhand, and I have never seen any evidence to corroborate it.

In 1836 a story went the rounds of the newspapers that LeGrand was a half-breed, his mother being Comanche and his father French, that he was educated in New York City, but had been a leading chief among the Comanche for fifteen years. *The Portsmouth Journal of Literature and Politics*, October 8, 1836, quoting the *Louisiana Advertiser* of September 17, 1836. At any rate, he was familiar with the *Llano-Estacado*, having surveyed a large claim in the Panhandle of Texas and eastern New Mexico in 1833. This feat alone entitles him to a place among great western explorers. The report of his survey is printed in William Kennedy, *Texas* (London, 1841), I, 183, ff. P. L. Chouteau regarded him as an authority on the Comanches. *Arkansas Gazette*, July 19, 1836.

8. LeGrand to Burnet, November 7, 1836, ms., *Texas Indian Papers*.

9. Extract from LeGrand's report of April 26, 1837, Yoakum, *History of Texas*, II, 228 ff.

| LeGrand's report implicates the Mexican emissaries as being chiefly responsible for the disgruntled attitude of the Comanches. However, it should be remembered that at this time Traveling Wolf was angry because he had just discovered that the treaty of Camp Holmes permitted the Border tribes to hunt in the Comanche country. |

10. Tex., 2 cong., called session of Sept. 25, *Journal of the House*, 82.

11. Among these was a law to raise a corps of regular cavalry, not to exceed 280 men rank and file, for the protection of the southwestern frontier. Gammel, *Laws of Texas*, I, 1480.

| 12. George W. Bonnell, Commissioner of Indian Affairs of the Republic of Texas, writing in the summer of 1838, stated that at this village some of the under-chiefs and warriors planned to kill their white guests, that a council was held in which a violent altercation took place among the different factions in regard to the matter, but that the council terminated favorable to the white men. Bonnell's report was published several years later in U.S. Senate, *Rep. Com.* No. 171, 30 cong., 1 sess., pp. 38–50.

However, Bonnell hated the Indians so bitterly and knew so little about them in spite of the position he held that one is justified in doubting every statement he makes.|

13. *Telegraph and Texas Register*, March 17, 1838.

14. Yoakum, *op. cit.*, II, 230.

15. Matagorda *Bulletin*, March 7, 1838.

16. W. P. Johnston, *The Life of Albert Sidney Johnston*, 88–91. The names of the chiefs have been spelled in various ways, Isowacony or Essowakkenny seems to be ēs'ă (wolf) and wăk'-kă-nȳ (turtle), Turtle Wolf. Essomanny, or Isomania as he was sometimes called, cannot be translated.

17. R. A. Irion, sec. state, to Houston, March 14, 1838, Corrsp. of Sec. State, bk. 36, 29–31, Texas State Library.

18. Smithwick, *The Evolution of a State*, 172 ff. Smithwick gives the name of the Eagle as Quinaseico, the Comanche equivalent for eagle, as he states. It is probably a combination of $kw\bar{e}'$-$n\bar{e}$, or $qu\bar{e}'$-$n\bar{e}$ (eagle) with some word which cannot be recognized. Smithwick thought Puestia had no meaning, and modern Comanches also are unable to translate it.

19. *Ibid*. Smithwick fixes these events as happening in the spring and summer of 1837. However, his memory must be at fault, for he stayed with the Comanches three months, when the treaty of May, 1838, was made at Houston.

20. Treaty with the Comanche Indians, May 29, 1838, Texas Indian Papers.

21. Anna Muckleroy, "The Indian Policy of the Republic of Texas," in *Southwestern Historical Quarterly*, XXVI, 23.

22. Smithwick, *op. cit.*, 194 ff.

23. *Ibid*.

24. | ". . . Observing that the other members of the family were all grown up, I asked the old man if that little boy was his child.

" 'Yes,' said he, taking the child in his arms, 'mine now.' He then told me that during the war between the Wacos and Comanches, the latter surprised an encampment of the enemy and killed all the occupants except that one little child." Said he:

" 'After the fight was over I went into a lodge and found this boy, about two years old, sitting beside its dead mother crying; and my heart was sorry for him, and I took him up in my arms and brought him home to my lodge and my wife took him to her bosom, and fed him, and he is mine now.' And the little orphan Waco, as well as the little white boy, was petted by the whole tribe."—*The Evolution of a State*, pp. 174, 175. |

25. *Telegraph and Texas Register*, April 28, 1838.

26. However, this was not the case with Smithwick. He lived with the savages long enough to come to appreciate the fact that they possessed many virtues in spite of some revolting practices they engaged in.

27. Issue of May 30, 1838.

28. "X.Y.," a correspondent of the *Telegraph and Texas Register*, June 16, 1838.

29. Later the Indians explained that they killed the traders because they believed the white men purposely introduced smallpox among them. Mary A. Maverick, *Memoirs*, 31. Concerning these depredations, see Seguin to the secretary of state, July 1, 1838, Corrsp. Sec. State, book 49, 68–70; *Telegraph and Texas Register*, July 7; Yoakum, *op. cit.*, II, 245; Morris to Irion, Oct. 15, 1838, Corrsp. Sec. State, book 49, 193–194.

30. *Journal* of the house of representatives, 3 cong., regular sess., 173–178.

31. Bonnell's report was published several years later in U.S. Senate, *Rep. Com.* no. 171, 30 cong., 1 sess., 38–50. See also Johnston, *The Life of Albert Sidney Johnston*, 106.

32. Gammel, *op. cit.*, II, 15–20, 30, 78, 84–85.

33. *Report* of the [Texas] secretary of war for 1839, 42; Smithwick, *op. cit.*, 215 ff.

34. Yoakum (*op. cit.*, II, 262), cites General Burleson's report to the secretary of war, March 2, 1839; Brown, *Indian Wars and Pioneers of Texas*, 61.

35. Yoakum, *op. cit.*, II, 263 ff.

36. Karnes to the secretary of war, January 10, 1840 (copy), Texas Indian Papers.

37. Johnston to Fisher, January 30, 1840, *Ibid.*

38. *Memoirs of Mary A. Maverick*, 31.

The council house fight has been described by almost every writer of Texas history of the time of the republic. McLeod reported the affair to President Lamar on the day following, and his account was published in the *Richmond Telescope and Register*, April 4, 1840. Except where otherwise indicated, I have followed this account.

39. *Memoirs of Mary A. Maverick*, 36, 37, 47. It was from the boy, B. L. Webster, who was later exchanged by the Indians, that Mrs. Maverick got her information as to the fate of the other prisoners.

40. *Ibid.*, 42 ff. Mrs. Maverick calls the chief Isimanica.

41. The girl had been a prisoner about two years. Mrs. Maverick, who saw her and probably helped to care for her, describes her plight in *Memoirs*, 44.

| "She was in a frightful condition, poor girl, when at last she returned to civilization. Her head, arms, and face were full of bruises, and sores, and her nose actually burnt off to the bone—all the fleshy end gone, and a great scab formed on the end of the bone. Both nostrils were wide open and denuded of flesh. She told a piteous tale of how dreadfully the Indians had beaten her and how they would wake her from sleep by sticking a chunk of fire to her flesh, especially to her nose, and how they would shout and laugh like fiends when she cried. Her body had many scars from fire, many of which she showed us. Ah, it was sickening to behold, and made one's blood boil for vengeance." |

42. Abner S. Lipscomb to General James Hamilton and A. T. Brumley, August 15, 1840, Republic of Texas, Executive Record, book no. 38, 148.

43. Another explanation of the raid is given by James N. Smith, who was in the battle of Plum creek. He states that when the plunder taken from the Indians was divided, there fell to him a beautiful, beaded shot bag with "Roman crosses" designed upon it. In this bag was a letter from a Mexican to an Indian chief or "officer" suggesting that the raid would be profitable. James N. Smith, *Autobiography*, ms., University of Texas Archives.

44. Yoakum, *op. cit.*, 11, 303; Brown, *Indian Wars and Pioneers of Texas*, 79 ff.; Z. N. Morrell, *Flowers and Fruits in the Wilderness*, 128–131.

45. Yoakum, *op. cit.*, II, 304, ff.; Brown, *op. cit.*, 83 ff.

| 46. On July 1, John C. (Jack) Hays, the illustrious ranger captain, reported having recently defeated a party of Comanches in the vicinity of the Canon de Uvalde. The Texans and a party of Mexicans who were operating with them killed eight of the Indians and captured the two remaining members of the party [Hays to the Secretary of War, July 1, 1841 (copy), Texas Army Papers]. A few weeks later he defeated a large band of Comanches, consisting of about fifty warriors with their families, on the head waters of the Llano. This party had about six hundred head of horses. When they reached the abandoned Comanche

camp the Texans found a Mexican prisoner swinging by the heels, shot and lanced to death.—Hays to Archer, August 13, 1841 (copy), *Ibid.* |

CHAPTER FOUR

1. See William Carey Crane, *The Life and Select Literary Remains of Sam Houston*, 295, 296.

2. Houston to Eldredge, April 17, 1843, Executive Record, book no. 40, 237. John Henry Brown, who was well acquainted with the family, spells the name Eldridge (*Indian Wars and Pioneers of Texas*, 96). The spelling I have adopted is that shown by numerous specimens of Eldredge's signature in the Texas archives.

3. Translated, He-who-has-relations-with-his-aunt.

4. Report of J. C. Eldredge to Houston, December 8, 1843, in West Texas Historical Association *Year Book*, IV, 131–132.

5. *Ibid.*, 136. John Henry Brown, who appears to have followed an account written some years later by Hamilton P. Bee, describes with a few variations the dramatic incidents set forth above. *Indian Wars and Pioneers of Texas*, 96 ff.

6. Treaty of peace between J. C. Eldredge and Pah-hah-yuco, Aug. 9, 1843, Texas Indian Papers.

7. Anna Muckleroy, "The Indian Policy of the Republic of Texas," in *Southwestern Historical Quarterly*, XXVI, 188–191.

8. Report of Daniel G. Watson to Houston, May 4, 1844, Texas Indian Papers.
General P. M. Butler, of the United States Indian service, had succeeded in getting in touch with the chief and inviting him to a council to be held on Red river, near the mouth of Cache creek, in December, 1843. But the chief had recently lost a son killed in the war with the Mexicans, and refused to attend the council because of his great grief. It was reported that he had killed his horses, destroyed his lodges, and had taken new skins to the Salt Plains, there to erect new lodges and try to overcome his grief in the new surroundings. Statement of Luis Sanches to Walter Winn, secretary to the commissioners at the council ground, May, 1844, Texas Indian Papers.

9. Minutes of the council at Tahwahkano creek, April 27, and May 13, respectively, Walter Winn, secretary, Texas Indian Papers.

10. Report of John Conner and James Shaw [written and] witnessed by Daniel C. Watson, October 2, 1844, Texas Indian Papers.

11. It is not likely that any of the chiefs present had participated in the agreements made with the Comanches in former years. Houston referred to the council house affair. However, Houston passed on to Lamar problems too difficult for the "bad chief" to have settled without an Indian war, even if he had wanted peace.

12. Minutes of a grand council held near the falls of the Brazos, between the Republic of Texas and the Indians, commencing on Monday, October 7, 1844, Texas Indian Papers. Hereafter referred to as Minutes of the Council.

13. Minutes of the Council.

14. Such a line would run roughly from Red river south to Comanche Peak in Hood county near the Brazos, thence almost exactly southwest to the old Spanish mission at Menard.

15. Letter of Mo-pe chook ko and others to Houston, March 21, 1844, Texas Indian Papers.

16. Treaty of peace, friendship, and commerce between the Republic of Texas and the Comanche, Keechi, Waco, Caddo, Anadahkah, Ionie, Delaware, Shawnee, Cherokee, Lepan, and Tahuahkano tribes of Indians, concluded and signed at Tahwaccaro creek, October 9, 1844, Texas Indian Papers.
The treaty was ratified January 24, 1845, being one of the few Indian treaties to receive the approval of the Texas senate. It is published in its corrected form in Gammel, *Laws of Texas*, II, 1192–1196.

17. These Indian names are rarely ever spelled alike in any two accounts. Evidently *pand-u-a* is a corruption of *pāh-dū-ă*, Comanche for bear. Probably the chief's name is Bear's Tail.

18. *Telegraph and Texas Register*, January 22, 1845, editorial.

19. Talk of Pahayeuca at trading house, January 19, 1845, Texas Indian Papers.

20. It was reported that he led a raid into Mexico in the winter of 1844–1845. *Telegraph and Texas Register*, February 12 and March 19, 1845.

21. Red Bear, a reliable Caddo chief, laid this to the Yamparikas. Notes taken at Torrey's trading house, July 22, 1844, Texas Indian Papers.
Torrey's trading house, near the council grounds on Tehuacana creek, about six miles southeast of the location of Waco, seems to have been a clearing house for all frontier news and gossip. The Torreys or

their clerks often made notes of reports and rumors brought in by the different Indians, and some of these notes found their way into the archives of the republic.

22. The Simpson lad had been taken by Wacoes or renegade Comanches from his home near Austin, the negro had run away from his master at or near the trading house, and the horses had been stolen by Wacoes from settlements on the Trinity.

23. Talk of Pahayeuca (Comanche chief) at trading house, January 10, 1845, as cited; *Telegraph and Texas Register*, February 5, 1845. | Päh'-häh-yō'-kō spoke of admonition he had given Buffalo Hump which indicates that he regarded that chief as subordinate, possibly another of his war chiefs. He states that Bear-with-a-Short-Tail is not war chief to Buffalo Hump. Perhaps this was to inform the white men that he, Päh-häh-yō'-kō, was the great head chief and that Buffalo Hump and the Bear were on the same level. The question of the relations that the different chiefs bore to the tribe and to each other is very difficult to determine. Evidently the Indians themselves were often confused on this point and there were many confusing claims. |

24. A party of hunters, including G. W. Kendall, the historian of the Texas Santa Fé expedition of 1841, found immense herds of these animals as far south as the San Gabriel. They reported that the oldest settlers stated that they had never known such great herds as far south at that season, April and May. *Telegraph and Texas Register*, May 28, 1845.

25. T. G. Western to Lieutenant A. Coleman, commanding the rangers of Travis county, May 5, 1845, Texas Indian Papers.

26. *Telegraph and Texas Register*, May 28 and June 11, 1845.

27. Western to Sloat and Williams, April 9, 1845; Sloat to Robert S. Neighbors, April 9, 1845, Texas Indian Papers.

It was stated that Jack Ned, a lawless Delaware, was at the head of the party.

28. Western to Sloat, *op. cit.*

29. Western to Sloat, July 10, 1845, and Sloat to Western, July 24, 1845, *ibid.*; *Telegraph and Texas Register*, June 11, 1845.

30. Western to Sloat, July 10, 1845, *op. cit.*

31. He had led in the raid when the Simpson boy (later restored by Päh'-häh-yō'-kō at Torrey's trading house) was captured. The youth's sister was killed at the time. Also, it was thought that he had led in the killing of Hornsby and Atkinson.

32. Report of B. Sloat, July 12, 1845, Texas Indian Papers. Although the report is dated as indicated, it covers some events that happened later. The report is headed, "Report of ten months with the Comanches."

33. Sloat to Western, July 24, 1845, *ibid*. Sloat makes a statement which is very significant, that is, that the chief, Cut-Arm, had planned to kill the young warrior because of depredations which that young renegade had already committed, but that the chief had not dared to execute his plan because of the superior strength of the young man's party. It seems, however, that at the time the chief was killed the chief's party was in the ascendency. Another case where Comanche shed Comanche's blood in the interest of peace with the white people is that of the slaying of Toroblanco, in the days of Anza, in New Mexico. Such instances were rare. Law enforcement among the Comanches generally went no further than admonition. The chiefs were not disposed to endanger tribal solidarity and harmony by enforcing severe penalties, particularly where the offenses committed had been against white persons.

34. Sloat's report of July 12, *op. cit*. The spacing in the quotation is partly my own. The goods with which the party purchased their lives were: 6 1/2 yds. of strouding; 4 butcher knives; 4 papers of paint; 4 looking glasses; 8 plugs of tobacco; 4 lbs. of powder; 8 bars of lead; and 4 cotton handkerchiefs.

35. Sloat to Western, August 18, 1845, *ibid*.

36. Western to the Indian commissioners, September 8, 1845, Texas Indian Papers.

37. Report of J. C. Neill, Thomas J. Smith and E. Moorehouse, September 27, 1845, *ibid*.

38. Williams and others to Western, November 23, 1845, being a report of a council held with the Comanche Indians, Texas Indian Papers.

39. Williams to Western, November 23, 1845, *ibid*. Williams's letter and an interesting account of this council is given by W. P. Webb, "The Last Treaty of the Republic of Texas," in *The Southwestern Historical Quarterly*, XXV, 167 ff.

40. In the matter of presents, the Anglo-Americans gave the Indians largely the same kinds of goods with which the Spanish had delighted them. At this council there were distributed among them: 21 silk handkerchiefs; 3 cotton handkerchiefs; 4 cotton shawls; 8 pieces blue prints; 40 1/2 yards blue and red strouding; 7 1/2 pieces blue drill; 75 lbs. brass wire; 4 3/12 dozen tin pans; 13 tin buckets; 12 lbs. ver-

million; 12 dozen six-inch butcher knives; 1 1/2 dozen cocoa handles, 7 inch; 5 dozen horn combs; 7 8/12 dozen ivory combs; 2 4/12 dozen files; 7 1/2 M brass tacks; 2 lbs. linen thread; 1 1/2 dozen fire steels; 1 1/2 M needles; 1 1/2 dozen looking glasses; 4 1/2 lbs. indigo and verdigris; 2 1/2 dozen squaw hatchets; 4 dozen tin cups; 1 1/2 [dozen] pair red blankets; 7 1/2 [dozen] pair white blankets; 42 small bars lead; 12 large bars lead; 2 pieces unbleached domestic, 32.12 yds.; 35 lbs. powder.

CHAPTER FIVE

1. Johnson and Barker, *A History of Texas and Texans*, I, 484.
2. Gammel, *Laws of Texas*, II, 1228 ff. Although the joint resolution of annexation did not specifically provide that the United States should assume responsibility for the Indians, it was so understood by both the state and federal governments. See Lena Clara Kock, "The Federal Indian Policy in Texas, 1845–1860," in the *Southwestern Historical Quarterly*, XXVIII, 259, 260.
3. *Telegraph and Texas Register*, December 10, 1845.
4. *Ibid.*, October 15, 1845.
5. Pierce M. Butler had served as governor of South Carolina from 1836 to 1838, and on September 17, 1841, was appointed agent to the Cherokee Indians. Foreman, *Pioneer Days in the Early Southwest*, 262, note 286.
 | As a matter of fact the United States Indian service had been trying for several years to make a treaty with the Comanches or to pacify them under the terms of the treaty of Camp Holmes, 1835. To this end Governor Butler and a party attended the council at Tehuacana Creek, in March and April, 1843. Since nothing was accomplished with the Comanches at this council, another was arranged to be held on Red river near the mouth of Cache Creek in the autumn following. But this council likewise was not effective because, it seems, that Päh'-häh-yō'-kō was grieving for his slain son and would not attend. Then it was planned to send a force to the Texas council ground at Tehuacana Creek in the autumn of 1844; but because of delay and reports of destructive prairie fires this was not done. It was at about this time that some Comanches participated in a raid against white and Choctaw settlers on Red river and it was necessary to send two companies from Fort Gibson to drive away the marauders. Foreman, as cited, pp. 293–295. |
6. *Cherokee Advocate*, July 2, August 6, 1846. For the report of Butler and Lewis, see 29 cong., 2 sess., *House Doc.* no. 76. I have followed a photostat copy of their original report filed with the commission of Indian Affairs.
7. *Cherokee Advocate*, July 2, August 6, 1846; Kappler, *op. cit.*, II, 557.
8. *Ibid.*, 554–557. The tribes participating were the Comanche, Ioni (Hainai), Ana-da-ca (Anadarko), Cadoe (Caddo), Lepan (Lipan), Longwha (Tonkawa), Keechy (Kichai), Tah-wa-carro (Tawakoni), Wichita (Wichita), and Wacoe (Waco).
9. The original treaty is printed in full in United States *Statutes at Large*, IX, 844–848, and the amended treaty in Kappler's *Indian Affairs Laws and Treaties*, II, 554–557.
10. Report of W. Medill, commissioner of Indian Affairs, November 30, 1846, 29 cong., 2 sess., *Sen. Ex. Doc.* no. I, 218.
 | Hicks states that the Comanches had only one white prisoner, a young man who was really not a prisoner but free to do as he pleased. The Indians agreed that he might return to his own people if he cared to do so. On the other hand the whites surrendered to the Comanches at the council at Tehuacana Creek four or five girls and one boy, "who had been kept in duress for a number of years by the Texans and who now speak the English." Hicks stated that these prisoners appeared well pleased on being returned to their people," although it was stated to the contrary by the whites."—*Cherokee Advocate*, July 2, 1846.
It is likely that the Comanches had more Anglo-American prisoners than the one young man referred to and it is certain that they had scores of Mexican captives. |
 | 11. The names appended to the treaty together with what is claimed to be their English equivalents are as follows: Pah-ha-u-ca (or the Amorous Man); Mon-ne-con-nah-heh (Ring); Mo-pe-chu-co-pe (or Old Owl); Santa Anna; Cush-un-a-rah-ah (or ravisher); Sa-ba-heit (Small Wolf); Ka-bah-ha-moo (or won't smoke); Quarah-ha-po-e (Antelope Road); O ka art-su (or Rope Cutter); Ka-nah-u-mah-ka (Nearly Dead); Moo-ra-que-top (or Nasty Mule); Ish-a-me-a-qui (Traveling Wolf); Ta-bup-pua-ta (or the winner); Mo-he-ka (Pole Cat); Kai-tia-tah (or Little); A-ka-chu-a-ta (No Horn); Kai-he-na-mou-rah (blind man); Ka-he-na-oo-ne (Blind Man); Ho-chu-cah (Bird House); Ma-war-ra (The Lost); Pah-moo-wah-tah (or No Tobacco); Ke-wid-da-wip-pa (Tall Women); Po-che-na-qua-heip (Buffalo Hump); Pa-na-che (Mistletoe). Kappler II, 556. |

12. These were: 1—Yam-pe-uc-coes, or root-diggers" (Yamparikas); 2—"Hoo'ish, or Honey Eaters" (Penatekas); 3—"Co-che-te-cah, or Buffalo Eaters" (Kotsotekas); 4—"Noonah, or People of the Desert" (Kwahadi); 5—"No-co-nee, or People in a Circle" (Nokoni); 6—"Te-naq-wash, or People in the Timber" (Tenawa).

13. Report of Butler and Lewis, *op. cit.*

14. Williams to Butler and Lewis, July 12, 1846, photostat copy of manuscript.

| Buffalo Hump was naturally a troublemaker. Concerning this affair Williams writes:

"I have since rec'vd a letter from Major Bryant stating that Buffalo Hump come to his place with 80 or 100 of his tribe and wanted him to give them corn, after giving them all he could spare they told him they must have more and He [Buffalo Hump] took from his pocket his medal and papers, threw them on the ground said the Americans was not friends and went on to take as much corn as they pleased then they went to the house Broke open trunks took Domestic Calico and various articles ... and left and are now [a] little above the settlements."

Williams stated that he was going at once to Bryant's and try to bring the chief to his senses. It seems that nothing further came of the affair. |

15. *Ibid.* Later on five companies of mounted volunteers were raised under the requisition of Colonel Harney. A. C. Horton, acting-governor of Texas, to President Polk, October 22, 1846, U.S. Indian Office, Misc., P 1793.

16. Medill to Neighbors, October 8, 1846, Ind. Off. Letter Book, 38.

17. Torrey to Houston, January 9, 1847, U.S. Indian Office, T 27. Except where stated otherwise, references to documents in the United States Indian Office at Washington, of date earlier than 1861, are in fact references to the University of Texas collection of photostatic copies of these papers. Generally the file number of the original document will follow, but in some cases this could not be ascertained from the photostatic copy.

Letters received at the Indian Office will ordinarily be designated by I.O., or I.O., L.R., followed by the file letter and number; and those sent will be designated by I.O., followed by the number of the letter book in which the copy is recorded.

18. Torrey to Medill, November 28, 1846, I.O., Misc., T 1520. | Torrey was much alarmed when the Indians began to come to the trading post to receive their presents and there was none to give them. On the advice of Sam Houston, Torrey supplied the goods. |

19. Torrey to Houston, January 9, 1847, I.O., T 27. In the Indian appropriation bill, approved March 3, 1847, congress appropriated $20,000 "for purchasing presents for the Comanche and other Indians of Texas." Of this sum an amount not to exceed $10,000 was to be used to pay Torrey for presents advanced. *United States Statutes at Large*, IX, 204.

The amount remaining was sufficient to purchase presents for the year 1847.

20. It was reported that the great chief had given away all of his property and had removed to a remote corner of the village, with scarcely enough skins to cover himself with, to die. In this matter he disappointed his heirs, however, for he recovered and lived for several years thereafter.

21. Medill to J. Pinckney Henderson, governor of Texas, April 3, 1847, I.O., L.R., 39.

22. R. L. Biesele, "The Relations between the German settlers and the Indians in Texas, 1844–1860," in *Southwestern Historical Quarterly*, XXXI, 118.

23. Neighbors to Medill, April 24, 1847, I.O., N 6.

24. *Texas*, 322, 323.

25. *Ibid.*, 324.

26. Neighbors to Medill, November 18, 1847, I.O., L.R., N 3.

27. Neighbors to Medill, April 13, 1847, I.O., Tex., N 6. At the request of Governor Henderson, Neighbors had been acting in that capacity since the first of February.

28. Neighbors to Medill, June 22, 1847, 30 cong., I sess., *Sen. Ex. Doc.* no. I, 892 ff.

29. *Ibid.* It will be recalled that Santa Anna had visited Washington the year before, 1846.

30. *Ibid.* | These upper Brazos bands, i.e., Waco, Wichita, and Tawakoni and some Kichai Indians brought about much confusion and bloodshed through their horse-stealing raids. They would return from the settlements through the villages of the faithful Caddoes and Anadarkoes and thus involve them in their theft. Also their depredations were often charged to the Comanches. | In 1844 the upper Kichai village was located on the east bank of the Brazos, fifteen or seventeen miles below the mouth of the Clear Fork. Statement of Luis Sanches, May, 1844, Texas Indian Papers.

31. Hays to Neighbors, July 15, 1847, I.O., N 31.

32. Neighbors to Medill, September 14, 1847, 30 cong., I sess., *Sen. Ex. Doc.* no. I, 899; Neighbors to Medill, October 12, 1847, *Ibid.*, 903, 904.

33. Buffalo Hump came in later with a number of his people and stayed several days while the agent furnished his party with provisions and presents. See Neighbors to Medill, December 13, 1847, 30 cong., I sess., *Sen. Rep. Com.* no. 171, 13.

34. Neighbors to Medill, November 18, 1847, *op. cit.*

35. Neighbors to Medill, March 2, 1848, 30 cong., I sess., *Sen. Rep. Com.* no. 171, 16 ff.

| 36. It will be remembered that Pah-ha-u-ca was a Penateka; but his band generally ranged north of the other Texas Comanches and, as this incident shows, he was intimately associated with the chiefs of the northern bands. It would be interesting to know how much authority he exercised among these bands of the north. The fact that Old Owl sent for him at this critical time indicates that he was a man of considerable power and influence. The greatest claim Old Owl ever made in the way of asserting his own power and dignity was to state that "even Pah-ha-u-ca" looked to him for council. It seems that wherever Pah-ha-u-ca went it was generally conceded that he was boss of all Comanches in his presence. On the other hand it could not be said that he was head chief of all the Comanches. Doubtless many Comanche warriors never heard of him and there is nothing to indicate that he claimed the allegiance of any warriors other than his own immediate followers. |

37. Neighbors to Medill, March 2, 1848, *op. cit.*

38. *Ibid.*, 24.

39. Neighbors to Medill, October 23, 1848, I.O., L.R. 74.

40. Article XI of the treaty between the United States and Mexico, concluded February 2, 1848, ratifications exchanged March 30. *International Acts, Protocols and Agreements*, 1776–1909, I, 61 cong., 2 sess., *Sen. Doc.* no. 357, 1112.

41. Medill to Neighbors, February 22, 1849, Ind. Off. Lettr. Bk., 41.

42. Neighbors to Brown, August 13, 1849, I.O., Tex. Specl. Agt., 94.

43. In the winter of 1847–1848 the ranger companies along the Texas frontier were as follows; the first company, stationed at the Elm Fork of the Trinity, was commanded by Captain Fitzburg; the second, commanded by Colonel M. T. Johnson, was stationed at the Waco village, not far from the present location of Waco; the third, commanded by H. E. McCulloch, was stationed on the Colorado; Captain Wm. G. Crump was stationed on the Medina, twenty-four miles northwest of San Antonio; Captain S. Highsmith was stationed sixty miles northwest of San Antonio; and another force was located at Laredo on the Rio Grande. *The Northern Standard*, January 22, 1848.

Apparently Neighbors thought that the ranger force was larger than necessary, and sometimes added to his troubles. At this time he wrote to Medill: "There is now eight companies of rangers on this frontier, which is more than was ever before stationed here, even when we were at war with the tribes on our borders." Neighbors to Medill, March 2, 1848, 30 cong., I sess., *Sen. Rep. Com.* 171, 24.

44. Buffalo Hump is hardly entitled to a place among this group.

CHAPTER SIX

1. L. H. Williams to Neighbors, October 9, 1849, I.O., L.R., N 91; W. Steele to Deas, September 22, 1849, I.O., W 370 (copy). Concerning the smallpox of 1848, see Neighbors to Medill, March 2, 1848, I.O., L.R., N 53.

2. The name means, he pays no attention to happenings, *i.e.*, the man of poise, or the dignified one.

3. Steele to Deas, September 22, 1849, *op. cit.*

| 4. In February, 1849, Neighbors wrote that with the consent of the Caddoes, Ionies, Anadarkoes, Wacoes, etc., who were being concentrated at the Kichai village, George Barnard was making arrangements to establish a branch trading house near them, adding that Barnard had always "stuck to legal trade." —Neighbors to Medill, February 15, 1849, O.I.A., Tex. Inds. N 84.

The expression "branch house" might indicate that Torrey's, who had for several years maintained the trading house near present Waco, were interested in this new project situated farther up the Brazos. An implication to this effect was made by agent John H. Rollins in September, 1850.—Rollins to the Commissioner of Indian Affairs [?], September 30, 1850, O.I.A., Tex. R 611.

Thomas T. Ewell, in his *History of Hood County* (Granbury, Texas, 1895), page 53, states that Barnard's Trading House was located "as far back as 1847." The date is surely incorrect, however, for Neighbors, who visited the Indians of this region several times a year, would certainly have made mention of the trading house if it had been located at that time. Ewell states that it was located in the Barnard or Fort Spunky community, which embraces that section of Hood. |

5. Rollins to the commissioner of Indian Affairs, September 30, 1850, I.O., Tex., R 611. The location of the trading house is marked by the present village of Fort Spunky. It seems that the Torreys had an interest in the business.

6. Rollins to the commissioner of Indian Affairs, November 2, 1850, 31 cong., 2 sess., *Sen. Ex. Doc.* no. I, 143–145; L. H. Williams to Neighbors, October 9, 1849, I.O., N 91.

7. "Treaty of peace entered into between John H. Rollins and the Indian Chiefs, at Spring Creek, near the San Saba, December 10, 1850." The treaty was never submitted to the senate because it was regarded as nothing more than a special agreement under the terms of the general treaty of 1846. Rollins to Lea, March 4, 1851, I.O., L.R., R 677.

At the place of the treaty, a few miles from the town of San Saba as now located, the agent caused to be erected a stone monument to impress the savages with the sacredness of their obligation. The original monument has been removed, but a marker has been erected in its place.

8. Hardee to Deas, May 28, 1851 (copy), I.O., L.R.

9. Rogers to Bell, November 25, 1851, ms., Texas adjutant-general's office; "List of Mexicans taken by Colonel John A. Rogers, Special Indian Agent in his treaty of Nov. 23, 1851," I.O., L.R.

10. Brevet-major H. W. Merrill, temporarily commanding at Fort Mason, to Rogers, March 9, 1852, I.O., L.R.

11. Stem to Lea, October 8, 1852, 32 cong., 2 sess., *House Ex. Doc.* no. I, 1, part 1, 433.

12. The system of giving presents to the Indians had been adopted again, and in 1851 the Texas Indians received annuities. Perhaps this made the northern Comanches jealous of their southern kinsmen.

13. Inman, *The Old Santa Fé Trail*; Lowe, *Five Years a Dragoon*; Froebel, *Aus Amerika*, II, 92 ff.; Grinnell, *The Fighting Cheyennes*; Grinnell, "Bent's Old Fort and its Builders," in Kansas Historical Society *Collections*, XV, 29 ff.

| 14. See Colonel Henry Inman, *The Old Santa Fé Trail* (New York, 1897); P. C. Lowe, *Five Years a Dragoon* (Kansas City, 1906); Julius Froebel, *Aus Amerika* (Leipzig, 1857), II, 92 ff.; George Bird Grinnell, *The Fighting Cheyennes* (New York, 1915), and "Bent's Old Fort and its Builders," Kansas Historical Society *Collections*, Vol. XV, 99 ff. |

15. Ralph P. Bieber, "The Southwestern Trails to California," in *Mississippi Valley Historical Review*, XII, 360.

16. Mabelle Eppard Martin, "California Emigrant Roads Through Texas," in *Southwestern Historical Quarterly*, XXVIII, 287 ff.

17. "Journal of a Trip from Dallas to the Passo del Norte, on the Route to California" [Gilbert Party], in *The Northern Standard*, February 16, 1850. The writer indicates that other routes were known and had been traveled.

18. Bent to the commissioner of Indian Affairs, report for 1859, 36 cong., I sess., *Sen. Ex. Doc.* no. 2, 506.

19. Bancroft, *Works*, XXV, 375, 376.

20. Some of the savages thought the white people were insane. George Bent, quoted by Grinnell, *The Fighting Cheyennes*, 119.

21. "Esculapas," an emigrant, to the editor, St. Louis [Missouri] *Republican*, July 25, 1858. For a brief biography of Jesse Chisholm, see Joseph B. Thoburn, *Standard History of Oklahoma*, I, 346, footnote 1.

22. Fort Mann, a crude log structure, was built in 1847 on the Santa Fé trail about five miles west of the present Dodge City, Kansas. Ralph P. Bieber, "Southwestern Trails to California," in *Mississippi Valley Historical Review*, XII, 366, footnote 49. In the same vicinity Fort Sumner, later called Fort Atkinson, was established in 1851 and abandoned in 1853. There was no other post on the upper Arkansas until Fort Larned was established at the mouth of Pawnee creek in 1859. Grinnell, *The Fighting Cheyennes*, 116, footnote 1.

23. Henderson to Neighbors, November 10, 1847 (copy), and Neighbors to Medill, December 13, 1847, I.O., L.R., N 36.

24. Neighbors to Medill, March 16, 1848, 30 cong., 1 sess., *Sen. Rep. Com.* no. 171, 14–16.

25. Päh'-häh-yŏ'-kō once said, "The Wichitas are like dogs. They will steal. You may feed a dog well at night, and he will steal all your meat before morning. This is the way with the Wichitas." "Talk of Pahayeuca (Comanche chief) at Trading House," January 10, 1845, Texas Indian Papers.

26. Jesse Stem to Colonel G. Loomis, January 9, 1853, I.O., L.R., S 347 (copy), and Stem to Lea, April 1, 1853, *ibid.*

27. Capron to Manypenny, about May 1, 1853, I.O., Univ. Tex. photostat copy.

One incident pertaining to the Wichita robber bands is of unusual interest. Koweaka, a chief, and a small band of squaws, children, and warriors had been seized by Major H. H. Sibley of the second infantry at a point near the Indian agency on the Clear Fork. They were informed that they would be held until certain other Wichitas brought in more horses which had been stolen. Concerning a tragic incident that occurred one night Sibley writes:

"They retired quietly to their tents at dark, manifesting not the slightest intention of an attempt to escape. The moon shone as bright as day. I had posted two distinct guards over them of six men each, with four sentinels. I had been up and moving about camp until about 20 minutes before 12. At 12 the sentinels were relieved. The sentinel posted more immediately over their camp, had gone near one of their tents to verify the number present, while the corporal of the guard, the old sentinel and a citizen who accompanied me, stood near looking on. Suddenly one of the Indians rushed forth from his tent towards the sentinel, and presenting a pistol fired, shooting him through the heart. This seemed to be the signal for a general 'break.' As the sentinel turned to retreat up the slope towards his companions, the chief Koweaka, rushed from his tent like a demon, threw himself upon the back of the sentinel, and with his reeking knife inflicted several wounds before he was shot down by the old sentinel. The rest succeeded in effecting their escape, running in different directions and answering the shots that were fired at them with yells of defiance. The chief, as was discovered on searching the tents, had purposely sacrificed himself, his wife, and boy seven years old, to secure the escape of his companions. The wife and child whom he had requested in the evening before to talk to and give them assurance of their safety, were found lying in their tent side by side, as if in deep sleep, but stabbed to the heart. The wife, at least, had consented to her fate, as we were informed by two old women who had [not?] attempted to escape."

"She seemed to have received the fatal blow without a struggle—both were carefully covered up to the breast, the child lying upon its mother's breast. The chief's moccasins were found near their heads, as a sign, the Indians told us, that he did not mean to leave the spot alive. Nothing in romance or history that I have ever read approximated to this act of devotion and self sacrifice. Cooper never could have ventured to paint such a scene?" *The Northern Standard*, June 11, 1853, quoting the *Southwest American*.

28. Stem to G. Loomis, commander at Fort Belknap, March 30, 1853, I.O. (copy). This was Koweaka's band.

29. The raids continued. As late as April, 1854, the Wichitas killed four persons within twenty miles of San Antonio and escaped unpunished. Neighbors to Manypenny, April 18, 1854, I.O., L.R., Texas, N 254.

30. Neighbors to Medill, March 2, 1848, 30 cong., 1 sess., *Sen. Rep. Com.* no. 171, 18 ff.

31. Wild Cat, who had fought in the Seminole War in Florida, was removed to Indian Territory and became a kind of scout and guide. He accompanied Butler and Lewis into Texas in 1846. Then, after his return from this trip, he took about 250 of his tribe on an exploring hunt into the prairies. His party secured credit at a frontier trading establishment and took along a considerable quantity of goods.

A few years later we hear of Wild Cat in Texas with a party of Seminoles and negroes, and about a hundred Kickapoo warriors and their families. He did not take seriously Agent Rollins's suggestion that he was a trespasser and had better move on. It seems that the chief finally took his Seminoles and negroes on to Mexico, where he appeared in a somewhat doubtful role in the Indian warfare along the Rio Grande. Survivors of his colony may still be found at Piedras Negras, opposite Eagle Pass.

32. Report of William Armstrong to the commissioner of Indian Affairs, September 30, 1845, 29 cong., 1 sess., *Sen. Ex. Doc.* no. 1, 508.

33. On his return from New Mexico by way of the north Texas route in 1849, Captain R. B. Marcy came across a band of Kickapoos near the Clear Fork of the Brazos. Concerning them he wrote: "They numbered one hundred warriors—fine, dashing-looking young fellows—all well mounted, and armed with good rifles, upon some of which we saw the familiar names of 'Darranger' and 'Tryon,' 'Philadelphia Makers.' They had their families with them; and were going to pass the winter hunting upon the Colorado, where they expected to find game abundant . . ." 31 cong., 1 sess., *Sen. Ex. Doc.* no. 64, 215.

| 34. Miller and Conner to Rogers, September 12, 1851, O.I.A. |

35. Whitefield to Cumming, September 27, 1854, 33 cong., 2 sess., *Sen. Ex. Doc.* no. 1, vol. 1, part 1, 298.

| 36. See the statement of Manypenny, 34 cong., 3 sess., *Sen. Doc.* no. 1, 566, 1856. |

37. Charles Joseph Latrobe, *The Rambler in North America*, 11, 203 ff.

38. Letter written at Fort Gibson, August 1, 1833, to the editor, *Skinner's American Turf Register*, quoted by the *Arkansas Gazette*, March 25, 1834.

39. Armstrong's report, 1841, 27 cong., 2 sess., *Sen. Ex. Doc.* no. 1, 338.

40. George F. Ruxton, *Adventurers in Mexico and the Rocky Mountains*, 254. This statement was written in 1846.

41. William Kennedy, *Texas*, I, 122.

42. Ruxton, *op. cit.*, 257; Roemer, *Texas*, 221 ff. In this connection see C. C. Rister, "The Significance of the Destruction of the Buffalo in the Southwest," in *Southwestern Historical Quarterly*, xxxiii, 34–49.

43. "Reminiscences of Mrs. Dilue Harris," in *Quarterly* of the Texas State Historical Association, IV, 161.

44. The *Standard* (Clarksville), May 28, 1853; "Report of Alex B. Hasson, Post Surgeon at Fort Phantom Hill, for 1852," in West Texas Historical Association *Year Book*, I, 75.

45. Report of S. P. Ross, Brazos agent, March 31, 1857, I.O., L.R., N 259.

46. Hill to Neighbors, April 3, 1855, I.O., L.R., N 424.

| 47. Vaughn to Cumming, October 21, 1853, 35 cong., 1 sess., *Sen. Exec. Doc.* 1, Part I, p. 354. |

48. Report of Robert Miller, agent for the upper Arkansas agency, October 14, 1857, 35 cong., 1 sess., *Sen. Ex. Doc.* no. II, 436.

49. Miller's report, August 17, 1858, 35 cong., 2 sess., *Sen. Ex. Doc.* no. 1, vol. 1, 450.

50. Whitefield to the commissioner of Indian Affairs, September 4, 1855, 34 cong., 1 sess., *Sen. Ex. Doc.* no. 1, part 1, 437.

CHAPTER SEVEN

1. See Grinnell, *The Fighting Cheyennes*, 35–59.

2. *Ibid.*, 60 ff.

3. The Bents evidently traded in the Canadian country as early as 1835, for one of the brothers returned from a trading expedition to the Kiowa and Comanche country while Colonel Dodge was at Bent's Fort in 1835. Grinnell, "Bent's Old Fort and its Builders," in Kansas Historical *Collections*, XV, 42, footnote 22.

Then the Bents built some kind of a post on the Canadian in the fall of 1842. In his journal of the Santa Fé trail, Captain Philip St. George Cook wrote, July 4, 1843, "With the Comanches and Kiowas Mr. Charles Bent made here last summer, a kind of peace or truce; they asked for traders amongst them, and in the fall he established a house about 200 miles to the south on the Canadian river . . ." "A Journal of the Santa Fé Trail" (ed. Connelley), in *Mississippi Valley Historical Review*, XII, 239.

The best known of Bent's posts, the one probably built in the winter of 1843–1844, was about a mile and a half up the Canadian river from the site of the new Adobe Walls built by the buffalo hunters in 1874. Another post was built, probably in the winter of 1845–1846, about two miles above the mouth of Red Deer creek, near the present town of Canadian. Dixon, *Life of "Billy" Dixon*, 108, 135, 151; Mooney, "Calendar History of the Kiowa Indians," *op. cit.*, 238.

4. "Journal of the Santa Fé Trail," *op. cit.*

5. "Bent's Old Fort and its Builders," *op. cit.*, 54.

6. Among such expeditions that of Lieutenant Abert, in 1845, may be mentioned. Along the upper Canadian he found the Kiowas friendly, but the Comanches fled at his approach. 29 cong., 1 sess., *Sen. Doc.* no. 438, 30 ff.

7. Marcy's report of this expedition is printed in the 31 cong., 1 sess., *House Ex. Doc.* no. 45, 26–89, and also in *Sen. Ex. Doc.* no. 64.

8. Fitzpatrick to D. D. Mitchell, superintendent of Indian Affairs, St. Louis, September 24, 1850, 31 cong., 2 sess., *Sen. Ex. Doc.* no. 1, 52.

It will be recalled that the year preceding, 1849, was the year that the cholera scourge carried away so many Penatekas. I have never seen an estimate of the number of northern Comanches and Kiowas who died from cholera that year, but Grinnell thinks that half, or almost half of the Cheyennes died, and the other plains tribes suffered severely. The scourge broke out while the Comanches were in attendance at a great Indian gathering to erect a medicine lodge on Bluff creek, south of present Dodge City, Kansas.

| Besides the Kiowas and Comanches there were Prairie Apaches, Cheyennes, Arapahoes, and a large camp of Osages. The Osages had recently made peace with the Kiowas and had come to the Kiowa village to trade. From the Cheyennes Grinnell got the following account which conveys a good conception of the helplessness of the savages before the onslaughts of the dread diseases:

"One day while all of the Indians were watching the Kiowa dancers in the medicine lodge an Osage man in the audience fell down with the 'cramps'—cholera—and died in a few minutes. White Face Bull, a Cheyenne chief, who was standing in the crowd with his son Porcupine Bull, was the first to realize what was wrong with the Osage man. He at once shouted out that it was 'cramps' and that all should take down their lodges and run. In a few minutes the plain was covered with bands of Indians fleeing in every direction." "Bent's Old Fort and its Builders," as cited, 47. |

9. Fitzpatrick to Lea, November 24, 1851, 32 cong., 1 sess., *Sen. Ex. Doc.* no. 1, part III, 332–336.

| 10. Henry Heith, Lieutenant Infantry, to Brevet Major General R. Jones, Adjutant General, September 4, 1851 (copy), O.I.A., L.R. |

11. Mitchell to Lea, October 17, 1852, 32 cong., 2 sess., *House Ex. Doc.* no. 1, vol. 1, part 1, 357.

12. Manypenny to Fitzpatrick, May 5, 1853, I.O., L.R., vol. 47.

13. Fitzpatrick to Cumming, November 19, 1853, 33 cong., 1 sess., *Sen. Doc.* no. 1, part 1, 360.

14. Kappler, *Indian Affairs Laws and Treaties*, II, 600–602. Fitzpatrick's report, *op. cit.*

15. 33 cong., 2 sess., *Sen. Ex. Doc.* no. 1, part I, 299; 35 cong., 1 sess., *Sen. Ex. Doc.* no. 11, 430; Froebel, *Aus Amerika*, II, 93 ff.

Some interesting characteristics of Shaved Head are given by Lieutenant Z. G. Beckwith of the Pacific Railway survey, whose party met the Comanches near Fort Atkinson, July 16, 1853.

"Shaved Head, with some of his principal men, paid us a visit just as Captain Gunnison and myself were dining. Blankets were spread for them in front of the captain's tent, and they did ample justice to the fare spread before them—carrying off, as usual, what they could not eat at the time. After the usual amount of talk, smoking, and ceremony, they took their leave, which, with Shaved Head—the principal chief of the Comanches of the plains—is a peculiar ceremony which he extends to all whom he esteems or deems of importance. He assumes an air of gravity and solemnity of features I have never seen equalled by more civilized performers, and taking you by the right hand, gives three shakes as slow and deliberate as the time to a funeral dirge, pressing your hand, with a firm grasp, and looking steadily in your eyes; releasing your hand he passes his arm through yours to the elbow, and thus facing in opposite directions he presses your arm firmly to his side; then the left arms perform the same measured functions; and during the whole of this leave-taking he repeats, 'bueno, mucho bueno,' with a grave accent." Pacific Railroad survey *Reports*, 11, 25.

16. Whitefield to Manypenny, September 4, 1855, 34 cong., 1 sess., *Sen. Ex. Doc.* no. 1, part 1, 435, 436.

17. The difficulty he had in suppressing violence with his little force of fifty men is set forth by R. H. Chilton, commanding at Fort Atkinson, in a letter to S. Cooper, July 27, 1853 (copy). I.O., L.R., N 355.

18. "Eldredge's Report on his Expedition to the Comanches," *op. cit.*, 124; report of Thomas H. Harvey, supt. Ind. Affrs., St. Louis, for 1844, 28 cong., 2 sess., *House Ex. Doc.* no. 2, 435; report of Harvey to T. H. Crawford, September 10, 1845, 29 cong., 1 sess., *Sen. Ex. Doc.* no. 1, 583; Harvey to Medill, report for 1848, 30 cong., 1 sess., *Sen. Ex. Doc.* no. 1, 835.

19. Richardson to the commissioner of Indian Affairs, March 27, 1848, I.O., L.R.

20. Whitefield to Cumming, September 27, 1854, *op. cit.*

21. George W. Hill, special agent, Texas Indians, to R. S. Neighbors, supervising agent, April 5, 1855, I.O., L.R., N 424; C. W. Dean, superintendent Indian affairs, southern superintendency, to the commissioner of Indian Affairs, September 13, 1855, 34 cong., 1 sess., *Sen. Doc.* no. 1, 441, 442.

22. Report of Robert C. Miller, Indian agent of the upper Arkansas, to the commissioner of Indian Affairs, August 17, 1858, 35 cong., 2 sess., *Sen. Ex. Doc.* no. 1, vol. 1, 449.

23. Report of D. Merriwether, governor and superintendent of Indian Affairs, Santa Fé, New Mexico, to Manypenny, September (no other date), 1855. 34 cong., 1 sess., *Sen. Ex. Doc.* no. 1, 509; Hill to Neighbors, April 5, 1855, *op. cit.* Hill stated that certain southern Comanches reported that many Nokoni and "Tanawish" Comanches, including some of their chiefs, were killed in a fight with the Osages during the winter of 1854–1855. Whitefield to Manypenny, September 4, 1855, 34 cong., 1 sess., *Sen. Ex. Doc.* no. 1, part 1, 331.

24. John Munroe to Jones, June 29, 1851, in A. H. Abel, *The Official Correspondence of James S. Calhoun*, 345–346.

25. Garland to Thomas, July 31, 1855, 34 cong., 1 sess., *Sen. Ex. Doc.* no. 1, part II, 71.

26. Report of the commissioner of Indian Affairs for 1853, 33 cong., 1 sess., *Sen. Ex. Doc.* no. 1, part 1, 252.

27. In 1856 some of the northern chiefs sent word to John R. Baylor, U.S. agent on the Texas reservation, that they wished to make a treaty with him. They stated that they had never made a treaty with Texas, that the treaty made in Kansas was a local affair. Baylor to Neighbors, November 18, 1856, I.O., L.R., N 198.

28. Neighbors to Manypenny, April 12, 1854, I.O., L.R.

29. That is, the portion of the southern Comanches then on the Texas reservation.

30. Report to the commissioner of Indian Affairs, September 16, 1857, 35 cong., 1 sess., *Sen. Ex. Doc.* no. II, 551, 552.

In this connection, see also General Twiggs to army headquarters, January 20, 1858, 35 cong., 2 sess., *Sen. Ex. Doc.* no. 1, vol. II, 249, 250.

31. Neighbors to Howard, January 7, 1855, I.O., L.R., J 859, N 360; Neighbors to Manypenny, September 18, 1856, 34 cong., 3 sess., *House Ex. Doc.* no. 1, 724.

32. For a biographical sketch of Jesse Chisholm, see Thoborn, *Standard History of Oklahoma*, 1, 364, footnote 1.

CHAPTER EIGHT

1. It should be stated that by Article 2 of the Gadsden Purchase treaty of 1853, Mexico released the United States from all liability for damages by United States Indians imposed by Article II of the treaty of Guadalupe Hidalgo and Article 33 of the treaty with Mexico made April 5, 1831. *United States Statutes at Large*, X, *1031*. However, when the United States amassed claims against the Mexican government for damages originating along the lower Rio Grande valley from lawless Mexicans and Mexican Indians, the Mexican government endeavored to offset these claims by compiling a long list of offenses committed in Mexico by Indians from the United States. In 1872 a commission sent by the Mexican authorities investigated the matter, examining the archives of the towns in the affected area, American newspaper files, and many works published in English including Gregg's *Commerce of the Prairies*. They could have strengthened their case by drawing on the archives of Texas and the United States. The report of this commission was printed in both Spanish and English. I have followed the English copy, entitled *Official Reports of the Committee of Investigation Sent in 1873 by the Mexican Government to the Frontier of Texas. Translated from the Original Edition made in Mexico* (New York, 1875). It will be cited as *Reports of the Mexican Commission*.

2. *Reports of the Mexican Commission*, 250.

3. "A Journal of the Santa Fé Trail" (ed. Connelley), in *Mississippi Valley Historical Review*, XII, 239, 240; *Telegraph and Texas Register*, February 12, 1845.

4. Western to Houston, April 25, 1844, Texas Indian Papers. Perhaps the chief was trying to avenge the loss of his son, who had been killed in a raid during the preceding year.

5. Watson to Houston, October 2, 1844, Texas Indian Papers.

6. *Telegraph and Texas Register*, March 19, and April 2, 1845.

7. Western to Coleman, May 5, 1845, Texas Indian Papers.

8. Western to Neighbors, May 11, 1845, *ibid*.

9. Sloat to Western, July 24, 1845, *ibid*.

10. Neighbors to Western, June 14, 1845, *ibid*. It seems that Bear's Tail, or Bear-with-a-Short-Tail, was Päh'-häh-yŏ'-kō's war chief.

11. Torrey to Houston, January 9, 1847, I.O., T 27.

12. Neighbors to Medill, September 14, 1847, 30 cong., 1 sess., *Sen. Ex. Doc.* no. 1, 899.

13. See John C. Cremony, *Life Among the Apaches*, 13 ff.

14. Neighbors to Medill, September 14, 1847, *op. cit.*

15. Neighbors to Medill, November 18, 1847, 30 cong., 1 sess., *Sen. Rep. Com.* no. 171, 9.

16. See L. H. Williams to Neighbors, October 9, 1849, I.O., N 97. In the treaty made with the southern Comanches in 1846, the matter of depredations against Mexico was not mentioned. In the treaty of Camp Holmes, made with some of the northern bands in 1835, there was nothing more than the statement that the United States did not desire to interrupt the "friendly relations" of the Indians with the Republic of Mexico. Article 9 of the treaty, *United States Statutes at Large*, VII, 476.

17. For an account of the appointment of the Mexican commission, see note 1.

18. Compare Whitefield to Cumming, September 27, 1854, 33 cong., 2 sess., *Sen. Ex. Doc.* no. 1, part 1, 299, and Neighbors to Manypenny, September 16, 1854, *ibid.*, 366.

19. *Reports of the Mexican Commission*, 293 ff.

20. *Ibid.*, 328 ff.

21. Ruxton, *Adventures in Mexico and the Rocky Mountains*, 111, 112; John Russell Bartlett, *Personal Narrative*, II, 467, 478, 492.

22. E. B. Babbitt, assistant quartermaster, San Antonio, to the secretary of war, October 15, 1849 (extract of letter), I.O., W 381; Froebel, *Aus Amerika*, 11, 219.

Notes

23. J. A. Rogers to the commissioner of Indian Affairs, June 29, 1851, I.O., Tex., R 686; Miller and Conner to Rogers, September 12, 1851, I.O., L.R., 706.
24. *Adventures in Mexico and the Rocky Mountains,* 112.
25. John Russell Bartlett, *Personal Narrative,* II, 442 ff.
26. Julius Froebel, *Aus Amerika,* II, 209-225.
27. *Reports of the Mexican Commission,* 305 ff. However, they were renewed, although not so extensively, after the Civil War in the United States. In fact, there were some during the period of the Civil War.
28. Howard to Lea, June 1 (?), 1852, O.I., L.R., Tex., H 105.
29. Neighbors to the commissioner of Indian Affairs, September 16, 1853, 33 cong., 1 sess., *Sen. Exec. Doc.* no. I, part I, pp. 425, 428.
30. Some of the new military posts in Texas were: Camp Lancaster, on the Pecos west of modern Ozona; Fort Bliss, near El Paso (1854); Camp Hudson, on Devil's river in Crockett county; Camp Verde, in what is now Kendall county; Camp Wood, on the Nueces river in what is now Real county; Camp Colorado, in what is now Coleman county; the re-occupation of Fort Inge, on the Leona river near the present town of Uvalde (1857); Fort Stockton, where that town now is located; and Fort Quitman, on the Rio Grande in what is now Hudspeth county (1859). One-fifth of the entire United States army was stationed in the state in 1860. On the whole the troops were aggressive, made many scouts, engaged in dozens of tilts with the Indians, and did well the service expected of them. A number of men who later became outstanding generals in the Union and Confederate armies were officers in these Texas Indian wars. Among them appear the names of Earl Van Dorn, J. B. Hood, Kirby Smith, N. J. Evans, George Thomas, Albert Sidney Johnston, G. Stoneman, Fitzhugh Lee, and Robert E. Lee. See W. C. Holden, "Frontier Defense, 1846-1860," in West Texas Historical Association *Year Book,* VI, 50, 54, 61, 63.
31. List of Mexicans taken by Colonel John A. Rogers, special Indian agent, in his treaty of 1851, *op. cit.*
32. Howard to Lea, June 10, 1852, I.O., L.R., Tex., H 104. It is possible that these were counted among the twenty-seven noted above.
33. Neighbors to Manypenny, November 21, 1853, I.O., L.R., Tex., N 190.
34. Neighbors to Manypenny, May 14, 1856, I.O., L.R., N 109.
| 35. Fitzpatrick to Cumming, November 19, 1855, 33 cong., 1 sess., *Sen. Exec. Doc.* no. 1, Part I, p. 363. |
36. Calhoun to Brown, March 31, 1850, 31 cong., 2 sess., *Sen. Ex. Doc.* no. 1, 137.

Indian traders, out of kindness or the hope of reward, sometimes purchased these Comanche and Kiowa prisoners. Among those who seem to have been actuated more by humanitarian impulses than by the hope of gain may be mentioned William Donoho who purchased several American prisoners in New Mexico, Josiah Gregg, and Jesse Chisholm.

Since the price of prisoners was generally about two hundred dollars, it is evident that a poor man could not afford to purchase one unless he was reasonably certain that the prisoner or his people could make good the purchase price.

37. Neighbors to Manypenny, May 14, 1856, *op. cit.*

CHAPTER NINE

1. See Butler and Lewis to Medill, April 1, 1846, I.O.
2. Neighbors to General W. J. Worth, March 7, 1849, I.O., N 93.
3. Message of the governor, in the *Northern Standard,* January 22, 1848.
4. Rollins to Lea, March 20, 1851, I.O., L.R.
5. Rollins to Brown, May 8, 1850, O.I.A., Tex. R 596.
6. Report of John A. Rogers, October 6, 1851, O.I.A.
7. Howard to Lea, June 1, 1852, I.O., L.R.
8. Capron to Howard, September 30, 1852, I.O., L.R., H 112.

Perhaps the reference to efforts made by the Comanches to plant crops should not be taken seriously.

9. I do not recall having read a single general description of the Comanches written by observers before 1850 that does not mention their disposition to refuse to drink liquor. But in 1853, Neighbors wrote:

"I am sorry to see that the Comanches, as they become more civilized from unrestricted intercourse with the numerous traders who visit our frontier, are becoming slaves to dissipation, and a large portion of their scanty means is squandered for whiskey. The chiefs, who are reliable, complain bitterly of the advantage taken of them by those who introduce whiskey, and say they cannot control their men so long as they are furnished with spirituous liquors." Neighbors to the commissioner of Indian Affairs, September 16, 1853, 33 cong., 1 sess., *Sen. Ex. Doc.* no. 1, part 1, 426.

Neighbors had been out of the Indian service for four years, and the increase in debauchery during that period especially impressed him.

10. Neighbors to Medill, March 2, 1848, 30 cong., 1 sess., *Sen. Rep. Com.* no. 171, 20.
11. Williams to Neighbors, October 9, 1849, I.O., N 97.
12. In the winter of 1851–1852, their villages were described as follows: Anadarko, 250 souls, chief José María, on the upper edge of the Cross Timbers, nine miles above the Palo Pinto creek; the Hainaies, 200 souls, chief Tow-y-ash, just across the Brazos from the Anadarkoes; the Caddoes, 200 souls, chief Ha-de-bah, on the west bank of the Brazos, six or eight miles above the Anadarkoes; the Kichaies, 280 souls, chief Cha-che-ruck, just opposite the Caddo village; the Tawakonies, 200 souls, chief O-che-dos, on the east bank of the Brazos, six or eight miles above the Kichai village; the Wacoes, chief A-cah-quash, 200 souls, just opposite the Tawakoni village. H. H. Sibley, captain and brevet-major, second dragoons, to Honorable G. W. Hill, January 3, 1852, in the *Northern Standard*, February 21, 1852.
13. Neighbors to Manypenny, August 6, 1853, I.O., L.R., Tex., N 140.
14. Gammel, *Laws of Texas*, III, 1495.
15. Report of Marcy and Neighbors, September 30, 1854, I.O., L.R., Tex., M 1296.
16. *Ibid.*
17. *Notes Taken . . . through Unexplored Texas*, 191 ff.
18. Neighbors to Manypenny, January 8, 1855, I.O., L.R., Tex., N 360, J 859.
19. Hill to Neighbors, August 31, 1855, 34 cong., 1 sess., *Sen. Ex. Doc.* no. 1, part 1, 502.
20. Hill to Neighbors, January 25, 1855, I.O., L.R., N 475.
21. Neighbors to Manypenny, March 5, 1855, I.O. This unfortunate affair, which illustrates so perfectly the lack of cooperation between some of the army officers and the Indian agents, provoked quite a tilt between these two agencies of the federal government. It appears that the foundation for the report that caused the trouble was a contemplated expedition from Fort Chadbourne north to punish the Nokoni and Tanima Comanches for depredations they had recently been guilty of. It seems that Neighbors had approved of the expedition with these objectives, provided the soldiers would not interfere with the reservation. Neighbors to Howard, San Antonio, January 7, 1855, *op. cit.* But the trader at Fort Chadbourne understood that the soldiers had instructions to attack all Comanches, both northern and southern, wherever they might meet them—and the trader was right. Captain Calhoun, who was in charge of the expedition (which did not leave Fort Chadbourne until February), stated to Hill, the acting Comanche agent, that his orders called for just that procedure. He did not propose to go on the reservation and fight the Comanches there, but all others he met would be chastised. Hill, at Fort Belknap, to Neighbors, at San Antonio, February 11, 1855, I.O., L.R., N 510. It was unfortunate indeed that of all the times the army might have sent an expedition to coerce the Indians, they chose to go at this critical period. On February 11, Hill wrote, "Half a million dollars will not produce the same quiet and calm condition of the Indian mind that existed on this frontier forty days ago." *Ibid.*
22. Hill to Neighbors, April 3, 1855, I.O., L.R., H 424.
23. Neighbors to Manypenny, June 10, 1855, I.O., L.R., N 491.
24. The different reports from the agents show numbers as follows: January 1, 1856, 450; September 18, 1856, 557; September, 1857, 424; January 17, 1858, 381; September 16, 1858, 371; October 30, 1858, 341; July, 1859, 382. The population in July, 1859, at the time the Indians were moved, was divided as follows: males over twelve, 80; males under twelve, 62; females over twelve, 118; females under twelve, 62.
25. It seems that Sanaco drifted from bad to worse. The last report of him was to the effect that he and his son had become notorious horse thieves. Ross to Neighbors, February 17, 1858, I.O., L.R., N 446.
26. Ross to Neighbors, July 23, 1856, I.O., L.R., N 144.
27. Leeper to Neighbors, June 1, 1857, I.O., L.R., N 284.
28. Neighbors to Leeper, July 16, 1857, I.O., L.R., H 1341.
29. Leeper to Neighbors, June 30, 1857, I.O., L.R., N 284.
30. Neighbors's report, September 16, 1857, 35 cong., 1 sess., *Sen. Ex. Doc.* no. II, vol. II, 551.
31. Leeper to Neighbors, June 4, I.O., L.R., N 479, and June 11, *ibid.*; H. P. Jones, reserve farmer, to Leeper, October 29, 1858, I.O., L.R., H 1341.
32. Baylor's report, September 12, 1856, 34 cong., 3 sess., *House Ex. Doc.* no. 1, 728.
33. These were companies A, E, F, and K, of the second (later the fifth) cavalry, under Major Hardee. Hardee arrived January 3, 1856, and established Camp Cooper, in the immediate vicinity of the reservation,

naming it in honor of the adjutant-general of the army. George F. Price, *Across the Continent with the Fifth Cavalry*, 41.

In September, 1856, there were two companies of infantry and two of cavalry at the post. Neighbors to Manypenny, September 18, 1856, 34 Cong., 3 sess., *House Ex. Doc.* no.1, 725.

34. George Stoneman, captain second cavalry, Camp Cooper, to Neighbors, September 25, 1857, I.O., L.R., H 1341. Neighbors to General Twiggs, commander department of Texas, March 29, 1858 (copy), I.O., L.R., N 454.

Neighbors alleged that Major Paul at Fort Belknap, Captain Stoneman at Camp Cooper, and Captain Givens, "who owns a stock farm about six miles from the Comanche reserve," had all interfered with the efforts of the agents and had tried to prejudice the citizens against the reserve Indians. Neighbors to Mix, May 18, 1858, I.O., L.R., N 464.

35. At this time Camp Cooper was merely an outpost of Fort Belknap.

36. Leeper to Neighbors, August 31, 1958, I.O., L.R., N 517; General Twiggs to army headquarters, September 17, 1852, 35 cong., 2 sess., *Sen Ex. Doc.* no. 1, part IV, vol. II, 263.

The reason given by the officer for the scant supply of ammunition was that since it was the last day the detachment was to remain at the post, they had shot away their ammunition in rifle practice.

37. John Withers, adjutant, to the commanding officer at Fort Belknap, September 15, 1858, I.O.

38. Leeper to Major Thomas, November 15, 1858, I.O., L.R., N 551; Neighbors wrote that General Twiggs was angry with him for not having the leaders among the Indians who had offered resistance to the troops arrested and punished, and that for this reason Twiggs would not continue to furnish protection for the agency. Neighbors to T. T. Hawkins, November 26, 1858, I.O., L.R., H 1341.

39. Neighbors to Greenwood, June 10, 1859, 36 cong., 1 sess., *Sen. Ex. Doc.* no. 2, vol. 1, 636.

40. H. B. Hubbard, United States district attorney for the western district of Texas, to Neighbors, January 12, 1859, 36 cong., 1 sess., *Sen. Doc.* no. 2, vol. 1, 592.

41. Neighbors to Denver, June 1, 1857, I.O., L.R., N 272. | Neighbors complained of this fact at this time and it does not appear that Congress ever took any action in the matter. |

42. Baylor to Neighbors, May 1, 1856, I.O., L.R., N 106. Ross to Neighbors, September 30, 1856, 34 cong., 3 sess., *House Ex. Doc.* no. 1, 730.

43. Baylor to Neighbors, June 8, 1856, I.O., L.R., N 125.

44. Baylor to Neighbors, July 6, 1856, I.O., L.R., N 144.

45. Leeper to Neighbors, April 9, 1858, I.O., L.R., N 452.

46. Thomas Lambshead (a citizen) to Manypenny, May 1, 1856, I.O., L.R., Tex., L 123; Hawkins to Mix, October 30, 1858, I.O., L.R., H 1317.

47. In this connection see Baylor's report, September 12, 1856, 34 cong., 3 sess., *House Ex. Doc.* no. 1, 725; Leeper to Neighbors, June 1, 1857, I.O., L.R., N 272; Leeper to Neighbors, August 20, 1858, 35 cong., 2 sess., *Sen. Ex. Doc.* no. 1, vol. 1, 527–530; H. P. Jones, reserve farmer, to Leeper, October 29, 1858, I.O., L.R., H 1341.

48. Hawkins to Mix, October 30, 1858, as cited.

49. Baylor to Neighbors, February 12, 1857, I.O., L.R., Ross to Neighbors, March 31, 1857, I.O., L.R., N 259; Neighbors's report, September 16, 1857, 35 cong., 1 sess., *Sen. Ex. Doc.* no. II, vol. II, 550–553.

50. Late in December, 1856, a party stole many horses, and killed or captured four or five persons in Erath and Bosque counties. It was charged that reserve Indians participated in this affair. John Forbes to Governor Runnels, January 13, 1857 (copy), I.O., L.R., H 1341.

In March, 1857, a marauding party stole a number of horses in the vicinity of the Brazos agency. Ross to Neighbors, March 31, 1857, I.O., L.R. See also Twiggs to army headquarters, January 31, 1858, 35 cong., 2 sess., *Sen. Ex. Doc.* no. 1, 249.

51. Leeper to Neighbors, November 20, 1857, I.O., L.R., N 405.

52. Neighbors to Denver, December 8, 1857, I.O., L.R., Tex., N 405.

The men who were killed were named Renfro, Renfro, and Lewis.

53. Ross to Neighbors, March 31, 1857, I.O., L.R., N 259.

The raids against these counties led to the establishment of Camp Colorado in Coleman county, in 1857. A. P. Porter, commanding at Camp Colorado, to Pease, July 6, 1857, Pease Papers, Texas State Archives.

For the scouts and engagement of the cavalry in the western portion of the state see Price, *Fifth Cavalry*, 57 ff. It was in July of this year that Lieutenant Hood, with twenty-four men, fought a desperate battle with a band of Lipans and Comanches near the head of Devil's river, after the Indians had raised a white flag and feigned friendliness. See J. B. Hood, *Advance and Retreat*, 9 ff.

228   COMANCHE BARRIER

54. For some reports of these numerous raids, see Thomas R. Carmack of the ranger company for Erath and Palo Pinto counties, to the governor, January 7, 1858 (copy), I.O., L.R., 6, H 1341; Carmack to the governor, January 11, 1858, *ibid.*; Thomas C. Frost, of the Comanche county rangers, to the governor, January 10, 1858, I.O., L.R., 5, H 1341; Runnels to Twiggs, January 9, 1858, 35 cong., 2 sess., *Sen. Ex. Doc.* no. 1, 248; Neighbors to Mix, January 17, 1858, I.O., L.R., Tex., N 414.

55. *The Standard*, June 5 and November 6, 1858; the Dallas *Herald*, September 29, quoting the Sherman *Patriot*.

56. A good general account of Indian raids against the Texas frontier and a treatment of the subject of frontier defense is given by W. C. Holden, "Frontier Defense, 1846–1860," West Texas Historical Association *Year Book*, VI, 35–64.

CHAPTER TEN

1. Neighbors to Twiggs, January 18, 1858, I.O., L.R., N 414.

2. See Whitefield to Manypenny, September 4, 1855, 34 cong., 1 sess., *Sen. Ex. Doc.* no. 1, part 1, 438; Robert Miller to Haverty, July 8, 1857, 35 cong., 1 sess., *Sen. Ex. Doc.* no. II, 429–436.

3. Royce, *op. cit.*, 808; Mix to Thompson, August 18, 1858, I.O., R.B. no. II.

| 4. The Indians reported that an agent from Indian Territory visited the different Comanche bands to discover their attitude towards coming on the proposed reservation. The Nokoni chief replied that he would camp near the Wichita Mountains if the agent would pay every man of his band a hundred dollars in silver. Leeper, at the Comanche Agency, to Neighbors, November 3, 1857, O.I.A. |

5. Twiggs to Thomas, July 6, 1858, 35 cong., 2 sess., *Sen. Ex. Doc.* no. 1, vol. II, 258.

| Possibly Twiggs would have adopted this aggressive policy sooner if the disturbed condition in Utah had not made it appear that the Second Cavalry would likely be called away for duty there during the winter of 1857–1858.

The following excerpt may be taken as a fair representation of public sentiment in Texas as regards the policy of frontier defense: ". . . No half way work will do. A sharp little skirmish, resulting in the killing of a few [Indians], might do temporary service. But for permanent service . . . a durable impression must be made upon the savages. . . . If an efficient force of Texans, will seek their villages in succession, and burn and kill as they come to them, as the early settlers of New England followed up the Pequods and Narragansetts, surrounding and exterminating them, follow them to their most secluded retreats—then there will be a finality about the work, which will thereafter ensure to the frontiersman the peaceable pursuit of his advocations."—Editorial, July 17, 1858. |

6. From the Indian agents comes the story of the exploits of one of these bands of reservation Indians that illustrates their cunning and resourcefulness. North of Red river twelve Delaware and two Caddo scouts came across a party of ten Yamparika Comanches returning from a raid in Texas and boasting of their accomplishments. That night the Delawares camped near the Comanches and visited their camp to gamble. While the games were going on, the Delawares cut the bow strings of the Comanches so that they would break when put into use. Then, at dawn, the Delawares attacked the Comanches and killed all but one, whom they permitted to escape in order that he might carry to his people the message of defeat. Among the trappings that they took from the Comanche camp was a shield with fifteen or twenty females' scalps attached to it, about half of which were scalps of white women. Ross to Neighbors, October 7, 1855, I.O., L.R., N 525; Baylor to Neighbors, *ibid.*

7. Ford's and Nelson's reports of the engagement were printed in the *Northern Standard*, June 12, 1858. See also Ford, "Memoirs," ms., University of Texas Archives; Thoburn, *A Standard History of Oklahoma*, I, 229.

| In his *Memoirs* Ford states that sixty prisoners were taken. I have not been able to locate Ford's Original Report, which included a map showing the route of the expedition. |

8. Pŏ'-ū-wā (metal), quă-sōō (shirt). Iron Jacket reminds one of Ecueracapa of Anza's time. Both were Kotsotekas.

9. At the mouth of Hubbard creek, on the Clear Fork.

| 10. A brief account of the Kotsoteka division of Comanches has already been given. The South Canadian river seems to have been more properly the home of this than of any other of the various Comanche divisions. In his reconnaissance down that stream in 1845, Lieutenant Abert found evidence of Kotsoteka camps in many places. He did not see many of the band because, as he finally learned, one of his Kiowa friends had played a joke on the Comanches by telling them that Abert's party were Texans. This caused Red jacket (Iron Jacket?) to flee down the stream ahead of Abert's party and gather his band at the Antelope Buttes

Notes 229

preparatory to meeting the enemy. Abert did not continue down the Canadian to that point, but turned south to the Washita.

A few of the Kotsotekas came to Abert's camp. Among other things given them was a cup of coffee. One fellow did not relish the beverage in the least; but tasted it sparingly, dipped his finger in it, and then made the sign of the cross—an evidence of Spanish Catholic influence. The saddles and bridles of these Indians were of Mexican make.

At this time, Red Jacket was reported to be angry with the Texans and evidently had not forgotten the wars between the Comanches and Texans which had been fought a few years before. Abert's report is given in 29 cong., 1 sess., *Sen. Doc.* no. 438, pp. 1 ff. |

11. Neighbors to Denver, December 9, 1858, I.O., L.R., N 563. They were not permitted to remain there since they were not regarded as Texas Indians.

12. At that time, however, the one hundredth meridian, north of Red river, which separated Texas and Indian Territory, was thought to be nearly a degree east of what has since been determined as its true location. Thus, as the maps were made at that time, the place of the battle might have appeared to be on Texas soil. But there is nothing to indicate that the rangers gave the matter any consideration.

13. T. C. Alexander, of Meridian, Bosque county, Texas, to President Buchanan, July 22, 1858 (copy), I.O., L.R.

14. Nelson's report, *op. cit.*

| 15. "Special Orders No. 71, by order of Brevet Major General Twiggs," in the *Northern Standard*, August 28, 1858. |

16. Van Dorn to Withers, assistant adjutant-general, September 26, 1858, 35 cong., 2 sess., *Sen. Ex. Doc.* no. I, vol. II, 268.

17. At this time the Wichita village was located at Rush Springs, not far from Fort Arbuckle. Mooney, in *Handbook*, II, 949.

18. L. S. Ross, son of S. P. Ross, Indian agent, was Texas governor, 1887-91.

19. Van Dorn to Withers, October 5, 1858, 35 cong., 2 sess., *Sen. Ex. Doc.* no. I, vol. II, 272-274.

20. Withers in "Orders no. 25," *ibid.*, 277.

21. W. E. Prince, commanding at Fort Arbuckle, to Major D. C. Buell, assistant adjutant-general of the west, enclosing a copy of Lieutenant Powell's report, dated Fort Arbuckle, August 26, 1858, *ibid.*, 421-423.

22. Rector to Smith, October 23, 1858, 36 cong., 1 sess., *Sen. Ex. Doc.* no. 2, vol. I, 586.

| 23. When General Twiggs learned of the negotiations that had been taking place between the army officers at Fort Arbuckle and the Comanches, Van Dorn's expedition had already left, but he made no effort to call it back. He made a vigorous protest at this ridiculous state of affairs insisting that the army headquarters should keep the different divisions informed as to the policy that was to be followed. Either all the department commanders should be instructed to fight the Comanches or all should be instructed to negotiate with them for peace.—Twiggs to Army Headquarters, October 7, 1858, 35 cong., 2 sess., *Sen. Ex. Doc.* no. 1, vol. II, p. 287. |

24. The *Northern Standard*, October 23, 1858, on authority of a "private letter" from Fort Belknap.

25. Price, *Fifth Cavalry*, 73, 76.

| 26. Twigg's orders of March 23 were that Major Van Dorn, with six companies of the Second Cavalry should scout the country along the Red, Washita, and Canadian rivers. His base was to be Camp Radziminski, which was to be guarded by Barton's company of the First Infantry.

In order to protect the frontier, a company of cavalry was to be stationed at Camp Colorado, under Captain C. S. Whiting and at Camp Cooper another company of cavalry was to be stationed under Major G. H. Thomas.—*The Northern Standard*, April 2, 1859.

Captains Ford and Bourland with their ranger companies were also in the field most of the spring. *Ibid.*, November 6, 1859. |

27. Price, *Fifth Cavalry*, 75.

28. Van Dorn's report, in the Dallas *Herald*, June 15, 1859.

29. *Ibid.*; Joseph B. Thoburn, "Indian Fight in Ford County," in Kansas Historical Society *Collections*, XII, 312-329; see also Price, *Fifth Cavalry*, 79, 80.

30. *Ibid.*, 82.

31. The Dallas *Herald*, September 28, 1858, quoting the *Sherman Patriot*.

32. *The Standard*, November 6, 1858; Ross to Neighbors, February 24, 1859, 36 cong., 1 sess., *Sen. Ex. Doc.* no. 2, 625; the Dallas *Herald*, March 9, 1859.

33. *The Standard*, April 16, 1859, quoting the *Belton Independent*; the Dallas *Herald*, May 4, 1859. For other accounts of raids, see the *State Gazette*, June 12, August 28, 1858; Dallas *Herald*, March 9, 23;

D. C. Cowan at camp 30 miles above San Saba, February 21, 1859, to Governor H. R. Runnels, ms., records of the adjutant-general's office (Texas); Henry Pendarvis, at Fredericksburg, to Runnels, April 9, 1859, *ibid.*; John Henry Brown, at Belton, to Governor Runnels, March 22, 1859, *ibid.*; Hillory Ryan, at Lampasas, to Runnels, March 26, 1859, *ibid.*

34. "N. P. C." in the *Standard* (Clarksville), January 15, 1859.

35. A more complete account than that which will be given here is Virginia Pink Noel, "The United States Indian Reservations in Texas, 1854–1859," M.A. thesis, University of Texas, June, 1927. I have treated the subject briefly in "The Comanche Reservation in Texas," in West Texas Historical Association *Year Book*, V, 43–66.

36. See Baylor to Neighbors, March 31, 1856, I.O., L.R., N 106; Ross to Neighbors, April 1, 1856, *ibid.*; Baylor to Neighbors, August 10 and 17, 1856, I.O., L.R., N 166; Neighbors to Manypenny, April 8, 1860, I.O.

| 37. The citizens denied this, and as the feeling against the Indians and agents became more and more bitter they frequently stated that the agents would not let them have their property when they discovered it at the reservation. Obviously no man, however tactful, could for long avoid a clash with the frontiersmen on this point; for the ranchmen expected the word of any white man to be accepted over the denial of any number of Indians. | That the agents did all they could to help the white men recover their property is virtually admitted by J. B. (Buck) Barry in a letter to Hawkins in 1858. He would say that Major Neighbors did treat him in a "clever and Gentlemanly manner" in connection with his efforts to recover horses which had been stolen from him. Barry to Hawkins, November 2, 1858, I.O., L.R., H 1341.

In his "Reminiscences" (ms., University of Texas Archives), Barry bitterly assails the reservation Indian.

38. Petition of the citizens of Williamson county, December 15, 1857, I.O., L.R., Tex., B 385; petition of citizens of Lampasas county, December 15, 1857, I.O., L.R., M 419.

39. W. G. Preston and others to M. Leeper, February 1, 1858, I.O., L.R. John R. Baylor, Comanche agent until he was dismissed in May, 1857, was among the signers of the letter to Leeper.

40. "Report of Select Committee on Indian Affairs," in *State Gazette*, March 27, 1858. Most of the report is printed in Johnson and Barker, *Texas and Texans*, 1, 513, 514. George B. Erath, Henry E. McCulloch, Forbes Britton, J. W. Throckmorton, and E. B. Scarborough composed the committee.

41. Neighbors to Mix, January 17, 1858, I.O., L.R., Tex., N 414; Leeper to Neighbors, February 12, 1858, I.O., L.R., N 433.

42. Leeper to Neighbors, December 5, 1857, I.O., L.R., N 405; Neighbors to Twiggs, December 8, 1857, *ibid.*

The immediate cause of Neighbors's action was that Stoneman had sent a sergeant on to the reservation to count the Indians without giving the agent notice of his intention. Evidently Stoneman was carrying on an investigation trying to show that there really were very few Indians at the reservation, and such a procedure on the part of a subordinate officer, without any general authority, naturally was regarded by the agents as conduct highly presumptuous and insolent. Furthermore, they alleged that the coming of the soldiers to the reservation and their counting operations, carried on as they were without the presence of the agents, alarmed the Indians and came near causing a general disturbance.

43. Neighbors to Manypenny, February 20, 1856, I.O., L.R., Tex., N 46; Neighbors to Manypenny, March 19, 1856, I.O., L.R., Tex., N 57.

44. Neighbors to Erath and others, June 16, 1859, 36 cong., 1 sess., *Sen. Ex. Doc.* no. 2, vol. 1, 659–662.

45. General E. H. Tarrant was a noted Indian fighter. He came to Texas from Kentucky in 1835 or 1836, and attained renown by commanding the expedition of Texans against an Indian confederation in 1841, defeating them at Village creek, west of Dallas. In 1858 he was living at Fort Belknap, and at the time of his death was on a speaking tour trying to arouse the people to a realization of the need for a better defense of the frontier. *Northern Standard*, May 28, June 12, 19, and August 14, 1858. The editor, Charles DeMorse, was at Weatherford at the time he spoke there.

46. Hawkins to Mix, October 30, 1858, I.O., L.R., H 1317.

47. Affidavit of John S. Ford and E. N. Burleson, November 22 and 24 respectively, I.O., L.R., H 1341.

48. Van Hogan to Neighbors, March 27, 1858, *ibid.*; petition of the citizens of Young county, January 20, 1857, I.O., L.R., N 238.

A letter, recently discovered in the Texas adjutant-general's office, indicates that much of the horse-stealing along the north Texas frontier was not the work of Indians, but of lawless white men. The letter, written at "Caddew Creek," Arkansas, December 15, 1859, is addressed to "Dear Chum" and signed by "O. L. M." The bearer of the letter, referred to as "Page, our faithful guide," who had to come down to the Clear Fork because "he had a small matter to settle with a couple of fellows on the Clear Fork," was killed and the letter was taken from his body by some troopers of the second cavalry from Camp Cooper and sent to the governor by the commanding officer of that post. The letter indicates that there was an organization of white men with representatives in the vicinity of the Texas reservations who stole horses in Texas and drove them north into Indian Territory and sold them. Their operations were so disguised and directed as to throw the blame for all their lawless acts on the Indians.

I am indebted to Dr. W. C. Holden of Texas Technological College for calling my attention to this letter.

49. Shirley to Barnard, May 6, 1858, I.O., L.R., N 466; Evans to Leeper, May 2, 1858, I.O., L.R., N 1341.

50. J. J. Sturm, farmer at the Brazos agency, to Ross, December 28, 1858, 36 cong., 1 sess., *Sen. Ex. Doc.* no. 2, vol. 1, 588; statement of Daniel Thorton, Peter Garland and others made at Palo Pinto, January 4, 1859, *ibid.*, 606 ff.

51. Statement of Garland and others, January 12, 1859, *ibid.*, 616.

52. Sturm to Ross, January 15, *ibid.*, 599.

53. Proceedings at Camp Palo Pinto, January 6 and 12, *ibid.*, 613 ff.

Sturm stated that these men at Palo Pinto would have broken up the reservation but that Major Thomas, in command at Fort Belknap, assured them that he would use the troops against them if they attempted it. Sturm to Ross, January 15, 1859, and Ross's report, February 12, 1859, as cited.

54. Proclamation of Governor Runnels, *ibid.*, 590.

55. E. J. Gurley, prosecuting attorney, to Neighbors, May 5, 1859, *ibid.*, 642. A copy of the report of the grand jury may be found in the Runnels Papers, Texas State Archives.

| 56. It must not be understood that these men were "thieves" and the "very worst frontier characters," as has often been maintained. Baylor later served the Confederacy in a responsible military position; R. W. Pollard of Palo Pinto county, Peter Garland, of Erath county, and J. B. Barry, of Bosque county, were prominent citizens in their communities and enjoyed the confidence of those who knew them. See Thomas T. Ewell, *A History of Hood County Texas*, 16 ff.

A secret agent sent out by Ross to determine the status of public sentiment in Jack and Palo Pinto counties gave him the name of a chief justice, a county commissioner and an assessor and tax collector as being parties to the plan to attack the reservation.

The years of bitter struggle with the Indians had hardened the hearts of the frontier people. They could not see that an Indian had any rights that a white man was obliged to recognize, and when the safety of citizens was involved they were wont to act first and investigate afterwards. See Ross to Neighbors, March 2, 1859, 36 cong., 1 sess., *Sen. Ex. Doc.* no. 2, vol. I, pp. 628, 629; W. R. Bradford, Ross's secret agent, to Ross, March 4, 1859, Runnels Papers, Texas State Archives. |

57. Ross to Neighbors, March 25, 1859, I.O., L.R.; Neighbors to Denver, March 28, 1859, I.O., L.R., N 626; Dallas *Herald*, March 12, 1859.

58. Neighbors to Denver, August 5, 1857, I.O., L.R., Tex., N 303.

59. Neighbors to Denver, February 14, 1859, 36 cong., 1 sess., *Sen. Ex. Doc.* no. 2, vol. 1, 603–605.

60. Neighbors to Denver, March 28, 1859, I.O., L.R., Tex., N 626.

61. *Ibid.*; Neighbors to Mix, April 11, 1859, I.O., L.R.; Mix to Neighbors, March 30, 1859, 36 cong., 1 sess., *Sen. Ex. Doc.* no. 2, vol. 1, 631.

62. "Resolution," April 25, 1859, I.O., L.R., G 120.

63. J. R. Worrall, of Jacksboro, June 1, 1859, to the editor. Dallas *Herald*, June 15, 1859. Fox was bringing dispatches from Fort Arbuckle, and was killed by a party of Jack county rangers.

64. *Ibid.*

65. Neighbors to Mix, May 12, 1859, I.O., L.R.; Ross to Neighbors, May 12, 1859, *ibid.*

66. Gurley to Runnels, records of the adjutant-general's office (Texas).

67. Report of Captain Plummer of the United States army, May 23, 1859, 36 cong., 1 sess., *Sen. Ex. Doc.* no. 2, vol. 1, 644; W. K. Baylor, "The Old Frontier; Events of Long Ago," in *Frontier Times*, October, 1924, 5, 6.

68. *Ibid.*

69. Runnels to Allison Nelson and others, June 6, 1858, *ibid.*, 655, 656; also "Memoirs of George B. Erath," in *Southwestern Historical Quarterly*, XXVII, 152, 153.

70. Erath to Ross and Neighbors, June 20, 1859, 36 cong., 1 sess., *Sen. Ex. Doc.* no. 2, vol. 1, 663; James Pike, *Scout and Ranger*, chap. ii.

71. Greenwood to Neighbors, June 11, 1859, 36 cong., 1 sess., *Sen. Ex. Doc.* no. 2, vol. 1, 649.

72. Neighbors, "Memorandum Travel Book from the Brazos Agency, Texas, to the False Ouachita Agency," C. N., July 31 and dates following, I.O.

73. *Ibid.*

| John Henry Brown, in command of the ranger force which had been established by order of the governor to watch the Indians pending their removal, offered to furnish escorts for the Indians to enable them to gather their stock, but Neighbors refused this proffered help. Probably he felt that no amount of precaution could prevent bloodshed if the Indians left the reservation. |

74. Leeper to the commissioner of Indian Affairs, September 15, 1859, 36 cong., 1 sess., *Sen. Ex. Doc.* no. 2, vol. 1, 701.

On their return from the leased district Neighbors and Leeper, who were traveling together, were attacked by wild Indians, and Leeper was seriously wounded.

After killing Neighbors, Cornett fled. He was pursued by a band of rangers, captured, "tried" without benefit of judge or jury, and executed.

75. Robert S. Neighbors was born in Virginia and came to Texas in 1836. He accompanied the ill-fated Mier expedition, and was imprisoned in Mexico for two years. After his release, he served the Republic of Texas and the United States government until the end of Polk's administration as Indian agent. Later, he served in the legislature as the representative from Bexar county. He was presidential elector from the Western district of Texas, voting for Pearce in 1852, and for the last six years preceding his death, he was supervising agent for Texas Indians. *The Southern Democrat* (Waco), clipping in the Neighbors Papers, University of Texas. The article was evidently written soon after his death; see also Neighbors to the governor's commissioners, June 16, 1859, 36 cong., 1 sess., *Sen. Ex. Doc.* no. 2, vol. 1, 659.

76. The correspondence pertaining to the Texas reservation indicates that syphilis in virulent form was common. Also the Comanches suffered severely from smallpox at different times. In 1837 the plague broke out among the Indians far to the north, and during the next year or two swept through the various plains tribes to the gulf. Again, in 1843, some of the Comanche bands brought it back with them from a raid against the Mexican country around Matamoros, and some bands suffered severely. In the spring of 1847, Neighbors reported that he was avoiding the southern Comanches because of the prevalence of smallpox, and he had information that the northern bands were suffering likewise. Again in 1848 the southern Comanches warned him of its presence in their camps, and while he was in the village of one band, several Indians died with that disease. In 1852 some of the chiefs of the southern Comanches asked if they could not have their people vaccinated, but it does not appear that this was ever done. In 1855 Neighbors wrote that Indians coming in from the north reported the prevalence of smallpox among the northern bands, and he was much alarmed when a few cases appeared at the reservation. However, it seems that his precautions managed to prevent a general scourge at that time.

77. A. H. McKisick, Wichita agent, to Colonel R. P. Pulliam, acting superintendent, April 15, 1858, I.O., L.R., Wichita, R 558; *The Northern Standard*, July 10, 1858, quoting the *Choctaw and Chickasaw Herald*, June 22, 1858; Lieutenant T. E. Powell, commanding at Fort Arbuckle, to the assistant adjutant-general, July 27, 1858; 35 cong., 2 sess., *Sen. Ex. Doc.* no. I, vol. II, 416 ff.; Dallas *Herald*, July 20, 1858; *The Northern Standard*, September 18, 1858.

78. Rector to Mix, October 23, 1858, 36 cong., 1 sess., *Sen. Ex. Doc.* no. 2, vol. 1, 586.

79. For instance, see the superintendent of Indian Affairs at Fort Smith, to the secretary of the interior, November (no other date), 1858, I.O., L.R.

80. See Blaine to Rector, March 3 and August 15, 1859, I.O., L.R.

81. *Ibid.*; Blaine to Rector, April 23, 1860, I.O., L.R., B 216.

82. John H. Clark, special agent at the Wichita agency, to Thompson, May 25, 1860, I.O., L.R., Wichita, C 553; Rector to Greenwood, May 3, 1860, I.O., L.R.

83. Miller's report, August 17, 1858, 35 cong., 2 sess., *Sen. Ex. Doc.* no. 1, vol. 1, 450 ff.

84. W. W. Bent, in report of October 5, 1859, 36 cong., 1 sess., *Sen. Ex. Doc.* no. 2, vol. 1, 506.

85. *Ibid.*

86. Collins to the commissioner of Indian Affairs, August 4, 1859, *ibid.*, 709.

87. *The Standard*, October 22, 1859, April 14, 1860; *Banner of Peace* (Nashville, Tennessee), April 5, May 10, January 3 and 24, 1860; Dallas *Herald*, December 7, 1859; R. B. Wells, Gatesville, to Governor Houston, February 16, 1860, records of the adjutant-general's office; report of the secretary of war for 1860, 36 cong., 2 sess., *Sen. Ex. Doc.* no. 1, vol. II, 193 ff.; Price, *The Fifth Cavalry*, 87 ff.

88. W. C. Holden, "*Frontier Defense, 1846–1860*," in West Texas Historical Association *Year Book*, VI, 62.

89. J. W. Wilbarger, *Indian Depredations in Texas*, 333 ff., gives Ross's report. See also J. T. Deshields, *Capture of Cynthia Anne Parker*, 58–68.

CHAPTER ELEVEN

1. A scholarly account of Pike's proceedings in this connection is given by Anna Heloise Abel in *The American Indians as Slaveholder and Secessionist*.
2. *Ibid.*, 180.
3. *Ibid.*, 188 ff. Pike acted as commissioner from the state of Arkansas as well as from the Confederacy.
4. These treaties are published in *War of the Rebellion, Official Records of the Union and Confederate Armies*, series IV, vol. 1, 542–554.
5. The "Ta-ne-i-weh" seem to have been closely associated with the Nokoni.
6. The Comanche form of these names is all that is appended to the treaty. The translations have been discovered from other accounts. Qui-na-hi-wi is well written, *i.e.*, *Quina*, or better *Quē'-nē* (eagle) *hē'-vē* (drinking); Bis-te-va-na has no meaning, or, at least, cannot be recognized by Comanches of our own day; Ma-a-we (*Māh'-wāy*), more accurately interpreted Trembling Hand, has nothing to do with salutation. For a brief account of Shaking Hand, see footnote 30.
7. Rector to Leeper, October 12, 1861, in Abel, *op. cit.*, 330; Pike to Rector, November 21, 1861, *ibid.*, 311.

In the autumn of 1861, the Confederate congress voted $64,862 for the Comanches in order that the government might comply with its treaty agreement. W. H. S. Taylor, auditor, to Pike, December 31, 1861, *ibid.*, 322.

8. *Ibid.*, 348.
9. Scott to Seddon, January 12, 1863, *War of the Rebellion, Official Records*, series IV, vol. II, 355; Abel, *op. cit.*, footnote 590; Joseph B. Thoburn, "H. P. Jones, Scout and Interpreter," in *Chronicles of Oklahoma*, II, 383, 384.

| In his letters to his superiors Leeper urged that the place be garrisoned, predicting that the Confederates would lose it unless this was done. Leeper's position was by no means an enviable one. He was located on the extreme edge of the frontier where dangerous Indians beset him on one hand and unsympathetic and arbitrary Confederate military officers on the other. His courage and patriotism were of the highest quality. |

10. Scott to Seddon, *op. cit.*; Colley to Dole, January 25, 1863, U.S. Indian Office, general files, upper Arkansas agency, C 50.
11. A letter from a soldier stationed at Fort Arbuckle, April 6, 1863, *The Standard*, May 2, 1863.
12. In this connection, see W. C. Holden, "Frontier Defense During the Civil War," *op. cit.*
13. Joseph Ward, captain Texas frontier regiment, to R. H. Graham, February 14, 1863, records of the adjutant-general's office, Austin; Wm. C. Twitty, at Gainesville, Cooke county, March 3, 1863, to General William Steele, *War of the Rebellion, Official Records*, series 1, vol. XXII, part II, 799; S. F. Mains, at Montague, April 28, 1863, to the editor, *The Standard*, May 16, 1863.
14. R. J. McKenzie, of Weatherford, to the editor, July 31, 1863, *Dallas Herald*, August 5, 1863.
15. Holden, *op. cit.*, 25.
16. Carson to Bourland, October 18, 1864, *War of the Rebellion, Official Records*, series 1, vol. XLI, part 1, 885; *Dallas Herald*, October 29, 1864.

One of the children taken in this raid was Millie Durgan. She grew to womanhood among the Indians and married a Kiowa chief. In 1930 her identity was established, and she visited her childhood home in Young county. Abilene *Daily Reporter*, October 26, 1930.

17. Throckmorton reported that he treated with all but one band of Comanches, with the Kiowas, and other plains Indians, and recovered from them nine prisoners. *Dallas Herald*, July 1, 1865.
18. *Report of the Commissioner of Indian Affairs for 1861*, 634.
19. A. G. Boone, Indian agent, upper Arkansas agency, at Fort Wise, to Major A. M. Robinson, superintendent of Indian Affairs, St. Joseph, Missouri, March 10, 1861, United States Indian Office, general files, upper Arkansas agency, R 1502. Hereafter documents in the United States Indian Office will be cited by giving the file description and number only.

For conditions along the upper Arkansas frontier at the opening of the Civil War, see also Boone to H. B. Branch, superintendent of Indian Affairs, April 25, 1861, *ibid.*, B 422; William Gilpin, governor of Colorado Territory, to the superintendent of Indian Affairs, June 19, 1861, *Report of the Commissioner of*

Indian Affairs for 1861, 709.

20. Boone to Robinson, March 10, 1861, *Upper Arkansas*, R 1502; Gilpin to Boone, August 26, 1861, *ibid.*, B 772.

21. Copy of treaty or agreement, September 6, 1861, *Upper Arkansas*, B 772. Among the signers were Hard Metal and Red Buffalo for the Comanches, Little Mountain, Sitting Bear, and Little Hart for the Kiowas. Little is known about the Comanches, but the Kiowas were influential Indians.

22. Boone to Mix, October 19, 1861, *Upper Arkansas*, B 861.

23. Boone to Dole, October 26, 1861, *Upper Arkansas*, B 900.

24. Boone to Dole, January 11, 1862, *Upper Arkansas*, B 1064.

25. In his report, the commissioner of Indian Affairs mentioned that their presents of goods had been given to them. 37 cong., 2 sess., *Sen. Ex. Doc.* no. I, vol. I, 634.

26. Copy of treaty or truce with the Comanches, May 13, 1861, ms., United States Indian Office, *Councils, Talks and Treaties*, file, C 1208. The chiefs, whose names come down to us in their Spanish form, probably in some cases corrupted, are hard to identify.

They are: Essaguipa (*cf. Es'-ă*, wolf, and *quĕ'-tä*, dung); Pluma de Aguila (Spanish for eagle feather); Gua Gunc (?); Paracasqua (probably *Par-rĭ'-ä*, Comanche for elk, plus *Kĭts-quā*, chewing); Parawausca (*cf. Par-rĭ'-ä*, elk, with a suffix that cannot be recognized); Pehores (corrupt Spanish, *cf. Pē-hōō'-ra*, Mexican frijole or bean).

27. Anderson to Chapman, June 29, 1861, *War of the Rebellion, Official Records*, series 1, vol. IV, 48; Canby to the assistant adjutant-general, July 14 and December 1, 1861, *ibid.*, 59, 77.

28. Colley to Dole, April 9, 1863, *Upper Arkansas*, C 131.

Ten Bears was perhaps the most influential Comanche chief during the years immediately following the Civil War. He was one of the leading spokesmen for his people at the council at Medicine Lodge creek, October, 1867, and thereafter until his death in 1872 he took a prominent part in all councils. He used his influence for peace, but he was exceedingly patriotic and was always ready to inquire how any treaty or proposal would affect his people.

At the council of August, 1872, he amused his audience by his speech which in part ran:

"You have got no presents for the young men, and that is bad. My heart is good, and I follow the white man's road. I want a house like the white men's houses and a barrel of sugar in the middle of it."

Immediately after this council the old chief again went with a party to Washington, but returned to the agency desperately ill and never recovered. One of his last acts was to give a picture of A. H. Love, president of the Peace society, to the Indian agent, expressing the desire that his people would quit raiding in Texas. Battey, *A Quaker Among the Indians*, 90.

29. United States Indian Office, special file, *Talks, Councils and Treaties*, treaty of April 6, 1863.

30. Shaking Hand [Mäh'wāy], principal chief of the Kotsotekas, whose name comes down to us as Ma-a-we or Mow-way, was one of the best-known Comanches of his day. He signed the treaty with the Confederates in August, 1861, but was broad-minded enough not to let that interfere with his peaceful relations with the men of the north. He seems to have been at home either along the Washita, the Arkansas, or the New Mexico border, and he apparently shifted his allegiance from time to time during the Civil War as the exigencies of the situation dictated. During the Indian troubles of 1868, Shaking Hand, or "Mohwee," was described, together with Horse's Back, the Nokoni, as being "true friends to the government and the whites, doing all they can to keep not only their own bands but all the wild Indians from committing depredations . . ." S. T. Walkley, acting Indian agent, to General W. B. Hazen, 40 cong., 3 sess., *Sen. Ex. Doc.* no. 18, 19. A little later the chief boasted that he had never done the government any harm, and had never fought against her.

However, it appears that he did not always live up to his reputation. In 1869 he was captured and taken prisoner to Santa Fé, but was soon released. Shaking Hand never did take kindly to the idea of the Comanches locating themselves on the reservation as long as there were buffalo to be had on the plains; and in the early seventies his band is referred to as the "most roving" of all the Comanche bands. At times his band was allied with the Mescalero Apaches as well as with the Kwahadi Comanches. Although Shaking Hand always represented himself to be friendly, his warriors no doubt participated extensively in raids against the Texas frontier. He stayed out on the plains with his band as long as possible, and his party was one of the last to be permanently located on the reservation. Once in council he commented on the matter of coming in as follows: "When the Indians in here are better treated than we are outside, it will be time enough to come in. I was promised lots of things, but I don't see them . . ." Report of the council of August 1872, *New York Herald*, September 8, 1872.

31. Colley to Dole, September 30, 1863, 38 cong., 1 sess., *House Ex. Doc.* no. 1, 252.

32. George K. Otis, general superintendent Overland Mail line, to Dole, written at Washington, August 31, 1864, *Upper Arkansas*, O 25.

33. Scott J. Anthony, major first cavalry of Colorado, commanding at Fort Larned, Kansas, to Captain G. H. Loving, acting assistant adjutant-general, district of upper Arkansas, Fort Riley, August 23, 1864, *War of the Rebellion, Official Records*, series 1, vol. XLI, part II, 827.

Anthony stated that if he should call together his forces stationed at Walnut creek, Fort Zarah, and the Cimarron crossing, he would have but 330 cavalry, 70 infantry, and 19 men for the battery.

34. Space does not permit our going into details pertaining to this Cheyenne war. A good short account is that given by F. L. Paxson, *The Last American Frontier*, 252 ff.

35. Colley to Dole, October 20, 1864, 38 cong., 2 sess., *House Ex. Doc.* no. 1, 386.

36. Boone to Dole, March 1, 1862, *Upper Arkansas*, B 1147; M. Stecke, superintendent of Indian Affairs, New Mexico, enclosing a letter from one Watrus to the commissioner of Indian Affairs, February 19, 1864, *Upper Arkansas*, S 265; Anthony to Loving, August 23, 1864, *op. cit.*

37. Carson's report is printed in *War of the Rebellion, Official Records*, series 1, vol. XLI, part 1, 939 ff. Another account is that of one of Carson's officers, George H. Pettus, entitled *Kit Carson's Fight with the Comanche and Kiowa Indians at the Adobe Walls on the Canadian river*, November 25, 1864.

38. Mooney, "Kiowa Calendar," 179, 314.

39. Carson to Carleton, December 16, 1864, *War of the Rebellion, Official Records*, series 1, vol. XLVI, part 1, 943.

| "We saw the tracks of three wagons going down the river," wrote Carson, "and you may be sure they belonged to the traders." Carson denounced Superintendent Steck in bitterest terms for giving passes to these traders. |

40. Ford to Dodge, March 17, 1865, *War of the Rebellion, Official Records*, series 1, vol. XLVIII, 1204.

41. Leavenworth to Colonel J. H. Ford, February 20, 1865, *War of the Rebellion, Official Records*, series 1, vol. XLVIII, part 1, 923.

42. Doolittie to Harlan, May 31, 1865, *ibid.*, part II, 868; Dodge to Harlan, July 13, 1865, *ibid.*, 1075, 1076.

43. Leavenworth to Major-general John B. Sanborn, August 4, 1865, *War of the Rebellion, Official Records*, series 1, vol. XLVIII, part II, 1164; also, Leavenworth to Sanborn, August 10, 1865, *ibid.*, 1176.

44. 39 cong., 1 sess., *House Ex. Doc.* no. 1, 578, 711–719.

CHAPTER TWELVE

1. These were the Nokonies, the Penatekas, the Tanimas, and several bands of Yamparikas. The treaty is given in Kappler, *Indian Affairs Laws and Treaties*, II, 891, 892.

2. Other commissioners were W. S. Harney, James Steele, Thomas Murphy, and J. H. Leavenworth. W. R. Irwin acted as secretary. Shirley interpreted for the Comanches, and Chisholm for the Kiowas. *Ibid.*, 895.

| 3. In response to the pleas of the frontier people Governor Throckmorton, by authority of the legislature, raised, or proposed to raise some companies of rangers for frontier defense, but General P. H. Sheridan, Commander of the military district including Texas, would not accept them or permit them to be organized. Sheridan to Throckmorton, October 9, 1866, and November 11, 1866, records of the adjutant-general's office, Texas. |

4. J. G. Stephens to the editor, Dallas *Herald*, October 6, 1866.

The Indians captured Mrs. Sarah Jane Luster and Biantha and Theodore Adolphus (Dot) Babb from the Babb home on Dry creek, twelve miles west of Decatur. Mrs. Luster soon escaped from the Indians, and the Babb children were ransomed. T. A. (Dot) Babb, *In the Bosom of the Comanches*.

| Mrs. Luster escaped from the Comanches only to fall into the clutch of a band of Kiowas. She escaped from her Kiowa captors also, and while in flight was chased for some distance by a detachment of United States cavalry before she learned to her delight that they were white men and friends. The soldiers gave her escort to Council Grove, Kansas, from which place she soon returned to her friends in Texas.

The Babb children were kept by the Indians several months before being ransomed by their father. The Indian who struck Babb's mother the fatal blow was Walking Face, nephew of chief Horse Back. Pernernay, Horse Back's brother, claimed the boy as his own. Finally the lad was rescued through the efforts of Milky Way, the Penateka. See, *In the Bosom of the Comanches*, by T. A. (Dot) Babb, Dallas, 1923. | See also

Leavenworth to Taylor, May 21, 1868, 41 cong., 2 sess., *House Misc. Doc.* no. 139, 8.

5. Throckmorton to Stanton, August 5, 1867, Records of Texas adjutant-general's office. Throckmorton's report was based on incomplete reports from county judges.

6. Both the Indian agents and the army officers charged that the others paid ransoms for captives too readily. Report of I. C. Taylor, Indian agent at Fort Larned, 39 cong., 2 sess., *House Ex. Doc.* no. 1, 280, 281.

Lawrie Tatum, agent for the Kiowas and Comanches, 1869–1873, paid one hundred dollars each for some captives, but secured others without ransom money by withholding rations from the offending Indians. Tatum, *Our Red Brothers*, 46–51.

7. Milky Way, or Ā'-sā-hä'-bi, recovered Dot Babb. *In the Bosom of the Comanches*, 58.

8. Smith, *The Boy Captives*; Lehmann, *Nine Years with the Indians*; Babb, *In the Bosom of the Comanches*, 144.

9. "Too much can hardly be said on this subject—the blankets were of a character very little superior to the kind ordinarily used for saddle blankets. The pants, which the invoice shows to have been purchased in Hartford, Conn., at a cost of $6.25 per pair, were of a very poor quality, a better article retailing at $5.00. per pair in the Sutler stores in the Indian country...." Report of Chas. Bogy and W. R. Irwin to Hon. Louis V. Bogy, December 8, 1866, United States Indian Office, special file, *Councils, Talks, and Treaties*, C 68.

10. In March, 1865, congress created a joint committee to investigate the entire Indian situation. The committee divided itself into three groups to investigate conditions on the Pacific slope, the northern plains, and the southern plains respectively. After months of labor, the committee reported, January 1867. This report of some 500 pages gives convincing proof that much inefficiency and some corrupt practice were to be found in almost every branch of the Indian service. 39 cong., 2 sess., *Sen. Rep.*, 156.

It should be stated that the special commission that visited the Comanche country commended the work of agents Wynkoop and Leavenworth of that region.

11. Major H. Douglass, commanding at Fort Dodge, to the assistant adjutant-general, January 13, 1867, 40 cong., 1 sess., *Sen. Ex. Doc.* no. 13, 53. This matter is treated at length by C. C. Rister in *The Southwestern Frontier, 1865-1881*, 78 ff.

| Among the traders named as supplying the savages was D. A. Butterfield, who had sold several cases of arms to the Cheyennes and Arapahoes, and Charley Rath, who had armed several bands of Kiowas with revolvers. |

12. Leavenworth to Taylor, May 16, 1867, 40 cong., 1 sess., *Sen. Ex. Doc.* no. 13, 104, 105.

13. Captain E. L. Smith to Colonel O. D. Green, assistant adjutant-general, department of Arkansas, February 16, 1867, 40 cong., 1 sess., *Sen. Ex. Doc.* no. 13, 82.

14. Sherman to Major George K. Leet, July 19, 1867 (copy), general files, *Central Superintendency*, W 454.

15. Leavenworth to Taylor, May 4, 1867, 40 cong., 1 sess., *Sen. Ex. Doc.* no. 113, 94.

16. During this time the Sioux and the northern Cheyennes had been at war against the United States, and the army had suffered the terrible Fetterman massacre. See Paxson, *The Last American Frontier*, chap. xvi.

17. General Sherman did not sit with the commission in its council with the southern Indians. The law named N. G. Taylor, commissioner of Indian Affairs, John B. Henderson, chairman of the senate committee of Indian Affairs, S. F. Tappan, and John B. Sanborn. The president appointed Major-general William S. Harney, Major-general A. H. Terry, and Major-general C. C. Augur.

The report of the commission, which gives its proceedings somewhat in detail, is published as *House Ex. Doc.* no. 97, 40 cong., 2 sess.

Several newspaper correspondents accompanied the commission. Interesting reports by "H.J.B.," the correspondent of *The Cincinnati Daily Gazette*, may be found in that paper for October 21, 26, and November 4, 1867. Henry M. Stanley was among the reporters.

| 18. Robert L. Boake, who knew George Bent, supplies the following terse description: "Over six feet tall, with a broad intelligent head, shoulders moderately broad, straight as an arrow at seventy years; fluent in Cheyenne, his mother's tongue; an accomplished 'sign talker' who was a master of English and understood the ways of the whites—unusual attainments rarely found even at a later date. He was honest and reliable and his attainments made him the premier of this trio of noted men, as it is not probable that Black Beaver and Chisholm spoke either of the four Indian languages sufficiently well to interpret without error. He was light in complexion and resembled the whites; yet his hair, eyes, and carriage were Cheyenne." |

19. Alfred A. Taylor, later governor of Tennessee, attended the council as a newspaper reporter. He has

contributed an account of the council in *Chronicles of Oklahoma*, II, 98–118. The quotation is taken from pp. 102, 103.

20. Papers relating to the peace commission of 1867, room 316, shelf I.S.P., 4, 5, and 6, U.S. Indian Office.

21. Little Mountain, for more than thirty years their recognized head-chief, had died the year before, and the tribe had no real leader.

22. Papers relating to the peace commission of 1867, *op. cit.*

23. Kappler, *Indian Affairs Laws and Treaties*, II, 977, 978.

24. This treaty, dated October 21, 1867, was ratified July 25, 1868, and proclaimed August 25, 1868. It is published in Kappler, *op. cit.*, 982–984.

25. The Comanche chiefs who signed the treaty were: "Parry-wah-say-man" [*Päh'-dū-ă* (bear) *Sā'-ĕr-mĭn* (ten)], Ten Bears, Yamparika; "Tep-pe-navon" [*Tĭp'-pĕ* (Lips) *Näh-vōōd* (painted)], Painted Lips, Yamparika; "To-sa-in" (*Tosh'-ā-wāy*), Silver Brooch, Penateka; "Cear-che-nika" [*Cĕ'-ah* (feather), *Chĕ'-nĕ-käk* (inserted)], Standing Feather, Penateka; "Ho-we-ar," Gap in the Woods, Nokoni; "Tir-ha-yah-guahip" (*Tā'-hā-yĕr-quŏip*), Horse's Back, Nokoni; "Es-a-nanaca" (*Ĕs'-ă-nan'-a-ca*), Hears a Wolf, Yamparika; "Ah-te-es-ta," translated Little Horn, Yamparika; "Pooh-yah-to-yeh-be" (*Pō'-ū-wā Tō'-yäh-vĭt*), Iron Mountain, Yamparika; "Sad-dy-yo," translated Dog Fat. Philip McCusker acted as interpreter.

| 26. That is this region may be regarded as their home. They ranged all the way from Coahuila to Idaho. See *The Boy Captives*, edited by J. Marvin Hunter giving an account of the prisoner Clinton Smith, who was with one of these Kwahadi bands. |

27. Clipping from *The New Mexican*, of Santa Fé, New Mexico, July 28, 1866, *New Mexico Superintendency*, W 69. Also, A. B. Norton to Cooley, July 31, 1866, 39 cong., 2 sess., *House Ex. Doc.* no. 1, 151.

28. Labadi's report is given in the *Report of the Secretary of the Interior, 1867*, part II, 214–215.

The Quitaque Draw or creek is about a hundred miles east of the Texas–New Mexico boundary, being one of the upper branches of Pease river. It flows eastward along and near the line of Floyd and Briscoe counties.

29. Besides Quitaque, a place referred to as Mucho Que, which may be Yellow House Canyon, near Muleshoe, the head of the Brazos river, was a favorite place for rendezvous. N. Badger to the secretary of interior, June 18, 1872, *Central Superintendency*, B 6; also Burton, *A History of the J. A. Ranch, op. cit.*, 95. Evidently a point near the head of the Colorado river was used for this purpose. Rister, *The Southwestern Frontier*, 85.

Captain R. G. Carter, who was with General Mackenzie in 1871, describes one of these trading stations which the command found on or near Duck creek, a little more than a day's march north of the Double mountains of the Brazos. He states: "We discovered this day the trading stations of the Mexicans with the Indians, consisting of curiously built caves in the high banks or bluffs, the earth propped up or kept in place by a framework of poles, giving these subterranean abodes the appearance of grated prison doors or windows, reminding us of the cave dwellers of Arizona and New Mexico. These trading stations were now abandoned." "Ridding West Texas of Comanches," in Fort Worth *Star Telegram*, magazine section, March 6, 1927.

30. J. Evetts Haley, *The XIT Ranch of Texas*, 26. The quotation is from the words of the veteran plainsman Charles Goodnight. | From Mr. Goodnight Mr. Haley secured the following account as to the nature and course of these cart trails:

"There was a north and south trade road. The north one left Las Vegas, where the traders outfitted, led northeast to the Canadian, followed down it to turn southeast about a day's drive from the Trujillo, near the state line. The traders left the river and pulled for the Door of the Plains, a large gap in the caprock which could be seen for miles. They watered at the Trujillo and then at the extreme head of the Palo Duro, in the XIT range. The trail led down this stream to near the site of MacKenzie Crossing. It led southeast again to the head of Rock Creek, thence to the foot of the Plains, by some spring, and on to the Tongue River. The Southern trail came back by the same route to MacKenzie Crossing, from where it turned west to Las Escarbadas, where one of the divisional headquarters of the XIT was later located. . . . The trail led to Laguna Salada, thence to La Laguna, eight miles north of Fort Sumner, and eight miles farther to join the main government road which led from the Fort to Santa Fe. From this road the traders dropped off to their homes." *Ibid.*, pp. 26, 27. |

31. C. C. Rister, *The Southwestern Frontier*, 82, quoting from the annual report of the commissioner of Indian Affairs, 1867–1868, part 1, 194.

| 32. It is not likely that the Mexican traders ever had to lend the Comanches either their pistols or their

horses, for the savages were always well mounted and generally well armed. A case in point is given by Haley:

"Jose Pena, once a trader, was on the trail with Goodnight in 1875. He told of a trip he made to the Quitaque. No cattle were there. He met a chief who told him to let his Indians have the goods, and the cattle would be there shortly. Pena was afraid to refuse to let his Indians have the goods, though he supposed he would never receive the cattle once he turned over the goods. But in a week or two the cattle were brought in, and Pena happily went his way." *The XIT Ranch*, p. 28. |

33. *Ibid*.

34. Rister, *op. cit.*, 82, footnote 73.

35. Report of C. C. Augur, commanding the department of Texas, September 28, 1872, 42 cong., 3 sess., *House Ex. Doc.* no. 1, part II, vol. 1, 54 ff.

36. *The Boy Captives*, 58.

37. McCusker, February 4, 1868, to Colonel Thomas Murphy, *Upper Arkansas Agency*, M 1386.

| McCusker stated that the Indians excused the taking of these scalps on the ground that the Caddo Indians had killed three of their Comanche warriors during the preceding summer. |

38. Leavenworth to Taylor, May 21, 1868, 41 cong., 2 sess., *House Misc. Doc.* no. 139, 5 ff.

39. Henry Shanklin, agent for the Wichita and associated tribes, to Taylor, April 23, 1868, *Wichita*, S 581.

40. S. J. Walkley, at Eureka valley, April 23, 1868, to Leavenworth, 40 cong., 2 sess., *Sen. Ex. Doc.* no. 60, 2.

The treaty did not expressly obligate the government to furnish the Indians with subsistence, but the agents as well as the army officers knew that this would have to be done if the savages were kept within the confines of their reservation for even a part of the time. Indeed, the whole reservation plan rested on this idea.

41. Shanklin to Taylor, May 30, 1868, general files, *Wichita*, S 611.

42. Shanklin to Wortham, superintendent of Indian Affairs, Fort Smith, Arkansas, June 6, 1868, *Wichita*, S 640.

43. Shanklin to Taylor, June 15, 1868, *ibid.*, S 627.

44. Leavenworth to the commissioner of Indian Affairs, April 23, 1868, 40 cong., 2 sess., *Sen. Ex. Doc.* no. 60, 3; Leavenworth to Taylor, May 21, 1868, 41 cong., 2 sess., *House Misc. Doc.* no. 139, 6.

45. *Ibid*. Leavenworth gave the names of some nineteen persons he had recovered.

46. S. T. Walkley to General W. B. Hazen, October 10, 1868, 40 cong., 3 sess., *Sen. Ex. Doc.* no. 18, 18. Leavenworth left May 26.

Leavenworth was succeeded by A. G. Boone, who had served as agent during the Civil War. Taylor to Boone, July 31, 1868, I.O. Letter Book 87, 220. Because of illness, Boone did not arrive in the Indian country until December, 1868.

47. Hazen to Sherman, November 10, 1868, 40 cong., 3 sess., *Sen. Ex. Doc.* no. 18, 15.

48. Walkley to Leavenworth, October 10, 1868, 40 cong., 3 sess., *Sen. Ex. Doc.* no. 18, 18.

| 49. Walkley commended some of these chiefs for their efforts in this direction. Shaking Hand and Horse's Back had followed bands of young warriors bound for the Texas frontier and had forced them to return. These chiefs had even given up their own horses and blankets in order to secure the release of captives.—*Ibid*. |

50. Sheridans's report, September 26, 1868, *Report of the Secretary of War for 1868* (abridgement), 50, 51.

51. General George A. Custer, *My Life on the Plains*, 109.

52. Thomas Murphy, superintendent of Indian Affairs, Atchison, Kansas, to General W. B. Hazen, September 21, 1868, *Central Superintendency*, M 1945.

| Really there was nothing left for the Indian Department to do but to leave the control of the tribes to the army. By an act approved July 20, 1868, Congress appropriated $500,000 to be expended under the direction of General Sherman in carrying out the treaty stipulations with the Indians dealt with by the peace commissioners. Thus the army had money while the Indian service was practically without funds. In carrying out the duty imposed upon him Sherman created two military districts; the first embracing all the country west of the Missouri river within the Sioux reservation, the other including the country between Kansas and Texas, bounded on the east by the Arkansas river and on the west by the hundredth meridian. | See George W. Manypenny, *Our Indian Wards*, 204, 205, 210.

53. Hazen to Sherman, November 10, 1868, 40 cong., 3 sess., *Sen. Ex. Doc.* no. 18, 14.

54. Custer, *My Life on the Plains*, chapts. XV, XVI; P. H. Sheridan, *Personal Memoirs*, chapt. XIII.

55. John Murphy, "Reminiscences of the Washita Campaign," in *Chronicles of Oklahoma*, 1, 266.

56. That they came in is vouched for by B. H. Grierson, Colonel 10th cavalry, commanding at Camp Wichita (Fort Sill), to the assistant adjutant-general, June 21, 1869, *Central Superintendency*, A 330.

| Among the chiefs arrested at Fort Bascom was Shaking Hand, the Kotsoteka. He had informed General Hazen that he did not propose to come to the agency until the agents arrived there with the goods for the Indians. He stated that he had been "fooled" too much already by the whites along that line, and if his people had to make their own living anyway they preferred to do it out on the plains away from the soldiers. He hoped that General Hazen would not "feel bad about it" [Mah-wee, chief of the Curtz-e-ticker to "My Friends," November 13, 1868, 40 cong., 3 sess., *Sen. Ex. Doc.* no. 18, p. 23]. It seems that as the troops approached the chief did the only thing he knew to do to protect his people—fled to the plains. But in this he was probably not successful, for it is likely that his band suffered in the attack by Colonel Evans on Christmas day 1868.

On this long journey Shaking Hand saw some objects which he later described to his tribesmen and an interpreter. "When we had traveled many days," he stated, "we came to where there was a new kind of road that I had never heard of. There was a very large iron horse hitched to several houses on wheels. We were taken into one of them which was the nicest house I ever saw . . . As soon as we were seated the iron horse made a snort, and away it went, pulling the houses! Our horses could not run half so fast."

Later he was taken to the Missouri river and concerning this he stated: "We were taken into a house that was built on the water (Missouri river), and it could swim anywhere. It made no difference how deep the water was, it could swim. There is where the sugar comes from. I saw men rolling great big barrels of sugar out of the house on the water, and so many of them!" Then the chief stated a conclusion similar to that often made by the Indians on their journeys to cities. "Nobody need talk to me about sugar being scarce after seeing the large amount come out of that house that was swimming on the water."—Lawrie Tatum, *Our Red Brothers*, pp. 75, 76. |

57. Hazen to Sherman, 41 cong., 2 sess., *House Ex. Doc.* no. 1, part III, 835, 836.

58. The statement must be modified as regard the Cheyennes. They had not been instructed to report at Fort Cobb. On the contrary, Black Kettle had visited the post a few days before his village on the Washita was attacked and had tried to become reconciled to the government, but General Hazen refused to give him any assurance of safety and instructed him to leave the vicinity. 40 cong., 3 sess., *Sen. Ex. Doc.* no. 18, 24, 25; Paxson, *The Last American Frontier*, chapt. XVIII.

| The Cheyennes in Kansas attracted wide attention. Some of their depredations had been committed near the great trans-plains communication routes in a region that was well "covered" by the large newspapers of the upper Mississippi Valley and the East. Furthermore, Kansas had not been stigmatized by joining the late rebellion as had Texas. Indian raids in Kansas provoked national indignation while Indian raids in Texas were taken as a matter of course and received little notice outside of the frontier counties which were directly affected by them. While in command of the military district that included Texas, General Sheridan had not permitted Indian raids to annoy him and had given but little attention to problems of frontier defense. He was more absorbed in matters pertaining to "reconstruction." When he was transferred to Kansas his attitude towards the savages changed and he became their most relentless pursuer. |

CHAPTER THIRTEEN

1. Laurence F. Schmeckebier, *The Office of Indian Affairs, Its History Activities and Organization*, 48.
2. *Ibid.*, 56, 57.

| 3. ". . . By the act of July 15, 1870 (16 Stat. L., 360), it was directed to inspect all goods purchased. The act of March 3, 1871 (16 Stat. L. 568), provided that not more than 50 per cent of the amount due any contractor should be paid until the accounts and vouchers had been submitted to the executive committee of the board, although the Secretary of the Interior could authorize payment to be made even if the voucher was disapproved by the board."—*Ibid.*, p. 57, n. 94. |

4. For instance, see the *Third Annual Report of the Board of Indian Commissioners to the President of the United States*, 1871.

5. Tatum, *Our Red Brothers*, XVII, XVIII.

| 6. According to General W. T. Sherman, nine field officers and fifty-nine captains and subalterns were detached from regular military duty and ordered to report to the Commissioner of Indian Affairs to serve as Indian superintendents and agents. This was distasteful to certain members of Congress who looked on these Indian positions as part of their proper patronage. Accordingly they passed an act, July 15, 1870, vacating the commission of any army officer who accepted a civil position. When some of the "politicians"

called on the President and admitted that the purpose of the army bill had been to save these Indian service jobs for their own followers, the President is said to have replied: "Gentlemen, you have defeated my plan of Indian management; but you shall not succeed in *your* purpose, for I will divide these appointments up among the religious churches, with which you dare not contend!"—*Memoirs of General William T. Sherman* (New York, 1889), vol. II, p. 437.

In setting forth this explanation of the origin of the "Quaker Policy" Sherman ignores the fact that more than a year before the events he described took place Grant had agreed to try out the Quaker plan. |

7. Reports by the various churches on the Indian work are given by the board of Indian commissioners in some of their *Reports*. See the *Report* for 1871, 161 ff.

8. *Our Red Brothers*, 25, 26.

9. *Ibid.*, 54.

10. The name of Philip McCusker occurs in the records of this frontier frequently. He was in the employ of the United States as early as 1865. During that year he worked under the direction of J. H. Leavenworth and was probably responsible for the recovery of certain prisoners by Leavenworth. He was interpreter at the council of Medicine Lodge creek in 1867. Thereafter for some time he seems to have been employed as special scout and interpreter to keep the commissioner of Indian Affairs informed on matters pertaining to the South Plains frontier. His reports are informative and manifest a thorough understanding of the Indians.

Not being a Quaker, he was not eligible to be an agent after the "peace policy" became operative. He was evidently popular with the Indians, for on more than one occasion they asked that he be officially recognized as a member of their tribes. It seems that after he left the Indian service he engaged in stock farming, for in 1871 he gave the Wichita agency a fine pair of Berkshire pigs.

During the disturbances of 1875 he accompanied a number of scouts and expeditions as volunteer interpreter and guide, and proved to be very useful to the military and the Indian agents at that time. He occasionally wrote letters to the Indian office, and was regarded as a sort of unofficial informant. See the Dallas *Herald*, January 13, 1866; McCusker to Murphy, February 4, 1868, *Upper Arkansas*, M 1386; petition of Indians, March 14, 1870, I.T. Misc., *Kiowa Papers*; McCusker to Smith, September 3, 1875, *Central Superintendency*, M 250; General Hazen's tribute to McCusker, 40 cong., 3 sess., *Sen. Ex. Doc*, no. 18, 11.

11. Hazen to McCusker, January 20, 1869, *Wichita*, W 134.

12. John B. Garrett, clerk of the executive committee of Friends, to the commissioner of Indian Affairs, rcvd. July 12, 1870, *Wichita*, G 453.

13. 41 cong., 2 sess., *House Ex. Doc.* no. 1, part III, 834.

14. For one hundred rations he allowed 150 lbs. beef, 75 lbs. corn meal, 25 lbs. flour, 4 lbs. sugar, 2 lbs. coffee, 1 lb. soap, 1 lb. salt. When the beef was poor he had to allow two and one-half pounds per ration. *Ibid.*, 832.

15. A considerable part of this band was transferred a little later to the Wichita agency.

16. 41 cong., 2 sess., *House Ex. Doc.* no. 1, part III, 836.

17. Sometimes translated The Chewer. The expression means something one chews and then throws away, as tobacco. The chief was generally associated with the Yamparikas. He always declared for the "white man's road" and his influence for good was a matter of consequence. During the disturbances of 1874, when so many of the Comanches were led off by the "Prophet," Quẽrts-quĭp stayed at the reservation and used his influence for peace and good order. Haworth to Hoag, May 9, 1874 (copy), I.T. Misc., *Kiowa*; Haworth to Hoag, June 3, 1874, *ibid.*; Haworth to Smith, July 7, 1874 (copy), *ibid.*

18. Tatum to Parker, July 24, 1869 (copy), *ibid.*

19. Tatum to Hoag, August 12, 1869, 41 cong., 3 sess., *House Ex. Doc.* no. 1, part III, 827.

20. *Ibid.*

21. Goods had to be hauled from Junction City, Kansas, on the Kansas and Pacific Railway, some three hundred miles to the northeast. The freight oxen contracted the Texas fever from the herds of Texas cattle driven over the trail, and some of the trains were thus left stranded without animals to move them. Report of Butler and Pugh, in the *Report* of the secretary of the interior for 1869, 563 ff.

| It is now known that this disease is transmitted by the Texas tick. Cattle raised on ranges infested with the tick develop immunity to the disease. Hence the Texas steers did not die like the "States" cattle.

The long overland freight journey made the price of goods at the agency seem exorbitant and delayed progress. For instance, Butler and Pugh found that inch boards, not of the best quality, sold at Camp Sill for ten dollars per hundred. This made the agency-building and store-house, then being erected, very costly. |

22. Hoag to Parker, April 26, 1870, *Central Superintendency*, 1871, H 1063.

Notes 241

23. The proceedings of this council, entitled "Friend Hoag's Report," were published in the Lawrence *Tribune*, April 12, 1870; clippings from this paper are deposited in *Central Superintendency*, 1871, H 1063.

24. Clipping from the *Western Home Journal*, April 21, 1870, *Central Superintendency*, 1871, H 1063.

25. Hoag to Parker, April 26, 1870, *ibid.*

26. Tatum's second annual report, August 12, 1870, 41 cong., 3 sess., *House Ex. Doc.* no. 1, vol. 1, 724–729.

27. *Ibid.*, 725, 726.

28. The claims against the Indians of the South Plains for damages reached an appalling sum. The following represents some of the principal claims against the Comanches and Kiowas which were recommended for allowance:

CLAIMANT	INDIANS	PLACE OF DEPREDATION	AMOUNT	DATE OF DEPREDATION
Andy Adams	Kiowas and Comanches	Kansas	$107,560	1867
John S. Chisum	Comanches	New Mexico	15,000	June, 1868
John Shirley	Kiowas and Comanches	Indian Territory	3,075	October, 1869
Henry Warren	Kiowas and Comanches	Texas	11,852	May 18, 1870
F. C. Bulkley	Comanches and Kiowas	Indian Territory	10,075	
D.G. & D.A. Sanford	Comanches	Texas	29,208	July, 1872

Selected from a list given in 43 cong., 2 sess., *House Ex. Doc.* no. 65.

29. Second annual report, as cited, 725.

30. *Ibid.*, 727.

31. *Ibid.*

32. See Mooney, "Calendar History of the Kiowa Indians," 242 ff.; Battey, *A Quaker Among the Indians*, chap. X; Grinnell, *The Cheyenne Indians*, II, 211–284.

33. Mooney, *op. cit.*, 327; report of J. A. Covington, acting agent for the Cheyennes and Arapahoes (not dated), Indian Ter. Misc., *Cheyenne and Arapaho*, 1870.

34. Tatum's second annual report, *op. cit.*, 727.

35. Tatum to Hoag, July 1, 1870, I.T. Misc., *Kiowa*.

36. Tatum's second annual report, *op. cit.*, 728.

37. Memorial of three hundred fifty citizens of the northwestern frontier of Texas (presented to congress May 28, 1870). 41 cong., 2 sess., *House Misc. Doc.* no. 142, 1–6.

| The petition read in part:

"Petitioners charge those in authority at Fort Sill as being protectors of the savage in his lawless pursuits, and against the distressed and humble citizens of the frontier of Texas; further charge, that they protect the savage holding a large amount of stolen property, to wit, thousands of heads of horses and mules, belonging to petitioners, to which petitioners offer evidence."

Concerning this matter of returning stolen property General Hazen wrote: "When the large force was here last winter I requested that examples might be made of the chief leaders in these crimes, and that the many stolen horses in their camps might be returned to their owners, many being present who had identified large numbers of the horses. I was given assurance that this should be done, but it was thought best afterward by the military commander to do nothing in the matter."—41 cong., 2 sess., *House Ex. Doc.* no. 1, Part III, p. 835. |

In August, 1870, Tatum wrote: "I am told that in no case have the Kiowas ever been required to return a horse or mule that they had stolen." 41 cong., 3 sess., *House Ex. Doc.* no. 1, part IV, vol. 1, 728.

38. The report of the secretary of war for 1869 (pp. 150, 151), shows that there were 3,672 soldiers in Texas, but nearly half of these were in the interior being used for "reconstruction" purposes. There were at this time 129 officers and soldiers stationed at Fort Concho, 234 at Fort Griffin, and 218 at Fort Richardson. The report for 1871 shows that there were 3,759 troops in the state, and that they were better situated to protect the frontier. There were at this time 369 officers and men at Fort Concho, 444 at Fort Griffin, and 499 at Fort Richardson. Likewise other frontier posts were comparatively well supplied with troops. At Fort McKavett, near the head of the San Saba, there were 560 officers and men, at Fort Stockton 259, and at Fort Davis 179. 42 cong., 2 sess., *House Ex. Doc.* no. 1, part II, 96, 97.

CHAPTER FOURTEEN

1. Rister, "The Significance of the Jacksboro Indian Affair of 1871," in *Southwestern Historical Quarterly*, XXIX, 181–201; H. H. McConnell, *Five Years a Cavalryman*, 273 ff.

2. Report of Brigadier-general Pope, at headquarters, department of the Missouri, October 2, 1871,

42 cong., 2 sess., *House Ex. Doc.* no. 1, part II, vol. 1, 34.

3. *Report of the Commissioner of Indian Affairs*, 1871, 503.

4. Tatum to Grierson and Mackenzie, August 4, 1871, I.T. Misc., *Kiowa* (copy).

5. This was Clinton Smith, son of Henry M. Smith, of Boerne, Randall county, Texas. The boy, together with a younger brother, was captured in 1869 by Apaches and Comanches. He was finally brought in and delivered up by the Comanche chief, Horse's Back, October 24, 1872. Battey, *A Quaker Among the Indians*, 83.

Clinton Smith's story has been told in *The Boy Captives*.

6. These were "Taba-nan-aca" and He Bear. The first chief's name might be written Tăb'-by or Tăb'-ĭ (sun) Nan'-ĭ-yŭt (name), or more properly Tăb'-by Nan'-ī-käh (Named Sun, or My Name is Sun). Named Sun was a man of fine appearance, an old-fashioned Comanche warrior who made no apologies for his roving habits and love for the prairie. He was a Yamparika, but was so closely associated with the wild Kwahadies that he was often described as belonging to that branch of the tribe. In the early winter of 1872 he came with his band to make the reservation his home. But he was disposed to be troublesome, and the agent was never sure of his attitude. Tatum to Hoag, December 9, 1872, I.T. Misc., Kiowa agency; Haworth to Hoag, June 13, 1874, *ibid*.

7. Quoted by Captain R. G. Carter, in "Ridding West Texas of the Comanches," in the Fort Worth *Star Telegram*, magazine section, February 27, 1927.

| 8. Among these had been an expedition under Captain John M. Bacon, who had gone into this region in October, 1869 with one hundred and sixty-nine men. On the "Fresh Water Fork of the Brazos" (White river or Catfish creek), the party was attacked by about five hundred Comanche and Kiowa warriors. The soldiers beat off the Indians and inflicted upon them the loss of eight men killed. | Rister, *The Southwestern Frontier*, 116 ff.; Burton, "A History of the J A Ranch," in *The Southwestern Historical Quarterly*, XXXI, 95.

| Again, in 1871, Mackenzie had led a force north from Fort Richardson into the region that is now Gray and Wheeler counties, without finding any considerable number of Indians. Harley True Burton, "A History of the J A Ranch;" The *Southwestern Historical Quarterly*, XXXI, 95. |

9. Carter, as cited. Captain Carter's articles appeared in the magazine section of the Fort Worth *Star Telegram* on February 27, March 6, 13, 20, 27, and April 3, 1927.

10. From Kent county east this stream is known as the Salt Fork of the Brazos; farther up it forms Blanco Canyon, and still higher it is known as Catfish creek. Sometimes the northwest part of Kent is called White river.

11. *Ibid.*, March 20, 1927.

12. Tatum to Hoag, February 21, 1872. I.T. Misc., *Kiowa*.

13. Tatum thought so. Tatum to Walker, May 1, 1872, *ibid*.

14. *Central Superintendency*, W 1568 and W 10 (copies).

15. Rister, *The Southwestern Frontier*, 148, 149.

According to Left Hand, a leading Arapaho, who was well acquainted with Kiowa affairs, Big Bow led this raid and the Kiowas took from the wagon train a large quantity of arms and ammunition. It was said that the son of Lone Wolf was wounded in the engagement. Beede's report of the council of June, 1872, *Central Superintendency*, H 181.

16. N. Badger, post chaplain, Fort Concho, Texas, to the secretary of the interior, June 18, 1872, *Central Superintendency*, B 6.

17. Tatum to Hoag, June 22, 1872, I.T. Misc., *Kiowa*.

18. Tatum to Walker, May 1, 1872, *ibid*.

19. Nearly all the Indians of the South Plains found fault with their agents. Tatum's Indians gave as their excuse for not liking their agency the fact that it was too close to Fort Sill. However, Tatum contended that they preferred to trade elsewhere because there was more laxity in the matter of contraband goods at other agencies, particularly at the Wichita and the Cheyenne and Arapaho agencies. Tatum to Hoag, April 9, 1872, *ibid*.

20. Tatum to Hoag, February 5, 1872, *ibid.*, Cyrus Beede's report of the council of 1872, *Central Superintendency*, H 181.

21. Tatum took charge of the agency July 1, 1869, and resigned March 31, 1873. During his incumbency he recovered fourteen white and twelve Mexican captives. He resigned in protest at the release of the Kiowa chiefs, Satanta and Big Tree. Tatum, *Our Red Brothers*, 154 ff.

Notes

22. A similar council, with indifferent results, had been held during the spring of 1870. *Ibid.*, 108-115.

23. A report of the council, together with the events that preceded and followed it, is given by Beede in his lengthy manuscript entitled "Report of the Condition of Indian Affairs in the Indian Territory," Lawrence, Kansas, August 13, 1872, *Central Superintendency*, H 181. The journal covers events in the Indian country from about the first of June up to the day it was written and filed in the office at Lawrence. Hereafter it will be referred to as Beede's report, and unless other sources are indicated, it represents the evidence upon which this part of the chapter is written.

24. The words quoted are those of Beede. Tatum stated that he left the council because the illness of his wife made it necessary that he return to his agency. Tatum to Hoag, August 3, 1872, I. T. Misc., *Kiowa*.

25. Tatum to Hoag, August 19, 1872, I. T. Misc., *Kiowa*.

26. "Report of Captain Henry E. Alvord, commissioner to the Kiowas, Comanches and other tribes in the western part of the Indian Territory," in the *Report of the Commissioner of Indian Affairs for 1872*, 128-148. I have followed Alvord's manuscript in the United States Indian Office, *Central Superintendency*, 1872, A 259. It will be cited hereafter as Alvord's report.

27. "Colonel" Horace P. Jones had served as a farmer on the Comanche reservation in Texas. Later he held a position at the Fort Cobb agency and was in the service of the Confederate government when the northern Indians swooped down on that agency and destroyed it, October, 1862. After the war, he served as scout and interpreter at Fort Arbuckle and Fort Sill, where his reputation for efficiency and honesty became a tradition. He was known among the Indians as "the man who never tells a lie." Joseph B. Thoburn, "Horace P. Jones, Scout and Interpreter," in *Chronicles of Oklahoma*, II, 380-391.

28. The New York *Herald*, September 25, 1872.

29. It seems that Red Food belonged to the Tanima or Liver-eater band of Comanches, a group that was fast disappearing. He was not regarded as an especially bad Indian, but he was never friendly toward the whites. He was largely the cause of an outbreak at the Wichita agency in August, 1874. Tatum to Walker, May 21, 1872, I. T. Misc., *Kiowa*; 43 cong., 2 sess., *House Ex. Doc.*, no. 1, part V, vol. 1, 529.

30. For a brief sketch of this chief, see footnote 6.

31. Alvord's report, *op cit.*

CHAPTER FIFTEEN

1. *Report* for 1872, 5, 6.

2. Captain Robert G. Carter, *The Old Sergeant's Story*, 82.

3. Mackenzie to the assistant adjutant-general, written at the camp on the Fresh Water Fork of the Brazos, October 12, 1872, *Central Superintendency*, W 542 (copy).

4. *The Old Sergeant's Story*, 85; *Report of the Commissioner of Indian Affairs*, 1872, 94.

5. Evidently some of the Indians had spent considerable time at the agency, for they recognized an officer of the fourth cavalry who had formerly been interpreter at the Kiowa agency. It is interesting that the Indians brought to Fort Sill a rather accurate account of their defeat, and the officers there knew of the engagement and made a report of it even before Mackenzie reported it. G. W. Schofield, major, tenth cavalry, commanding at Fort Sill, October 10, 1872, *Central Superintendency*, W 542 (copy).

6. Tatum to Hoag, November 15, 1872, I.T. Misc., *Kiowa*.

7. Tatum to Hoag, March 3, 1873, I.T. Misc., *Kiowa*; 43 cong., 1 sess., *House Ex. Doc.* no. 257, 25.

| 8. Thomas Battey paid a fine tribute to Horse's Back, stating:

"Horseback is a chief of no ordinary capacity, having about two hundred people in his band. He is probably about fifty years of age, and though not a Quahada, yet possesses a very great influence with the chiefs of that band of Comanches. He, being sick at the time the Washington delegation left, had to remain at home, and has become active in his demonstrations of his friendship to the whites, probably more from policy than from any inherent good feeling towards them. However that may be, he has not only secured the delivery of the white children held in captivity by the Quahadas, but also from twelve to fifteen Mexicans, since the delegation left, and has now made out all the horses and mules stolen by the tribe. He, being a man of great determination, has exercised his firmness and resolution this fall and winter, by visiting and bringing into the Agency, on peaceful relations, the Quahada band of the tribe...."—*A Quaker Among the Indians*, pp. 113, 114. |

9. Tatum to Hoag, January 11, 1873, *op. cit.*

| 10. Haworth made a number of changes in the personnel of the agency. "My object in selecting employees," he said, "is to get them of a different class from the floating population of the frontier." Some

conception of the various activities of the agency as well as of the cost of administration may be had by scanning the list of Haworth's employees:

NAMES	OCCUPATION	COMMENCEMENT OF SERVICE	COMPENSATION
Thomas Chandler	Interpreter	1" mo. 1–1873	$ 400.00 per annum
William Wykes	Carpenter	5" " 12–1871	75.00 per month
James Storey	Farm Laborer	4" " 1–1873	40.00 " " & rations Discharged 4" mo. 8"
Montgomery Sherwood	Farm Laborer	4" " 1–1873	40.00 per month
Thomas C. Battey	Teacher at Kiowa Camps	10" " 17–1872	100.00 " "
Josiah Butler	Teacher Boarding School	1" " 1–1871	1000.00 " annum
Lizzie Butler	Asst. Boarding School	8" " 23–1872	50.00 " month
Peter Young	Herder at Agency	4" " 1–1873	40.00 " " & rations
John Leonard	Farm Laborer	10" " 1–1872	40.00 " " "
William F. Miller	" "	1" " 1–1873	40.00 " " "
Fred Klann	Cook for Farm	2" " 26–1872	40.00 " " "
Wilson Jones	Cutting and Hauling Logs	12" " 2–1872	35.00 " " "
Wilson Jones	Breaking Prairie for Indians	2" " 26–1873	5.00 " acre	

11. Battey, *op. cit.*, 164; Haworth to Hoag, June 12, 1873, I.T. Misc., *Kiowa*.

So bitter was the feeling against the Indians at Jacksboro, Texas, that a large crowd gathered and threatened to intercept the train and do violence to the Indians. McClermont heard of the threats and sent the train with the prisoners around the town while he drove in and waited, apparently expecting the Indians to follow. In this way he gave the squaws and their escort time to pass around the town and get safely out of the community before the ruse was discovered. Carter, *The Old Sergeant's Story*, 87.

12. Haworth to Hoag, July 14, 1873, I.T. Misc., *Kiowa*.

| 13. The excellent discipline among the Kiowas at this critical time serves as some foundation for the statement frequently made by frontiersmen that the chiefs could control their braves when they really wanted to do so. Such a statement contains only a measure of truth. Overwhelming sentiment of the group, the emphatic approval or disapproval of any course of action, represents a powerful sanction among backward as well as civilized people and at times the most reckless individual will not dare oppose it. |

14. Haworth to Hoag, August 18, 1873, I.T. Misc., *Kiowa*.

15. Haworth to Hoag, August 21, 1873, I.T. Misc., *Kiowa*.

16. See *A Quaker Among the Indians*, 190 ff.

17. Davis's principal demand was that "all of the horse [mounted] Indians bordering on Texas be gathered into reservations, their arms and horses taken from them, and supplies of food be issued to them for not longer than one day at a time." Battey, *A Quaker Among the Indians*, 199, quoting a letter from Governor E. J. Davis to Hon. C. Delano, secretary of the interior.

18. The account of the proceedings at Fort Sill is given briefly by the commissioner of Indian Affairs in 43 cong., 1 sess., *House Ex. Doc.* no. 1, part 5, vol. 1, 375–376. A much fuller account may be found in *A Quaker Among the Indians*, chap. XII. Battey was present at the council.

19. Haworth to Hoag, December 1, 1873, I.T. Misc., *Kiowa*.

20. Haworth to Beede, December 8, 1873. According to Tah-vah-nah, a Comanche interpreter and a brother-in-law of Chēē'vĕrs, this name is not Comanche and has no meaning.

21. *A Quaker Among the Indians*, 230.

22. Battey, *op. cit.*, 239.

23. George E. Glenn to the adjutant-general, January 15, 1874, *Central Superintendency*, W 204 (copy); Haworth to Hoag, March 28, 1874; I.T. Misc., *Kiowa*.

24. Report of F. W. Smith and J. W. Smith to the commissioner of Indian Affairs, September 26, 1874, *Central Superintendency*, S 1328.

25. Report of Brevet major-general John Pope, 43 cong., 2 sess., *House Ex. Doc.* no. 1, part 2, vol. 1, 29–31.

26. Haworth to Beede, April 25, 1874, I.T. Misc., *Kiowa*; Haworth to Hoag, April 27, *ibid*.

27. Haworth to Hoag, May 6, 1874, *ibid.*
28. Report of F. W. and J. W. Smith, *op. cit.*; Battey, *op. cit.*, 302–303.
29. Davidson to the assistant adjutant-general, department of Texas, July 20, 1874, *Central Superintendency*, W 1371 (copy). Davidson got his information from Milky Way and other Penateka chiefs.
30. Haworth to Hoag, May 13, 1874, I.T. Misc., *Kiowa*.
31. Haworth to Hoag, June 8, 1874, *ibid.*
32. Haworth to Smith, September 1, 1874, 43 cong., 2 sess., *House Ex. Doc.* no. 1, part V, vol. 1, 528.
33. See chap. VI, The Failing Buffalo Supply.
34. Rister, "The Significance of the Destruction of the Buffalo in the Southwest," in *Southwestern Historical Quarterly*, XXXIII, 34–50; Holden, *Alkali Trails*, 5–19; Dixon, *Life of "Billy" Dixon*. See also two articles by J. Wright Mooar in the West Texas Historical Association *Year Book*, III, 89–92, VI, 109–111.
35. Haworth to Hoag, June 6, 1874, I.T. Misc., *Kiowa*.

| 36. The Treaty of Medicine Lodge Creek has been referred to as obligating the United States to keep hunters out of the territory south of the Arkansas river. There was no such provision in the treaty. In fact, much of that territory was a part of the State of Kansas. Furthermore, after what is now the narrow strip comprising the Panhandle of Oklahoma was crossed, the hunters coming south from the Dodge City country would be in the Panhandle of Texas. Obviously the United States army had no authority to keep them out of this region and while in that country they were in no sense trespassers. Article Eleven of that treaty gave the Indians "the right to hunt on any lands south of the Arkansas river so long as the buffalo may range thereon in such numbers as to justify the chase" and the United States was obligated to prevent settlements on lands included within their old range for a period of three years. [Kappler, as cited, vol. II, Treaties, p. 980]. Time had rendered this last provision obsolete.

J. Wright Mooar states that the buffalo hunters understood that if they crossed to the south side of the Cimarron, then supposed to be the south line of Kansas and the north line of the Indian Territory, their property would be seized and confiscated. However, when he and a companion visited General Dodge to inquire about this matter the general indicated that they need not take the regulation seriously.—West Texas Historical Association *Year Book*, VI, p. 110. |

37. The "New Adobe Walls" were on East Adobe Walls creek, near the Canadian, in Hutchinson county. The place was about a mile and a quarter from the ruins of Bent's trading post. Dixon, *op. cit.*, 108, 135, 151.

| 38. Dixon, *op. cit.*, 161; Mooney, "Calendar History of the Kiowa Indians," 203. |

39. Davidson to the assistant adjutant-general, July 7, 1874 (copy), *Central Superintendency*, W 1186.
40. Haworth to Smith, July 2, 1874, I.T. Misc., *Kiowa*.

| 41. The place is described by Dixon as follows: "Myers & Leonard built a picket house twenty by sixty feet in size. James Hanraban put up a sod house, twenty-five by sixty, in which he opened a saloon. Thomas O'Keefe built a blacksmith's shop of picket, fifteen feet square . . ." [p. 135]. He adds that a little later Rath and Wright built a sod house sixteen by twenty feet and Myers and Leonard built a stockage corral of cottonwood logs hauled a distance of six miles [pp. 136–137]. |

42. *Ibid.*, 156. I have treated the attack on Adobe Walls in a slightly different way in "The Comanche Indians and the Adobe Walls Fight," in *Panhandle Plains Historical Review*, IV, 24–39.
43. *Ibid.*, 163. It has been said that their bugler was a negro soldier who had deserted.
44. *Ibid.*, 176, 177. The Indian accounts vary from this slightly. Lieutenant-colonel J. W. Davidson, at Fort Sill, who received the Indian account through Jones and Stillwell, interpreter and scout respectively at that post, stated that the Indian losses were seven Comanches and four Cheyennes. Davidson to the assistant adjutant-general, *op. cit.*
45. Report of F. W. and J. W. Smith, September 26, 1874, *Central Superintendency*, S 1328.
46. Grinnell, *The Fighting Cheyennes*, 313. At any rate, he made that excuse some years later when talking to some white men about the defeat.
47. Report of F. W. and J. W. Smith, September 26, 1874, *op. cit.*
48. The words in quotations are those of General Sherman on reading Miles's dispatch. *Central Superintendency*, W 1073.
49. Lieutenant H. F. Wichester, at Sun City, to the post adjutant, Dodge City, August 31, 1874, *Central Superintendency*, W 1518.
50. Jones to the adjutant-general, December 1, 1874, records of the adjutant-general's office, Texas.

The following report of J. F. Williams, an employee at the Cheyenne agency, was accepted by F. W. and J. W. Smith in their report on general Indian affairs in the Indian Territory. His report of September 9, 1874 (*Central Superintendency*, S 1328) is in part as follows:

"we have had well-authenticated accounts from Texas and other sources that the number of individuals killed in New Mexico amount to 40
Colorado 60
Lone Wolf's 1st raid into Texas 7
Big Bow's 1st raid into Texas 4
The Adobe Walls Fight 3
S. West from C. Supply buffalo hunter 3
Between Supply and Dodge (hunters) 5
Vicinity of Med. Lodge and Sun City 12
                                                                                                                    Total 134

On Crooked creek 2
On Trail north from Cheyenne agency 5
On A.T. & S.F.R.R. 4
Washita and Ft. Sill agencies and vicinity 14
Dr. Halloways's son—Charge agency 1
Mr. Dougherty, beef contracter for these agencies, reports at least 30 persons recently killed in Texas 30
                                                                                                                    Total 56

51. Orders of July 17, 1874, I.T. Misc., *Kiowa* (copy).

| 52. He Bear's identity is hard to follow because writers have done such violence to his name. It is even difficult to determine to which band he belonged, although it is certain that he spent much time with the Kwaharies. In August, 1869 the chief is mentioned by the subcommittee of the board of Commissioners as being in council with them at the agency. Here he is listed as a Kotsoteka and the name is given "Pat-ro-o-kome (He Bear)." [41 cong., 2 sess., *House Exec. Doc.* no. 1, Part III]. On August 4, 1871, Tatum reported, "Taba-nan-a-ca's & He Bear's bands have been away from here more than a year & frequently raiding." [I.T. Miscl., *Kiowa*].

At Alvord's council in 1872 He Bear visited the commissioner on the first day but could not find time to remain at the council. The *New York Herald* correspondent in terms not at all complimentary described him as the "high cockalorum of 200 Staked Plains Comanches or Quah-ah-das" known "for his unrelenting hatred of the whites, his proud record of murder of defenseless men, women and children, and his triumphant career as a horse and mule thief . . ." The *New York Herald*, September 23, 1872. In his report Alvord referred to him as "Paduacomb (He Bear)." Report of the Commissioner of Indian Affairs for 1872, p. 137. In December, 1872, after MacKenzie had defeated the Comanches on McClellan's creek, this chief came in together with Shaking Hand and "Tab-a-nan-a-ka." In his report to Hoag Tatum calls the chief "Parry-o-coom." I.T. Misc., *Kiowa*.

Again, in November, 1873, Tatum states that "Parry-o-coom, one of the most prominent of the Quaha-des Chiefs," as camped "in the Mts. within reasonable distance of the Agency with near five hundred of those Indians . . ." To Tatum all wandering Comanches were Quahadas. He Bear was a Kotsoteka, but like Shaking Hand and other chiefs who belonged to the eastern bands he took up with the Quahadas when life on the reservation failed to appeal to him, and is, therefore, easy to confuse with that band. Still later in that year Tatum refers to him as the head chief of the "Qua-ha-das." But in the grizzly old breast of He Bear there was some sentiment. One Presciliano Gonzalez, a Mexican boy of ten, was captured at his home in Mexico by Apaches and traded to a Comanche. He soon became a favorite among the Comanches, but when he was brought to the agency and told that he might leave the Indians he chose to do so, at which He Bear wept! [Tatum to Hoag, March 3, 1873, I.T. Misc. *Kiowa*; 43 cong., 1 sess., *House Ex. Doc.* no. 257, p. 25]. |

53. Haworth to Smith, July 28, 1874, *ibid*.
54. Haworth to Hoag, August 5, 1874, *ibid*.
55. Beede to Hoag, August 13, 1874, I.T. Misc., *Kiowa*.
56. The Indians claimed that the chief merely wished to confer with another Indian he saw some distance away, that he yelled to attract the other's attention, and dashed away to meet and confer with him, not realizing that his act would be taken as an effort to escape from his guard.
57. Lone Wolf had wanted to register, but had not been permitted to do so because of alleged participation in recent outrages. He had recently returned from Texas (or possibly Mexico) where he had gone to recover the body of his son killed in a raid some time before. The chief denied that he had been guilty of serious wrongs. There is little positive information concerning his conduct during the year. Haworth to

Beede, June 13, 1874; Haworth to Hoag, June 15, 1874, Indian Territory Misc., *Kiowa;* also John F. Williams, employee at Cheyenne agency, to Smith, September 9, 1874, *Central Superintendency,* 1874, S 1328.

58. Haworth to Smith, November 14, 1874, I.T. Misc., *Kiowa.*

59. F. W. and J. W. Smith estimated the number of hostiles as follows: Cheyennes, 1800; Comanches, 1700; Kiowas, 1000; representing altogether 800 warriors.

60. Hoag to Smith, October 20, 1874, 43 cong., 2 sess., *House Ex. Doc.* no. 1, part V, vol. 1, 522.

61. Nicholson to Smith, October 16, 1874, *Central Superintendency,* N 125.

| In his annual report Hoag wrote: ". . . I desired, further, that these Indians should be counseled with, and their faith and reliance in the friendship of the Government strengthened, and to this end, unable to leave my official duties, I subsequently directed Cyrus Beede, my chief clerk, accompanied by E. F. Hoag, clerk, to proceed to the three southwestern agencies in pursuance of this important service, under special instructions; but this legitimate and appropriate service so much needed was denied by the military, as evinced in their report herewith . . ."—43 cong., 2 sess., *House Ex. Doc.* no. 1, part 5, vol. 1, p. 522. |

62. See Rister, *The Southwestern Frontier,* 158 ff.

63. *Ibid.,* map opp. 156.

64. 44 cong., 1 sess., *House Ex. Doc.* no. 1, part II, vol. 1, 73 ff.; Nelson A. Miles, *Personal Recollections,* chap. xi; Price's report to the adjutant-general, September 23, 1874, *Central Superintendency,* W 1708; Burton, "History of the J. A. Ranch," in *Southwestern Historical Quarterly,* XXXI, 101 ff., map 233; Carter, *The Old Sergeant's Story,* chap. xi.

65. *Central Superintendency,* W 1583 (copy). Counting armed teamsters, Lyman had sixty-six men with him. W. H. Lewis, lieutenant-colonel 19th U.S. infantry to the assistant adjutant-general, September 12, 1874, *ibid.*

66. Miles, *Personal Recollections,* 172, 173.

67. Price's report, September 23, 1874, *Central Superintendency,* W 1708 (copy); Dixon, *The Life of "Billy" Dixon,* 199 ff.; Miles, *op. cit.,* 173, 174.

The privates were Z. T. Woodhall, Peter Rath, John Harrington, and George W. Smith. Smith died of his wounds before the engagement ended.

68. Carter, *The Old Sergeant's Story,* 113, 114.

69. Haworth's report, September 20, 1875, 44 cong., 1 sess., *House Ex. Doc.* no. 1, part V, vol. 1, 773–777.

70. *Central Superintendency,* 1875, S 1253.

71. See the report of Major John B. Jones, commanding frontier battalion, to the adjutant-general (Texas), March 8, 1876, printed in *Frontier Echo,* Jacksboro, April 14, 1876.

72. Martha Leota Buntin has treated this subject in an interesting way in a Master of Arts thesis, prepared at the University of Oklahoma, entitled "History of the Kiowa, Comanche, and Wichita Indian Agency," Ms. In preparing the work she used the files of the agency, which is in charge of her father, J. A. Buntin.

The Comanches soon gave up their old habit of leaving the reservation, even in small parties. Quanah Parker and others served as police, and arrested recalcitrant Indians. Many of the men soon acquired herds of cattle (sheep raising did not prove successful), and took great interest in caring for their herds and protecting their property from thieves. After a few years, the larger bands began to break up, and the different families to move away and locate separately in localities where the grass was especially good and the soil rich. They even gave up the old habit of moving from a location whenever death visited their group. Some of the men earned considerable money by hauling freight from the railroad to the reservation. In 1886 an Indian court was established, the judges of which were selected by the Indians themselves, with the assistance of the agents.

The Indians of the Kiowa, Comanche, and Apache agency had more land than they needed for their own use, and leases to cattlemen brought in considerable revenue to the tribes. In 1892 the Jerome agreement or treaty was made, whereby the Indians, for two million dollars consideration, relinquished their rights to a part of their land, retaining enough for a one hundred sixty acre allotment for each person, some additional acreage for schools and public purposes, and four hundred eighty thousand acres to be held as common property. Many friends of the Indians, together with some of the most influential red men, alleged that the Jerome agreement was made through fraud and duress, and urged congress not to ratify it. In June, 1900, it was finally ratified, nevertheless, and the reservation was thrown open to settlement. The Indians were given the choice of the lands, each individual to hold his land as a ward of the government for a period of twenty-five years or longer, as the president might decide. In most cases the time has been extended, and the Indians still do not have a title in fee simple to their land.

The reports of the agents indicate that the coming of white settlers brought debauchery and much imposition upon the Indians. But in spite of bad influences, they have, thanks to their agents, teachers, missionaries, and native leaders, made considerable progress. Most of them have comfortable houses, their young people have a good elementary or high school education, and they have acquired the characteristics of their white neighbors. In 1926, they numbered 1,790 persons.

Bibliography

Abel, Annie Heloise. The American Indian as Slaveholder and Secessionist (Cleveland, 1915).
———. History of Events resulting in Indian Consolidation west of the Mississippi River: in American Historical Association *Annual Report*, 1906, vol. 1.
Arkansas Gazette [Little Rock], 1829–1838.
Babb, Theodore Adolphus (Dot). In the Bosom of the Comanches (Amarillo, Texas, 1923).
Banner of Peace [Nashville, Tenn.], 1858–1861.
Barry, James B. (Buck). Reminiscences and Memoirs (University of Texas Archives, Ms.).
———. A Texas Ranger and Frontiersman: the Days of Buck Barry in Texas, 1845–1906, ed. James K. Greer (Dallas, 1932).
Bartlett, John Russell. Personal Narrative (New York, 1854), 2 vols.
Battey, Thomas C. The Life and Adventures of a Quaker among the Indians (Boston, 1875).
Bancroft, Hubert Howe. History of the North Mexican States and Texas (San Francisco, 1888), 2 vols.
———. History of Arizona and New Mexico (San Francisco, 1889).
———. History of Nevada, Colorado, and Wyoming (San Francisco, 1890).
Becker, Daniel A. Comanche Civilization; History of Quanah Parker: in *Chronicles of Oklahoma*, vol. 1 (Oklahoma City, 1923).
Bexar Archives (University of Texas Archives, Austin).
  This is a large collection of official papers that were accumulated at San Antonio during the Spanish period.
Bieber, Ralph P. The Southwestern Trails to California in 1849: in *Mississippi Valley Historical Review*, vol. xii (Cedar Rapids, Iowa, 1925).
Bollaert, W. Observations on the Indian Tribes in Texas: in London Ethnological Society *Journal*, vol. II (London, 1850).
Bolton, Herbert E. Athanase de Mézieres and the Louisiana–Texas Frontier, 1768–1780 (Cleveland, 1914), 2 vols.
———. Texas in the Middle Eighteenth Century: in University of California *Publications in History*, Vol. III (Berkeley, 1915).
Board of Indian Commissioners. Third Annual *Report*, 1871 (Washington, 1872).
Biesele, R. L. The German Settlers and the Indians in Texas: in *Southwestern Historical Quarterly*, vol. XXXI (Austin, 1927).
Brown, John Henry. Indian Wars and Pioneers of Texas (St. Louis, n.d.).
Bugbee, Lester G. The Texas Frontier, 1820–1825: in Southern History Association *Publications*, vol. IV (Washington, 1910).
Buntin, Martha Leota. History of the Kiowa, Comanche, and Wichita Indian Agency (M.A. thesis, University of Oklahoma, Ms. Norman, 1931).

Burton, Harley True. A History of the J. A. Ranch: in *Southwestern Historical Quarterly*, vols. XXXI, XXXII (Austin, 1927–1928).

Burnet, David G. American Aborigines, Indians of Texas: in Cincinnati *Literary Gazette*, vols. I, II (Cincinnati, Ohio, 1824–1825).

Calhoun, James S. Official Correspondence, while Indian Agent at Santa Fé and Superintendent of Indian Affairs in New Mexico, ed. Annie Heloise Abel (Washington, 1915).

Carter, Captain Robert G. The Old Sergeant's Story (New York, 1926).

Catlin, George. North American Indians (reprinted at Edinburgh, Scotland, 1926), 2 vols.

Cherokee Advocate [Talequah, Cherokee nation], 1846.

Clark, W. P. The Indian Sign Language (Philadelphia, 1885).

Clift, W. H. Warren's Trading Post: in *Chronicles of Oklahoma*, vol. II (Oklahoma City, 1924).

Cincinnati [Ohio] Daily Gazette, 1874.

Custer, George A. Life on the Plains and Personal Experiences with Indians (New York, 1876).

Dallas [Texas] Herald, 1858–1866.

Davis, Theodore R. The Buffalo Range: in *Harper's New Monthly Magazine*, vol. XXXVIII (New York, 1869).

Detrich, L. C. Comanche Vocabulary (Fort Sill, Indian Territory, 1895, Ms.): in Bureau of American Ethnology Library, Washington, D.C.

DeShields, James T. Border Wars of Texas (Tioga, Texas, 1912).

Dixon, Olive K. Life of "Billy" Dixon (Dallas, 1927).

Dodge, Richard Irving. Our Wild Indians (Hartford, Conn., 1882).

Dunn, William E. Apache Relations in Texas: in Texas State Historical Association *Quarterly*, vol. XIV (Austin, 1911).

Eldredge, Joseph C. Report on Expedition to the Comanches, ed. R. N. Richardson: in West Texas Historical Association *Year Book*, vol. IV (Abilene, Texas, 1928).

Erath, Major George Bernard. Memoirs, ed. Lucy A. Erath: in *Southwestern Historical Quarterly*, vol. XXVI (Austin, 1922–1923).

Farnham, Thomas J. Travels in the Great Western Prairies: in Early Western Travels, ed. R. G. Thwaites, vol. XXVIII (Cleveland, 1904–1908).

Ford, John S. Memoirs (University of Texas Archives, Austin, Ms.).

Foreman, Grant. Pioneer Days in the Early Southwest (Cleveland, 1926).

Fowler, Jacob. Journal, ed. Elliott Coues (New York, 1898).

Froebel, Julius. Aus Amerika (Leipzig, 1857), 2 vols.

An English translation of this work was published at London in 1859 entitled Seven Years' Travel in Central America, Northern Mexico, and the Far West of the United States. I did not have access to the English edition.

Gregg, Josiah. Commerce of the Prairies: in Early Western Travels, ed. R. G. Thwaites, vols. XIX, XX (Cleveland, 1904–1908).

Gammel, H. P. N. The Laws of Texas (Austin, 1898), 10 vols.

Gittinger, Roy. The Formation of the State of Oklahoma: in University of California *Publications in History*, vol. VI (Berkeley, 1918).

Grinnell, George Bird. The Story of the Indian (New York, 1898).

———. The Fighting Cheyennes (New York, 1915).

———. The Cheyenne Indians (New Haven, 1923), 2 vols.

———. Bent's Old Fort and its Builders: in Kansas Historical Society *Collections*, vol. XV (Topeka, 1922).

Haley, J. Evetts. The X I T Ranch of Texas (Chicago, 1929).

Hodge, Frederick Webb, ed. Handbook of American Indians North of Mexico (Washington, 1907 and 1910), 2 vols.

Published as Bureau of American Ethnology *Bulletin 30*.

Holden, William Curry. Alkali Trails (Dallas, 1930).

———. Frontier Defense in Texas during the Civil War: in West Texas Historical Association *Year Book*, vol. IV (Abilene, Texas, 1928).

———. Frontier Defense, 1846–1860: in West Texas Historical Association *Year Book*, vol. VI (Abilene, 1930).

James, General Thomas. Three Years Among the Indians and Mexicans, ed. Walter B. Douglas (St. Louis, 1916).

Kappler, Charles J. ed. Indian Affairs Laws and Treaties (Washington, 1903), 3 vols.

Kennedy, William. Texas (London, 1841), 2 vols.
Koch, Lena Clara. The Federal Indian Policy in Texas, 1845–1860: in *Southwestern Historical Quarterly*, vols. XXVIII, XXIX (Austin, 1925–1926).
Lee, Nelson. Three Years Among the Comanches (Albany, New York, 1859).
Lehmann, Herman. Nine Years Among the Indians, ed. J. Marvin Hunter (Austin, Texas, 1929).
Long, Stephen H. Expedition from Pittsburgh to the Rocky Mountains, performed in the years 1819–1820, ed. Edwin James: in Early Western Travels, ed. R. G. Thwaites, vols. XIV–XVII (Cleveland, 1904–1908).
Lowe, P. G. Five Years a Dragoon (Kansas City, 1906).
Lowie, Robert H. Dances and Societies of the Plains Shoshone: in Museum of Natural History *Anthropological Papers*, vol. XI, part X.
McConnell, H. H. Five Years a Cavalryman (Jacksboro, Texas, 1889).
Marcy, Randolph B. Thirty Years of Army Life on the Border (New York, 1866).
———. Report [on the route from Fort Smith to Santa Fé] 1849: in 31 cong., 1 sess., *Sen. Ex. Doc.* no. 64..
———. and George B. McClellan. Exploration of the Red River of Louisiana, in the year 1852. *Sen. Ex. Doc.* 54, 32 cong., 2 sess., and *House Doc.* (no number), 33 cong., 1 sess.
Margry, Pierre. Découvertes et établissements des Francais dans l'ouest et dans le sud de l'Amérique Septentrionale, 1614–1754. Mémoires et documents originaux (Paris, 1875–1886), 6 parts.
Matagorda [Texas] Bulletin, 1838–39.
Maverick, Mary A. Memoirs (San Antonio, Texas, 1921).
Mexico, Archivo General de la nacion, Mexico City, Provincias Internas, t. 12, 65, and 201 (University of Texas transcripts). These documents pertain to affairs in Texas, New Mexico, and other north Mexican provinces during the last half of the eighteenth century.
Mexican Border Commission. Official reports of the Committee of Investigation sent in 1873 by the Mexican government to the frontier of Texas. Translated from the original edition made in Mexico (New York, 1875).
Mooney, James. The Ghost-dance Religion and the Sioux Outbreak of 1890: in Bureau of American Ethnology Fourteenth Annual *Report*, part II (Washington, 1896).
———. Calendar History of the Kiowa Indians: in Bureau of American Ethnology Seventeenth Annual *Report*, part II (Washington, 1899).
Morrell, Z. N. Flowers and Fruits in the Wilderness (Dallas, 1886).
Muckleroy, Anna. The Indian Policy of the Republic of Texas: in *Southwestern Historical Quarterly*, vols. XXV, XXVI, 1922–23.
New York Herald, 1872.
Northern Standard [Clarksville, Texas], 1842–1862.
Pacific Railroad Survey Reports. Reports of Explorations and Surveys to ascertain the most practicable Route for a Railroad from the Mississippi River to the Pacific Ocean, 1853–1854 (Washington, 1855–1860), 13 vols.
Parker, W. B. Notes taken during the Expedition Commanded by Captain R. B. Marcy through unexplored Texas, in the Summer and Fall of 1854 (Philadelphia, 1856).
Paxson, Frederick Logan. The Last American Frontier (New York, 1918).
Perrine, Fred S. and Grant Foreman. The Journal of Hugh Evans Covering the First and Second Campaigns of the United States Dragoon Regiment in 1834, 1835: in *Chronicles of Oklahoma*, vol. III (Oklahoma City, 1925).
Pike, Albert. Narrative of a Journey in the Prairie: in Arkansas Historical Association *Publications*, vol. IV (Conway, Arkansas, 1917).
Pike, James. Scout and Ranger, ed. Carl L. Cannon (reprinted from the edition of 1865, Princeton, 1932).
Pike, Zebulon Montgomery. Expeditions, ed. Elliott Coues (New York, 1895), 3 vols.
Plummer, Rachel. Narrative, ed. James W. Parker (1926).
Price, George F. Across the Continent with the Fifth Cavalry (New York, 1885).
Richardson, Rupert N. The Comanche Indians and the Adobe Walls Fight: in *Panhandle Plains Historical Review*, vol. IV (Canyon, Texas, 1931).
———. The Comanche Reservation in Texas: in West Texas Historical Association *Year Book*, vol. V. (Abilene, Texas, 1929).
Rister, Carl C. The Southwestern Frontier, 1865–1880 (Cleveland, 1928).
Roemer, Ferdinand. Texas (Bonn, 1849).
Royce, Charles C. ed. Indian Land Cessions in the United States: in Bureau of American Ethnology

Eighteenth Annual *Report*, part II (Washington, 1899).

Ruxton, George A. F. Adventures in Mexico and the Rocky Mountains (New York, 1855).

Schmeckebier, Laurence F. The Office of Indian Affairs, its History, Activities, and Organization: in Institute for Government Research, Service Monograph of the United States Government, no. 48 (Baltimore, 1927).

Schoolcraft, Henry R. Historical and Statistical Information Respecting the History, Condition and Prospects of the Indian Tribes of the United States (Philadelphia, 1851–1857), 4 parts.

St. Louis [Missouri] Republican, 1858–1859.

Santa Fé Trail, Journal, ed. William E. Connelley: in *Mississippi Valley Historical Review*, vol. XII (Cedar Rapids, Iowa, 1925).

Smith, Clinton L. and Jeff. D. The Boy Captives, ed. J. Marvin Hunter (Bandera, Texas, 1927).

Smithwick, Noah. The Evolution of a State (Austin, 1898).

Stephens, H. Morse, and Herbert E. Bolton. The Pacific Ocean in History (New York, 1917).

Sowell, A. J. Early Settlers and Indian Fighters in Southwest Texas (Austin, 1900).

Tatum, Lawrie. Our Red Brothers (Philadelphia, 1899).

Taylor, Alfred A. The Medicine Lodge Peace Council: in *Chronicles of Oklahoma*, vol. II (Oklahoma City, 1924).

Telegraph and Texas Register [Houston], 1835–1849.

Texas Army Papers, Texas State Library, Austin.

A collection of several hundred manuscripts pertaining mainly to the Republic of Texas.

Texas Executive Record Books, State Library, Austin.

These are the blotters of the president. Books number 38 and 40 as well as correspondence book number 49, of the secretary of state, were drawn upon for a number of items.

Texas Governor's Papers, State Library.

This is a collection of a part of the correspondence of Texas governors, and contains many items bearing on the frontier. The papers of Henderson, Wood, Pease, Runnels, and Throckmorton were used extensively.

Texas House of Representatives Journal, 2 congress, called session, and 3 congress, regular session.

Texas Indian Papers, Texas State Library.

A comparatively complete collection of the official Indian papers of the Republic of Texas and some material bearing on the period of statehood.

Texas State Gazette [Austin], 1849–1855.

Thoburn, Joseph B. Standard History of Oklahoma (Chicago, 1916), 5 vols.

———. Horace P. Jones, Scout and Interpreter: in *Chronicles of Oklahoma*, vol. II (Oklahoma City, 1924).

Thomas, Alfred B. Forgotten Frontiers; a Study of the Spanish Indian Policy of Don Juan Bautista de Anza, Governor of New Mexico, 1777–1787 (Norman, Oklahoma, 1932).

———. An Eighteenth Century Comanche Document: in *American Anthropologist*, vol. XXXI (Washington, 1929).

Twitchell, Ralph Emerson. Leading Facts of New Mexican History (Cedar Rapids, Iowa, 1911), 4 vols.

———. The Spanish Archives of New Mexico (Cedar Rapids, Iowa, 1914), 2 vols.

United States Commissioner of Indian Affairs. Annual *Reports* for 1861, 1867, 1869, 1871, 1872.

United States House of Representatives Documents: 23 congress, 2 session document no. 2; 25 congress, executive document no. 351; 28 congress, 2 session, document no. 76; 31 congress, 1 session, executive document no. 45; 32 congress, 2 session, executive document no. 1, part 1, vol. 1; 34 congress, 3 session, executive document no. 1; 41 congress, 2 session, executive document no. 1, part 3; 38 congress, 2 session, executive document no. 1; 39 congress, 1 session, executive document no. 1; 39 congress, 2 session, executive document no. 1; 41 congress, 2 session, executive document no. 1; 41 congress, 2 session, miscellaneous documents, no. 137, 139, 142; 41 congress, 3 session, executive document no. 1, vol. 1; 42 congress, 2 session, executive document no. 1, part 2, vol. 1; 42 congress, 3 session, executive document no, 1, part 2, vol. 1; 43 congress, 1 session, executive document no. 257; 43 congress, 2 session, executive document no. 1, part 2, vol. 1.

United States Office of Indian Affairs, Interior Building, Washington, D.C.

Every division of the general files and every special file that might furnish information on the Comanches was examined, except material already included in the University of Texas photostat copy collection. Those drawn from most extensively are: Central Superintendency, 1863–1878; Upper Arkansas Agency, 1856–1868; Wichita Agency, 1860–1869; New Mexico Superintendency, 1860–1865; Abstract of letters Sent,

1860–1876; Talks, Councils, and Treaties (special file); and Indian Territory Miscellaneous, Kiowa and Comanche Papers, 1869–1874 (one or two quarters missing). These last named papers appear to be originals in some cases and copies in others of the correspondence from the Kiowa and Comanche agency which was sent to or passed through the Central Superintendency, at Lawrence, Kansas. They contain much information not found in the General Files.

United States Congress, Senate Documents: 22 congress, 1 session, executive document no. 90; 27 congress, 2 session, executive document no. 1; 29 congress, 1 session, executive document no. 1; 29 congress, 1 session, executive document no. 438; 29 congress, 2 session, executive document no. 1; 30 congress, 1 session, reports of committees, no. 171; 31 congress, 1 session, executive document no. 64; 31 congress, 2 session, executive document no. 1; 32 congress, 1 session, executive document no. 1, part 3; 33 congress, 2 session, executive document no. 1, part 1, vol. 1; 34 congress, 1 session, executive document no. 1, part 1; 35 congress, 1 session, executive document no. 11; 35 congress, 2 session, executive document no. 1; 36 congress, 1 session, executive document no. 2; 36 congress, 2 session, executive document no. 1; 37 congress, 1 session, executive document no. 11; 37 congress, 2 session, executive document no. 1, vol. 1; 38 congress, 2 session, executive document no. 1; 39 congress, 2 session, reports of committees no. 156; 40 congress, 1 session, executive document no. 13; 40 congress, 2 session, executive document no. 60; 40 congress, 3 session, executive document no. 18; 61 congress, 2 session, executive document no. 357.

United States Secretary of War. Annual *Reports* (abridged) for 1868 and 1869.

University of Texas Collection of photostat copies of documents in the United States Indian Office.

This collection contains copies of all documents bearing on Texas Indians and Indian affairs not available in printed government documents. It contains also considerable correspondence from Indian agents and army officers north of Texas. The period covered is from 1845 to 1860.

War of the Rebellion. Official Records of the Union and Confederate Armies, series 1, vols. IV, XLI, and XLVIII; series IV, vol. II.

Wilbarger, J. W. Indian Depredations in Texas (Austin, Texas, 1899).

Wissler, Clark. North American Indians of the Plains (New York, 1927).

———. The American Indian (New York, 1922).

———. The Influence of the Horse in the Development of Plains Culture: in *American Anthropologist*, XVI (Washington, 1914).

Index

A-cah-quash, 55, 56
Acer-quash. *See* A-cah-quash
Adelsverein, 70
Alamo Gordo, 141
Alvord, Captain Henry E., 162, 180, 181, 183
American Revolution, 24, 28
Anadarkoes: as guides, 73; location of, 19; meetings with, 73; plight of, 108
Anglo-Americans: arrival of, 21, 30, 31; early treaties of, 337–4; and Indians, 32; during Texas revolution, 39
Anza, Governor Don Juan Bautista de, 3, 4, 24–27
Apaches: alliance of, 142; attacks of, 84, 89; and Comanches, 1, 20, 21, 23, 24–28, 101; cooperation of, 195; councils with, 145, 178; decline of, 87–88; meetings with, 91; raids of into Mexico, 100; relocation of, 162; territory of, 33; treaties with, 142, 151, 155; visit Washington, 183
Arapahoes: alliance of, 142; attacks of, 84, 89, 161; councils with, 145, 178; decline of, 87–88; location of, 18, 33; meetings with, 91; treaties with, 142, 147, 151; visit Washington, 183
Arbuckle, General Matthew, 35, 37
Armstrong, Major F. W., 35
Austin, Stephen F., 39

Babb, Dot (captive), 148
Baker, Mosely, 42
Bannock Indians, 2
Barnard, Charles, 79
Barry, "Buck," 128
Battey, Thomas C., 187, 189
Baylor, John R.: and end of reservations, 127, 128, 130–31; and hatred of Neighbors, 126; and purchase of boy, 104; as resident agent, 112
Bear-with-a-Short-Tail, 61
Bear's Tail, defeat of by Mexicans, 99
Becknell, William, 33
Bee, Hamilton P., 55
Beede, Cyrus, 166, 178, 179, 186
Bent (agent in 1859), 133

Bent, George, 151
Bent, W. W., 147
Bent, William, 33, 89, 90
Bent's Fort, 89, 90, 98
Big Bow, 147
Big Tree: imprisonment of, 175, 179, 188; surrender of, 199
Bis-te-va-na, 136, 140
Black Beard, cooperation of, 187
Black Beaver, 151, 178
Black Duck, 187
Black Horse, 182
Black Kettle, 143, 162
Bogy, Charles, 149
Bonnell, George W., 47
Boone, A. G., 140, 141
Bowl, 40
Brother (agent?), 69
Buell, Lieutenant-colonel, 190, 197
buffalo: as food, 3; hunters of, 192–93, 194, 200; hunting of, 6, 7; supply of, 85–88
Buffalo-eaters. *See* Kotsotekas
Buffalo Hump: attacks on, 122, 123; and councils, 57, 58–59, 60, 67, 69, 74; description of, 71–72; expeditions of, 63–65, 70, 111–12; fleeing of, 110; leadership of, 69, 78, 79, 122; meetings with, 72–73; raids of into Mexico, 98, 99; on the reservation, 111, 138; treaties with, 65, 70, 80
Burleson, E. N., testimony of, 127
Burleson, Edward, 52
Burnet, David G., 41
Butler, Governor (Cherokee agent), 37
Butler, Governor P. M., 67, 68

Cabello, Governor Domingo, 29
Caddoes: at council, 178, 182; as guides, 112; location of, 19; meetings with, 73; plight of, 108; treaties of, 57, 67, 68
Caldwell, Matthew, 52
Calhoun, James S., 94
Camp Holmes, treaty at, 35, 36, 90

Camp Radziminski, 123
Capron, Horace, 83
captives, treatment of, 105, 148–49
Carleton, General James H., 143
Carson, Christopher (Kit), 143–44, 147
Castro (Lipan chief), 52
Catlin, George, 8, 9, 34, 37
Chapman, Amos, 199
Cheevers, 188–89, 195
Cherokees: at council, 178; relocation of, 19, 83–84; and Texans, 48
Cheyennes: alliance of, 142; battles of, 89, 149, 161, 193; at council, 178, 180; decline of, 84, 87–88; depredations of, 190, 194; and Kiowas, 18; meetings with, 91; surrender of, 199; territory of, 33; treaties with, 142, 147, 151
Chisholm, Jesse, 67, 81, 90, 96, 151; son of, 145
Chivington, Colonel J. M., 143
Choctaw Tom, 128
Chom-o-pand-u-a, 59
Chouteau, Colonel A. P., 36
Chouteau, Major P. L., 37
Christian Indians, 21–22. See also Jicarillas
Clear Fork, 126
Coffee's traders, 35, 41, 86
Cogswell, 64
Coleman, Lieutenant, 98
Colley, S. G., 142
Collins, J. L., 141
Comanche Peak, council at, 67–68
Comanchería, 17, 18, 23, 31
Comanchéros, 3, 37, 144, 156–57
Comanches: alliances of, 28; appearance of, 8; arrests of, 200; attacks of, 40, 192–93, 194; attacks on, 53, 119, 121; bands of, 2, 4, 5; burial of, 15–16; characteristics of, 5, 17, 38; colonization of, 26; cooperation of, 195; council of, 2, 11; councils with, 24, 25, 34–35, 42–43, 151, 178–83; country of, 17–20; dances of, 2; death of, 15; decline of, 88, 107–08, 109; dress of, 8–9; food of, 9; family of, 2; games of, 16; and the horse, 6–8; hunting methods of, 6, 7; knowledge of, 16–17; language of, 4, 5; leadership of, 2, 11–12; marriage of, 2, 9–10; medicine of, 15; medicine dance of, 190–91; names of, 1–2; organization of, 5; origins of, 1, 17; and Osages, 93; and peace, 49, 89; population of, 4, 37; raids of into Mexico, 97–105; range of, 18; religion of, 13–14; removal of, 131; at the reservation, 200; speech of, 2; taboos of, 14; treaties with, 35, 59, 136, 146, 147, 155; tribe of, 2; wars of, 19, 24–28; war parties of, 12–13
Comanches, northern: and agents, 89; independence from Texans, 95–96; and Indians of New Mexico, 94; and southern Comanches, 80
Comanches *Orientales*, 29. See also Kotsotekas;

Penatekas
Comanches, southern: alliance of, 142; crises of, 78; decline of, 109. See also Penatekas
Conner, John, 55, 57, 67, 84
Cooke, Colonel William G., 49
Cornett, Edward, 131
Cota de Malla. See Ecueracapa
Council House affair, 49–51, 65
Council Springs. See Tehuacana creek
Cox, J. D., 169
Creeks, 37, 136, 178
Croix, El Cavallero de, 24
Crow Indians, 91
Cuchanec. See Kotsotekas
Cuerno Verde, 24
Custer, General George A., 162
Cut-Arm, 62
Cutscrip. See Quĕrts-quĭp

Dakotas, and Kiowas, 18
Davidson, Lieutenant-colonel J. W., 194, 195–96, 197
Davis, Governor E. J., 175, 188
de Mézieres, Athanase, 28
Delawares: attacks of, 62, 138; at council, 178; as guides, 55, 73; relocation of, 83–84; territory of, 88
Detsanayuka. See Nokonies
Dixon, "Billie," 199
Dodge, Colonel Henry, 34, 35, 36; expedition of, 37
Doolittle, Senator J. R., 145
Drinking Eagle, 136, 142, 147, 156

Eagle, the, 43, 45
Eagle Feathers, 94
Eagle Heart, 175
Eastland, Captain W. M., 48
Ecueracapa, 25–26
Eldredge, Colonel J. C., 54–57, 64
England, 23, 24
Erath, George B., 130, 131
Es-ă-wäk'-kä-ny, 45, 52. See also Isowacony
Evans, Captain, 128
Evans, Governor John, 143
Evans, Lieutenant-colonel A. W., 162

Faraon, 20. See also Apaches
Fast Bear, at council, 183
Fischer, Rudolph (captive), 156
Fisher, Colonel William S., 49
Fitzpatrick, Thomas: and northern Comanches, 91; and treaty of Fort Atkinson, 92, 104
Flacco (Lipan chief), 48
Ford, Captain John S., 119, 120, 127
Fort Adobe, 89
Fort Arbuckle, 81

Index

Fort Atkinson, 81; treaty of, 92–97, 142
Fort Belknap, 81, 117
Fort Chadbourne, 81
Fort Cobb, 132, 136
Fort Gibson, 34, 41
Fort Griffin, 87
Fort Mann, 81
Fort Phantom Hill, 81, 95
Fort Sill, 162
Fort Sumner. *See* Fort Atkinson
Fowler, Jacob, 32
Fox Indians, 84
France, 23, 27
Friends. *See* Orthodox Friends

Gaignard, 28
Garland, Peter, 128
Gente de Palo. *See* Yupes
gentile system, 2
German colonists, 70
Gilpin, Governor, 140
Givens, Captain N. C., 126
Goodnight, Charles, 157
Grant, Ulysses S., 165, 169
Green Horn, 24
Grierson, Colonel, 172, 175
Guadalupe Hidalgo, treaty of, 76, 100
Gurley, Edward J., 130

Hainaies, location of, 19; plight of, 108
Hardee, Lieutenant-colonel W. J., 80
Harry, Jack, 55 ?, 123
Hatch, Major John P., 177
Hawkins, Thomas T., investigations of, 116, 127
Haworth, J. M., 186, 187, 188, 189, 190, 195
Hays, Captain John C., 63, 73; and Buffalo Hump, 99
Hays, Robert, 73
Hazen, General W. B., 161, 162, 167, 168
He Bear, 168, 182; at agency, 185; cooperation of, 195, 201
Heith, Lieutenant Henry, 91
Henderson, Governor J. Pinckney, 66, 70, 82
Hicks (Cherokee), 68
Hitson, John, 157
Hoag, Enoch, 166, 168, 178, 186, 196–97
Honey-eaters. *See* Penatekas; Comanches
Horse's Back, 147; and captives, 148; cooperation of, 180, 185, 187, 189; at Medicine Lodge Creek, 156; on the reservation, 168
Houston, Sam, 41, 44, 54–65
Howard Wells massacre, 177
Howe, Captain, 73
Howeah, 195
Hudson, Lieutenant, 190
Huston, Felix, 52

Indian Affairs, house committee on: board of commissioners, 164–65; commissioners of, 47, 67, 76, 84, 129, 184, 195; recommendations of, 41, 106–07, 196; superintendents of, 55, 62, 91, 98; tactics of, 187, 188
Indian fighters, payment of, 101
Ionies. *See* Hainies
Iron Jacket, death of, 119
Iron Mountain, 147, 155; cooperation of, 195; on the reservation, 168
Iron Shirt, 147
Irwin, W. R., 149
I'sătaí, 190, 191, 193, 194
Isomania, 42, 45, 51
Isowacony, 42, 45
Is-sa-keep, 7

James, Thomas, 32
Jicarillas, 20, 29–22. *See also* Apaches
Johnson, Colonel M. T., 130
Johnston, General Albert Sidney, 42, 47, 49
Jones, Anson, 65, 66
Jones, H. P., 138, 179 ?, 180 ?
Jumper, Colonel John, 178
Jupes, 26. *See also* Comanches

Kansa Indians, 2, 33
Karnes, Colonel Henry W., 42, 47, 49
Kătŭm'sĕ: complaints of, 102, 107; cooperation of, 79, 83, 103, 110, 114, 125; decline of, 109; on the reservation, 111–12; treaties with, 80; visits of, 78
Kellogg, Mrs. Elizabeth (captive), 40
Kichaies: as guides, 73; history of, 19; plight of, 108; population of, 37; problems with, 83
Kickapoos: attacks of, 116; relocation of, 83–84
Kicking Bird, 147; cooperation of, 185; at council, 180
King, Captain, 129
Kinney, Colonel, 63; and Buffalo Hump, 99
Kiowa Apaches: history of, 18; population of, 37; treaties with, 36, 92, 147
Kiowas: alliances of, 142, 196; arrests of, 200; attacks of, 40, 41, 84, 89, 116, 139, 143, 193; attacks on, 144; characteristics of, 38; communication with, 91; cooperation of, 195; councils with, 145, 178–79, 180, 183; decline of, 87–88; history of, 18; and the horse, 8; and the Indians of New Mexico, 94; and northern Comanches, 96, 97; population of, 37; raids of into Mexico, 97–105; and reservations, 137, 161, 187, 200; restrictions on, 188; treaties with, 36, 92, 142, 147, 151, 155
Kotsotekas: attacks on, 120; cooperation of, 74; councils with, 25; history of, 3; location of, 111; population of, 4; raids of, 28, 150; and reserva-

tions, 168; treaties with, 29, 90, 136, 147. See also Comanches
Kwahadies: as distinct band, 2, 136, 147, 156–58; history of, 4; and reservations, 168; surrender of, 200. See also Comanches; Staked Plains Comanches
Kwaharies. See Kwahadies

Labadi, Lorenzo, 156
Lamar, Mirabeau B., 44, 47
Leavenworth, Colonel J. H., 144–45, 147, 150, 158; change in attitude, 159–60
Leavenworth, General Henry, 34, 35
Lee, Lieutenant Fitzhugh, 123
Leeper, Matthew: in Confederate service, 137, 140; killing of, 138; as resident agent, 112, 113–14, 116, 131
Leeper's Creek, council at, 180–83
Legrand, Major A., 37, 41, 45
Lewis, Colonel M. G., 67, 68
Lipans: complaints of, 102; history of, 20; and Kickapoos, 84; plight of, 108; relocation of, 83; treaties with, 64, 68, 69, 80; and whites, 48, 52. See also Apaches
Little Arkansas treaty, 145, 147–48
Little Crow, surrender of, 199
Little Hart, 142
Little Mountain, 89, 133, 144; at council, 35, 183; and farming, 20; meetings with, 145; treaties with, 93, 147
Little Raven, 87; at council, 182
Little Wolf. See Yellow Wolf
Liver-eaters. See Tanimas
Llano Estacado: as Comanche country, 17, 134; and Kwahadies, 4
Lockhart, Andrew, 48
Lockhart, Matilda (captive), 48, 50, 51
Lone Wolf, 142, 155, 170; at council, 179, 180, 183; surrender of, 199
Long, Major, 32
Lyman, Captain W., letter of, 198

Mackenzie, Colonel R. S., 157, 175–77, 184–85, 197–98, 200
Marcy, Randolph B., 90, 174–75; and chiefs, 7; as surveyor, 108
María, José: complaints of, 108; indictment of, 128 strategy of, 111–12
Mason, Major, 85
McClellan's creek, attack at, 184–85
McClermont, Captain Robert, 186
McCulloch, Ben, 52
McCusker, Philip, 158, 159, 167, 179
McLeod, Colonel Hugh, 49, 50, 51
Medicine Lodge Creek, treaty of, 151–56, 158
Mescaleros, 20. See also Apaches

Mexican War, 61, 69–77, 99
Mexico: Indian raids into, 97–105; in treaty of Fort Atkinson, 97
Miles (agent), 178
Miles, A. P., 43
Miles, Colonel Nelson A., 197–98, 199
Miles, John D., 194
Milky Way, 147; and captives, 148; at council, 181; on the reservation, 168
Miller and Fisher contracts, 70
Mix, Charles E., 129
Moore, Colonel John H., 48, 52
Mow-way. See Shaking Hand
Muguara, 44, 48, 50, 51
Mukewarrah. See Muguara
Mu-la-que-top, 16, 123

Named Sun, 147; at agency, 185; and captives, 148 at council, 181; surrender of, 199, 201
Navajoes, attacks on, 156
Naytana, 28. See also Yamparikas
Neighbors, Robert S.: at councils, 67; and encroachment, 82; enemies of, 126; and Indian raids into Mexico, 98, 99; and Indians, 90, 95; and Indians' removal, 129, 131; murder of, 131; and Penatekas, 69–77; removal of, 125; reports of, 11, 14; suggestions of, 106, 118, 129; as supervising agent, 112; as surveyor, 108. See also Penatekas
Neill, J. C., 69
Nelson, Lieutenant Allison, 120, 128?
New Mexico, 141; Comanches in, 21–27, 31, 94
Nicholson, William, 196
Nokonies: attacks of, 116; attacks on, 196; cooperation of, 74, 81, 191; history of, 3–4; location of, 111; on the reservation, 168; treaties with, 90, 136, 147. See also Comanches
Norton, A. B., 156, 157

Oh-he-wek-ku, 90
Ola Mocohopie, 123
Old Owl: cooperation of, 57, 61, 77, 83; councils with, 64, 67; death of, 78; description of, 71; meetings with, 58, 72, 74; raids of into Mexico, 98; treaties with, 59, 64–65, 70, 72; village of, 62
"One who rides the Clouds," 92
Orthodox Friends, 165, 166, 189, 196
Ortiz Parilla, Colonel Diego, 27–28
Osages: attacks of, 84, 110; and Comanches, 93–94; history of, 19; territory of, 33, 88
Over the Buttes, 142, 147
Overland Mail Company, 142

Päh'-häh-yō'-ko: cooperation of, 61, 62, 77; councils with, 55–57, 64–65, 67, 68, 69; hostilities of, 98; leadership of, 4, 78; meetings with, 72, 74,

Index

80; treaties with, 60, 72
Painted Lips, 155
Palmer, Dr., 159
Palmer, V. R., 43
Paranuarimuco, 26
Parker, Cynthia Ann, 40, 134
Parker, Elder John, 40
Parker, John, 40
Parker, Quanah, 168, 176, 193, 201. *See also* Comanches
Parker, Silas, 40
Parker, W. B., observations of, 108–09
Parker's Fort, 40
Parrish, Professor Edward, 180
Pawnee Picts. *See* Wichitas
Pawnees, 19, 33
Pecan (Kickapoo), 67
Penatekas: attacks of, 28, 84; attacks on, 123; cooperation of, 90, 191; councils with, 68; decline of, 78–80; fleeing of, 138; history of, 2–3, 4, 9; hunting of, 87; leadership of, 78; and the northern Comanches, 112; population of, 52; and the reservation, 110, 137, 168; and Texas Americans, 44; treaties with, 29, 41–42, 60, 136, 147. *See also* Comanches; Pä′h-häh-yō′-ko
Pike, Albert, 32, 135–38, 140
Plum creek, 52
Plummer, James Pratt, 40
Plummer, Mrs. Rachel (captive), 40
Pohebits Quasho, death of, 119
Pollard, R. W., 128
Powell, Lieutenant, 122
Price, Major, 197–98
Prick-in-the-Forehead, 142
Puestia, 43

Quakers. *See* Orthodox Friends
Quĕrts-quĭp, 168; cooperation of, 187, 191

Red Arm, 90
Red Food: cooperation of, 187, 195–96; at council, 181; surrender of, 199
Red Otter, at council, 183
reservation system, 108–31; and liquor, 114–15
Richards, Jonathan, 167
Richardson, John M., 93
Rivera, Tito (captive), 104
Roemer, Dr. Ferdinand, 70–71
Rogers, John A., 80
Rollins, John H., 67, 76; as Neighbors' replacement, 79–80; recommendations of, 106
Root-eaters. *See* Yamparikas
Ross, Captain L. S., 121, 134
Ross, Captain S. P., 75, 111–12, 119, 131
Rubí, Marqués de, 23
Runnels, Governor, 123

Salt Creek massacre, 174
San Antonio. *See* Council House affair
San Carlos de los Jupes, 26
San Jacinto, 40
San Saba mission project, 31
Sanaco: captive of, 104; complaints of, 107–08; cooperation of, 79, 83, 110; fleeing of, 109–10; and his horse, 7; on the reservation, 111; selection of as chief, 78; and treaty, 80
Sanborn, General John B., 145, 147
Sanchez, Luis, 67
Sand Creek massacre, 143
Santa Anna (Penateka chief): cooperation of, 69, 77; and councils, 60, 64, 67; death of, 78; description of, 71; meetings with, 73; raids of into Mexico, 98; treaties with, 65, 70, 72; widow of, 109
Santa Fé trail, 81, 90, 93, 94, 143; creation of, 33
Sa-tank, 147, 175
Satanta, 93, 147; imprisonment of, 174–75, 179, 188; on the reservation, 169; speech of, 152; surrender of, 199
Sauk Indians, 84
Schmalsle, William F., 199
Second-Eye, 55
Seminoles: at council, 178; relocation of, 83–84
Serna, Captain, 21
Shaking Hand, 136, 142, 150, 156; attack on, 185; cooperation of, 163, 170; at council, 182; surrender of, 199
Shanklin, Henry, 159
Shaved Head, 89, 92
Shaw, Jim, 55, 57, 62, 64; with Buffalo Hump, 99 as interpreter, 67, 71, 112
Shawnee Jim, 123
Shawnees, 42; attacks of, 138; relocation of, 83–84
Sheridan, General, 161, 162
Sherman, General William Tecumseh, 150?, 174–75
Shoshonies, 2, 3
Sibley, Major, 95
Silver Brooch, 147, 168
Sioux, 91; alliance of, 142; battles of, 149, 161; and the horse, 8
Sitting Bear. *See* Satanta
Sleeping Wolf, at council, 183
Sloat, Benjamin, 61, 62–64; with Buffalo Hump, 99; with Texas Indian service, 98
Smith, Clinton (captive), 9, 157–58, 185
Smith, Edward P., 195
Smith, T. J., 69
Smithwick, Noah, 10, 43, 44, 48, 50, 51
Society of German Noblemen, 70
Son of the Sun, at council, 183
Spaniards, 21–32
Staked Plains Comanches, 136, 159, 162, 163. *See also* Kwahadies

Steen, Major E., 110
Stem, Jesse, 80, 83, 90
Stokes, Governor Montford, 35, 37
Stoneman, Captain, 126
Stumbling Bear, 183
Sturm, Dr. J. J., 200
Sun Eagle, 35, 36, 90

Ta-na-wahs, 80–81
Tanimas: associations of, 4; location of, 111; treaties with, 136, 147
Taos, council at, 24
Tarrant, General E. H., 127
Tatum, Lawrie, 166–77, 178, 186
Tavores, Rosalie (captive), 105
Tawakonies: alliances of, 28; and Comanches, 61; history of, 19; meetings with, 73; plight of, 108; population of, 37; relocation of, 83; treaties with, 36
Tawehash, 28
Taylor, General, 69
Tehuacana creek, councils at, 57–59, 67
Ten Bears: and captives, 148; at council, 179, 182; as delegate to Washington, 142, 183; at Medicine Lodge Creek, 152–54, 155; on the reservation, 168; and treaties, 92, 147
Tenawas, 90; associations of, 4; location of, 111; threats of, 74; treaties with, 136
Texas Emigration and Land Company, 82
Texas government: and Indian rights, 42; overtures of, 55–57
Texas, Republic of, 20, 41
Texas revolution, 39
Throckmorton, General J. W., 139
Tonkawas: history of, 20; plight of, 108; relocation of, 83; as scouts, 185; treaties with, 64
Toroblanco, 25
Torrey, Thomas, 55, 64, 69; trading post of, 60, 61, 86
Tosacondata, 25
Toshua, 78, 80
Toyash. *See* Wichitas
Traveling Wolf, 35, 36, 41; treaties: difficulty of, 5, 60, 65; provisions of, 59, 68, 80, 92, 97, 137, 145, 154–55
Twiggs, General, 114, 118, 119, 121, 123, 126

Ugalde, Cañon de, 28
Ugalde, Juan de, 28
Ugarte (Spanish commander-general), 26

United States government: efforts on behalf of Mexico, 102; and South Plains Indians, 34, 82, 139, 147, 161
Utes, 2, 18, 21, 25, 26

Van Camp, Lieutenant Cornelius, 113–14, 121
Van Dorn, Major Earl, 121, 122, 123
Vaughn, Alfred D., 87
von Meusebach, Baron, 70, 71

Wacoes: attacks of, 62, 74; and Comanches, 45, 61; history of, 19; meetings with, 73; population of, 37; relocation of, 83; treaties of, 57, 67
Wainwright, Captain R. A., 141
Walker, Francis J., 184
Walkley, S. T., 160
Warren, "Captain" Henry, 174
Watson, Daniel G., 57, 98
Western, Thomas G., 62, 98
Wheelock (of Dodge expedition): descriptions of Comanches, 37–38
White Antelope, 143
White Bull, 142
White Eagle, 92
White Horse, 179
White Wolf, surrender of, 199
Whitefield, John W., 20, 87–88
Wichita agency, battle at, 195–96
Wichitas: alliances of, 28; characteristics of, 38; councils with, 35, 178, 182; history of, 19; meetings with, 73; population of, 37; relocation of, 83; treaties of, 67, 68; visit Washington, 183
Wild Cat, 84
Williams, Colonel, 79
Williams, L. H., 64–65, 69
Wolf creek, battle of, 89
Wolf Turtle. *See* Isowacony
Woman's Heart: at council, 183; surrender of, 199

Xavier Ortiz, Francisco, 4

Yamparikas: attacks of, 61, 159; councils with, 25; history of, 3; location of, 111; population of, 4; and reservations, 161, 168, 191; treaties with, 28, 92, 136, 147; visits of, 81. *See also* Comanches
Yellow Buffalo, 142
Yellow Wolf, 67, 78, 79; treaties with, 80
Yupes: councils with, 25; population of, 4. *See also* Comanches

www.ingramcontent.com/pod-product-compliance
Lightning Source LLC
Chambersburg PA
CBHW080836230426
43665CB00021B/2857